THE *EXCELLENCIES* OF ROBERT BOYLE

broadview editions
series editor: L.W. Conolly

From R.T. Gunther, *Early Science in Oxford*, Vol. III (Oxford: Oxford University Press, 1925).

THE *EXCELLENCIES* OF ROBERT BOYLE

The Excellency of Theology and The Excellency and Grounds of the Mechanical Hypothesis

edited by J.J. MacIntosh

broadview editions

Library and Archives Canada Cataloguing in Publication

Boyle, Robert, 1627-1691
The excellencies of Robert Boyle / edited by J.J. MacIntosh.

Includes bibliographical references and index.
Contents: The excellency of theology–The excellency and grounds of the mechanical hypothesis.
ISBN 978-1-55111-466-8

1. Religion and science—Early works to 1800. 2. Theology—Early works to 1800. I. MacIntosh, J.J. (John James) II. Boyle, Robert, 1627-1691. Excellency of theology. III. Boyle, Robert, 1627-1691. Excellency and grounds of the mechanical hypothesis. IV. Title.

BT50.B66 2008 215 C2008-903289-6

Broadview Editions
The Broadview Editions series represents the ever-changing canon of literature in English by bringing together texts long regarded as classics with valuable lesser-known works.

Advisory editor for this volume: Colleen Franklin

Broadview Press is an independent, international publishing house, incorporated in 1985. Broadview believes in shared ownership, both with its employees and with the general public; since the year 2000 Broadview shares have traded publicly on the Toronto Venture Exchange under the symbol BDP.

We welcome comments and suggestions regarding any aspect of our publications—please feel free to contact us at the addresses below or at broadview@broadviewpress.com.

North America
Post Office Box 1243, Peterborough, Ontario, Canada K9J 7H5
2215 Kenmore Avenue, Buffalo, NY, USA 14207
Tel: (705) 743-8990; Fax: (705) 743-8353;
email: customerservice@broadviewpress.com

UK, Ireland, and continental Europe
NBN International, Estover Road, Plymouth PL6 7PY UK
Tel: 44 (0) 1752 202300 Fax: 44 (0) 1752 202330
email: enquiries@nbninternational.com

Australia and New Zealand
UNIREPS, University of New South Wales
Sydney, NSW, 2052 Australia
Tel: 61 2 9664 0999; Fax: 61 2 9664 5420
email: info.press@unsw.edu.au

Broadview Press acknowledges the financial support of the Government of Canada through the Book Publishing Industry Development Program (BPIDP) for our publishing activities.

www.broadviewpress.com

This book is printed on paper containing 100% post-consumer fibre.

Typesetting and assembly: True to Type Inc., Claremont, Canada.

PRINTED IN CANADA

Contents

Acknowledgements

Work on this book has been supported by a Social Sciences and Humanities Research Council of Canada research grant, by a fellowship from the Humanities Institute of the University of Calgary, and by a sabbatical leave from the University of Calgary. Like every worker on the Boyle manuscripts, I have been considerably helped by the work of Michael Hunter, who has not only provided workers on Boyle with microfilmed versions of the Boyle manuscripts as well as a mass of information about them, but has been constantly generous with both his time and expertise on matters concerning Robert Boyle and the seventeenth century generally.

I have received a great deal of help from the librarians and staff of the Royal Society Library in London, as well as from librarians at the University of Calgary. For permission to publish my transcriptions of various items from the Boyle Papers, I am grateful to the Librarian and Fellows of the Royal Society. For permission to make use of previously published material, I am grateful to the publishers and editors of *International Studies in the Philosophy of Science*, the *Croatian Journal of Philosophy*, *Dialogue*, *Enlightenment and Dissent*, the *Stanford Encyclopedia of Philosophy*, and the Cambridge University Press. The work has benefited from the helpful comments and suggestions of Peter Anstey, and of an anonymous referee for Broadview. The letter from John Evelyn to Boyle (Appendix K) has been previously published in *The Correspondence of Robert Boyle*, edited by Michael Hunter, Antonio Clericuzio, and Lawrence M. Principe, and I am grateful to the editors and to Pickering and Chatto for permission to reprint it.

Karen Walde's help and advice have been invaluable throughout.

Introduction

Robert Boyle's Life and Works[1]

Childhood and Adolescence: The Conversion to Committed Christianity

Robert Boyle was born in Lismore, in Ireland, 25 January, 1627. He was his parents' fourteenth child, and the youngest to survive to adulthood. A fifteenth child, Margaret, born a year and a half after Boyle, died at the age of eight. Boyle's mother, who was about fifteen when she was married, died when Boyle had just turned three. Boyle's upbringing was then in the hands of his father, the first Earl of Cork, and his older siblings. His sister Katherine, some twelve and a half years older, was to play an extremely important part throughout his life.

Boyle's references to his parents are fond, but he did not really know either of them. Of his mother's death, he said that he would

> ever reckon it amongst the Cheefe Misfortunes of his Life, that he did ne're know her that gave it him: her free & Noble Spirit (which had a handsome Mansion to reside in) added to her kindnesse & sweete carriage [made] her hugely regretted by her Children, & so lamented by her Husband; that not only he annually dedicated the Day of hir Death to solemne Mourning for it; but burying in her Grave all thoughts of Aftermarriage, he rejected all Motions of any other Match, continuing a constant Widdower till his Death.[2]

---

1 This is a short sketch of those periods of Boyle's life that are most relevant to his views in the *Excellencies*. For further details of Boyle's life, see Hunter 1994, which contains an excellent introduction by Hunter, as well as the best transcription of Boyle's own third-person autobiographical "An Account of Philaretus During His Minority" (BP 37:170r-184v, with some misordering), written between Boyle's coming of age in January, 1648, and July of the next year, and Maddison 1969. Recent and reliable accounts of shorter stretches of Boyle's life include Hunter 1993, 1995a, and 2000, and Principe 1994 and 1995. I have discussed Boyle's early years in slightly more detail in Boyle 2006. A much fuller biography of Boyle by Michael Hunter is due to be published by Yale University Press shortly. It is a definitive biography which will supersede current biographies, including this brief account.

2 BP 37:173r; Hunter 1994, 3. For conventions regarding transcriptions from the Boyle Papers see "A Note on the Text," p. 98.

Nor did Boyle know his father well, though he always spoke highly of him and believed himself to be his father's favourite. Views about the Great Earl of Cork vary widely. He arrived in Ireland as a young man, nearly penniless, and contrived to amass a great fortune. En route, many believe, he managed to destroy Munster economically, a result that is perhaps unsurprising in someone whose interest throughout his life lay centrally in money. Even when he is remarking on the way in which he values his wife more than money, the money is clearly important:

> I was married in Dublin to my 2d wife Katherine Fenton the only daughter of Sir Jeffery Fenton Kt Principal Secretary of State Privy Councellour of Ireland, with whom I never demanded any Marriage Portion neither had promise of any, it not being in my consideration, yet her Father after our Marriage gave me a thousand pound in Gold with her, but that gift of his Daughter, I must ever thankfully acknowledge to Almighty God, as the Croune of all his manifold blessings, for she was a most religious, vertuous, loving & obedient wife unto me all the dayes of her Life, and the happy mother of all my hopeful children, whom with their Posterity I beeseech God to bless.[1]

"I have never been able to think of the Great Earl of Cork without loathing and without anger," wrote George Sarton. "My main quarrel against him," he said, "is not that he was corrupt and greedy beyond measure but that he was the most sanctimonious devil I have ever heard of."[2] Such sanctimony was, however, common at the time, and the young Boyle, like others, felt that his various escapes from injury as a child should be seen as the result of divine intervention.

Boyle was sent off to Eton at the age of eight. He was popular with his first tutor, who wrote to his father: "M[R] Robert … is growne very fatt and joviall and pleasantly merry, and of the rarest memory that ever I knew; he prefers Learning afore all

---

1 BP 37:126, from "An Acompt of my Fathers life written out of his booke" (BP 37:122), "Taken from a Copy written by the Lady Vicountess Ranelaugh, Daughter to the Said Earle of Corke" (BP 37:127).

2 Sarton 1950, 158. For an admiring if somewhat uncritical account of Boyle's father see Townshend 1904. A good, and balanced, account of the elder Boyle is given in Canny's *The Upstart Earl* (Canny 1982), which is also extremely interesting on Robert.

other vertues or pleasures; M[R] Provost does admire him for his excellent genious."[1]

Boyle's sister Katherine was also noted for her memory.[2] "She hath a memory that will hear a sermon and goe home and penn itt after dinner verbatim," said Sir John Leeke.[3] Boyle had, throughout his life, a speech impediment, the result, he believed, of his imitating some other children, "whose stuttring Habitude he so long Counterfeited that he at last contracted it."[4] At Eton, the Headmaster, Sir Henry Wooton, wrote to Boyle's father, "My good Lord, I have commended seriously, and with promise of a good reward, your spirity Robin to the master of our choristers here, who maketh profession (and hath in one or two before given good proof thereof) to correct the errors of voices and pronunciation; for which he shall have fit hours assigned him." Later he wrote that when Boyle's sister Lettice, sees him during the long vacation, "Robert will entertain her with his pretty conceptions now a great deal more smoothly than he was wont."[5] However, when Magalotti visited England in the late 1660s, the problem remained:

> One could not say so much in praise of this wise and virtuous gentleman that he would not merit much more. He is full of religion towards God, of magnanimous charity towards his

---

1 Maddison 1969, 11n.

2 Throughout his writings Boyle assumes, what was in fact the case at the time, that both his readers and the "philosophers" he mentions would be male. However, his sister Katherine was a striking example of the fact that women could be intellectually far more able than most males, though as Antonia Fraser points out, she was obviously comfortable in her role as supporter of her acclaimed younger brother (Fraser 1984, 131 ff.). After her death, Bishop Gilbert Burnet wrote, "She lived the longest on the publickest Scene, she made the greatest Figure in all the Revolutions of these Kingdoms for above fifty Years, of any Woman of our Age. She imployed it all for doing good to others, in which she laid out her Time, her Interest, and her Estate, with the greatest Zeal and the most Success that I have ever known.... She had with a vast Reach both of Knowledg and Apprehensions, an universal Affability and Easiness of Access, a Humility that descended to the meanest Persons and Concerns [and] an obliging Kindness" (Hunter 1994, 52-53).

3 Verney 1892, 1:203.

4 Maddison 1969, 4.

5 Wooton to the Earl of Cork, 6 December, 1635, and 6 June, 1636, in Smith 1907, 2:359, 2:360.

> neighbour, of generosity, of affability, of courtesy, of gentleness towards all. He is still quite young, but of a constitution so weak that it does not promise him all his days. He speaks French and Italian very well, but has some impediment in his speech, which is often interrupted by a sort of stammering, which seems as if he were constrained by an internal force to swallow his words again and with the words also his breath, so that he seems so near to bursting that it excites compassion in the hearer.[1]

Throughout his life, Boyle stressed the virtue of truthfulness. In later life, he habitually recorded negative as well as positive experimental results, and consistently reported the various experimental disasters that occurred in his laboratory. Speaking of himself in the third person, he notes that, as a child,

> Lying was a Vice both so contrary to his nature & so inconsistent with his Principles, that as there was scarce any thing he more greedily desir'd then to know the Truth, so was there scarce any thing he more perfectly detested; then not to speake it. Which brings into my Mind a foolish Story I have heard him Jeer'd with, by (his Sister,) my Lady Ranalagh; how she having given strict order to have a Fruit-tree preserv'd for his sister in Law, the Lady Dungarvan, then big with Childe; he accidentally comming into the Garden, & ignoring the Prohibition, did eat halfe a score of them: for which being chidden by his sister Ranalagh; (for he was yet a Childe:) & being told by way of aggravation, that he had eaten halfe a dozen Plumbs; Nay truly Sister (answers he simply to her) I have eaten halfe a Score. So perfect an enemy was he to a Ly, that he had rather accuse himselfe of another fault, then be suspected to be guilty of that.[2]

When Boyle was at Eton, various escapes from injury impressed him considerably, and raised in him feelings "both of Gratitude and Wonder."[3] One night the wall of his room collapsed, but Boyle and the others present escaped without harm. On two occasions he fell from his horse, and was almost trampled

1 Magalotti 1980, 135.

2 BP 37:173v; Hunter 1994, 4-5. Boyle tells this story as though it happened before he went away to Eton on 9 September, 1635. At the time Boyle would have been eight, his sister Katherine (Lady Ranelagh), twenty.

3 BP 37:175v; Hunter 1994, 7.

in the first instance and almost crushed under the horse in the second. On yet another occasion, an apothecary mistakenly gave him "a very strong vomit[1] prepared & intended for another" instead of the prescribed "refreshing Drinke":

> after a long struggling, at last the Drinke wrought with such violence, that they fear'd, <that>[2] his Life would be disgorg'd together with his Potion. This Accident made him long after apprehend more the Fisitian then the Disease & was possibly the occasion that made him afterwards so inquisitively apply himselfe to the study of Fisicke, that he may have the lesse need of them that professe it. But Philaretus[3] wud not ascribe any of these Rescues unto Chance, but would be still industrious to perceive the hand of Hev'n in all these Accidents: & indeed he would professe that in the Passages of his Life he had observ'd so gratious & so peculiar a Conduct of Providence, that he should be equally blind & ungratefull, shud he not both Discerne & Acknowledge it.[4]

This piety in the young Boyle was not unusual. Michael Hunter notes that "the spiritual autobiography, aimed at chronicling God's purpose for the individual in question by recounting providential escapes, spiritual trials and conversion experiences," was "a characteristic genre of autobiographical writing in seventeenth-century England,"[5] and Nicholas Canny points out that "The invocation of providence as an explanation for accidental or chance happenings in this life was so commonplace among sincere Protestants in the early seventeenth century that it had come to be considered irreverent or profane not so to attribute them."[6] There is no doubt, though, that these protestations of gratitude were sincere in Boyle's case. Moreover, he continued to believe throughout his life in the possibility not only of divine, but

---

1 Strong laxatives ("purges," or "purgatives"), and strong emetics ("vomits," or "vomitives"), were common medical prescriptions of the time. An apothecary was the seventeenth century equivalent of a pharmacist.

2 Angle brackets enclose Boyle's insertions. For other conventions see p. 98.

3 In this early autobiographical fragment Boyle refers to himself throughout in the third person as "Philaretus" (Greek: "lover of virtue") or "P."

4 BP 37:175v-176r; Hunter 1994, 7-8.

5 Hunter 1994, xx.

6 Canny 1982, 28.

also of angelic and diabolic intervention, though in any given case he tended toward scepticism. About the *possibility* of such intervention he had no doubts; about the actuality of its having occurred in the cases reported to him he was in general (though not inevitably) very dubious.

Shortly after this time, Boyle's father arranged a marriage between Boyle's brother Francis and Elisabeth Killigrew,[1] but then arranged for Francis and Robert to leave for France and a continental tour four days after the marriage. Boyle's father writes, "his Ma^{TY} and the queen both staied in the bedchamber till they saw my son & his wife in bed together; and they bothe kissed the bride and blessed them, as I did."[2] Boyle was twelve at the time, his brother fifteen, and the bride sixteen. Boyle was happier about the proposed trip than his brother. He writes:

> But to render this Joy [of Francis and Elizabeth] as short as it was Greate, P. & his Brother, were within 4 dayes after commanded away for France, & having Kiss't their Majesties hands; they tooke a differing farewell of all their Friends; the Bridegroome extreamely afflicted to be so soone deprived of a Joy; which he had tasted but just enuf of, to encrease his Regrets, by the Knowledge of what he was forc't from; but Philaretus as much satisfy'd; to see himselfe in a Condition to content a Curiosity to which his Inclinations did passionately addict him.[3]

Francis and Robert travelled on the continent with their tutor Isaac Marcombes, a Frenchman who lived in Geneva. Boyle tells us of Marcombes, who had formerly been "a Traveller & a souldier," that "he was well fashion'd, & very well knew, what belong'd to a Gentleman.... Schollership he wanted not, having in his greener[4] Yeares been a profess'd Student in Divinity; but he was much lesse Read in Bookes then men. And hated Pedantry as much as any of the seaven Deadly sins."[5] Marcombes

---

1 In fact Boyle's father wanted to delay the marriage, and was angling for a marriage contract only, but the bride's mother wanted a marriage and since she won the King's approval, the marriage duly took place (Maddison 1969, 24n).

2 Maddison 1969, 25n.

3 BP 37:179r; Hunter 1994, 13.

4 I.e., younger.

5 BP 37:177v-178r, Hunter 1994, 11.

was Cynically[1] Dispos'd; & a very nice Critick both of Words & Men; which Humor he us'd to exercise so freely with Filaretus; that at last he forc'd him to a very cautious & considerate way of expressing himselfe; which after turn'd to his no small advantage. The Worst Quality he had, was his Choller, to Excesses of which he was excessively prone: & that being the onely Passion to which Philaretus was (much) observ'd to be inclin'd: his Desire to shunne clashing with his Governor; & his accustomednesse to beare the sudden sallys of his impetuous humor, taught our Youth, so to subdue that Passion in himselfe, that he was soone able to governe it, habitually & with ease. The Continuance of which Conquest he much acknowledg'd to that Passage of St. James; For the Wrath of Man worketh not the righteousnesse of God.[2] And he was ever a strict observer of that Precept of the Apostles, Let not the Sun go downe upon Your wrath....[3]

In Geneva, Boyle studied with interest "the most Practicke Part of Arithmetick, Geometry (with it's subordinades) the Doctrine of the Sphere, that of the Globe, & Fortification,"[4] but in later life he "often wish'd that I had imploy'd about the Speculative part of Geometrie, and the cultivating of the Specious Algebra I had been taught very young, a good part of that Time and Industry that I spent about Surveying and Fortification ... and other Practick parts of Mathematicks."[5]

He also, while in Geneva, learned Fencing (which, Marcombes wrote, "he is soe desirous to Learne that I am almost afraid that he should have left a quarell unperfect[6] in England"),[7] and dancing, "the former of which Exercises he ever as much affected as he contemn'd the latter."[8] He remembered as an adult, however, "the giddines acquir'd by turning on ones Toes,"[9]

---

1 Boyle, particularly the young Boyle, often left himself with a choice of words separated by a slash. In this case the MS reads: "Stoically/Cynically."

2 Jam. I.20 [RB's note].

3 Eph. 4.26 [RB's note]. BP 37:178r, Hunter 1994, 11-12.

4 BP 37:180; Hunter 1994, 14-15.

5 "Usefulness II," *Works*, 6:440.

6 Unfinished.

7 Maddison 1969, 31n.

8 BP 37:180v, Hunter 1994, 15.

9 BP 2:143 (Boyle 2006, 4.5.4, 372).

and retained throughout his life a fondness for fireworks ("which I have often seen with pleasure").[1]

During his stay in Geneva, Boyle, though already something more than a nominal believer, had what amounted to a conversion experience. In the middle of the night he was awakened by a thunderstorm with lightning strikes that were so severe "that P. began to imagine them the Sallyes of that Fire that must consume the World," convincing him "of the Day of Judgement's being at hand." This made "him Resolve & Vow, that if his Feares were that night disappointed all further additions to his life shud be more Religiously & carefully[2] employ'd."[3]

This vow, however, appeared to be simply the result of his terror during the storm. Realizing this, Boyle repeated his vow the next day under a sunny and unfrightening sky, so that it should be clearly the result of reason, not fear. Boyle's faith from then on was strong, though not unassailed by doubts, and indeed, hard on the heels of his thunderstorm experience, doubts about his faith began to trouble him.[4] In April, 1641,

> spending some of the Spring in a Visit to Chambery, (the Cheefe Towne of Savoy) Aix (fam'd for its Bathes) Grenoble the head Towne of Dauphiné & Residence of a Parliament, his Curiosity at last lead him to those Wild Mountaines where the First & Cheefest of the Carthusian Abbeys dos stand seated; where the Devil taking advantage of that deep raving Melancholy, so sad a Place; his humor, & the st[r]ange storys & Pictures he found there of Bruno the Father/Patriark/ of that order, suggested such strange & hideous thoughts, & such distracting Doubts of some of the Fundamentals of Christianity/Religion;/ that tho his lookes did little betray his Thoughts, nothing but the Forbiddenesse of Selfe-dispatch, hindred his acting it. But after a tedious languishment of many months in this tedious perplexity; at last it pleas'd God one Day he had receiv'd the Sacrament, to restore unto him the withdrawne sense of his Favor. But tho since then Philaretus ever look't upon those impious suggestions, rather as Temptations to be suppress't/rejected/ then Doubts to be satisfy'd; yet never after did these fleeting Clouds, cease now & then to darken/obscure/ the clearest seren-

---

1 BP 2:142v.

2 Once more Boyle left himself a choice in the MS, here duplicating "carefully" by "watchfully."

3 BP 37:181r-v, Hunter 1994, 16.

4 Such doubts were not less common in the seventeenth century than in any other. See, e.g., Thomas 1973, 6.4, "Scepticism," 198-206.

ity of his quiet: which made him often say that Injections of this Nature were such a Disease to his Faith as the Tooth-ach is to the Body; for tho it be not mortall, 'tis very troublesome. However, (as all things worke together to them that love God,) P. deriv'd from this Anxiety the Advantage of Groundednesse in his Religion: for the Perplexity his doubts created oblig'd him (to remove them) to be seriously inquisitive of the Truth of the very fundamentals of Christianity: & to peruse what both Turkes, & Jewes, & the cheefe Sects of Christians cud alledge for their severall opinions: that so tho he beleev'd more then he could comprehend, he might not beleeve more then he cud prove; & not owe the stedfastnesse of his Fayth to so poore a Cause as the Ignorance of what might be objected against it.[1]

Boyle's doubts, like his interest in proving the truth of Christianity, continued throughout his life, though their nature varied. Michael Hunter points out that

> Boyle's notes show that, as his death approached, he still struggled with religious doubts, echoing those which he had so graphically described in the aftermath of his conversion experience in his *Account of Philaretus*. In addition, he clearly shared with many earnest Christians of his day an anxiety that he might have committed the Sin against the Holy Ghost, as described in chapter 12 of St. Matthew's Gospel.[2] As his friends saw, there could be no doubt whatever about the genuineness of a faith so repeatedly scrutinised, but it probably made Boyle an uncomfortable colleague....
>
> Equally significant is the evidence that exists of Boyle's acute scruples over matters of conscience concerning his own affairs.... the Restoration settlement of impropriations on former church lands ... clearly lay on Boyle's conscience, partly because those in possession of such rights could be regarded as guilty of the sin of sacrilege, and partly because he had had the benefit of perquisites which might otherwise have been used for ecclesiastical ends.[3]

---

1 BP 37:182r-v, Hunter 1994, 17-18.

2 Hunter's reference is to Matthew 12.31-2, which reads: "Wherefore I say unto you, All manner of sin and blasphemy shall be forgiven unto men: but the blasphemy against the Holy Ghost shall not be forgiven unto men. And whosoever speaketh a word against the Son of man, it shall be forgiven him: but whosoever speaketh against the Holy Ghost, it shall not be forgiven him, neither in this world, neither in the world to come."

3 Hunter 1994, lxxiii-iv. See further "Casuistry in Action" in Hunter 2000, especially 83.

In the fall of 1641, Robert, Francis, and Marcombes crossed the Alps into Italy, where Boyle read the works of "greate Star-gazer Galileo; whose ingenious Bookes, perhaps because they could not be so otherwise were confuted by a Decree from Rome."[1] While in Italy (in the winter of 1641-42) he had what seems to have been one of the very few sexual encounters of his life:

> Nor did he sometimes scruple, in his Governor's Company, to visit the famousest Bordellos; whither resorting out of bare Curiosity, he retain'd there an unblemish't Chastity, & still return'd thence as honest as he went thither. Professing that he never found any such sermons against them, as they were against themselves. The Impudent Nakednesse of vice, clothing it with a Difformity, Description cannot reach, & the worst of Epithetes cannot but flatter. But tho P. were noe Fewell for forbidden Flames, he prov'd the Object of unnaturall ones. For being at that Time not above 15, & the Cares of the World having not yet faded a Complexion naturally fresh enuf; as he was once unaccompany'd diverting himselfe abroad, he was somewhat rudely presst by the Preposterous Courtship of 2 of those Fryers, whose Lust makes no distinction of Sexes; but that which it's Preference of their owne creates; & not without Difficulty, & Danger, forc't a scape from these gown'd Sodomites. Whose Goatish Heates, serv'd not a little to arme Filaretus against such Peoples specious Hyprocrisy; & height-n'd & fortify'd in him an Aversenesse for Opinions, which now the Religieux discredit as well as the Religion.[2]

Leaving Rome they pressed on to Marseilles where distressing news awaited them. The money Boyle's father had been sending was now cut off since, as a result of the rebellion in Ireland, the Earl was in a "dangerous and poore estate." He had "with much difficulty gott together two hundred and fifty pounds by selling of plate," but to pay Marcombes' bills punctually as he had in the past, "I am noe waies able." However, this final £250 was in fact used by Cork's London agent to pay off some other bills, and so, unknown to the Earl, no money accompanied his letter, which went on to advise Marcombes to use the (confiscated) money to bring the two boys

1 BP 37:183v-184, Hunter 1994, 19.

2 BP 37:184r-v, Hunter 1994, 20.

out of some meet port in France to land either at dublin, Corke, or Youghall, (for all other Cities and Sea townes are possessed by the enemy), or else my two sonnes, till this generall rebellion and waste contynues, must of necessitie upon receipt of these my lettres, presently begin their journey from the place where these lettres shalbe delivered you, and travaile into Holland, and putt themselues into entertaynement under the service and conduct of the Prince of Orange; for they must henceforward maintayne themselves by such entertaynements as they gett in the warres.... It wilbe a worke worthy your consideration, how you governe my two sonnes, and how you with their owne consents will dispose of them, either for Ireland or Holland.... in any case, I pray be very circumspect how you spend this last 250^{li} now made over unto you....[1]

Francis decided to return to Ireland, and arrived in time to fight in the Battle of Liscarrol (3 September, 1642). Robert decided that his health, youth, and lack of money made both a return to Ireland and a career of soldiering in Holland undesirable, and wrote from Lyons to tell his father that Marcombes had offered to let him stay with him in Geneva.[2] He remained in Geneva before finally returning to England in the summer of 1644.

During this stay in Geneva, Boyle met François Perreaud (1572-1657), who later wrote *Démonographie, ou traité des démons et Sorciers*,[3] which Boyle subsequently arranged to have translated into English by Peter du Moulin (the younger, 1601-84). In a letter prefixed to this English edition, Boyle recalled that "the conversation I had with that pious author during my stay at Geneva, and the present he was pleased to make me of this treatise before it was printed, in a place where I had opportunities to enquire both after the writer, and some passages of the book, did at length overcome in me (as to this narrative) all my settled indisposedness to believe strange things."

In the manuscript draft "Loose papers whence some things are to be extracted for the Discourse of the causes of Atheism," Boyle considered three objections to belief in "the storys of

1 Earl of Cork to Marcombes, 9 March, 1641/2, Maddison 1969, 47.

2 Boyle to his father, 25 May, 1642, *Correspondence* 1:19-20.

3 Geneva, 1653, subsequently retitled in the second edition (1656) *L'Antidemon de Mascon*. The English translation, *The Devil of Mascon*, is reprinted in *Works*, 13.

witchcrafts and apparitions of spirits," namely, the specific improbability of our being able to affect incorporeal beings by the use of material entities or activities such as drugs or magical ceremonies, the general implausibility of the claims involved which required the possibility of immaterial things interacting with material ones, and the implausibility of the suggestion "that *proud* spirits, such as the Devills; should submit to be at the becke of a silly and despicable[1] old woman, and at her command doe things extravagant & even ridiculous."[2]

In reply Boyle points out that we know very little of "the nature, customes, & government of the Intelligent creatures of the *spirituall world*: and particularly what concernes the Falne Angells or bad Dæmons," so we are in no position to remark on the plausibility or implausibility of any particular claim about them. However, he adds, we may well be suspicious of this or that *account* of interaction with spiritual beings, since whether such interaction is likely or unlikely in itself, there is no doubt that most (at least) of the claims concerning such interaction are suspect. As to the claim that there is a problem about the material and the immaterial interacting, Boyle simply rejects it out of hand, on the ground that the human soul and body provide a counter example, and though we have no idea how this interaction occurs, there is no doubt that it *does* occur.[3]

When Boyle arrived back in England in mid-1644, he was 17, and the Civil War had already begun. He was quickly reunited with his sister Katherine, who re-adopted the semi-maternal role she so often played after the death of their mother. Katherine had been married, shortly before the death of her mother, and within a fortnight of her fifteenth birthday, to "the foulest churl in Christendom, whose best point was that he was nightly dead drunk and so probably not quarrelsome,"[4] and thus became Katherine Ranelagh. It was to this household in London that Boyle repaired, but shortly thereafter removed to an estate in Stalbridge, settled on Boyle though entailed on Francis.

At this time Boyle was interested in both ethics and theology, and was indeed shortly to produce treatises in both fields. Much

1 In this period "despicable," could mean merely "miserable," or "wretched," a now obsolete, but milder, sense than ours.

2 Similar objections had been strongly urged by Reginald Scot (Scot 1584) in the previous century.

3 BP 2:105 (Boyle 2006 3.5.21, 258-59).

4 Sir John Leeke, in a letter introducing Katherine to the Verneys (Verney 1892, 1:203; Townshend 1904, 234).

of his time during the early part of his Stalbridge period was spent working on moral philosophy: "My *Ethics* go very slowly on," he wrote to Katherine on 30 March, 1646.[1] He already resembled the "Lay-Bishop" that Anthony Walker was later to find him to be.[2] He was, in fact, a serious, somewhat priggish young man, though no doubt the light-heartedness that led him to enjoy fencing and other sports and which kept breaking out in later life was not absent during these up and down years.

In his funeral service for Boyle, Bishop Burnet said that "As for Joy, he had indeed nothing of Frolick and Levity in him ... he did not waste his Time, nor dissipate his Spirits into foolish Mirth," a judgement accepted by Steven Shapin, but both Burnet and Shapin fail to allow for the lighter moments that Boyle undoubtedly enjoyed.[3] The two *Excellencies* show plainly Boyle's delight in experimenting and the joy he took in his discoveries. His light-hearted delight in experimenting comes out clearly in his report of his replication of Archimedes' displacement result, which he reported to the Royal Society in 1664:

> filling a large and deep glass to a convenient height with fair water, we plac'd in it another deeper glass, shap'd like a *Goblet* or Tumbler, that it might be the fitter for swimming; and having furnish'd it first with Ballast, and then, for merryment sake, with a wooden Deck, by which a tall Mast, with a Sayle fasten'd to it, was kept upright; we fraughted[4] it with wood, and by degrees pour'd Sand into it, till we had made it sinck just to the Tops of certain conspicuous marks, that we had fasten'd on the outside of the Glass to opposite parts thereof.[5]

The man who fitted out this little container with a tall mast and a sail "for merryment sake" was not a man who "had indeed nothing of Frolick and Levity in him."

---

1 *Correspondence* 1:34. For the young Boyle's views on ethics, see Harwood 1991.

2 "[T]hat Honourable, and well known name *R. Boyl*, Esquire, that *profound Philosopher, accomplished Humanist,* and *excellent Divin*e, I had almost said *Lay-Bishop*," (Walker 1678, 45).

3 Gilbert Burnet, *A Sermon at the Funeral of the Honourable Robert Boyle*, in Hunter 1994, 55; Shapin 1994, 187. Burnet had noted a few paragraphs earlier, however, that Boyle "allowed himself a great deal of decent chearfulness."

4 I.e., loaded.

5 "Hydrostatical Paradoxes" *Works*, 5:231.

Boyle was intended by his father to marry "my Robins yonge Mrs," Anne Howard, but it unlikely that Boyle was comfortable with this project. He was against marrying, as he told Burnet late in life, "at first out of Policy afterwards more Philosophically."[1] When he was "very young" he wrote to his niece Katherine (a year younger than Boyle), who had heard that Boyle was married, telling her

> to suspend your belief of a marriage celebrated by no priest but fame, and made unknown to the supposed bridegroom. I may possibly e're long give you a fit of the spleen upon this theme; but at present it were incongruous to blend such pure raillery, as I ever prate of matrimony and amours with, among things I am so serious in as those this scribble presents you. I shall therefore only tell you, that the little gentleman[2] and I are still at the old defiance.... But though this untamed heart be thus insensible to the thing itself called love, it is yet very accessible to things very near of kin to that passion; and esteem, friendship, respect, and even admiration, are things, that their proper objects fail not proportionably to exact of me.[3]

Stalbridge and Oxford: The Conversion to Science[4]

Around the age of twenty, sequestered in Stalbridge, occupied with the penning of tracts on morality and theology, Boyle's interest in experimental philosophy was steadily developing, despite his suffering from the ill health that was to follow him throughout his life. In the summer of 1647 he suffered "a severe fit of the stone, to which distemper he was extremely subject." He was also worried

1 Hunter 1994, 27.

2 I.e., Cupid.

3 *Correspondence* 1:27-28, Birch 1772, I:cxxxvii-cxxxviii. The date and recipient of this letter are somewhat conjectural. Birch mentions the "lady Barrymore, his niece" as the recipient (*Works* 1772 I:cxxxvii). If this is Katherine Barry, it is slightly odd to refer to her as the "lady Barrymore." Another possibility is that she is Susan Barry, Richard Barry's wife (*Correspondence* 1:27). However, a plausible dating of the letter, in view of its content, is 1645; but Richard did not marry Susan Killigrew until 1649. As Alice Boyle's daughter, Katherine would be Robert's niece; as Alice's son's Richard's wife, Susan would be his niece by marriage, so either of them could be construed as Birch's "his niece." Both were equally young: Katherine was born in 1628, and Susan in 1629.

4 See the note on the terms "science," "natural philosophy," and "experimental philosophy" in the section "A Note on the Text."

about smallpox ("very rife in these parts"), but was attempting to "court nature as eagerly as such a disaccommodated solitude will permit," and was suffering "necessitated idleness" while awaiting "a great earthen furnace" and a number of associated "Vulcanian implements."[1] The furnace was necessary to subject a variety of items to the fire, the then standard method of checking the composition of things. The later Boyle was to be critical of separation by fire as the most important method of discovery,[2] but at the time he was eager to make use of it.

However, the road to Stalbridge was long and in poor repair, and the furnace arrived "crumbled into as many pieces, as we into sects," so that "the fine experiments ... I had built upon its safe arrival, have felt the fate of their foundation," leaving Boyle to attempt "such experiments, as the unfurnishedness of the place, and the present distractedness of my mind, will permit me." Receiving the furnace broken, he wrote to his sister, "is a defeat, that nothing could recompence but that rare lesson it teaches me, how brittle that happiness is, that we build upon earth."[3]

As his remark about the diversity of sects shows, Boyle was already troubled by the fragmentation of Christianity and was to continue so throughout his life. He was worried that among "the Giddy Multitude here in England ... this Multiplicy [*sic*] of Religions will end in none at all,"[4] and in his will funding the Boyle Lectures against atheism, he charged the lecturers with "proveing the Christian Religion against notorious Infidels (*viz*ᵗ)[5] Atheists, Theists, Pagans, Jews and Mahometans, not descending lower to any Controversies that are among Christians themselves."[6]

When finally a furnace did arrive, Boyle found himself "so

---

1 Boyle to Worsley, *Correspondence* 1:49. The recipient of this letter is not certainly known; Worsley is the very plausible conjecture of the *Correspondence* editors. Vulcan is the Roman god of fire and metalworking.

2 See, for example, the "Excellency of the Mechanical Hypothesis," *Works*, 8:110 [240]; and see further Principe 1998, 35-36.

3 Boyle to Katherine Ranelagh, 6 March 1647, *Correspondence*, 1:50; Boyle to Hartlib, 8 May, 1647, *Correspondence*, 1:60.

4 Boyle to John Mallet, 2 March, 1652, *Correspondence* 1:133; see also Underdown 1971, 331.

5 A contraction of videlicet (Latin): that is to say, or namely; now, more usually "viz."

6 Maddison 1969, 274. Hunter points out that the earliest draft of the will mentions only "Atheists and Theists" (Hunter 1994, lxxxiv, n 76).

transported and bewitch'd [as to] fancy my laboratory a kind of Elysium.... I there forget my Standish[1] and my Bookes, and almost all things."[2] Henry Stubbe wrote to him despairing of "this empirical ignorant age," but Boyle was partial towards "sooty Empiricks," and did not despise "a study which [many Learned Men] scarce think fit for any but such as are unfit for the rational and useful parts of Physiology."[3] Two years before the writing of *The Excellency of Theology*, Boyle emphasized his interest in experimenting and his willingness to get his hands dirty doing so:

> For my part, If I durst think my Actions fit to be Examples, I should tell you, that I have been so farre from that effeminate squeamishness, that one of the *Philosophical Treatises*, for which I have been gathering Experiments, is of the Nature and Use of Dungs. And though my condition does (God be praised) enable me to make Experiments by others Hands; Yet I have not been so nice, as to decline dissecting *Dogs, Wolves, Fishes*, and even *Rats* and *Mice*, with my own Hands. Nor, when I am in my Laboratory, do I scruple with them naked to handle Lute and Charcoal.[4]

Despite the distractions of poor eyesight,[5] recurrent illnesses, and delight in experiment, his standish and his books were not

---

1 Elysium, or the Elysian fields, is the area at the ends of the earth where heroes fortunate enough to be favoured by the gods enjoy immortality. A standish is a stand that contains ink, pens, and writing materials.

2 Boyle to Katherine, 31 Aug, 1649, *Correspondence* 1:83.

3 Henry Stubbe to Boyle, 17 December, 1669, *Correspondence* 4:155; "Certain Physiological Essays," *Works*, 2:85.

4 "Considerations touching the Usefulness of Experimental Natural Philosophy," *Works*, 3:211. Lute was a substance, typically sticky and dirty, used to seal joins between, for example, a glass vessel and a tube leading out of it. In his experiments with a vacuum pump, Boyle would have been using lute constantly. Richard Mathew, alluded to by Boyle in *Works* 10:86, suggests making a lute of "blood, lome, hair, and sharp sand ... moisten[ed] with strong Brine," while Boyle's friend Robert Sharrock, in a volume dedicated to Boyle, offers as a lute for grafting plants one "made with horse-dung & stiff clay well mix'd together" (Mathew 1662, 143; Sharrock 1659, 68).

5 Boyle often mentions his weak eyesight—even "the flame of a Candle," he wrote, "is offensive to my weak eyes"—but it was not allowed to interfere with his scientific endeavours. And though a candle was offensive to his eyes he used to look at the sun through "a Telescope ...

neglected. He was also reading,[1] particularly Gassendi, "a very profound mathematician, as well as an excellent astronomer," "a great favourite of mine,"[2] and also perhaps the most important single influence on the seventeenth century revival of atomism.[3] It is clear from the manuscripts and his printed works that he also immersed himself in the works of Descartes and Aristotle. He tells us that his knowledge of Aristotle, and his scepticism about Aristotelian explanations, came very early:

> Having ever [sinc]e I first addicted my Time & Thoughts to the more serious parts of Learning, found my selfe by a secret but strong Propensity, inclin'd to the Study of Naturall Philosophy, the first course I tooke to satisfy my Curiosity, was to instruct my selfe in the Aristotelian Doctrine, as that whose Principles I found generally acquiesc'd in by the Universitys & Schools, & by numbers of celebrated Writers, celebrated for little lesse, then Oraculous. But I had scarce <well> acquainted my selfe with the Peripateticke Theory, before I was strongly tempted to doubt it's Solidity. For the Commands of my Parents engaging me to visit divers forreigne Countrys, I could not but in my Travells meet with many things capable to make me distrust the Doctrine <wherewith> I had freshly been imbu'd. For first I found Aristotle's Principles much more strongly asserted then prov'd by his Admirers & by not inconsiderable arguments oppos'd, not only by the Chymists[4] in generall & great store of Moderne Physitians but [by many] acute & fam'd Philoso[phers] ... In the next place I observ'd many things in my Travells which were wholly unintelligible from Aristotles Theory which being grounded but upon [a] few obvious & not thoroughly examin'd appearances of things as much too narrow <&

---

though thorow a thick, red, or blew glass, to make its splendor supportable" ("Colours," *Works*, 4:27, 30-31).

1 Boyle's views on reading may be gathered from his mentioning to Oldenburg in November, 1665, that the "necessary things" of life were "Eating, & Sleeping, & Reading and Writing" (*Correspondence* 2:581). Nonetheless, earlier, in 1657, he had noted that "the Weakness of my Eyes has this long time kept me from reading almost any Books, save the Scripture, with some Critical Expositions of it, and here and there some Portions of the Writings of those that pretend to teach their Readers Experimental Matters" ("Proemial Essay, CPE," *Works*, 2:33).

2 Boyle to Hartlib, 8 May, 1647, *Correspondence* 1:59.

3 See Osler 1994 for details.

4 That is, the followers of Paracelsus.

> slight> to reach either all or the more abstruse effects of Nature, & lastly I found the same Theory alltogether barren as to useful productions & that with the assistance of it I could doe noe more then I could have done when I was a stranger to it. And tho I deny not that wee owe divers useful discoveryes & Inventions to the Embracers of the Doctrine wee mention yet I find not but that themselves ow'd them not to Aristotles principles but to some luckynes or Sagacity of their owne genius or to some other notions or Experiments which they might have acquir'd tho they had never heard of Aristotles writings, wherefore tho I much reverenced the rare abilityes of that <Greate> Philosopher who what he would have done had his vast reason had experiments to worke upon wee may g[ue]sse by his excellent Treatises concerning Animalls yet finding so many things in nature either not intelligible from his principles or not consistent with them I could not acquiesse in them....[1]

However, though he found Aristotelian explanations implausible, and though he felt Aristotle's views (particularly on the eternity of the world) were (at least) contributory to atheism, he nonetheless retained a considerable admiration for him, ranking him among "those Philosophers ... that have improv'd Reason to the greatest height."[2] He also thought highly of his writings on animals: "I must confesse I have with some delight observ'd how much more honestly Aristotle writes of God in some Passages of his Bookes De Animalibus then in his other Workes & was pleas'd to find Speechlesse Creatures preach Providence so powerfully to a Philosopher so venerated; & draw honest Confessions from a Person sufficiently indispos'd to such kind of Acknowledgments."[3]

By the end of 1649 he had already finished or was working on some thirty-six theological or moral pieces, many though not all of which have survived in one form or another.

While living in Stalbridge, Boyle made two visits to that "illiterate country," Ireland, for a year from June 1652, and for eight months from October, 1653. While there he wrote to Clodius, in the spring of 1654:

---

1 BP 38:80r-v. The MS is both torn and badly blotted. Conjectural readings are shown in square brackets; Boyle's insertions, as usual, are within angle brackets.

2 *Works* 3:204.

3 BP 8:29v, and cf. *Works* 5:295.

> For my part, that I may not live wholly useless, or altogether a stranger in the study of nature, since I want glasses and furnaces to make a chemical analysis of inanimate bodies, I am exercising myself in making anatomical dissections of living animals: wherein (being assisted by your father-in-law's friend Dr *Petty*, our general's physician) I have satisfied myself of the circulation of the blood, and the (freshly discovered and hardly discoverable) receptaculum chyli, made by the confluence of the venae lactae;[1] and have seen (especially in the dissections of fishes) more of the variety and contrivances of nature, and the majesty and wisdom of her author, than all the books I ever read in my life could give me convincing notions of.[2]

It was also during this period, no doubt in large part due to Cromwell's extremely harsh treatment of the Irish,[3] that Boyle's Irish properties were returned to him and began to yield rents. The fact that Boyle's friend Petty conducted the survey on which the disposal of the lands was based can hardly have been to Boyle's disadvantage though, as mentioned earlier, Boyle continued throughout his life to worry about the legitimacy and morality of his title to these possessions.

In the mid-1650s Boyle moved to Oxford, a place to which he was already favourably disposed. Writing from Eton to Samuel Hartlib in September 1655, he tells him,

> After then my occasions had drag'd me out of Towne I made Oxford my way (though it were many miles out of it) on

---

1 The "freshly discovered ... receptaculum chyli" is the thoracic duct. Remarking that he had made the discovery earlier, Jean Pecquet (1624-74) first published his discovery in 1651 in his *Experimenta nova anatomica*. In 1652 Johannes van Horn (1621-70) published the same result, having apparently achieved it independently (Foster 1924, 49). The venae lactae (the "milky" veins) are the vessels that carry the chyle (lymph given a milky look from the absorption of emulsified fats) from the small intestine to the thoracic duct. (I owe these points to Andrew Cunningham.)

2 *Correspondence* 1:167, Birch 1772, VI:55.

3 See Barber 1999 for further details. Parker 1993 points out that a likely figure for Ireland during the Civil War is a population loss of over 40% (618,000 out of a total pre-war population of 1,500,000), compared with a loss of approximately 3.7% for England and 6% for Scotland. For comparison Parker estimates a population loss due to enemy action and war-related disease for Britain during World War II of 0.6%.

> purpose to visit our Ingenious Freind DR Wilkins with whom I spent a day with noe Small Satisfaction, his entertainement did as well speake Him a Courtier as his discourse & the reall Productions of his Knowledge a Philosopher. But tho I were used with a huge deale of Civility in divers Colledges during my short stay at Oxford (where I continu'd not full two dayes) yet that which most endear'd to me my Entertainment was the delight I had to find there a Knot of such Ingenious & free Philosophers, who I can assure You doe not only admit & entertaine Reall Learning but cherish & improve It, & have done <& are like to doe> more toward the Advancement of it then many of those Pretenders that doe more busie the Presse & presume to undervalue'um, & during the little time I spent there I had the Satisfaction to heare both the Cheife Professors & Heads of Colledges maintaine Discourses & Arguments in a way so far from Servile that if all the New Paradoxes <have> not found Patrons there, tis not their Dissent from the Ancient or the Vulgar Opinions but some juster Cause that hinders their admission, so that <much of> what you & I had bin inform'd of concerning the Servilnes & Disaffection to reall Learning of that University may perchance have bin true when the Informers liv'd there but certainely now the Persons are mistaken & so injur'd, they being so far from being Censurable for their Predecessors failings that it ought to be their Praise not to have imitated them.[1]

In the autumn of 1655 Katherine travelled to Oxford to decide upon suitable lodgings for Robert. She decided upon two rooms in the house that stood on what is now the site of the Shelley Memorial in University College. Neither room, she felt, was really warm enough, but one of them might do with the help of a folding screen to cut down on the wind that would otherwise blow in by the door.[2]

In Oxford Boyle's tremendous output of published works in philosophy, theology, and experimental philosophy began. It was here that he published *New Experiments Physico-Mechanical, Touching the Spring of Air and its Effects; Certain Physiological Essays; The Sceptical Chymist; Some Considerations Touching the Usefulness of Experimental Natural Philosophy*, and a number of other works including *The Origine of Forms and Qualities*.

---

1 Boyle Papers 37:189r, *Correspondence* 1:190-91.

2 *Correspondence* 1:193.

Lawrence Principe has pointed out the change in Boyle's style that occurred with his new interest in scientific pursuits.[1] Although no piece of Boyle's tends to arouse our (as opposed to his contemporaries') stylistic admiration, his style is certainly crisper in his natural philosophy pieces than it is in his overtly theological and moral writings. As the otherwise obsequious Eustace Budgell noticed after his death,

> It must ... be confessed, that his Stile is far from being correct; that it is too wordy and prolix; and that though it is for the most Part plain and easy, yet, that he has sometimes made use of harsh and antiquated Expressions: Yet under all these Disadvantages, so curious is his Matter, and so solid are his Observations, that the hardest Thing we can say of his most careless Piece, is, That it appears like a beautiful Woman in an Undress. Besides his Philosophical Works, Mr. Boyle has wrote several Pieces of Divinity: In these last, he is still more wordy, and makes Use of more Circumlocutions than in the former. To say the Truth, I think his Theological Works, much inferior to his Philosophical ones: It cannot however be denied, That he has often blended Religion and Philosophy happily enough together; and made each serve to illustrate and embellish the other.[2]

The London Years

Boyle's years in London (off and on from 1665, and then continuously from 1668 to his death) saw the continuation of his experimental work, along with the publishing of a number of works on philosophy and theology, including *The Excellency of Theology, Compar'd with Natural Philosophy; Considerations About the Excellency and Grounds of the Mechanical Hypothesis; Free Enquiry into the Vulgarly Receiv'd Notion of Nature; Discourse of things above Reason; Disquisition about the Final Causes of Natural Things*; and *The Christian Virtuoso, Part I.*

It was in 1665 that the bulk of *The Excellency of Theology* was written, though Boyle presumably made some alterations before its publication in 1674. *The Excellency and Grounds of the Mechanical Philosophy* was written later—its precise date of composition is not known. It was also in 1665 that Boyle published his *Occa-*

1 See Principe 1994 and Principe 1995.

2 Budgell 1732, 124-25.

sional Reflections upon Several Subjects, dedicated to his sister Katherine, though the *Reflections* were in the main written much earlier, around 1647-48, "under an Usurping Government."[1] The *Occasional Reflections* are interesting as revealing the ethical views of the young Boyle (then aged twenty or twenty-one), and as showing the way in which, in his opinion, morality and religion interacted.[2] The work was favourably received, particularly though by no means solely by Boyle's friends, and continued to be so into the eighteenth century, though by then some found the selections somewhat wearying, and Dean Swift (1667-1745) famously penned his "Meditation on a Broom-Stick" as a satire upon them.[3]

Though Boyle does not explicitly mention his writing of *The Excellency of Theology*, he touches upon one of its main motivations in a letter to "my Reverend & highly Esteemd Freind Mr Richard Baxter" in June 1665. Boyle had previously sent Baxter copies of *Seraphic Love, Style of the Holy Scriptures*, and *Occasional Reflections*, which led Baxter to say "I read your Theologie as the Life of your Philosophie, & your Philosophie as animated & dignifyed by your Theologie."[4] In his reply to Baxter's letter Boyle says "there are divers things that speake you to be none of those narrow-Sould Divines, that by too much suspecting Naturall Philosophy, tempt <many of> Its Votaries to suspect Theology."[5] Persuading natural philosophers not to yield to what Boyle saw as the completely understandable temptation to place natural philosophy above the investigation of theological topics was certainly one of the main reasons for his writing *The Excellency of Theology*.

The time of its writing was a troubled one, but Boyle's output was, in general, not affected by external circumstances. Nonetheless it must have been difficult for him to work at this time, for 1665 was the year of the Great Plague of London.[6] The figures are necessar-

---

1 *Works*, 5:93; for the dating see *Works* 5:xi. The "Usurping" government was the government during the Interregnum.

2 Boyle 2006 treats of this subject in more detail. It might be worth saying explicitly that modern readers may find the *Reflections*, much admired by Boyle's sister Katherine, somewhat sententious.

3 See Appendix H for Swift's satire, for the occasion of his writing it, and for an example of the "Meditations" that Swift was satirizing.

4 *Correspondence*, 2:473.

5 *Correspondence*, 2:486.

6 Thomas Sydenham had already, "upon Boyle's 'persuasion and recommendation,' [begun] the clinical study of London epidemics" (Dewhurst 1966, 30), but the plague of 1665 was unusually virulent, and caught

ily imprecise, but out of an estimated population of roughly 460,000, nearly 100,000 died in 1665, the majority being victims of the plague, and many of the other deaths being plague-related.[1]

The plague reached the western suburbs of London in May, and by the end of that month many of those who could were leaving London to escape it. Though living in London, Boyle moved to Oxford in late May or early June, 1665, to escape "the fatall Plague wherewith God is now pleas'd to afflict & punish us,"[2] and though earlier Katherine had prayed throughout the night at the bedside of infected friends, by the end of July she too had left London and was in Leese, in Essex, where her sister Mary, Countess of Warwick, lived.[3]

In September of 1665, Samuel Pepys, who stayed on in London longer than most who were able to leave, wrote to Lady Carteret:

> I having stayed in the city till above 7400 died in one week, and of them above 6000 of the plague, and little noise heard day nor night but tolling of bells; till I could walk Lumber-street [Lombard Street] and not meet twenty persons from one end to the other, and not fifty upon the Exchange; till whole families (ten and twelve together) have been swept away; till my very physician, Dr Burnet, who undertook to secure me against any infection ... died himself of the plague; ... till I could find neither meat nor drink safe, the butcheries being everywhere visited, my brewer's house shut up, and my baker with his whole family dead of the plague.
>
> Yet, Madam, through God's blessing ... your poor servant is in a perfect state of health.[4]

The following year the Great Fire of London, which irrevocably changed the face of London,[5] lengthened Boyle's stay in

London and Londoners unprepared despite the work of Sydenham and others. Sydenham, "the *English Hippocrates* and most accurate Observer of Distempers that ever *Europe* produc'd," as Benjamin Marten called him in 1720 (139-40), was Boyle's neighbour in Pall Mall. Readers wishing to know more about Sydenham may usefully consult Dewhurst 1966 and Duchesneau 1970.

1 Moote and Moote 2004, 10.

2 Boyle to Oldenburg, 14 June, 1665; *Correspondence* 2:480.

3 BP 14: 28-42; Moote and Moote 2002, 68-9; *Correspondence* 2:498.

4 Pepys 1932, 24-25.

5 For details, see Ross 1965.

Oxford, though he seems to have been living near London at the time of the fire. Because of the large number of visitors he had to cope with in Oxford, Boyle also took a place in nearby Stanton St. John's to which he could flee when the influx of visitors became too distracting. Boyle spent 1667 mainly in London, but also in Oxford, before settling finally in London in 1668.

By this period Boyle's interest in natural philosophy had replaced his interest in producing works of ethics, but his interest in theology remained, as did his view, clearly stated in *The Excellency of Theology*, that both revealed and experimentally discovered truth should be of interest to the practising scientist.

In his experimental work Boyle happily made use of assistants, and though he often performed experiments himself, he also relied on others both to make observations and to perform experiments. Like scientists in our own time, he was not a solo worker; he effectively *managed* a laboratory. However, all too often, allowing others to help in the work resulted in problems of one sort or another. For example, having obtained from another person a fluid that had been compounded accidentally, and which continued moving for a number of days (under a scum on its surface), Boyle made a number of observations about it which he reported to the Royal Society. "The motion of this Liquor was not only brisk, but very various." Moreover:

> Tho' the motions of the ... Liquor did not seem to be always equally brisk, yet they appeared to continue manifest and various in some diversities of Weather, as to cold and heat; and when I lookt on it by Candle light, as well as by Day light. And when being not well enough to visit it my self, I sent one purposely to look upon it, about ten a Clock at night, he brought me word that it continued to move as formerly, and so it has done for ten days. And how much longer it will continue to do so; Time must determine.

Boyle, here as ever, was more interested in accurately reporting his observations than in producing theoretical explanations of what he had observed. Moreover he was quite happy, when necessary, to rely on the observations of others,[1] and to leave matters

1 "I do not pretend," Boyle wrote in *Relations about the Bottom of the Sea*, "to have visited the Bottom of the Sea, but since none of the Naturalists whose writings I have yet met with, have been there any more then I, ... I presume it will not be unpleasant, if ... I recite in this place, what I

open, as depending on future results.[1]

However, though Boyle hoped that time would determine how long the self-moving liquid continued to move, he found that, as not infrequently happened in his laboratory, accidents intervened:

> Some time after the foregoing Account had been written, when I came to look upon the Liquor (which in the mean time had been severall times viewed, and appeared to retain its motions) I found to my trouble, that some body's impertinent curiosity and heedlessness had crackt the lower part of the Earthen Pot; at which overture the Liquor, tho' not the Scum, was run out; which had put a period to our Observations, but that, foreseeing that such an Accident might happen, I had long before taken out some spoonfulls of the Liquor, and kept it close stopt in a Vial. [Later, Boyle took it out of the vial and put it in a "*China* Cup" to gratify the curiosity of a foreign minister "and that of some ingenious men there present." He put] the Vessel into divers postures in a Window, the better to discover the true cause of this *Phænomenon*; but whilst I was busy about this, which ingrossed my attention; a mischance overturned the Cup, and by throwing down the liquor, put an end to my speculation.[2]

Boyle's laboratory was in the same house as his sleeping chamber, and the two were in such close proximity that on one occasion, as he was getting ready for bed, an assistant, clearly being aware that Boyle would be interested, brought him the news that a servant had discovered a piece of meat with luminescent spots. Boyle at once had the meat sent for, and despite the lateness of the hour and the fact that he had to rise before five the next morning to visit a sick niece, made a number of observations

---

have learn'd by Enquiry from those Persons that among the many Navigators and Travellors I have had opportunity to converse with, were the likeliest to give me good Information about these matters" (*Works* 6:357).

1 Thus, when reporting a negative result concerning the expected difference in rate of a pendulum in air and in a vacuum, Boyle wrote, "the event of this Experiment being other then we expected, scarce afforded us any other satisfaction, then that of our not having omitted to try it. And whether in case the tryal be made with a *Pendulum* much less disproportionate to the Air then Steel is, the event will much better answer expectation, experience may be consulted ("Spring of the Air," *Works* 1:229)."

2 "An Historical account of a strangely self-moving Liquor," *Works* 9:450-1.

on the luminous spots both in the air and in his vacuum pump, which he subsequently related to the Royal Society.[1]

Although Boyle was about to retire for the night, it was clear to his assistant that he would be interested in anything new and strange, and would want to be informed of it at once. Those about him were aware of his very strong interest in observing the world and in experimenting on any new phenomenon. He was no doubt sincere in his claims to value experimental philosophy because of its theological import, but there is also no doubt that he was also interested, whatever he may himself have thought, simply in experiment for its own sake.

Throughout Boyle's life, what stands out is the fact that he retained that "unsatisfy'd Appetite of Knowledge, that is yet as greedy, as when it first was rays'd," which he found in himself as an adolescent. This greedy curiosity continued. In *The Excellency of Theology*, Boyle noted that

> in the book of nature ... the things we would discover are so darkly or incompletely knowable by those that precede them, that the mind is never satisfied till it comes to the end of the book, till when all that is discovered in the progress, is unable to keep the mind from being molested with impatience to find that yet concealed, which will not be known till one does at least make a further progress. And yet the full discovery of nature's mysteries is so unlikely to fall to any man's share in this life, that the case of the pursuers of them is at best like theirs, that light upon some excellent Romance, of which they shall never see the latter parts.[2]

Towards the end of his life Boyle began to have fears about the possibility of an unhappy afterlife, and he consulted frequently with Bishop Burnet in an effort to lay these fears at rest. Burnet tried hard to convince him of the groundlessness of these worries in his case, but it is not clear that Boyle was convinced.[3]

Throughout his life Boyle's health was poor and when, in December 1691, Katherine died, Boyle died the following week. After his death, Burnet wrote:

---

1 *Works* 7:457-62. This incident is discussed in more detail in Boyle 2006, 45-47.

2 *Works* 8:57 [171].

3 For details of the whole issue, see Hunter 1993.

he had the purity of an angell in him, he was modest and humble rather to a fault. He despised all earthly things, he was perhaps too eager in the pursute of knowledge, but his aim in it all was to raise in him a higher sense of the wisdome and glory of the Creator and to do good to mankind, he studied the Scripture with great application and practised universall love and goodnes in the greatest extent possible, and was a great promoter of love and charity among men and a declared enemy to all bitternes and most particularly to all persecution on the account of religion.[1]

Structure, Purpose, and Overview of the *Excellencies*

The Excellency of Theology ("a work which influenced me wonderfully," Leibniz wrote to Oldenburg) provides us, as Hunter and Davis point out, with an important "exposition of [Boyle's] epistemological views," while *The Excellency and Grounds of the Mechanical Hypothesis* gives a succinct view of Boyle's reasons for favouring that hypothesis.[2] Though some of the material they contain may be found in Boyle's other works, the two *Excellencies* together provide an important insight into Boyle's views on theology and natural philosophy.

Boyle tells us straightforwardly at the beginning of *The Excellency of Theology* how he plans to structure the work:

> I shall divide the following epistle into two distinct parts. In the former of which I shall offer you the chief positive considerations by which I would represent to you the study of divinity as preferable to that of physics; and in the second part I shall consider the allegations that I foresee your friend may interpose in favour of natural philosophy. From which distribution you will easily gather that the motives on the one hand, and the objections on the other, will challenge to themselves distinct sections in the respective parts whereto they belong.

However, as often happens with Boyle, other matters arise, enter into, and even take over the exposition. He kept finding, he

1 "A Rough Draught of my own Life," quoted in Maddison 1969, 185. It is possible that Boyle's own views may not have been, for the England of his time, strictly orthodox, though he would certainly have attempted to make sure that they were in accord with his reading of Scripture.

2 *Works* 8:xiii-xiv.

tells us, "new things springing up ... under my pen." Thus we find him launching out towards the end of *The Excellency of Theology* into a discussion of whether natural philosophers should have *systems*, that is, all-encompassing accounts of natural phenomena. Boyle clearly had no desire to provide such a system, nor did he make any attempt to do so. It is, he suggests, the "judicious modesty of the corpuscularians" which has "made them backward"[1] in the matter of system building and, clearly, he sees himself as sharing this "judicious modesty." There were additional reasons. Boyle felt that it was, to put it no stronger, highly unlikely that any one system might contain the whole truth. He writes,

> Right Reason may be look'd upon as a Catholick Principle of which Philosophy is but an Application, and the Dictates of particular Philosophy's, such as the Peripatetick, the Platonick the Epicurean, &c. are but particular Corollary's which are not alwayes truely drawn, and on that account may alwayes be Question'd or Examin'd; and may I fear, oftentimes be justly Rejected. <And this holds> Especially, when in the *Examen*, He that makes it is assisted by the Discoveries made by Revelation; from whose Heavenly Light, in reference to divers subjects, the Intellect may receive such a benefit, as the Air dos in a clear day from the Beams of the Sun; by which it is both Enlighten'd and Expanded.[2]

The complaints he makes concerning systems in *The Excellency of Theology* echo his earlier views: "I must freely acknowledge to you, that it has long seem'd to me none of the least impediments of the real advancement of true Natural Philosophy, that men have been so forward to write Systems of it, and have thought themselves oblig'd either to be altogether silent, or not write less than an entire body of Physiology: for from hence seem to have ensu'd not a few Inconveniences." Boyle mentions: (1) that experts in one branch of science are tempted to write as experts in all; (2) that the reader is misled by the compendious-

1 *Works* 8:86 [211].

2 BP 1:11. Boyle makes a similar point in the *Appendix to the Christian Virtuoso I* (*Works* 12:405) where he suggests that the wise philosopher will select portions from many different philosophical systems, "selecting and picking out of each that, which seemed most consonant to truth and reason, and leaving the rest to their particular authors and abettors."

ness of the table of contents into thinking that all the work is already done; (3) that the writer's own good thoughts will be lost among the borrowed bits needed to fill up the systematical tract; and worst of all, (4) that people with a small good result suppress it: "many excellent Notions or Experiments are by sober and modest men suppress'd, because such Persons being forbidden by their Judgement and Integrity to teach more than they understand, or assert more than they can prove, are likewise forbidden by Custome to publish their Thoughts and Observations, unless they were numerous enough to swell into a System."[1]

This attitude towards the construction of systems was not Boyle's alone, as Peter Anstey has pointed out,[2] but was central to the early Royal Society's favouring of experimental over speculative philosophy. This was an almost complete reversal from an earlier period when it was sometimes assumed that *only* speculative philosophy was scientifically acceptable. In the late fifteenth century, the Aristotelian Petrus Garsia, Bishop of Ussellus in Sardinia, said, "To assert that ... experimental knowledge is science or a part of natural science is ridiculous, wherefore such magicians are called experimenters rather than scientists. Besides, magic, according to those of that opinion, is practical knowledge, whereas natural science in itself and in all its parts is purely speculative knowledge."[3]

Boyle's lack of interest in system building was noted by Eustace Budgell in the next century:

> I believe I may truly venture to assert, That no Philosopher, either before, or after him, ever made so great a Number of curious and profitable Experiments. He very rightly judged,

---

1 *Certain Physiological Essays, and other Tracts* (1661), "Proemial Essay," *Works* 2:10.

2 Anstey 2005.

3 Quoted in Partington 1961, 2:10. Bishop Garsia was an Aristotelian, but Aristotle himself was at times slightly more accommodating. Although he held that scientific propositions had to be universal and necessarily true, he also allowed a place, even if a smaller, incidental, one, for other truths: "It is clear," he said, "that if the propositions from which a deduction proceeds are universal, then it is necessary for the conclusion of such a demonstration, i.e. of a demonstration simpliciter, to be eternal. There is therefore no demonstration of perishable things, nor any understanding of them simpliciter but only incidentally, because nothing holds of them universally but only at some time and in some way" (Aristotle 1994, 1.8, 75b 21-6).

> that this was the only proper Method to become a Master of the Secrets of Nature; and there is one Particular, for which he can never be too much admired or commended; it is evident, that he made all his Experiments without any Design to confirm or establish any particular System. He is so much in earnest in his Search after Truth, that he is wholly indifferent where he finds it. We may truly say, That he has animated Philosophy; and put in Action what before was little better than a speculative Science. He has shewn that we inhabit a World, all the Parts of which, are incessantly in Action; that Nature is every Moment carrying on her grand Scheme; and, that even our own Bodies are affected by an infinite Number of Agents more than we imagined.[1]

Earlier, Boyle's lack of interest in system building was lamented by Leibniz, shortly after Boyle's death:

> It is astonishing that Mr. Boyle, who has so many fine experiments, did not come to some theory of chemistry after meditating so long on them. Yet in his books, and for all the consequences that he draws from his observations, he concludes only what we all know, that everything happens mechanically. He is perhaps too reserved. Excellent men should leave us even their conjectures; they are wrong if they wish to give us only those truths that are certain.[2]

Boyle's intent, then, was to uphold the study of theology as not only worthwhile in itself, but as preferable even to the study of natural philosophy. Boyle thought each subject worthy of pursuit, and believed too that they could be usefully combined, but he is here initially intent on establishing priorities. Interestingly, even when he is most intent on extolling the virtues of theology, Boyle cannot refrain from admiring comments about experimental philosophy. And it is relevant, too, that he decided to publish *The Excellency and Grounds of the Mechanical Hypothesis* in the same volume with *The Excellency of Theology*. Nonetheless, even though experimental philosophy has its delights for the experimenter, and even though "the mechanical arts are highly beneficial ... to those places and perhaps those states, where such improvements are found out

1 Budgell 1732, 119-20.

2 Leibniz to Christiaan Huygens, 29 December, 1691, in Huygens 1888, 10:228.

and cherished,"[1] there are two caveats to be noted. One is that the real delight for the experimenter comes from the increased knowledge of the world that such experimentation brings, and this increased knowledge of the world amounts simply to an increased knowledge of God's design. Boyle was a constant employer of the "two books" metaphor, and though for him the "Booke call'd Scripture" was paramount, we also gain insight into the nature of God by studying the book of nature: "indeed, the World is the great Book, not so much of Nature, as of the God of Nature, which we should find ev'n crowded with instructive Lessons, if we had but the Skill, and would take the Pains, to extract and pick them out."[2]

The second point Boyle wants to draw to our attention is this. Very often the "advantages" that accrue to states do so at the expense of people, "of which we have an example in the invention of extracting gold and silver out of the ore, with mercury. For though it has vastly enriched the Spaniards in the West Indies, yet it is not of any solid advantage to the world, no more than the discovery of the Peruvian and other American mines, by which (especially reckoning the multitudes of unhappy men that are made miserable, and destroyed in working them), mankind is not put into a better condition than it was before."[3]

Throughout Boyle is explicitly writing for believers. He is not trying to convert atheists, but to convince scientists who are also Christians of the value of cultivating theology as well as natural philosophy. Although there is no denying the delights of scientific investigation and progress, his argument goes, there is nonetheless a nobler and better pursuit: "I consider in general that, as there are scarce any motives accounted fitter to engage a rational man in a study than that the subject is noble, that it is his duty to apply himself to it, and that his proficiency in it will bring him great advantages, so there is not any of these three inducements that does not concur in a very plentiful measure to recommend to us the study of theological truths."[4]

In the seventeenth century and earlier, "practical" matters were often matters of *ethical practice*, and since one's ethical doings involved one's soul's salvation, self-interest was also

---

1 *Works* 8:62 [179].

2 *Occasional Reflections*, *Works* 5:39. Boyle sometimes adds a third book, the book of conscience (see, e.g., BP 8:123), but in the main he stays with the more common dichotomy. For the background to the two books metaphor see Howell 2002.

3 *Works* 8:62 [179].

4 *Works* 8:13 [111].

involved. Acting ethically was a *practical* matter, which would have a heavenly reward, even if that was not supposed to be one's *reason* for so acting. So theological issues were also *practical* issues. Nowadays the preamble "Let's be practical" is inevitably followed by an immoral suggestion, but it was not always so.

For Boyle, however, "practical" also had a use closer to ours: the practical arts were the useful as opposed to the merely speculative parts of knowledge. As mentioned above in the *Life*, the young Boyle studied "Surveying and Fortification ... and other Practick parts of Mathematicks," but later regretted his lack of knowledge of pure as opposed to applied mathematics.[1] Also, Bishop Garsia's distinction between "experimenters" who produced only "practical knowledge," as opposed to the purists who produced the more desirable "purely speculative knowledge," remained as a distinction but not as a disparagement. Boyle very clearly wanted both experimental (practical) knowledge and theoretical knowledge; in general, in fact, he was more interested in acquiring straightforward factual knowledge, being content to let theory follow when it could.

In *The Excellency of Theology*, Boyle treats theology as paramount. For though Boyle was enamoured of the new experimental philosophy, he was worried about its possible negative effect. On the one hand, it had clear positive value. It could lead to cures for diseases, it could improve agriculture, it could lessen the hazards of voyaging by sea, it could be useful in the mining and refining of metals, and so on and on and on. At least as important as this, it could lead the thinking virtuoso to a greater appreciation of the wonders of creation, and hence of the greatness of the Creator. On the other hand, it contained a danger: it was so enchanting that it could lead its practitioners to value it over the study of, and concentration on, theology. Moreover, it could lead the unthinking to ignore the need for God in the creation and sustaining of natural laws in favour of a belief that those laws were themselves as much explanation as was needed. So, "you are not to expect that I should give philosophy the wounds of an enemy. For my design being not to discourage you, nor any ingenious man, from courting it at all, nor from courting it much, but from courting it too much, and despising divinity for it, I employ against it not a sword to wound, but a balance, to show that its excellencies, though solid and weighty, are less so than the preponderating ones of theology."[2]

---

1 "Usefulness II," *Works* 6:440.

2 *Works* 8:56 [169].

Boyle's constant harping on the conceit that a natural philosopher may have, that would lead him to devalue theology, shows us something of what Boyle takes to be the temper of the times. It also reveals what he takes to be a completely understandable reaction to the pleasures of experimental philosophy (that is, science). Throughout the *Excellencies* we find Boyle lauding theology while at the same time being unable to resist praising experimental philosophy. Indeed, his publisher tells us that he postponed publication of *The Excellency of Theology* in order not to allow it to be "misapplied by some enemies to experimental philosophy."[1]

Notably, his love of theology did not extend to an uncritical fondness for theologians. Clerics and commentators, he felt, often made mistakes:

> [T]he greater reverence I owe to the Scripture itself than to its expositors, prevails upon me to tell you freely that you will not do right either to theology, or (the greatest repository of its truths) the Bible, if you imagine that there are no considerable additions to be made to the theological discoveries we have already, nor no clearer expositions of many texts of Scripture, or better reflections on that matchless book, than are to be met with in the generality of commentators, or of preachers, without excepting the ancient fathers themselves.[2]

Thus while reverencing Scripture, and allowing due weight for the pronouncements of clerical authority, in this as in all matters, we should, while realizing its limitations, trust our own reason:

> In matters of Religion, the Authority of the church with the general consent of Learned Men, may sway with me, as long as I have no cogent Reason to be of another opinion; but if I can light upon any demonstrative proof for a differing opinion, I would follow my own private judgement against the general consent. As, if I[3] set my watch in weather that hides the sun from us, I am content to set it by the Town clock, or that which belongs to the church ..., but if I have the opportunity of con-

1 *Works* 8:5 [102].

2 *Works* 8:29 [133]. Later Boyle remarks that he hopes that "a philosophical eye ... may pierce a great deal farther than has yet been done ... by divines" (*Works* 8:36 [142].

3 Altering the MS "As if I be to set my watch" to "As, if I set my watch."

> sulting a good sun-dial I shal not scruple, in case of difference (for some hours after) to prefer the Information of my own watch to that of the Town clock, & as many other clocks & watches as were set by it, and agree with it.[1]

Boyle was cautious in matters of belief. He accepted, for example, that there were supernatural beings. He accepted that they sometimes interacted with mortals. Unlike many Protestants of the time, he accepted that miracles were still possible. But on any specific occasion his tendency was to reject or downplay such accounts. Thus though "The famous Sennertus, and some other learned physicians, tell us of diseases which proceed from incantation,"[2] Boyle points out the practical uselessness of such accounts. In this he was followed in the next century by Immanuel Kant, who held the same view:[3]

> In the affairs of life ... it is impossible for us to count on miracles or to take them into consideration at all in our use of reason (and reason must be used in every incident of life). The judge (however credulous of miracles he may be in church) listens to the delinquent's claims to have been tempted of the devil exactly as though nothing had been said; although, were the judge to regard this diabolical influence as possible, it would be worth some consideration that an ordinary simple-minded man had been ensnared in the toils of an arch-rogue.... As regards miracles of the good variety, they are employed by men in the affairs of life as mere phrases. Thus the doctor says that there is no help for the patient unless a miracle occurs—in other words, he will certainly die.[4]

Should anyone, Boyle asks, "take up the articles of faith concerning matters of great and everlasting consequence, upon the authority of men fallible as themselves, when satisfaction may be

---

1 BP 5:91 (Boyle 2006, 4.2.10, 362-63).

2 *Works* 8:108 [236].

3 Kant, like Boyle, was a sincere believer. But, also like Boyle, he felt that we should be modest in our claims about religious *knowledge*. In the *Critique of Pure Reason*, while emphasizing the need for *belief* in God, he argued that there was no possibility of *demonstrating* God's existence. He had, he said, "found it necessary to deny *knowledge*, in order to make room for *faith*" (Kant 1787, Bxxx).

4 Kant 1793, 82.

had without them from the infallible word of God?"[1] Boyle's answer is a clear *No*. In the *Sceptical Chymist* Boyle has Carneades remark, regarding van Helmont's claim to have a universal solvent: "I cannot but say on this Occasion what ... our Friend Mr. *Boyle* is wont to say, when he is askt his Opinion of any strange Experiment, That He, that hath seen it hath more Reason to beleeve it, than He that hath not,"[2] and Carneades' report is upheld in Boyle's second "Essay concerning the Unsuccessfulness of Experiments" where, discussing reports of locating metals by dowsing with hazel rods, he says, "of this Experiment I must content my self to say, what I am wont to do when my opinion is ask'd of those things which I dare not peremptorily reject, and yet am not convinc'd of; namely, that they that have seen them can much more reasonably believe them, than those that have not."[3] Ever cautious, Boyle was not quick to accept unlikely accounts, but not quick to reject them out of hand either.

An Overview of the Excellencies: The Excellency of Theology

Part 1: The positive reasons for studying theology

Section 1: The Nobility of Theology's Object

The *object* of the study is greater than any other, and God's account of God's nature and attributes is preferable to any less direct knowledge. Reason will tell us something of God, but revelation will tell us much more, and provide us with otherwise unobtainable details.

Revelation also provides us with knowledge of God's intended positive laws. Additionally, we may learn directly of God's thoughts and actions in the history of the world. (Boyle gives a number of examples.) Through the study of theology we learn of God's judgements, and vitally, of his promise to "accept, forgive, and reward those that sincerely obey him."

We also learn from revelation about angels, the universe, and the bodies, immortal souls and creation of humans, knowledge which, though inferior to knowledge of God, is nonetheless

1 *Works* 8:43 [152].

2 *Works* 2:244.

3 *Works* 2:69.

"highly preferable to any that natural philosophy has been able to afford its votaries."[1]

There are also issues of importance and interest with which theology deals, but which lie outside the province of natural philosophy. These concern questions such as Christ's sacrifice, God's judgement of humans, the production and possible preexistence of human souls, the fate of the soul after death, the state of the universe after its ultimate transfiguration, the post-mortem continuance of our earthly relations, whether social, or marital, and many others questions the answers to which the study of theology may provide some answers, however incomplete.

Boyle now turns to questions of possible inconsistency, either internal to the scriptures, or external by comparison with the knowledge that natural philosophy gives us. And here he spends some time noting that both commentators and translators are likely, unwittingly, to lead us astray. On the other hand, some commentators (such as those mentioned by Boyle) can give us genuine help.

Just as in natural philosophy close empirical work is better than mere speculation,[2] so in theology a "close and critical account" is better than the remarks of "superficial writers, though never so florid or witty."

Finally, we should realize that the results of natural philosophy, important though they are, do not exhaust "the nature, counsels, and works of God." For there are also the communities of incorporeal things: the good and bad angels, as well as human souls—three areas where natural philosophy, dealing as it does with material things, is unable to provide us with knowledge. And it is "probable that the grand attributes of God are more signally exercised, and made more conspicuous in the making and governing of each of the three intellectual communities, than in the framing and upholding the community of mere bodily things."

---

1 It is worth noting that though these studies and the results which natural philosophy can give us are of less importance than our knowledge of God, they receive, in terms of length in this section, rather more attention than that knowledge of the divine, perhaps because of our having more easy access to such knowledge, but also, perhaps, because of Boyle's abiding and passionate interest in them.

2 A "skillfully dissected" eye, Boyle remarks in passing, reveals more to the philosopher than a poetic excursion on its beauty.

Section 2: Our Obligation to Study Theology

The obligation (of those "that have the capacity and opportunity") to study theology is based on two main grounds: "*obedience*, and *gratitude*." The need for obedience is shown not only through the nature of the study, but because he who commands it is "the supreme and absolute lord of all his creatures" and thus "has a full right to make what laws he thinks fit, and enjoin what service he thinks fit, as well as a power to punish those that either violate the one, or deny the other."[1]

Secondly, we "are extremely great debtors unto God" both for our creation and "the higher blessings ... we may receive from him as Christians." Boyle now offers a strange but interesting reason for gratitude to God. Not only has God made us rational creatures (and reason is "a ray of divinity"), God has also created the material world so that we, as natural philosophers, may gain knowledge of it.

Thus we have good reason to praise God, and "men's hearty praises [are pleasing] to God."

Boyle now considers the suggestion of some natural philosophers that there is no *need* to study theology since a very little knowledge of that subject will suffice for salvation. Against this Boyle points out (1) that even if a little knowledge is enough, it is not easy to be sure that this or that account of the "fundamental articles" *is* the sufficient collection; (2) that besides the *beliefs* we should have, we also need to know the requisite *rules of life*; (3) even if certain things are not absolutely necessary, they may help us "more clearly understand, more rationally and firmly believe, and more steadily practise, the points that are necessary"; finally (4) "searching into the matters of religion" may be necessary as a result of God's command, whether or not such searching is otherwise necessary for our soul's salvation.

In the next century Kant suggested that for rational entities to neglect the development of their talents was, in a certain sense, a contradiction in terms: morally, they have a duty to develop their talents.[2] And here we find Boyle making a similar point in the key of theology: people who "have received from God a greater measure of intellectual abilities than the generality of Christians" should not "willingly ... come short ... in the knowledge of the

1 For an argument in favour of this currently unfashionable stance see Geach 1969, ch. 9.

2 Kant 1956, 90.

mysteries and other truths of Christianity." And so even if "not all the evangelical truths are precisely necessary to be known, it may be both a duty not to despise the study of them, and a happiness to employ ourselves about it."

Section 3: The Advantages Accruing from a Study of Theology

Simply contemplating such "noble and worthy objects" provides delight. Moreover, such pleasures have an "affinity with the pleasures that shall make up men's blessedness in heaven." We shall have a "contentment" from such study that comes from our awareness of having performed our duty. (This is one of those duties which, "upon the bare account of their being duties, [are] not only tolerable but pleasant.")

"Another advantage ... is the improvement of the contemplator ... in point of piety and virtue." Someone who does study theology is likely to be "more disposed than others" to admire, trust, and love God, and accept his governance. Again, such a study will "afford us very powerful consolations" when "afflictions, and the approaches of death" are troubling us, something which natural philosophy, despite its charms, cannot offer. Finally, "though heaven abound with inexpressible joys ... not of the least [will be] that the knowledge of divine things that was here so zealously pursued shall there be completely attained."

Part II: A comparison of the advantages of natural philosophy and theology

Section 1: The Delights and Drawbacks of Natural Philosophy

In this section Boyle does not deny the pleasures that natural philosophy brings, but points out that they must not be allowed "to surpass, or even equal" those of "theological contemplations." His intention is not "to give philosophy the wounds of an enemy," but rather to show that experimental philosophy's "excellencies, though solid and weighty," are out-weighed by "the preponderating ones of theology."

First then, there are the many *practical* inconveniences that beset the experimenter such as, as Boyle elsewhere points out, the difficulty of getting "unsophisticated," that is, pure, samples of chemicals; the difficulty of getting glass tubes of the right bore and thickness; the difficulty of getting accurate measuring instruments, etc. The experimenter will need to rely on "a variety of mechanic people (as distillers, drugsters, smiths, turners, etc.)," which will take up considerable time and energy and often lead to nothing but disappointment—"a drudgery greater than any who has not tried it will imagine, and which yet, being as inevitable as unwelcome, does very much counter-balance and allay the delightfulness of" experimental philosophy.

A further problem, or at least relevant point, is that experimental investigations are never finished. Knowledge is never complete, and additionally one can never be sure that some error in the experiment or in the apparent truths deduced from it has not led us down a blind alley. However, the experimenter who also interests himself in theology knows that every such discovery, partial though it may be, nonetheless reveals something further about God's "transcendent excellencies."

Section 2: The Practical Goods Resulting from Natural Philosophy and from Theology

Boyle, once again, not only accepts the point that natural philosophy brings practical goods, he endorses it, but is concerned to emphasize equally that the study of "the divine may benefit [us] much more." The argument is interesting. First and immediately there is the fact that "he who effectually teaches men to subdue their lusts and passions does as much as the physician contribute to the preservations of their bodies by exempting them from those vices [which lead to] wars, and duels, and rapines, and the pox ... and all the train of other diseases that attend" such vices. However, and perhaps less obviously, Boyle believes that failure to withhold from such vices provokes "God to punish [the offenders] with temporal as well as spiritual judgements, such as plagues, wars, famines, and other.... calamities, that sweep away a great part of mankind."[1]

---

1 Boyle is here untroubled, apparently, by the *scope* of the punishment of offenders, which seems to destroy a number of innocent others in its train. Elsewhere he suggests a standard eschatological solution to the implicit problem of evil which is lurking here: "There, [in the Cœlestiall Court, about the Majestick Throne of Christ] I hope, we shall have clearly expounded to us those Riddles of Providence, which have, but too often, Tempted ev'n good men, to question Gods Conduct in the Government of the World; whil'st the Calamities and Persecutions of Vertue, and Innocence seem approv'd by him, who Accumulates Prosperities on their Criminall Opposers ("Seraphic Love," *Works* 1:126)."

Moreover, though the results of the natural philosophers may improve both medicine and trade, not all such results are to the general advantage of humanity. The ability to extract gold and silver from the ore has proved advantageous to Spain but not to the miners who are "destroyed in working" the mines in question. Even if such advances in experimental philosophy do provide us with benefits, those benefits are for this life alone. They will not follow us "to the other world," whereas the benefits of divinity will still hold "when we are arrived at our journey's end." They "reach beyond the end of time itself."

Section 3: The Supposed Certainty and Clearness of Physics as Opposed to the Darkness and Uncertainty of Theological Matters

Boyle's first point: so far from being unclear, the "fundamental and necessary articles of religion" are "evident, and capable of a moral demonstration." Secondly, the truths of religion have a "moral certainty," and the truths of physics cannot claim any higher degree of certainty. Moreover, many apparent scientific truths have themselves simply a moral certainty. For example, what corporeal substances are is by no means clear to "modern philosophers." Indeed, there are difficulties in the very notion of material substance, for either matter is infinitely divisible or it is not, and both sides of the disjunction are subject to difficulties that their proponents seem unable to overcome: "the more candid ... have confessed the objections on both sides to be insoluble."

We also do not know how perception, which involves an interaction between a corporeal entity, the brain and nervous system of humans, and an incorporeal entity, the mind, occurs: "this union of an incorporeal with a corporeal substance (and that without a medium) is a thing so unexampled in nature, and so difficult to comprehend, that I somewhat question whether the profound secrets of theology, not to say the adorable mystery itself of the incarnation, be more abstruse than this."[1] Boyle goes

---

1 Boyle's awareness of this lack of knowledge about ourselves was constant. In the posthumously published *Christian Virtuoso II*, he wrote:

> [T]he very notion we have of spirits in general, is, to me, no small argument how little we really and particularly know of them. For though superficial considerers take up with the vulgar definition, that a *spirit is an immaterial substance*, yet that leaves us exceedingly to seek, if we aim at satisfaction in particular enquiries. For it declares rather what the

on to give more examples of the difficulty involved in the notion that humans have incorporeal minds without, however, drawing the conclusion that there are no such entities.[1] In certain areas at least, then, the claimed certainty and clarity of scientific investigations is clearly lacking.

Boyle now points out that even a dim or approximate grasp of *important* truths is more worthwhile than a complete grasp of unimportant ones. It is better, from the point of view of the naturalist, to have even a rough estimate of planetary distances than to have a precise measurement of a farmer's field. Since theological truths are among the most important we can have, a "dim and imperfect knowledge of God and the mysteries of religion may be more desirable, and upon that account more delightful, than a clearer knowledge of those inferior truths that physics is wont to teach."

Section 4: The Natural Philosopher's Unjustified Pride of Achievement

Once again, Boyle does not want to denigrate natural philosophy, but only to limit the "overweening opinion" natural philosophers may have of their successes. To this end he points out, first, that the theological truths we have through revelation are not only of nobler objects but are truths that natural philosophy could never uncover. Secondly, if there is room for pride in achievement, we should notice that it is only the *originators* of a particular doctrine

---

thing *is not*, than what *it is*; and is as little instructive a definition, as it would be to say, that *a curve line is not a straight one*....

The terms we use of moving, perceiving, exciting, enlightening, determining, restraining, commanding, &c. do not suggest true notions of the things we would signify, being but applications of corporeal actions or qualities, to things of an incorporeal, and so of a quite differing nature and condition....

The knowledge we have of our own souls, is but partly by consciousness or internal sensation, the rest we must learn as we can.

What the soul does in the body, as when we remember and speak, and blush, and see, she knows not how she does it, nor so much as what instruments, or parts are employed in her work.

The operations of spirits upon bodies and vehicles, and much more upon one another, we are in the dark about. (*Works* 12:474-75)

1 Boyle's admiring friend, John Locke, felt that it was possible for God to superadd thought to matter, but the prevailing view was that thinking matter involved a contradiction in terms. See the section on Descartes in Part 5 of this Introduction, "Predecessors and Influences."

(such as corpuscularianism) that are entitled to such pride. After these main principles are established, routine scientific endeavour can lead to results which "may fall to the lot of persons not endowed with any extraordinary sagacity or acuteness of parts."

Boyle then points out that, in fact, our achievements in natural philosophy are all too slight. We know almost nothing of the "vast bodies that are above us" and our knowledge of the earth, minute though the earth is by comparison with the rest of the universe, "seems confined to but a small share of the superficial part of a physical point!"

Finally, God understands the universe far better than we possibly could, and it is his judgement that the truths of theology are "more valuable than those which relate but to the objects, that he has exposed to all men's eyes."

Section 5: The Value of the Fame that Scientific Attainments Bring

In this section Boyle is concerned to point out, at length, the difficulties inherent in seeking fame through scientific endeavours, not to mention the problems that "that perfumed smoke, applause" brings in its train. Naturalists must either publish their "thoughts or experiments" or refrain from publishing, but both produce problems. Not publishing simply intensifies the amount of intrusive questioning that, if rejected, will lead to the blackening of the character of the non-responder, while if the naturalist disingenuously responds the danger will be that of "having his notions or experiments arrogated" by others. And attempts at a compromise between these two extremes also, Boyle argues, fail in their aim.

So perhaps it is better to publish? Well, no, says Boyle, clearly writing from the heart. For either the works will be systematical, or they will not. If they are the writer will be obliged to include many things that are well known as well as many things that are *not* well known to the author. And if "declining the systematical way, one shall choose the other of writing loose tracts and discourses, he may indeed avoid some of the lately mentioned inconveniences, but will scarce avoid the being plundered by systematical writers."

Thus, if the naturalist writes large books they will almost certainly contain things which are inaccurate or irrelevant, while if "he writes but small tracts, as is the custom of the most judicious authors, who have no mind to publish but what is new and considerable, as their excellency will make them to be the sooner dispersed so the smallness of the bulk will endanger them to be quickly lost, as experience shows us of divers excellent little tracts which, though published not many years ago, are already out of print."

Moreover, lasting fame rests as much on the judgement of "compilers [who] frequently leave far better things than they take ... for the want of skill to understand the author they cite and epitomize, or candour to do him right."

Besides these specific difficulties there is the general point that reputations are subject to the whims of fashion.[1] Sometimes one branch of learning finds general favour, sometimes another, "by which you may see how little certainty there is that, because a man is skilled in natural philosophy, and that science is now in request, his reputation shall be as great as now, when perhaps the science itself will be grown out of repute."

Moreover, Boyle points out, science progresses, and new discoveries and technological advances may overturn a previously accepted assumption or theory. So, Boyle remarks, "*it is far less easy than he thinks, to be as sure that he shall have the praises of future ages, as that (though he have them) he shall not hear them.*"

Further, Boyle argues, even if that were not the case, we still should not turn away from the study of divinity. For first, there is no reason for industrious and clever people not to work in both areas, and second, if a good reputation is the desired end, that may be obtained in divinity as well as in natural philosophy. But finally, even if the study of divinity led necessarily to a "neglect [of] the acquisition of reputation," this would be minor inconvenience in view of the heavenly reward that "will make a rich amends for the declining of a fading wreath here upon earth."

---

1 "Fame," said Bacon, "is like a Riuer that beareth vp things light, and swolne; and drownes things waighty and solid. But," Bacon added, offering a ray of hope, "if persons of quality & iudgement concur, then it is as the Scripture saith, *Nomen bonum instar vnguents fragrantis* [Latin: a good name is like a fragrant ointment]; It filleth all round about, and will not easily away. For the odors of ointments are more durable then those of flowers" (Bacon 1612, 204-5). [The Vulgate has *melius est nomen bonum quam unguenta pretiosa*, and the King James Version agrees: "a good name is better than precious ointment" (Ecclesiastes 7.1).]

The Conclusion

Boyle concludes by reminding the reader that *The Excellency of Theology* is expressly aimed at readers who accept the Gospels. It is not an attempt to convert unbelievers, but to persuade the *Christian* virtuoso not to devalue theology in favour of natural philosophy.

An Overview of the Excellencies: The Excellency and Grounds of the Mechanical Hypothesis

Boyle begins by identifying the doctrines of Aristotle and Paracelsus as the two main views that are opposed to his favoured corpuscularian or mechanical position. His argument will be to show that such opposing views must either fail or be shown to be compatible with the mechanical hypothesis.

Boyle himself provides (in his Recapitulation [246]) a clear summary of the points in *The Excellency of the Mechanical Hypothesis*. He points out that he is arguing for "a philosophy [that] reaches but to things purely corporeal." He believes, and immediately tells us, that God created the material world, "gave motion to matter, ... so guided the various motions of the parts of it, as to contrive them into the world he designed ... and established those rules of motion and that order amongst things corporeal, which we are wont to call the laws of nature." However, given that as background, the naturalist may treat of the world as a "great automaton, or self moving engine, wherein all things are performed by the bare motion (or rest), the size, the shape, and the situation or texture of the parts of the universal matter it consists of."[1]

In our explanatory principles, he suggests, we cannot make do with fewer notions than matter and motion. These two together will generate a number of other properties such as the shape, size, situation, etc. of the individual parts of matter, which in turn account for the bodies and their kinds that we perceive,[2] as well

---

1 "The Excellency of Theology," *Works* 8:75 [198].

2 In *Forms and Qualities*, Boyle points out that "That, upon whose account [we] really distinguish any one Body from others, and refer it to this or that *Species* of Bodies, is nothing but an Aggregate or Convention of such Accidents [that is, properties or qualities], as most men do by a kind of Agreement (for the Thing is more Arbitrary then we are aware of) think necessary or sufficient to make a Portion of the Universal Matter belong to this or that Determinate *Genus* or *Species* of Natural Bodies" (*Works* 5:323).

as the qualities that we perceive them to have.[1] Finally these principles are intelligible, and any other explanation will of necessity be less general and so be reducible to a special case of the corpuscular hypothesis.

God and the World

For Boyle, God created the world, gave it natural laws, and constantly sustains both the created objects and the laws which describe their behaviour.[2] Boyle accepted the Genesis account in its broad outline, and so he held that the world was fairly recently created, as his admired friend, James Ussher, archbishop of Armagh, had suggested. (Boyle accepted most of the Bible literally, as may be seen from his unquestioning account of the nature and actions of good and evil spirits.)[3] Scientific investigation, Boyle held, can give us many important results, but revelation gives us truths that we would otherwise never attain, and gives us otherwise unsuspected details even of the truths that can be ascertained naturally. Without revelation we could not know, for example, of the existence of Adam and Eve, and of other truths revelation yields details that we can without revelation obtain only "very dimly, incogently, and defectively,"

> such as ... That the World had a beginning, that 'tis upheld and govern'd by Gods general concourse & providence; that God has a peculiar regard to mankind; and a propitious one to good men; that he foresees those future things, we call *contingent*: that mens souls shall not dye with their bodyes, and many

---

1 *How* the texture, etc., of bodies, interacting with our sensory organs, produce precisely the sensations they do is, according to Boyle, the result of a lawlike connection instituted by God. The particular connections were made by God for reasons which are no doubt weighty, but which are to us unobvious and arbitrary: "the intimate Union between [mind and body] as well as most of the Laws of it, depends upon the free or arbitrary institution of God" (BP 2:62; Boyle 2006, 3.5.1, 248).

2 Boyle has, and uses, the notion of "laws of motion," but his general notion of *law* is not always quite ours. "When a Man shoots an Arrow at a Mark, so as to hit it," Boyle says, "though the Arrow moves towards the Mark, as it would if it could and did design to strike it, yet none will say, that this Arrow moves by a law, but by an External, tho' well directed, Impulse" ("Notion of Nature," *Works* 10:458).

3 *Works* 8:18-20 [118-20].

other articles of the Philosophers, as well as the Christians Creed.[1]

Boyle's creation story, then, is that of Genesis, spelled out in a slightly different idiom. God, Boyle believed, created the matter of the world, then broke it up and started it moving.[2] He provided laws for the particles of matter, but the laws he chose could have been different, and it is possible, Boyle thought, that other regions of our Universe might have different laws. There are also laws that are not laws of nature, with the laws that govern interaction between mind and matter providing a clear example. Under certain conditions we have a perception of a red object (when looking at a cherry, for example), but this is not a necessary connection: God might have decided that we should have a mental experience of blue under such conditions. Nor are such laws *laws of nature*—that is, laws for which a natural philosopher can provide an explanation—for they have to do not with the interaction of material corpuscles, but with the interaction of the material with the immaterial, which, though regular and lawlike, remains mysterious and inexplicable: "the very conditions of the *Union* of the Soul and Body; which being setled at first by God's *arbitrary institution*, and having nothing in all Nature parallel to them, the manner and Terms of that strange Union, is a Riddle to Philosophers, but must needs be clearly known to *Him*, that alone did Institute it, and, (all the while it lasts) does preserve it."[3]

Boyle was very aware that "law" in such contexts has to be interpreted with care, for non-rational entities can only metaphorically be law-governed. Hence God is required not only to sustain the objects he has created, but to sustain the laws he has decided upon. One more factor was required. God made matter, broke it up and started it moving in accordance with laws, but it was also necessary for him to give the particles *directed* motions that he foresaw would lead to the "orderly, beautifull & many ways admirable ... systeme ... we call the world."[4]

1 BP 7:242. For the difficulties to which God's foreseeing *contingent* events gives rise, see Appendix F, "Future Contingents."

2 Sometimes Boyle considers the possibility that God created matter "incohærent," that is, already broken into particles (so that the matter is not "cohering"), as at "Usefulness I," *Works* 3: 248, but in general he opts for the creation of formless matter first.

3 "Of the High Veneration Man's Intellect owes to God," *Works* 10:188-9. See also "CV 1, Appendix," *Works* 12:380; BP 9:40; BP 36:46v (Boyle 2006 2.2.32, 242-43).

4 BP 7:188v.

All this is true of the corporeal universe, but God also created immaterial entities: angels, good and bad, and human souls. Indeed, God continues to create new human souls. Their production and the "physical miracle" required to attach them to their respective bodies is a daily occurrence.[1] Because God created humans it might be thought (and was commonly thought at the time) that the universe was created for humans, but Boyle is clear that this is not the only possibility:

> [I]f God be allowed to be, as indeed he is, the Author of the Universe, how will it appear that He, whose Knowledge infinitely transcends ours, and who may be suppos'd to operate according to the Dictates of his own immense Wisdom, should, in his Creating of things, have respect to the measure and ease of Humane Understandings, and not rather, if of any, of Angelical Intellects, so that whether it be to God, or to Chance, that we ascribe the Production of things, that way may often be fittest or likelyest for Nature to work by, which is not easiest for us to understand.[2]

The universe, that is, might be too complicated for us to understand and, in any case, it follows that while simplicity may often be our best guide as to what working hypothesis to choose, we should not think it to be inevitably a reliable guide to truth.

Since philosophers such as Descartes (whom Boyle admired, though not uncritically) held that God created the world as a going concern, why did Boyle believe God created the universe in this piecemeal way?

Two points stand out. First, Boyle has a very limited view of omnipotence. He is, for example, amazed by the swiftness of God's creative activity:

> As great a Number & variety of parts as a living Humane Body

1 BP 7:243, BP 2:62 (Boyle 2006, 3.5.1, 247). In an earlier tradition time and the angels, along with the heavens and the earth, were co-created, so that there was never a time when the angels did not exist. See St. Thomas Aquinas, ST, 1a 61.3 c; 1a 66.4 c; *QD de Potentia Dei*, 3.18 ad 20.

2 "Usefulness 1," *Works* 3:257. "[W]e presume too much of our own abilities," Boyle wrote, c. 1680, "if we imagine that the omniscient God can have no other Ends in the framing & managing of Things Corporeal, than such as we Men can discover" (Boyle MS 198:120; also at BP 7:116, Boyle 2006 3.6.3, 267).

> consists of, 'tis highly probable that the Lump of Stupid matter out of which they were fashion'd, was contriv'd into this admirable System; if not in a moment, yet in a very short time. For the sacred story relates, that man was not created till <about> the end of the six dayes work; and since in One day God created all the four footed Beasts, (wilde & tame,) and all the numerous Reptiles that creep upon the Earth after their kind; 'tis no way improbable that among so great a multitude of differing *species* of Animals, or Living Engines, that were made in one Part of the same sixth day, God should make a Humane Animal in an extreamly short time, not to say *in a trice*.[1]

So it is not surprising that he thinks of God as proceeding step by step. Additionally there are historical reasons. Earlier thinkers typically treated matter in motion as giving rise to the present world, and some past thinkers had held that the matter in question had always existed until some particular changes occurred that gave rise to the present world. The notion of a step-by-step creation fits Boyle's views of God's abilities, fits Genesis, and fits the views of previous thinkers. It is unsurprising that Boyle adopted such a view.

Boyle's contemporary, Ralph Cudworth, and, following him, the biologist John Ray, argued that it was beneath God's dignity to work immediately, and that furthermore there were considerations against it. For example, if God wanted things to be a certain way, he would simply bring about that state of affairs immediately, and the present "Slow and Gradual Process that is in the Generation of things ... would seem to be a Vain and Idle Pomp, or a Trifling Formality, if the Agent were Omnipotent."[2] Moreover, "It is not so decorous in respect of God ... that he should ... set his own hand ... to every work, and immediately do all the meanest and triflingest things himself drudgingly."[3] Hence we should posit the existence of a "plastic nature" between God and the world, which would not only relieve God of these constant chores, but would also provide an explanation of the fact that there are, apparently, mistakes in the design. The

1 BP 4:85 (Boyle 2006, 2.2.68, 161). In quotations here and throughout, the emphasis is in the original unless otherwise noted.

2 Cudworth 1678, 150.

3 Cudworth 1678, 149. Cudworth attributes this point to "the writer [of] *De Mundo*," Thomas White. Boyle and Cudworth's contemporary Leibniz realized that all tasks were of equal (because of no) difficulty to Omnipotence.

plastic nature would allow for "*Errors* and *Bungles* ... Whereas an *Omnipotent Agent* ... would always do [its Work] *Infallibly* and *Irresistibly*; no *Ineptitude* or *Stubbornness* of Matter, being ever able to hinder such a one, or make him *Bungle* or *Fumble* in any thing."[1] Boyle disagreed, partly because he realized, some of the time at any rate, that it would not be demeaning for God to have all causal activity in his immediate control, partly for the philosophically more interesting reason that such intermediaries would not provide us, as they were meant to, with anything other than the bare *form* of an explanation:

> They that, to solve the phenomena of nature, have recourse to agents which, though they involve no self-repugnancy in their very notions, as many of the judicious think substantial forms and real qualities do, yet they are such that we conceive not how they operate to bring effects to pass. These, I say, when they tell us of such indeterminate agents as the soul of the world, the universal spirit, the plastic power, and the like, though they may in certain cases tell us some things, yet they tell us nothing that will satisfy the curiosity of an inquisitive person, who seeks not so much to know, what is the general agent, that produces a phenomenon as, by what means, and after what manner, the phenomenon is produced.[2]

"God," then, "may be said to have been at the Formation of the world, not only like the wind that moves the ship, but like the Shipwright, that contriv'd it, and the Pilote, that guided it."[3] Boyle sums up in *The Excellency and Grounds of the Mechanical Hypothesis*: "the universe being once framed by God, and the laws of motion being settled and all upheld by his incessant concourse and general providence, the phenomena of the world thus constituted are physically produced by the mechanical affections of the parts of matter, and how they operate upon one another according to mechanical laws."[4]

1 Cudworth 1678, 150.

2 "Excellency and Grounds of the Mechanical Hypothesis," *Works* 8:108 [235].

3 BP 1:36 (also BP 7:163v; Boyle 2006, 3.4.34, 244).

4 *Works* 8:104 [230]. These views bring Boyle very close to the doctrine of occasionalism, though Boyle seems not to be clearly aware of this. See further Anstey 1999 and Anstey 2000.

Demonstration, Proof and Revelation[1]

A number of factors combined to make the notions of *demonstration* and *proof* of considerable interest in the seventeenth century. *Demonstration*, as seventeenth-century logic books emphasized, still had its central Aristotelian meaning of the derivation of necessary truths from necessary truths by valid arguments. In matters of science these primary necessary truths were called principles (Aristotle's *archai*), and *science* properly conceived was held to consist of such universal truths as these *demonstrations* yielded. To *prove* something, in its central sense, was to *test* it. Having proved it, it might be found acceptable, or it might be necessary to reject it. However there were a number of areas where *demonstration* seemed a tool which was either unnecessarily strong, or which was, simply, unavailable.

In particular, it was inappropriate in legal areas, and in the judicial realm the notions of evidence, testimony, and the new notion of *matters of fact* began to be developed and clarified.[2] In matters of religion, too, the question of reliable testimony arose. Clearly it was necessary to find a way to make scriptural revelation acceptable without licensing every sort of claimed revelation. And in natural philosophy, as Descartes had stressed and perhaps over-stressed it was necessary to find a reliable foundation for empirical knowledge. For Boyle, this amounted to the need to know just which reports of experimental results were reliable, and could therefore be treated as vicarious direct observation. There were paradigm cases of reliable reports such as Tycho Brahe's report of the nova of 1572, but there were also large numbers of unreliable reports. Many writers, particularly writers of alchemical texts, had reports of experiments which, as Boyle complained, were incomplete or unreliable. He remarks, for example, of an experiment reported by "the learned *Berigardus*" that "he must have good luck, that performs it only by the directions here given by our Author, who by omitting one of the chief ingredients, and some requisite circumstances, appears indeed manifestly enough to have *heard* of such an Experiment, but without seeming to have sufficiently *known*, what he pretends to teach (at least as far as his bringing this Experiment as a proof, and the obscure style,

1 On these topics see also Appendix G, "Moral Demonstrations," and Appendix I, "Coke, Boyle, and Edwards on Testimony."

2 On this issue see Shapiro 1983, 1994, 1999, and 2002, and Daston 1988 and 1991.

he is wont to imploy in the little I have yet read of his Book, permits me to judge.)"[1] Boyle later adds that "*Berigardus* is not the only author of Note I have met with, that having made particular mention of the Experiment, has given the Curious but a Lame and unsatisfactory Account of it."[2]

In law, in theology, and in experimental science, the question of the reliability of testimony was all important, and developments in any one of these areas soon affected the other two. In *The Excellency of Theology*, Boyle remarks that he "will not here engage myself in a disquisition of the several kinds or, if you please, degrees, of demonstration (which yet is a subject that I judge far more considerable than cultivated),"[3] but elsewhere he goes into more detail:

> [B]esides the Demonstrations wont to be treated of in vulgar Logick, there are among Philosophers three distinct, whether *kinds* or *degrees*, of Demonstration. For there is a *Metaphysical* Demonstration, as we may call that, where the Conclusion is manifestly built on those general Metaphysical Axioms that can never be other than true; such as *Nihil potest simul esse & non esse*[4].... There are also *Physical* Demonstrations, where the Conclusion is evidently deduc'd from Physical Principles; such as ... *ex nihilo nihil fit*:[5] ... which are not so absolutely certain as the former, because, if there be a God, He may (at least for ought we know)[6] be able to create & annihilate Substances.... And lastly, there are *Moral* Demonstrations, such as those where the Conclusion is built, either upon some one *such* proof cogent in its kind; or some concurrence of Probabilities, that it cannot but be allowed, supposing the truth of the most receiv'd Rules of Prudence and Principles of Practical Philosophy.
>
> And this *third* kind of Probation, though it comes behind the two others in certainty, yet it is the surest guide, which the *Actions of Men*, though not their *Contemplations*, have regularly allow'd them to follow.[7] ... And this is considerable in *Moral*

1 *Works* 4:450-1. Boyle gives a corrected version of the experiment at *Works*, 4:515-16.

2 *Works* 4:516.

3 *Works* 8:65 [182].

4 Latin: Nothing can simultaneously be and not be.

5 From nothing, nothing comes.

6 This parenthetical caution with respect to knowledge claims, including theological knowledge claims, is characteristic of Boyle.

7 This certainty, Locke remarked, "is not only *as great* as our frame can attain to, but *as our Condition needs*." (Locke 1975, 4.11.8.)

Demonstrations, that such may consist, and be as it were made up of particulars, that are each of them but probable; of which the Laws establisht by God himself among his own People, as well as the practice our Courts of Justice here in *England*, afford us a manifest Instance in the case of Murder, and some other Criminal Cases.[1] For, though the Testimony of a *Single* Witness shall not suffice to prove the accus'd party guilty of Murder; yet the Testimony of *two* Witnesses, though but of equal Credit, that is, a second Testimony added to the first, though of it self never a whit more credible then the former, shall ordinarily suffice to prove a Man guilty; because it is thought reasonable to suppose, that, though each Testimony *single* be but probable, yet a concurrence of such Probabilities, (which ought in Reason to be attributed to the Truth of what they jointly tend to prove) may well amount to a Moral certainty, *i.e.* such a certainty as may warrant the Judge to proceed to the sentence of death against the Indicted party.

To apply these things, now to the *Christian Religion*: If you consider, with how much approbation from discerning Men, that judicious Observation of *Aristotle* has been entertain'd, where he says, that 'tis as unskilful and improper a thing to require *Mathematical* Demonstrations in *Moral* Affairs,[2] as to take up with Moral Arguments in matters Mathematical; you will not deny, but that those Articles of the Christian Religion that can be prov'd by a Moral, though not by a Metaphysical or Physical, Demonstration, may without any blemish to a Man's Reason be assented to; and that consequently (by vertue of the foregoing Considerations) those other Articles of the Christian Faith, that are clearly and legitimately deducible from the so demonstrated Truths, may likewise without disparagement, be assented to.[3]

Boyle was well aware that, in general, people believed in the religion they did for insufficient reasons:

---

1 Correcting "causes" (*Works* 8:282) to MS "Cases" (BP 2:113).

2 "It is the mark of an educated man to look for precision in each class of things just so far as the nature of the subject admits; it is evidently equally foolish to accept probable reasoning from a mathematician and to demand from a rhetorician scientific proofs" (*Nicomachean Ethics*, Aristotle 1984, 1094b11-27).

3 "Reason and Religion," *Works* 8:281-2. Boyle makes similar points in "The Notion of Nature," *Works* 10:442, and "Things Above Reason," *Works* 9:366-69 and 398.

> Though it be little taken notice of, and less laid to heart, yet 'tis much to be lamented, that the generallity of those that call themselves Christians, assume that title upon motives Injurious, and dishonourable, both to themselves, and the Religion they make profession of. For there are some who like those Americans that worship all the day the first thing they chance to meet with in the morning, own the Christian Religion all their life because tis that which was taught them in their youth. Others there are who out of lazines springing from an undervaluation of every thing that chiefely concerns another life, chuse rather to take up with the Christian Religion, then put themselves to the trouble of Examineing whether or no, it be the best. And others againe, who I fear make farr the greatest number of those that pass for Christians, profess themselves such only because Christianity is the Religion of their Parents, or their Country, or their Prince, or those that have been, or may be, their Benefactors: which is in effect to say, that they are Christians but up on the same grounds that would have made them Mahometans if they had been born & bred in Turky.[1]

Boyle makes the same point in the *Excellency of Theology* about the way in which too many people form their beliefs: "is it not, think you, a great piece of respect, that these men pay to those truths, which God thought fit to send, sometimes prophets and apostles, sometimes angels, and sometimes his only son himself to reveal, that such truths are so little valued by them, that rather than take the pains to study them, they will implicitly, and at adventures believe, what that society of Christians they chance to be born and bred in, have (truly or falsely) delivered concerning them?"[2]

Boyle, however, thinks that we can find moral demonstrations which will show us that the Christian religion is indeed the right one: "as to the fundamental and necessary articles of religion, I ... take those articles to be both evident, and capable of a moral demonstration."[3] There are, Boyle holds, arguments from natural theology which will yield the existence of a deity. Given that, he suggests, it is reasonable to expect God will have *instituted* a religion to let humans know about his nature, attributes and desires: "God knows himself infinitely better then purblind man knows him, so the informations he is pleased to vouchsafe us, touching his own nature and attributes, are exceedingly preferable to any

1 BP 4:60 (Boyle 2006, 3.7.5, 302).

2 *Works* 8:43 [152].

3 *Works* 8:64 [182].

account, that we can give ourselves of him, without him."[1] And the way in which God institutes such a religion is by performing miracles which signal that the religion to which they point is the right one.[2]

Boyle also has various arguments to show that biblical accounts are reliable, and indeed he accepted them, subject to there not being compelling evidence against them, without question.[3] We need, however, to look to experimental philosophy for additional knowledge about the world, knowledge that is infinitely preferable to "the empty and barren physiology that is taught in the schools."[4] But, while valuing experimental philosophy, we should not neglect scripture, for "The last and correctest edition of the law of nature is the Gospel."[5]

Predecessors and Influences

Aristotle (384-22 BCE)

Boyle mentions many earlier and contemporary thinkers in his various works and in the manuscripts, but the most important ones are (in chronological order) Aristotle, Epicurus, Francis Bacon, Thomas Hobbes, Pierre Gassendi, and René Descartes. Additionally Boyle refers often to both Paracelsus and Johannes Baptista van Helmont.[6]

Aristotle, effectively the inventor of logic, was, after his works were recovered in the Latin West, so admired by the mediaevals for his depth and range that he was referred to simply as The Philosopher. Partly because of this enormous respect, many of his followers were effectively, if un-Aristotelianly, anti-empirical, feeling that since Aristotle had provided the truth, there was no need to look further. Boyle almost always writes of Aristotle with respect, and it is clear that Aristotle's works (unlike those of Plato) were much read by him. In what follows I shall mention, briefly, only some of the views of the "infinitely thought-provoking" Aris-

---

1 *Works* 8:14 [112].

2 For a more detailed discussion of this point see MacIntosh 1994.

3 See for example, BP 7:95-99 (Boyle 2006, 3.6.29. 286-90).

4 *Works* 8:56 [170].

5 BP 5:96 (Boyle 2006, 3.4.31, 243).

6 In non-intellectual areas there are also numerous references to Moses, St. Paul, and Solomon, and there were tracts written specifically against Linus, Hobbes and More.

totle,[1] concentrating on those which are most relevant to Boyle's views.[2]

Aristotle's influence on subsequent thinking was enormous. Quite apart from his logic, his views, mainly empirically based, though sometimes, partly at least, intra-systemic, on the plausibility of the atomists' doctrine of atoms and the void, on the notion of light "travelling,"[3] on Platonic forms, on causality and explanation, on the correct analysis of matter and material things, on the soul, and on a host of other topics were central to philosophical discussion for centuries.

Aristotle had a number of ingenious, mainly empirical, arguments against the possibility of a vacuum and thereby against atomism. One straightforward argument depends on the empirically plausible view that velocity through a medium, given a constant impelling force, varies with the density of the medium. For the same expenditure of energy, an object will travel more swiftly in a less dense medium (air, say) than in a denser one (water, for example). But if that is so, positing a vacuum apparently leads to a contradiction.[4]

If there is no vacuum, then any atomistic account of matter should be rejected. What is the alternative? Aristotle's alternative is meant to provide us with an explanation of the fact that individuals fall into classes, and of the fact that things in the world come into being and pass away. Aristotle suggested that this is because any given thing is matter *formed* in a certain way, where "form" is, in effect, a technical term. Any given cow is a cow because it shares a bovine *form* with all other cows. What makes it *this* cow rather than *that* is the matter of which it is composed, but the explanation of its bovine nature is its possession of a bovine form. And when our cow passes to the great pasture in the sky what has happened is that its matter is no longer structured by that form, but by some different one.

We may think of a statue as being marble, say, with a certain

---

1 Ackrill 1981, 3.

2 For readers interested in discovering more about Aristotle, Ackrill 1981 and Barnes 1982 both provide clear, readable, interesting, and short accounts of Aristotle's philosophy. Ross 1923 remains a valuable, more detailed, work on Aristotle's entire corpus. Anstey 2000 discusses the direct relevance of many of Aristotle's views to Boyle's philosophical outlook.

3 For Aristotle on light having a velocity see Appendix C: "Aristotle's arguments against the void" [288].

4 For details, see Appendix C: "Aristotle's arguments against the void."

form, but the marble's structure, too, is to be explained in terms of some underlying matter with a particular form. Underlying all material things is unformed *prime matter*—a theoretical notion, for there is no actual matter which does not have some specific form or other. St. Thomas Aquinas (and other Christian Aristotelians) held that though it was impossible to have unformed matter, it was nonetheless possible to have form without matter. There is certainly a basis for this view in Aristotle, but opinions on the matter vary. C.S. Peirce wrote, "The notion that the form can antecede matter is, to Aristotle, perfectly ridiculous. It is the result of the development of matter. He looks upon the problem from the point of view of a naturalist. In particular, the soul is an outgrowth of the body."[1]

Change is explained in terms of an underlying matter losing one form and acquiring another. The underlying matter itself is composed, Aristotle held, of four primary or basic elements, earth, air, fire, and water. No individual thing is made up purely of a single element, though for any given item one of the elements may predominate. Associated with the notion of four basic elements is the notion that there are four basic or primary qualities, the hot, the dry, the cold, and the moist. Elements and qualities are connected: earth is dry and cold, water cold and moist, air is moist and hot, fire is hot and dry, with the first quality in each case predominating. In terms of these basic qualities change consists in something that could have that quality, but currently does not, causally interacting with something that does. A dry thing becomes wet by causally interacting with something wet, a cold thing becomes hot by causally interacting with something hot, and so on.[2]

Flowing from this account is the view that individual kinds of things have a *nature* which at least partially *explains* the way they behave. It is in the nature of an acorn, if the appropriate conditions obtain, to grow into an oak. One way of looking at the difference between the corpuscularian account championed by Boyle and the Aristotelian account of Boyle's scholastic contemporaries is this: for the scholastics, each individual thing had its nature in terms of which its behaviour could be explained; for the corpuscularians, each individual thing was made up of essentially the same types of corpuscles, and it was their behaviour according to the God-given

1 Peirce 1931, 6:356.

2 See Anstey 2000, part I, for a detailed discussion of Boyle's account of qualities, and its relation to Aristotle's account.

(and God-sustained) laws of nature that accounted, given the initial parameters, for the behaviour of individual things.

Aristotelian forms provided a solution (or a "solution") to a problem which was difficult for the corpuscularian doctrine, that of cohesion (why, if things are merely collections of particles, don't they simply fall apart?). The solution to this problem eluded corpuscularians until Newton moved fairly radically away from pure corpuscularianism.[1] Individual substances, Aristotle held, as opposed to mere aggregates, had a "substantial form" that provided the explanation of their continuing structure. When this form was lost, the matter of which the object was formed could acquire a new form. Examples apparently abound: fire transforming wood to smoke and ashes, the decay of animals after death, etc. In the case of humans, this substantial form was the human soul.[2] Boyle, although in general accepting a more Platonic/Cartesian view of the soul, was nonetheless cautious about rejecting the Aristotelian one: "when ever I shall speake indefinitely of Substantiall forms, I would alwayes be understood to except the Reasonable Soule, that is said to inform the humane Body; which Declaration I here desire may be taken notice of, once for all."[3] In the same work Boyle comments more generally on Aristotle: "where in the following Tract, or any other of my writings, I do *indefinitely* depreciate *Aristotle*'s Doctrine, I would be understood to speak of *his Physicks*, or rather of the Speculative part of them (for his Historical Writings concerning Animals I much esteem,) nor do I say, that even These may not have their Use among Scholers, and even in Universities, if they be retain'd and studied with due cautions and Limitations."[4]

1 Ernan McMullen points out that "Around 1692, in some notes for the *Opticks*, [Newton] speculated that the cohesion of solid bodies may well be due to "attractive virtues" that decrease with distance by an inverse power greater than the fourth. These would decrease so rapidly that "great bodies composed of such particles shall not attract one another sensibly" (McMullen 1978, 88). For further discussion of Boyle on cohesion, and of the difficulties that cohesion posed for the corpuscularian doctrine, see MacIntosh 2001 and Hill 2004. For a brief but very helpful discussion of Leibniz's sharp criticism of the alternative positions, see the Bennett/Remnant note on *cohesion* in Leibniz 1981, xxxiv. See also Bennett and Remnant 1978.

2 There are considerable difficulties for this doctrine, as there are for every doctrine positing immaterial souls. For discussion of these difficulties see, e.g., Penelhum 1970, and Kim 2001.

3 "Forms and Qualities," *Works* 5:300.

4 "Forms and Qualities," *Works* 5:295.

Aristotle did not have an inertial view of motion. Every change, he held, required a cause. It followed that motion from A to B, even for something already in motion, required an explanation. It was necessary, from an Aristotelian point of view, to explain *why* moving things continued in motion. If something continued in motion, something must be providing the propelling impulse. Thus some Aristotelians held, as Boyle notes, that the planets orbiting the earth (as they believed, but the same point holds for heliocentric planets) must have *something* providing the impelling force, and this *something* was by some held to be angels or some equivalent "intelligences." It is worth noting that Newton and other holders of inertial views did not provide an answer to the question "Why do moving things keep moving?" It is not an answer to that question to say, as Newton did, "Objects in motion keep moving in a straight line unless acted on by an external force." That is a refusal to answer, not an answer; it is a way of saying that the very question itself is mistaken. From an Aristotelian point of view what needs to be explained is every change; from an inertialist point of view what needs to be explained is every change of state, which is a different matter. The implications of inertial laws took some time to be realized, and Kant still found it worthwhile to make this point explicitly a century later.[1]

Not everyone accepted the shift happily. Late in the seventeenth century the biologist John Ray, strongly and explicitly influenced by Ralph Cudworth's *True Intellectual System* (Cudworth 1678), could still write:

> an intelligent Being seems to me requisite to execute the Laws of Motion. For First Motion being a fluent thing, and one part of its Duration being absolutely independent upon another: it doth not follow that because any thing moves this moment, it must necessarily continue to do so the next; but it stands in as much need on an Efficient to preserve and continue its motion as it did at first to produce.... And as for any external Laws or established Rules of Motion, the stupid Matter is not capable of observing or taking any notice of them; neither can those Laws execute themselves: Therefore there must besides Matter and Law be some Efficient; and that either a Quality or Power inherent in the Matter itself, which is hard to conceive, or

1 Kant 1787, A207n/B252n. For a detailed discussion of Boyle on this issue, see Anstey 2000, ch. 5.

> some external intelligent Agent, either God himself immediately, or some *Plastick Nature*.[1]

Ray's point here is that, contra Newton and the inertialists, inertial laws require something *extra* for objects to "obey" them. *All* laws of nature require God's constant support if they are to continue to hold: but for Ray, inertial laws require something more. Up to a point Boyle agreed—something was required, but for Boyle the something was God's sustaining of the inertial laws, not an active force (whether "God ... himself, or some *Plastick Nature*") doing the actual pushing.

As noted in the section on "Demonstration, Proof and Revelation," above, Boyle often refers, as did others, to Aristotle's dictum that we should in our investigations only expect the degree of certainty that any given discipline allows, thus clearing the way for accepting the truths of religion on a footing less solid that that required for mathematics or logic. He was worried that Aristotle's apparent championship of the past infinity of time would lead to atheism, a worry that might have been set to rest had he known of the arguments of Albertus Magnus, St. Thomas Aquinas, and others to the effect that it was possible for God to have created a universe which was past infinite in time (though, as was always made clear, it was known by revelation that this was not the case).

Epicurus (341-270 BCE)

Epicurus was the most influential early atomist. He was also one of the most important philosophical influences on seventeenth-century thinkers. Boyle's contemporary, Thomas Stanley, devotes more space to Epicurus in his *History of Philosophy* (Stanley 1687) than he does to any other single philosopher. The *History* deals only with classical philosophers, and Epicurus and the Epicureans get one hundred pages, which is about a tenth of the three volumes. For comparison, Plato receives 41 pages and Aristotle, just over 42.

Epicurus' views clearly depend on those of Leucippus and Democritus, though Diogenes Laertius reports claims that he denied the existence of the former and spoke disparagingly of the latter.[2] (Whether these claims are true is a debatable matter.)

1 Ray 1691, 32-35.

2 Diogenes Laertius 10:8, 13.

Epicurean atoms had weight, size, and a variety of shapes. They were, as the name suggests, indestructible. The present world has a beginning in time as a result of the combining of these atoms, which are, however, themselves eternal. Thus, for Epicurus, the view that there was a time when nothing material existed is simply false. Moreover, as Boyle notes, since the world was not created, Epicurus, though accepting that there were gods, saw no need for a creator. Additionally, since all things are made of atoms, humans are made of atoms, and similarly human souls are made of atoms. And though atoms are indestructible, the items they compose are not. So immortality is not to be looked for in an Epicurean universe.

Moreover, since Epicurus did not confine his views to the study of nature, there were also, from the point of view of later thinkers, his moral views to consider. And here they found a great deal to condemn, for Epicurus, though distinguishing different types of pleasure (natural and necessary, natural but unnecessary, and neither natural nor necessary), clearly felt that, in general, pleasure was good. However, the world being as it is, not every pleasure is desirable, since some come with concomitant drawbacks (in particular, pain) which outweigh their intrinsic value. Seventeenth-century writers, concentrating on a doctrine of pleasure that was more theirs than Epicurus', but that they happily attributed to him, found him, in Meric Casaubon's words, a "detestable monster" characterized by "lewd doctrine, notorious stupiditie, and grosse ignorance."[1] Since his atomism and his (im)morality came together as a package, it was necessary to separate the two before atomism could be accepted. It was not a simple task. Atomism, said Cudworth, "was again revived by *Epicurus*, but so blended ... with Immorality and Impiety, as that it soon sunk again."[2] And that, indeed, was the problem. Atomism was associated with Epicurus, and Epicurus was asso-

---

1 Casaubon 1999, fol. 22, 149. Casaubon was writing in 1667.

2 Cudworth 1731, 62. Throughout the seventeenth century, Epicureanism, in common parlance, stood for atheism and immorality, particularly sexual immorality. Thus Shakespeare in *King Lear* has Gonerill say,

> Heere do you keepe a hundred Knights and Squires,
> Men so disorder'd, so debosh'd and bold,
> That this our Court infected with their manners,
> Shewes like a riotous Inne; Epicurisme and Lust
> Makes it more like a Tauerne, or a Brothell,
> Then a grac'd Pallace. [Act 1, Scene 4, 750-55]

ciated with "impiety and immorality," and guilt by association is always hard to shake off. Boyle does not accept Epicureanism as such, as is clear from his all-out attack on Epicurus' own doctrine of atomism,[1] but in *The Excellency and Grounds of the Mechanical Hypothesis* he is explicitly aiming to promote a corpuscularian doctrine which is *not* that of Epicurus.[2] Indeed, the publisher of the earlier *Origine of Formes and Qualities* felt able to assure readers that "though the most *noble Author* hath herein, for the main, espoused the *Atomical Philosophy*," it has been "corrected and purged from the wild fancies and extravagancies of the first *Inventors* of it, as to the *Origine* of the *Universe*."[3]

Thus it was necessary for Gassendi to reclaim Epicurus. Gassendi explicitly rejected the Epicurean view that the material world was eternal, and in this he was followed by Boyle. The corpuscular portion of Epicureanism could be accepted while the cosmological, theological, and eschatological views were jettisoned. To help Gassendi's project of de-villainizing Epicurus, Boyle made a point of stressing that the charge of atheism was misplaced, for Epicurus not only explicitly stated that there were gods, but the Epicurean version of the gods was such as *not* to appeal to the vulgar (a common charge was that Epicurus was only paying lip service to the existence of gods in order to placate the populace). However, Epicurus' gods, though possessed of personal attributes, were material,[4] and were not particularly interested in the doings and fate of terrestrial creatures, including humans. Clearly, then, in seventeenth-century eyes, the Epicurean doctrine must be wrong, since humans are extremely important, both to themselves and to the Deity. Alexander Ross, writing against Kenelm Digby, says:

[*You thinke* Epicurus *to be no Atheist, for denying Gods providence*

---

1 See Boyle 2006, 4.1.

2 *Works* 8:103-04 [229-30].

3 "The Publisher to the Ingenious Reader,' "Forms and Qualities," *Works* 5:283.

4 Epicurus apparently found some difficulty with the gods' materiality. The gods, Cicero reports him as saying, "have a human shape but nonetheless their form [*species*] is not that of a body, but is like that of a body, it contains not blood, but something blood-like" (*De Natura Deorum*, I.xviii). Boyle says wryly that he is not surprised that Cicero's "Opposer ... of this Paradox should take the freedome to make himselfe pleasant with it" (BP 2:35 [Boyle 2006, 4.1, 356]; see also BP 6:312 [Boyle 2006, 1.2, 58]).

over the triviall actions of inferiour creatures.][1] But, I say, hee is no lesse an *Atheist* that denies Gods providence, or any other of his Attributes, then hee that denies his Essence. Though *Epicurus* and *Democritus* babbled something of a Deity, yet in holding the world to be casually and rashly agglomerated of small *atomes*, they were very *Atheists*.... Reade *Tully*, and hee will tell you whether *Epicurus* were not an *Atheist*, who wrote against the gods; & that both he & *Democritus* were *Atheists*, for denying that the gods did either help or shew favour to men: And, that as *Xerxes* were an *Atheist* in his hands, by pulling downe the Temple of the gods; so was *Epicurus* in his tongue, who pulled them downe with his reasons.[2]

In the next century, the times had changed sufficiently to allow David Hume to offer a sustained and interesting defence of Epicurus.[3]

Bacon (1561-1626)

Francis Bacon (Baron Verulam of Verulam, Viscount St. Albans) was the great publicist for the new method in natural philosophy. All was to be done by induction and the gathering of facts, and the old, Aristotelian, logic was to be set aside. No longer would experimental matters be decided by appeal to authority, and the age was delighted to be told so by such an authoritative figure. Aristotle, Bacon held, was only an apparent experimentalist, "For he had come to his conclusion before; he did not consult experience, as he should have done, for the purpose of framing his decisions and axioms, but having first determined the question according to his will, he then resorts to experience, and bending her into conformity with his placets,[4] leads her out like a captive in a procession. So that even on this count he is more guilty than his modern followers, the schoolmen, who have abandoned experience altoge-

1 Square brackets are Ross's. He uses them to interpolate the points he is attributing to Digby.

2 Ross 1645, 33-4.

3 Hume 1975, XI.

4 Literally a vote of assent ("it pleases me"; "it is acceptable to me"), here used in a slightly wider sense to mean the propositions that are already accepted.

ther."[1] People, he suggested, "must force themselves for a while to lay their notions by and begin to familiarize themselves with facts."[2] Boyle refers to Bacon often and respectfully, and though his own practice did not follow Bacon's precepts in detail,[3] he certainly was more interested in ascertaining matters of fact than in providing support for preconceived theories. Bacon's views on the necessity of observation and experiment strongly influenced the founders of the Royal Society.

Bacon stands on the divide between Aristotelianism and atomism. In his early works such as the *Cogitationes de natura rerum* and *Ded principiis atque originibus* he speaks favourably of the atomism of Democritus. However these works were only published posthumously (in 1653), and in the *New Organon* (1620) he assures us that by following his method we shall not "be led to the doctrine of atoms, which implies the hypothesis of a vacuum and that of the unchangeableness of matter (both false assumptions); we shall be led only to real particles, such as really exist."[4]

Hobbes (1588-1679)

"I love," said Boyle, "to speak of Persons with Civility, though of Things with Freedom,"[5] and indeed the only person he habitually seemed willing to disparage was Hobbes. Concerning Hobbes's attack on "the whole Society at *Gresham* Colledge," Boyle observed that "the Vindication of such an Assembly against Mr. *Hobbs* deserves a better Pen than mine, though it doth not need it," and remarked, "I never envied Mr. *Hobbes*'s forwardness

1 *New Organon*, Book I, Aphorism 43. Letting theories preempt observation is all too easy. Bacon himself provides an example of this when speaking of things that are hot: "Animals, especially and at all times internally; though in insects the heat is not perceptible to the touch by reason of the smallness of their size" (*New Organon*, Book II, Aphorism 11, "Instances Agreeing in the Nature of Heat," 20; Bacon *Works*, vol. 1; English translation, vol. 4).

2 *New Organon*, Book I, Aphorism 36.

3 They are, in fact, not particularly easy to understand, still less to follow. Harvey, "speaking in derision," said, "He writes Philosophy like a Lord Chancellor" (quoted by John Aubrey in "Harvey," Aubrey 1957).

4 Bacon, *New Organon*, Book 2, Aphorisms VIII. Helpful discussions of Bacon's philosophical views may be found in Anstey 2002, Gaukroger 2001, and Broad 1952, Section II. Hunter 2007 presents documentary evidence for the important influence of Bacon on Boyle's work from the 1660s onwards.

5 "Certain Physiological Essays," *Works* 2:26.

to triumph, and am content, his Conjectures be recommended by the confidence, that accompanies them, if mine be by the success that follows them."[1]

Boyle disliked Hobbes personally, thought him to be an incompetent (natural) philosopher and mathematician, and believed, in common with many others, that Hobbes was straightforwardly an atheist, and was responsible for turning others to atheism. David Berman draws our attention to the comment of the first Boyle lecturer, Richard Bentley:

> And then for Theists you say, they have books written, but Atheists have only talk. Must we then pass by the Atheists, against the judgement and command of my Honble Benefactor, who hath put them in the very first place as the most dangerous enemies? Atheism is so much the worse that it is not buried in books, but is gotten [into life]; that taverns and coffee-houses, nay Westminster-hall and the very churches, are full of it ... But are the Atheists of your mind, that they have no books written for them? Not one of them but believe Tom Hobbes to be a rank one; and that his corporeal God is a meer sham to get his book printed. They understand that Cabbala well enough, that all that is but juggle; and that a corporeal infinite God is downright nonsense. I have said something to this in my first sermon, and I know it to be true by the conversation I have had with them. There may be some Spinosists, or immaterial Fatalists, beyond seas; but not one English Infidel in a hundred is any other than a Hobbist; which I know to be rank Atheism in the private study and select conversation of these men whatever it may appear to be abroad.[2]

Hobbes was, from Boyle's point of view, a survivor from a past age, both chronologically and intellectually, a person who was willing to make *a priori* pronouncements about matters of fact with a confidence as large as it was unjustified. Finally, in Boyle's view, Hobbes had not really got the hang of what had come to count as an acceptable explanation. When we add to this the clear fact of Hobbes's irascibility, not to say bellicosity, his love of profanity, and the kind of tunnel vision that seemed to let him ignore plain facts, it is not surprising that Hobbes, despite his clear philosophical ability (in our sense) was never admitted to the

1 *Works* 3:117; *Works* 8:173.

2 Berman 1988, 49-50.

Royal Society. Boyle's view of Hobbes was shared by his assistant, Robert Hooke:

> I should have sooner given you an account of an interview I had of Mr. *Hobbes*, which was at Mr. *Reeve*'s, he coming along with my lord *De.*[1] to be assistant in the choosing a glass.[2] I was, I confess, a little surprised at first to see an old man[3] so view me and survey me every way, without saying any thing to me; but I quickly shaked off that surprizal, when I heard my lord call him Mr. *H.* supposing he had been informed to whom I belonged. I soon found by staying that little while he was there, that the character I had formerly received of him was very significant. I found him to lard and seal every asseveration with a round oath, to undervalue all other men's opinions and judgments, to defend to the utmost what he asserted though never so absurd, to have a high conceit of his own abilities and performances, though never so absurd and pitiful, &c. He would not be persuaded, but that a common spectacle-glass was as good an eye-glass for a thirty six feet glass as the best in the world, and pretended to see better than all the rest, by holding his spectacle in his hand, which shook as fast one way as his head did the other; which I confess made me bite my tongue.[4]

Nowadays, Hobbes is frequently considered only in his character as a political philosopher, but this is too narrow a view of his interests and abilities. Hobbes was an excellent philosopher (in our sense of the term). He was a materialist, and his attempt to marry his materialism with his mathematics led him into a mathematical quagmire (see Jesseph 1999 for details),[5] but his

---

1 William Cavendish, Earl of Devonshire.

2 Telescope.

3 Hobbes (born 5 April, 1588) would have been 75 at the time.

4 Hooke to Boyle, 3 July, 1663, *Correspondence* 2:97.

5 There is a deep, and general, problem here, one that Hobbes confronted with his materialist account of mathematics. If we are *Platonists* in mathematics—if we believe that abstract entities such as numbers *exist* (in some sense or other), even though they have no spatio-temporal location and are causally inert—then our philosophy of mathematics becomes straightforward, though our metaphysics becomes ontologically well-endowed (over endowed, many would say). If, on the other hand, we deny the existence of abstract objects in favour of a *nominalist* ontology and opt for a world that contains only entities for which there is empiri-

philosophical ability is nonetheless clear. In the early modern period he was also highly thought of as a natural philosopher. This evaluation was not shared by Boyle, and Boyle's view is that of posterity, though Shapin and Schaffer 1985 makes a valiant attempt to defend Hobbes's ability in natural philosophy. In that work, the views of Hobbes find considerably more sympathy than they do in the writings of Boyle. Extending such sympathy to Hobbes, however, requires them to write explicitly as non-realists in their philosophy of science, and also to speak in terms of "accepted knowledge" and "rejected knowledge," so that what Boyle would have regarded as the simply false claims of Hobbes become pieces of knowledge, albeit pieces of *rejected* knowledge.

Two main issues, discussed in detail by Steven Shapin and Simon Schaffer in Shapin and Shaffer 1985, may be mentioned here. First, there was a clash over the question of whether or not designed or artificial experiments should be preferred to simple observation. Boyle was clear on the matter:

> [A]lthough the Peripatetic, and some other Philosophies do also pretend to be grounded upon *Reason* and *Experience*; yet there is a great difference betwixt the use that is made of these two Principles, by the School-Philosophers, and by the *Virtuosi*. For *those*, in the framing of their System, make but little use of Experience; contenting themselves for the most part to employ but few and obvious Experiments, and vulgar Traditions, usually Uncertain, and oftentimes False; and superstructing almost their whole Physicks upon *Abstracted Reason*; by which, I mean, The rational Faculty endowed but with its own Congenit, or Common Notions and *Idea's*, and with Popular Notices; that is, such as are common among men, especially those that are any thing Learned. But now, the *Virtuosi* I speak of, and by whom, in this whole Discourse, I mean those, that Understand and Cultivate Experimental Philosophy, make a much greater and better use of Experience in their Philosophical Researches. For they consult Experience both frequently and heedfully; and, not content with the *Phænomena* that Nature spontaneously affords them, they are solici-

cal evidence of one sort or another, our metaphysics becomes more appealing, but our philosophy of mathematics becomes much more difficult. Various philosophers have attempted various compromises between extreme Platonism and extreme nominalism, but no view has currently been found universally satisfactory.

> tous, when they find it needful, to enlarge their Experience by Tryals purposely devis'd; and, ever and anon Reflecting upon it, they are careful to Conform their Opinions to it; or, if there be just cause, Reform their Opinions by it. So that our *Virtuosi* have a peculiar Right to the distinguishing Title that is often given them, of *Experimental Philosophers*.[1]

Hobbes, by contrast, coming to the situation with his theoretical views already firmly in place, felt that either *no* experiments were necessary or, to the extent that they were, they (or better, it—for one should suffice) should simply be obvious observations without the need for contrived experiments. Boyle was aware that the situation was more complex: the naturalist,

> at least if he be a considering man ... will oftentimes find reason to doubt, whether the experiment or observation have been so skillfully and warily made in all circumstances, as to afford him such an account of the matter of fact, as a severe naturalist would desire. And then, supposing the historical part no way defective, there are far more cases than are taken notice of, wherein so many differing agents may produce the exhibited phenomenon, or have a great influence upon the experiment or observation, that he must be less jealous[2] than becomes a philosopher, to whom experiments do not oftentimes as well suggest new doubts, as present new phenomena.[3]

The second issue concerned the plenist/vacuist debate. Hobbes, though a mechanist, was a confirmed denier of the vacuum. Boyle, experimenting with his vacuum chamber, noted that animals died in the vacuum he was able to produce. He came, not unreasonably, to the conclusion that the lack of air was causally relevant.

Hobbes, however, had a different answer, and indeed a different type of answer. He had a set of explanatory devices which included suction, and a congenite "simple circular motion" that corpuscles have, along with the possibility that the corpuscles themselves could be "infinitely subtle." These additions to the mechanists' tool chest were never themselves explained. "Simple circular motion" was to be the answer to all the problems but, as Boyle pointed out,

---

1 "Christian Virtuoso I," *Works* 11:292.

2 "Jealous," in this context means "vigilant in scrutinizing."

3 *Works* 8:57-8 [171].

how it is to be the answer is never made clear. So, with these infinitely subtle particles of the air, to which glass is permeable, how does Hobbes try to explain the deaths in the evacuated receivers, the extinguishing of candles, the loss of sound transmission, etc.? He simply denies the point about sound. Defending Hobbes, Shapin and Schaffer report his views on the other two:

> In dealing with phenomena which did not obviously involve the air's spring, Hobbes's task was straightforward, given his stipulation of the meaning of the term "vacuum." For example, he agreed with Boyle that animals died in the "evacuated" receiver; they were, however, literally blown to death by a violent circulatory wind, not deprived of vital air.... Candles went out for the same reason.... In the case of animals' death within the receiver, Hobbes offered a choice of non-Boylean explanations: either the violent wind or some form of suction that interrupted respiration.[1]

This is not a very *plausible* account. For it is noticeable that there are no *other* phenomena associated with the putative "wind"—in particular the "violent circulatory wind" that blows out a candle fails to move a feather, even when augmented by a pair of bellows.[2] As Bacon said of Aristotle, so Boyle might have said of Hobbes, "he had come to his conclusion before; he did not consult experience, as he should have done, for the purpose of framing his decisions and axioms, but having first determined the question according to his will, he then resorts to experience, and bending her into conformity with his placets, leads her out like a captive in a procession[70]."

Gassendi (1592-1655)

"*Gassendus*, a great favourite of mine, I take to be a very profound mathematician, as well as an excellent astronomer, and one that has collected a very ample treasure of numerous and accurate observations of all that belongs to the abstruse science of those sublimer bodies,"[3] the young Boyle wrote to Samuel Hartlib in

---

1 Shapin and Shaffer 1985, 121-22, and note.

2 "A continuation of New Experiments Physico-Mechanical touching the Spring and Weight of the Air, and their Effects," Experiments 38 and 39, *Works* 6:128-37.

3 Boyle to Hartlib, 8 May, 1647, *Correspondence* 1:59.

1647, and this admiration for Gassendi was retained throughout his life. Pierre Gassendi was a Catholic priest whose revival of the views of Epicurus and the early atomists profoundly affected the direction taken by natural philosophy in the seventeenth century. "It is clear," Margaret Osler points out, "that a number of Boyle's claims about the theological and epistemological ramifications of his corpuscularianism are remarkably similar to Gassendi's views on these questions."[1] Boyle was apparently aware of this similarity, for he made a point of telling his readers that his views had been arrived at independently. In 1661, he notes he had

> purposely refrain'd, though not altogether from transiently consulting about a few Particulars, yet from seriously and orderly reading over those excellent (though disagreeing) Books[2] or so much as Sir *Francis Bacon's Novum Organum*, that I might not be prepossess'd with any Theory or Principles till I had spent some time in trying what Things themselves would incline me to think; yet beginning now to allow my self to read those excellent Books, I find by the little I have read in them already, that if I had read them before I began to write, I might have enrich'd the ensuing Essays with divers truths, which they now want, and have explicated divers things much better than I fear I have done.[3]

And in the *Origine of Forms and Qualities*, published in 1666, but with parts of it written much earlier, Boyle tells us, after mentioning several authors' works, that

> though some of their books I could not procure when I had occasion to have recourse to them; and though the weakness of my eyes discouraged me from perusing those parts of others that concerned not the subject I was treating of, yet I hope I have been benefited by those I have consulted, and might have been more so by the learned *Gassendus's* little, but ingenious, *Syntagma Philosophiae Epicuri*, if I had more seasonably been acquainted with it.[4]

---

1 Osler 1992, 178.

2 Descartes' *Principles*, and Gassendi's "little *Syntagma* of *Epicurus*'s Philosophy."

3 "Certain Physiological Essays, and other Tracts" (1661), "Proemial Essay," *Works* 2:12-13.

4 *Works* 5:295. On Gassendi's influence on Boyle see further Osler 1992 and Osler 1994.

Gassendi was not a sceptic, but he happily used the recently recovered sceptical doctrines of Sextus Empiricus against Aristotle and the Aristotelians. Like Boyle and Newton (whom he also directly and strongly influenced), he was a mechanist, but not a materialist. It was largely as a result of his efforts that atomism was seen as a viable candidate for the vacancy created by the increasing unsatisfactoriness of both the Aristotelian and the Paracelsan accounts of the structure of the world.

Descartes (1596-1650)

René Descartes was the most influential philosopher as well as one of the greatest mathematicians and natural philosophers of the seventeenth century. While disagreeing with Descartes about some fundamental points of natural philosophy and theology, Boyle read Descartes with care and respect. Descartes was a plenist, but Boyle saw him as a fellow "corpuscularian"—one who was willing to ground all natural phenomena in the interaction of minute particles of matter.[1] Boyle's defence of Descartes against More—"though not confining my self to any Sect, I do not profess my self to be of the Cartesian: yet I cannot but have too much value for so great a wit as the founder of it, and too good an opinion of his sincerity in asserting the existence of a Deity, to approve so severe a Censure as the Doctor is pleased to give of him"[2]—is obviously sincere.

Descartes was a major influence on Boyle, as he was on every later seventeenth-century writer. Whether thinkers agreed or disagreed with him, he was never ignored. It is through Descartes' *Meditations* that contemporary readers are most commonly introduced to him, but Boyle paid more attention to Descartes' scientific works for which the *Meditations* were intended to provide a metaphysical underpinning. Descartes, in addition to his work on mechanics, optics, etc., transformed mathematics by algebraizing geometry, giving us our familiar Cartesian coordinates and our ability to transform geometrical propositions and theorems into algebraic ones.

Notoriously, Descartes espoused a species of dualism (substance dualism), that supposes humans to be composed of two distinct parts, a material body and an immaterial mind or soul.

---

1 For Boyle on corpuscularianism see Appendix B, "Boyle's 'Corpuscularianism'."

2 *Works* 7:142.

The interaction between these two supposed entities is, to put it mildly, mysterious. They are, said Descartes, clearly distinct, yet so closely intertwined that they form, "as it were," a unit. Descartes' version of the soul as an incorporeal entity separable from the body was a reversion to the earlier Platonic view, and away from the Aristotelian concept in which the soul was the form of the body (a view that led the Aristotelian mediaeval philosopher and theologian St. Thomas Aquinas to remark, "If my soul alone survives then I survive not, and nor does any man"). Boyle, although not denying that the *human* soul *might* be an Aristotelian one,[1] was a Cartesian dualist—more so, perhaps, than Descartes himself, in view of Descartes's view of the body-mind complex as a quasi-unit. For Boyle, on the other hand, "the rational soul ... is a kind of imprisoned angel."[2]

Of course there were questions about how these two entities, mind and body, interacted.[3] How in particular was perception possible? The mediaeval doctrine of perception, largely accepted by Descartes, held that perception required an internal sense, that would be responsible for a number of features of perception. In particular, said Roger Bacon (Boyle's "Friar Bacon"), it was required (a) to judge "diversity in the sensibles, as, for example, that in milk whiteness is different from sweetness," a distinction which no individual sense can make; (b) to judge of the senses that they do just what they in fact do: that vision sees, and hearing hears, for "vision does not perceive that it sees," and so for the other senses; and (c) "to receive the [information] coming from the particular senses and to complete a judgement concerning [it],"[4] to allow you to know that it is one and the same thing that you are both seeing and hearing, for example. This sense was referred to as the "common sense" because it was common to all the other senses: it could combine information from the sense of smell and the sense of sight, and so on. This seemed like a plausible theoretical entity to bridge the gap between body and soul, and the question was, where in the brain might it be located?

When Descartes observed the brain he noted that it appeared, at least in the detail available to him, to be symmetrical in terms of its hemispheres, with one exception: the pineal gland, or *conar-*

1 *Works* 5:300.

2 *Works* 12:504.

3 Boyle highlights some of the problems in "The Excellency of Theology," *Works* 8:68-69 [188-89].

4 Bacon 1733, part V.1, Dist.1, chapter 2, 258.

ion, was the one asymmetrical feature. Moreover, it was small, and easily moveable. So a plausible hypothesis seemed to be that this was the gateway to the soul. Perception involves the "animal spirits" arriving in the brain and interacting with the pineal gland to affect (somehow) the incorporeal soul or mind, a possibility that Boyle accepted, hesitantly, and with which he was clearly not very happy.[1]

This Cartesian view of the nature of humans gives rise to many problems and not a few criticisms. The twentieth-century philosopher Peter Geach writes:

> It is a savage superstition to suppose that a man consists of two pieces, body and soul, which come apart at death; the superstition is not mended but rather aggravated by conceptual confusion, if the soul-piece is supposed to be immaterial. The genius of Plato and Descartes has given this superstition an undeservedly long lease of life; it gained some accidental support from Scriptural language, e.g. about flesh and spirit—accidental, because a Platonic-Cartesian reading of such passages is mistaken, as Scripture scholars now generally agree.[2]

Boyle, however, was fairly straightforwardly Cartesian in his views about the soul, though, with his usual caution, he points out that it is one view among others, and that indeed it is subject to considerable difficulties. As noted in the "Overview," he remarks "that this union of an incorporeal with a corporeal substance, (and that without a medium) is a thing so unexampled in nature, and so difficult to comprehend, that I somewhat question, whether the profound secrets of theology, not to say the adorable mystery itself of the incarnation, be more abstruse than this."[3]

Nonetheless, Boyle adopted the Cartesian account, not least because he held, as did most, that it was conceptually impossible for matter to think,[4] and also because he held, again in common with many others, that there were a variety of intelligent operations that could not be produced materially. His younger con-

1 See further MacIntosh 1983.

2 Geach 1969, 38.

3 *Works* 8:68 [188].

4 "Matter, however vastly extended," he wrote, "and how curiously shaped soever, is but a brute thing that is only capable of local motion and its effects and consequents on other bodies, or the brain of man, without being capable of any true, or at least any intellectual, perception, or true love or hatred (*Works* 8:33 [138])."

temporary Leibniz produced a thought experiment to show the impossibility of matter thinking:

> [P]erception and what depends on it are *inexplicable by mechanical reasons*, that is, by figure and motion. If we imagine a machine whose structure enables it to think, feel, and perceive, we could conceive it as enlarged, with the same proportions, so that one could enter it as one does a mill. If we did this, we should find nothing there but parts which push one upon the other, but nothing which would explain a perception.[1]

Against this popular and widely accepted view, John Locke argued that it was, given God's omnipotence, *possible* for (suitably organized) matter to think, since God could superadd thought to matter. Locke dismissed our apparently inability to conceive the way in which this could happen by noting the "weakness of our apprehensions [that] reaches not the power of God."[2] We have, Locke agreed, no idea *how* matter could think, but this is balanced by the fact that we also have no idea how an incorporeal mind could think. "Pray tell us," he wrote in the margin of his copy of Thomas Burnet's attack on the *Essay*, "how y^{u} conceive cogitation in an unsolid created substance. It is as hard, I confess, to me to be conceived in an unsolid as in a solid substance."[3]

The problem was a difficult one for seventeenth-century thinkers, since non-humans animals apparently *did* think and apparently were simply material entities. Moreover, since *soul* still had the Aristotelian property of being that—whatever it was—that explained the difference between living and non-living entities, it was assumed that non-human animals had souls of *some* sort. The question was whether they had rational, conscious souls. Theory said no; experience said yes, or at least, maybe. Jean Baptiste Duhamel, writing to the secretary of The Royal Society, Henry Oldenburg, said,

> I regard it as a difficulty which does not lead me to take away all kinds of consciousness from animals, being convinced of the contrary by thousands of experiences.
>
> Thus I am almost certain, because I see that they have feeling and consciousness, although the manner in which they

1 *Monadology*, 17, Gerhardt 6:609.

2 Locke 1823, 4:468.

3 Porter 1984, 48; Burnet 1989, 85.

are conscious is unknown to me; and this happens with almost all the facts of nature, whose existence is quite apparent, although we cannot know their essence or manner of existence, as with gravity, the magnet, and an infinity of other things. Most geometers and philosophers believe in the infinite divisibility of matter as indubitable and evident from demonstrations, yet there is nevertheless nothing more inconceivable. Thus, although there is nothing more shocking to the mind than granting some consciousness to matter, it nevertheless seems to me that we should first thoroughly examine the fact and see whether animals who have every appearance of being nothing but matter do not have some consciousness, rather than be dismayed by the absurdities, either real or apparent, which occur in this matter.... However this question may be among the number of those which are never resolved.[1]

Pierre Bayle noted the religious overtones of the controversy: "It is a pity that Descartes' view is so implausible and difficult to sustain, because it is otherwise very advantageous to the true faith, which is the only reason why some people continue to hold it."[2] The first Boyle lecturer, Richard Bentley, after a discussion on the nature of matter, sums up: "we have proved, and 'tis agreed on all hands, that in our conception of any quantity of Body, there is nothing but Figure, and Site, and a Capacity of Motion. Which Motion, if it be actually excited in it, doth only cause a new Order and Contexture of parts."[3] But, argues Bentley, indulging himself in whimsy at the atheist's expense, the motion of which matter is capable can never give rise to thought. Flint and steel produce sparks, but

what a strange and miraculous thing should we count it, if the Flint and the Steel, instead of a few Sparks, should chance to strike out Definitions and Syllogisms? and yet it's altogether as reasonable, as this sottish opinion of the Atheists; That dead senseless Atoms can ever justle and knock one another into

1 Jean Baptiste Duhamel to Oldenburg 16/26 October, 1673 (Oldenburg 1965, 10:298,299-300). For further discussion of this point see MacIntosh 1996.

2 "C'est dommage que le sentiment de M. Des Cartes soit si difficile à soutenir, & si éloigné de la vraisemblance; car il est d'ailleurs très-avantageux à la vraie foi, & c'est l'unique raison qui empêche quelques personnes de s'en départir." "Rorarius," Bayle 1734, 4:906.

3 Bentley 1699, 51.

> Life and Understanding. All that can be effected by such encounters of Atoms, is either the imparting or receiving of Motion, or a new determination and direction of its Course. Matter, when it acts upon matter, can communicate nothing but motion.[1]

What, however, of the fact, or apparent fact, that the "actions of some Brutes ... visibly discover some glimpses of Understanding"?[2] Earlier in the seventeenth century such questions caused considerable unease. For *soul* seemed to have two main jobs to do. One was its apparent explanatory power with respect to such functions as perception, intentional action, and rational behaviour. The other was that it conferred immortality on its possessor. There were hangovers from the Aristotelian notion of soul, in which one could speak of a corporeal soul, but even there the problem arose. For if the possession of a corporeal soul could explain the apparent reasoning abilities of non-human animals, why couldn't it do the same for humans? And if non-human animals had a *mortal* soul, mightn't humans have such a soul as well? The view that human souls might be mortal was accounted not only startling but dangerous, and the Blasphemy Ordination of May 1648 imposed "the death penalty on Mortalists or those who denied the Trinity or that the Scriptures were the word of God."[3]

Descartes' disciple, Antoine Le Grand, attributing to Plato the view that animal and human souls were alike, resolutely refused to treat it as worthy of any refutation other than a rhetorical shudder:

> this *Opinion* hath long since grown out of date, and is reckoned by the *Fathers* among *Plato's Childish Fictions*, so that there is no necessity of encountring them with *Arguments*: Let it suffice to take notice what enormous absurdities must needs arise from the admitting of this *Opinion*, and what confusion in Nature would follow: For if the *Souls* of *Beasts* be *eternal* and invested with *immortality*, what distinction will there be between *Men* and other *Animals*? Doth the same felicity attend them as us?[4]

---

1 Bentley 1699, 56.

2 Bentley 1699, 59.

3 Hill 1972, 143-44. Hill adds that the Ordination "proved unenforceable." For further details on the Mortalists, see Hill 1977, ch. 25, and Burns 1972.

4 Le Grand 1694, Book III, 226.

Boyle suggested a psychological reason to explain why atheists might cling to mortalism:

> if to [a] Brute Animal, there belongs a Being more noble than Matter, that can actuate and inform it, and make it self the Architect of its own Mansion [and] perform all the Functions of a vegetable Soul; and besides those, See, Hear, Taste, Smell, Imagine, Infer, Remember, Love, Hate, Fear, Hope, Expect, *&c.*, and yet be a mortal thing, and perish with the Body; it will not be difficult for those Enemies of Religion, who are willing to think the Soul Mortal, because their brutish Lives make them wish she were, to fancy, that human Minds are but a somewhat more Noble, but not for that less Mortal kind of Substantial Forms.[1]

Bentley, however, simply sidestepped the issue. Either Descartes was right, and animals were simply complex machines, or he was not. If he was, we should "admire and adore the divine Artifice and Skill in such a wonderful contrivance."[2] If he was not, the brutes have immortal souls and God will either annihilate them at death, or he will not. In either case "what need we be concerned about it? 'tis only by the good pleasure of their Maker, who doth all things for the best."[3] One thing, however, is very

1 "Christian Virtuoso 1," *Works* 11:298. Although Boyle was contemptuous of "the great noise made by vulgar Philosophers of their Substantial Forms" (BP 9.28r), he entered the following caveat:

> when ever I shall speake indefinitely of Substantiall forms, I would alwayes be understood to except the Reasonable Soule, that is said to inform the humane Body; which Declaration I here desire may be taken notice of, once for all.... Nor am I willing to treat of the Origine of Qualities in beasts; partly because I would not be engaged to examine, of what Nature their Soules are, and partly because it is difficult enough in most cases (at least for one that is compassionate enough) either to make experiments upon Living animals, or to judge what influence their life may have, upon the change of Qualities, produc'd by such Experiments. ("Origine of Forms and Qualities," *Works* 5:300)

2 Bentley 1699, 59-60.

3 Bentley 1699, 59, first edition phrasing. Clarke was later to make a similar point in his dispute with Dodwell ("A Second Defence of ... the Immateriality and Natural Immortality of the Soul," Clarke *Works* 3:795). The casual acceptance of these possibilities by Bentley and Clarke shows clearly that the earlier furore centring around the question of animal souls was now comparatively quiescent. On this issue see further, MacIntosh 1996, and Lennon 1993, 23, "The Bestial Soul."

clear to Bentley: “Omnipotence it self cannot create cogitative Body.” This is not “any imperfection in the power of God, but an incapacity in the Subject. The Ideas of Matter and Thought are absolutely incompatible ... none but besotted Atheists, do joyn the two Notions together.”[1]

1 Bentley 1699, 62.

Robert Boyle: A Brief Chronology

1615 Katherine Boyle born
1627 Robert Boyle born
1630 Katherine Boyle (age 15 on 22 March, 1630) marries Richard Jones (Lord Ranelagh) 4 April, 1630
1635 Boyle enters Eton 2 October, with brother Francis (later Viscount Shannon)
1638 Boyle leaves Eton
1639 Boyle to France *en route* to Geneva with Francis and tutor Isaac Marcombes
1640 Boyle's thunderstorm "Conversion"
1641 Boyle visits the Carthusian Abbey in the spring, has suicidal thoughts, travels to Italy in the fall, reads Galilei Galileo
1642 Civil War begins in England. Boyle in Florence, visits brothels in company with his tutor, retains "an unblemish't Chastity"; to Rome in March, and then to Marseilles to find that because of the War there will be no more money forthcoming from his father; Robert goes to Geneva, Francis travels to Ireland in time to fight at Battle of Liscarrol (where their brother Lewis is killed); all theatres in England closed until end of Commonwealth (however, Sir William Davenant, despite his background as a Royalist, managed to persuade the Parliamentarians that operas were not plays, so various "operas" were performed that, after the Restoration, turned out to be plays as well)
1643 Boyle's father Richard Boyle, first Earl of Cork, dies; Boyle in Geneva converses with François Perreaud (which conversation, plus Perreaud's later book (1653), "did at length overcome in me (as to this narrative) all my settled indisposedness to believe strange things")
1644 Boyle returns to England
1645 Boyle in Stalbridge (until 1655, with various trips to France, Holland, Ireland); notebooks on ethics 1645-46
1647 Probable date of composition of Boyle's *An Invitation to a free and generous Communication of Secrets and Receits in Physick* (published 1655), and his *Free Discourse against Customary Swearing* (published posthumously 1695)

1648 Boyle's autobiographical *Philaretus* written sometime between January 1648 and July 1649; *Seraphic Love* probably written while visiting his sister Mary, published 1659; *Occasional Reflections* started; Boyle visits Leiden

1649 Charles I tried and executed, Commonwealth declared; Cromwell's conquest of Ireland begins

1652 First Anglo-Dutch war begins; Cromwellian settlement of Ireland; Boyle to Ireland in June

1655 Boyle, *Invitation to Free Communication* (probably written c. 1649)

1656 Henry Oldenburg engaged by Ranelaghs to tutor their son, Richard Jones, probably meets Boyle 1657; Boyle in Oxford from late 1655 or early 1656 (till 1668)

1658 Robert Hooke invents balance spring for watches, makes Boyle an air pump (possibly 1659)

1659 Boyle's brief residence in Chelsea; Boyle arranges (perhaps in conjunction with Samuel Hartlib) for Peter Sthael ("a Lutheran and a great hater of women ... a very useful man"—Anthony à Wood) to come to England and give chemistry classes at Oxford; among his students was "Jo. Lock[1] ... a man of a turbulent spirit, clamorous and never contented," who was "prating and troblesome" (Wood). (Other students included John Wallis and Christopher Wren)

1660 Boyle, *Spring and Weight of the Air* (second edition and *Defence*, 1662); Samuel Pepys begins his diary; Charles II restored to the throne (29 May); foundation of Royal Society; Hooke's Law of elasticity

1661 Boyle, *Certain Physiological Essays* (second edition, 1669), *The Sceptical Chymist, Style of the Scriptures*; Christiaan Huygens visits London (April/May), meetings with Boyle and others

1662 Grant of royal charter to Royal Society; Hooke recommended by Boyle to be Curator of the experiments of the Royal Society; Boyle becomes first Governor of the Corporation for Propagation of the Gospel in New England

1663 Boyle, *Usefulness of Experimental Philosophy* (Tome II, 1671); René Descartes' writings put on Index; Huygens elected Fellow of the Royal Society; Isaac Newton, binomial theorem

---

1 I.e., the philosopher John Locke (1632-1704).

1664	Boyle, *Experiments and Considerations touching Colours*
1665	Great Plague of London; Boyle, *Occasional Reflections* (some portions as early as 1648); *Experimental History of Cold; Excellency of Theology* (probable date of composition, published 1674); Hooke, *Micrographia*, appointed Professor of Geometry at Gresham College; 1665-66: Newton's calculus; 8 September, Boyle created Doctor of Physic at Oxford
1666	Great Fire of London; Boyle, *Hydrostatical Paradoxes*; *Origine of Formes and Qualities*; founding of the Académie Royale des Sciences, Paris; France and Holland declare war on England
1667	Peace of Breda between Holland, France and England; Jean-Baptiste Denis transfers about 350 ml of lamb's blood into a sick boy (who lived), later two patients die, Denis tried for murder, acquitted, transfusions banned in France
1668	Edme Mariotte discovers blindspot; Hooke, *Discourse on Earthquakes*; Newton makes reflecting telescope; Boyle in London, lives in Pall Mall with his sister, Katherine, Lady Ranelagh, till death in 1691; Locke's constitution for Carolina approved
1669	Boyle, *Of Absolute Rest in Bodies*; Lorenzo Magalotti ill during visit to London, Boyle visits for two to three hours daily
1670	Boyle, *Cosmical Qualities*, Boyle has a serious stroke (June); posthumous publication of Pascal's *Pensées*; Benedict Spinoza, *Tractatus theologico-politicus*; present day Alberta included in territory granted to Hudson's Bay Company
1671	Boyle, *Usefulness of Experimental Philosophy* Tome II (Tome I, 1663), *Rarefaction of the Air*; Henry More visits Boyle, they discuss Descartes' philosophy
1672	Boyle, *Origine and Virtues of Gems*, *Relation betwixt Flame and Air*; Clarendon Press founded
1672-76	Gottfried Leibniz in Paris (meets Huygens, invents differential calculus, improves Pascal's calculating machine)
1673	Boyle, *Essays of Effluviums*; Leibniz visits London (from Paris), meets Boyle
1674	Boyle, *Saltness of the Sea*, *Excellency of Theology* (mainly written 1665), *Excellency and Grounds of the Mechanical Hypothesis*, *Hidden Qualities of the Air*

1675 Ole Rømer estimates speed of light; Boyle, *Reconcileableness of Reason and Religion, Possibility of the Resurrection, Mechanical Origin of Qualities*

1676 Leibniz to Hanover; influenza epidemic in England; Thomas Sydenham, *Observationes medicae*; Mariotte publishes *Discours de la nature de l'air* (contains statement of Boyle's/Mariotte's Law and coined word "barometer")

1677 Open air fair (January) on frozen Thames; ice cream popular dessert in Paris; Robert Plot, elected to Royal Society, publishes *The Natural History of Oxfordshire* (contains earliest description and drawing of a dinosaur bone: the end of the thigh bone of Megalosaurus); punishment for heresy reduced from death by burning to excommunication

1678 Boyle, *Degradation of Gold*; Huygens writes *Treatise on Light* (published 1690)

1679 Boyle experiments with vacuum preservation of foodstuffs; European discovery of Niagara Falls by Jesuit Father Louis Hennepin

1680 Boyle, *Aerial Noctiluca, Producibleness of Chymical Principles*; Boyle elected president of the Royal Society (30 November, 1680), December 8, refuses position on grounds of oath taking after consulting three lawyers; dodo becomes extinct

1681 Boyle, *Things above Reason*; first street lamps (oil) in London; Wren becomes president of the Royal Society, Plot secretary

1682 Boyle, *Icy Noctiluca*; Edmond Halley observes Halley's Comet, predicts return in 1759 (first correct prediction of its kind)

1683 Boyle, *Salt Water Sweetened, Humane Blood* (1683-84); Antony van Leeuwenhoek draws bacteria; Newton's theory of tides; first Vienna coffeehouses; worst of a series of cold winters, market on frozen Thames

1684 Boyle, Porosity of Bodies, Mineral Waters (1684-85)

1685 Boyle, *High Veneration to God, Languid and Unheeded Motion, Specifick Medicines*; Charles II dies, accession of James II

1686 Boyle, *Free Inquiry into the Vulgarly receiv'd Notion of Nature*; Newton, *De Motu Corporum* (first book of *Principia*) presented to the Royal Society; Leibniz, *Discourse on Metaphysics*, 1686-87; in Russia the Tsar liberates a prisoner convicted of two crimes: swearing and playing chess

1687 Boyle, *Martyrdom of Theodora* (probably written 1647); Newton, *Principia*; Venetians capture Corinth and Athens, Parthenon destroyed by Venetian mortar (September 26, 1686, at about 7:00 p.m.)

1688 Boyle, *Medicinal Experiments, Final Causes and Vitiated Sight, Loss of his Writings*; William of Orange lands in England, James II flees

1689 William and Mary proclaimed King and Queen; Huygens in London (June-August), meetings with Boyle, Halley, Locke and Newton; because of ill health Boyle resigns Governorship of the Corporation for Propagation of the Gospel in New England

1690 Anne Finch Conway, *Principles of the Most Ancient and Modern Philosophy* (written before 1679, published posthumously, transcribed by Francis Mercury van Helmont); Locke, *Essay Concerning Humane Understanding*; Boyle, *Medicina Hydrostatica, The Christian Virtuoso* (Part I published, Part II probably written or at least assembled by 1690, published 1744)

1691 Boyle, *Experimenta et Observationes Physicæ*; Boyle's final illness, failing sight, and fear of blindness; Katherine Boyle dies (December 23, 1691); Boyle dies the following week (December 31, 1691)

1692 Boyle, *History of the Air* (written 1691); Boyle buried 7 January at St. Martin's in the Fields; Burnet's funeral sermon delivered

1693 Wallis, *Algebra* (using fluxions)

1695 Boyle, posthumous publication of *A Free Discourse against Customary Swearing* (probably written 1647)

A Note on the Text: Conventions, Terminology, Transcriptions

General

For this modernized edition of Robert Boyle's *The Excellency of Theology* and *The Excellency and Grounds of the Mechanical Hypothesis*, I have altered the spelling and punctuation to conform, as far as possible, to modern conventions. I have, very occasionally, changed a word, for example substituting "overlook" for Boyle's "over-see," where leaving the original would alter the meaning for a modern reader. I have also altered Boyle's Latin-based pronouns (typically "she" and "her") for references to words such as "soul," "nature," "reason," "philosophy," etc., and have replaced "Cartesius" by "Descartes." I have introduced or suppressed pronouns as necessary when breaking up some of Boyle's often lengthy sentences, some of which run to over three hundred words. I have, similarly, divided some of Boyle's lengthy paragraphs. Boyle's biblical references have been standardized, and his Greek has been transliterated. I have added headings to Boyle's internal sections in *The Excellency of Theology*.

Otherwise, I have altered the text as little as possible, explaining in footnotes words that may be unfamiliar, particularly those whose central meanings have changed since the seventeenth century, while trying not to cross the line between informing and insulting the reader. If a term is well-known, but typically nowadays substituted by another ("explicated" and "explained" for example) I have simply left the text as is. If, however, the original term may be confusing ("amel" for our "enamel" for example) I have used the modern term. When I have quoted from other seventeenth-century sources, including Boyle's manuscripts and printed works, I have left spelling (which in this period was anything but standardized) and punctuation unchanged so that readers may see something of seventeenth-century orthography and style.

Throughout references to Boyle's *Works* are to the now standard (and definitive) edition of Michael Hunter and Edward B. Davis. References to the Boyle *Papers* (BP) are to the 46 volumes of the Boyle Papers in the Royal Society Library, London now available on microfilm, ed. Michael Hunter, as *Letters and Papers of Robert Boyle* (Bethesda, MD: University Publications of

America, 1990). For permission to publish my transcriptions of various items from the Boyle *Papers*, I am grateful to the Librarian and Fellows of the Royal Society.

Terminology

Some words of frequent occurrence may be noticed here. "Catholic," in Boyle's usage, always has the meaning simply of "universal." Thus when Boyle speaks of the "primitive and Catholick Affections of Matter, namely, bulk, shape and motion,"[1] he means simply that these are the properties that every piece of matter has. The terms "virtuoso," "mathematician," or simply "philosopher," could be applied to anyone who was a practising natural philosopher or scientist. In particular, the term "mathematician" has sometimes our narrow sense of someone versed in mathematics, but was also used of someone who was simply a person with a wide range of practical and theoretical abilities. Thus Boyle speaks of "those excellent Mathematicians, Dr. *I. Wilkins*, and Mr. *Christopher Wren*,"[2] neither of whom was a mathematician in our sense of the word. Boyle does not use the term to cover alchemists, however. Chemistry and alchemy are not distinguished in this period.[3] When Boyle speaks of *chemists* he usually has the followers of Paracelsus in mind, though he also uses the term and its cognates in a more general sense.

A "virtuoso," in Boyle's use, is not merely someone talented, but more restrictedly is someone versed in, and adept at, natural philosophy—the members of the early Royal Society would be styled *virtuosi* by Boyle. When Boyle speaks of the "Peripatetics," the "Scholastics," or the "School-men," he is referring to the followers of Aristotle who dominated intellectual thought during the high Middle Ages and whose influence remained strong throughout the Renaissance and into the early modern period.

A "creature" is anything which in Boyle's view was created by God; thus the stars, grains of sand, and living things are all creatures. "Vulgar," for Boyle as for his contemporaries, simply meant "common" or "ordinary" and had no more derogatory connotation than those terms have. "Specious" is used in its commendatory sense, meaning "beautiful" or "appropriate." For Boyle a

1 CPE, *Works* 2:21.

2 *Usefulness I*, *Works* 3:327.

3 See further Principe and Newman 1998.

specious argument is a good argument (even if it is ultimately rejected), not, as it is for us, an initially plausible but ultimately untrustworthy argument. "Physiology" is the study of nature, particularly that branch of it that we now call physics. When Boyle speaks simply of "history," he is typically using the term in our sense; but when he speaks of "a history," or of "convincing historical proofs," he is referring to a collection of data in a given area. He lamented the absence of such collections of data and set himself the task of providing them in a number of areas. His publisher tells us in *Tracts about The Cosmical Qualities of Things, &c.* (1671), that "his main Designe in these as well as his other Physicall Writings, was to provide Materialls for the History of Nature,"[1] and Boyle himself tells us in his *Defence of the Doctrine Touching The Spring and Weight of the Air* (1662) that "it was not my chief Design to establish Theories and Principles, but to devise Experiments, and to enrich the History of Nature with Observations faithfully made and deliver'd; that by these, and the like Contributions made by others, men may in time be furnish'd with a sufficient stock of Experiments, to ground Hypotheses and Theorys on."[2]

"Divine" as an adjective has its usual meaning; "divine" as a noun refers typically to clerics. Save in quotations, and the titles of works, I have changed Boyle's "chymistry" to "chemistry," but it should be remembered that chemistry as an independent science is really a production of the eighteenth century,[3] and that the subject Boyle has in mind is as close to alchemy as it is to the later chemistry. (For a detailed discussion of this point see Principe and Newman 1998.) For Boyle and his contemporaries a common sense of the term "stupid" was "insensible." Thus when Boyle speaks of matter as "stupid," he is simply referring to the generally accepted view that matter was non-sensing, that is, *stupid*. The word "divers," though etymologically connected with "diverse," is a distinct term, and in Boyle's use it has the sense, common in the seventeenth century, of "various," or "several."

1 *Works* 6:261.

2 *Works* 3:12.

3 In his 1704 lectures on chemistry, John Freind remarked that "No Body has brought more light into this Art than Mr. *Boyl*, that famous Restorer of Experimental Philosophy: Who nevertheless has not so much laid a new Foundation of Chymistry, as he has thrown down the old; he has left us plentiful Matter, from whence we may draw out a true Explication of things, but the explication it self he has but very sparingly touch'd upon" (Freind 1737, 3-4).

"Science," "natural philosophy," "experimental philosophy," "corpuscular philosophy," "mechanical philosophy": Although the term "science" (from Latin *scientia*-knowledge) is to be found in English from the Middle Ages on, in our sense of the word it is comparatively late, and the endeavours that we consider paradigmatically scientific were, in the early modern period, thought of as springing from a particular philosophical outlook, the kind of philosophy that had a special interest in nature and its experimental observation. Thus Boyle, like his contemporaries, speaks commonly of *experimental philosophy*, or of *natural philosophy*, where we might speak of *science*.

Henry More distinguished between the "mechanical philosophy" (which he thought might lead to atheism) and "experimental philosophy"; it is the latter, More suggests, that members of "the celebrated Royal Society" practice. Many people, More says, mistakenly confound the two notions; but in his view they should be kept distinct. Most, however, like Boyle, ran the two together. Samuel Parker, the future Bishop of Oxford, preferred "the Mechanical and Experimental Philosophie before the *Aristotelean* ... because it puts inquisitive men into a method to attain [certainty], whereas the other serves only to obstruct their industry by amusing them with empty and insignificant Notions."[1]

The issue is not merely terminological, for there is currently a debate among historians about the appropriateness of using the term "science" at all to refer to the activities of the natural philosophers in this period. To oversimplify the debate considerably, writers who want us to eschew the use of the word "science" as being misleadingly anachronistic in this context point out that natural philosophers in this period typically had as their aim the uncovering of God's works and the testimony those works provided to God's glory, so that the point was only incidentally the uncovering of theologically neutral truths; the main thrust of the enterprise was to discover God's handiwork. Contemporary scientists, by contrast, are held to be engaging in apparently similar activities for quite different reasons; they are acting ir- or non-religiously for the love of truth (or money, or fame, or perhaps tenure). In discussing the activities of Boyle and his contemporaries I have normally used the terms "natural philosophy," or "experimental philosophy" and their cognates, but I have also used "science" and its cognates when use of the alternative terms might strike modern readers as unnecessarily cumbersome.

1 More 1671, "Preface to the Reader," §11; Parker 1666, 45.

It is true, and important, that almost all the natural philosophers of the seventeenth century were believers,[1] and felt that their work was a matter of uncovering the work of God. "The World," said Boyle, "is the great Book, not so much of Nature, as of the God of Nature, which we should find ev'n crowded with instructive Lessons, if we had but the Skill, and would take the Pains, to extract and pick them out."[2] It is also true, however, that their work makes it clear that the experimental pursuit of truth was for most if not all of them an end in itself. Things can have intrinsic as well as extrinsic value, and there is no reason to suppose that seventeenth-century natural philosophers were not motivated by both religious *and* scientific desires and interests.[3] Indeed, half a century after Boyle's death, the poet Mark Akenside happily united "the lamp of science" with the discovery of the fruits of the hand of the author of nature:

Or shall we touch that kind access of joy,
That springs to each fair object, while we trace,
Thro' all its fabric, wisdom's artful aim
Disposing every part, and gaining still
By means proportion'd her benignant end?
Speak, ye, the pure delight, whose favour'd steps
The lamp of science thro' the jealous maze
Of nature guides, when haply you reveal
Her secret honours: whether in the sky,
The beauteous laws of light, the central pow'rs
That wheel the pensile planets[4] round the year;
Whether in wonders of the rowling deep,
Or smiling fruits of pleasure-pregnant earth,
Or fine-adjusted springs of life and sense,
You scan the counsels of their author's hand.[5]

---

1 Thomas Hobbes was considered by most to be both a natural philosopher *and* an atheist, but Descartes had already warned his readers that an atheist could not correctly claim *any* knowledge since the atheist could not correctly claim to be *certain* about anything (Replies 2, AT 7:141). Not being a believer, the atheist cannot depend on the existence of a benevolent God who will ensure that she or he is not being systematically deceived. See further Newman 2005.

2 "Occasional Reflections," *Works* 5:39.

3 On intrinsic and extrinsic value, see Hurka 2006.

4 I.e., planets *hanging* or *suspended* in the void (cf. Job 26.7: "He stretcheth out the north over the empty place, and hangeth the earth upon nothing").

5 Akenside 1744, Book II, 121-35.

Nonetheless, it was almost a century later that William Whewell used the term "scientist" for the practitioners of scientific endeavours in our current sense.

Transcriptions

In my transcriptions from the Boyle Papers, I have followed most of Michael Hunter's suggestions in Hunter 1995b and Hunter 2006. Boyle's insertions are in angle brackets (<, >), and for this edition I have omitted Boyle's deletions. I have printed in full standard manuscript shortened forms. Thus instead of printing abbreviations with the thorn as "yt," ye," I have printed "that," "the," and similarly for other contractions. I have retained Boyle's (or Boyle's amanuenses') ampersands and contracted forms that often found their way into print. Where there is doubt as to whether or not an initial letter is upper or lower case, I have opted for the current (usually lower-case) version. Seventeenth-century English had an alphabet of twenty-four letters, with the pairs "u," "v," and "i," "j," treated as single letters. In transcribing I have, again following Hunter, used the modern forms, writing "have" for "haue," etc. in transcriptions. However, where a word such as "haue" occurs in a quoted printed work I have left it as is.

Volume and folio number in the manuscripts are shown between slashes, with *recto* usually omitted. Thus /7:165/ refers to *Boyle Papers*, volume 7, folio 165, recto, while /7:165v/ refers to *Boyle Papers*, volume 7, fol. 165, verso. A number of fragments relating to theology in the Boyle Papers are collected in *Boyle on Atheism* (Boyle 2006), and where these have been quoted I have also given the Boyle 2006 section and page numbers. References to *The Excellencies* are to the *Works* with the page number of this modernized edition following in brackets. Cross references within the current text are similarly shown in brackets.

As noted in *Works* 8:xii, parts of the text survive in a manuscript version, as does a Latin translation of the *Excellency of the Mechanical Hypothesis*, and on the rare occasions when the text has been altered to take account of manuscript readings, or of the Latin, this has been noted in a footnote. Boyle's marginal references and comments are shown as footnotes followed by a bracketed "[RB's note]"; when I have added something to his marginalia my addition follows. Otherwise footnotes are mine.

The text I have used is that of the first edition, checking it against Hunter and Davis's printing of the first edition in Volume

8 of *The Works*. Their version has a helpful and interesting introduction and numerous helpful footnotes. For the reader who wishes to read Boyle in his original seventeenth-century form, *The Works* edition can be unreservedly recommended. I have also consulted M.A. Stewart's modernized version of *The Excellency and Grounds of the Mechanical Hypothesis* in Stewart 1979, pp. 138-54.

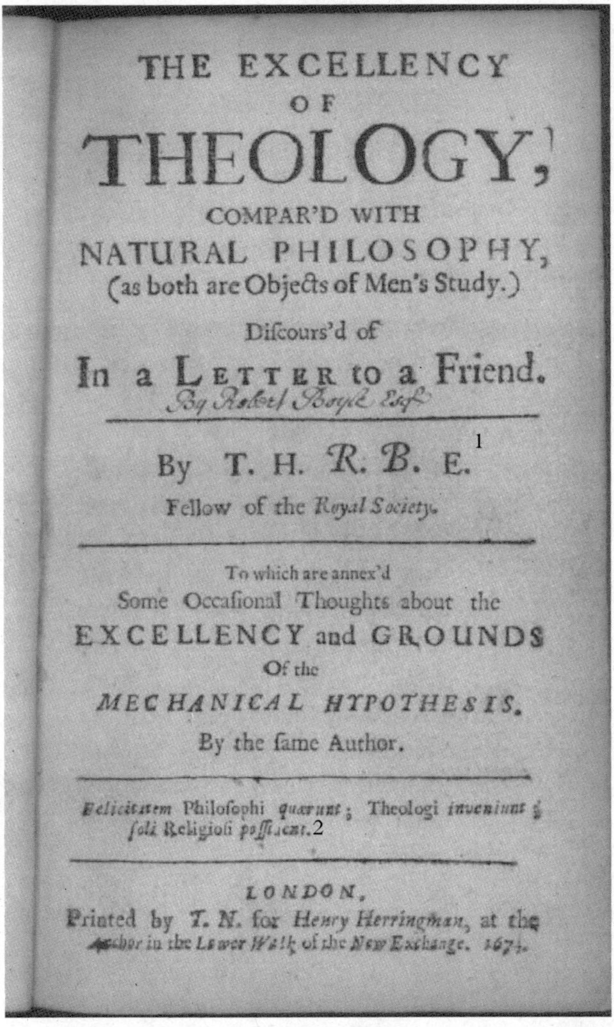
THE EXCELLENCY
OF
THEOLOGY,
COMPAR'D WITH
NATURAL PHILOSOPHY,
(as both are Objects of Men's Study.)
Discours'd of
In a LETTER to a Friend.
By Robert Boyle Esq
By T. H. R. B. E.[1]
Fellow of the *Royal Society*.
To which are annex'd
Some Occasional Thoughts about the
EXCELLENCY and GROUNDS
Of the
MECHANICAL HYPOTHESIS.
By the same Author.
Felicitatem Philosophi *quaerunt*; Theologi *inveniunt* & *soli* Religiosi *possident*.[2]
LONDON,
Printed by *T. N.* for *Henry Herringman*, at the *Anchor* in the *Lower Walk* of the *New Exchange*. 1674.

1 That is, The Honourable *Robert Boyle* Esquire. This at best half-hearted attempt at anonymity is also given away by the first line of "The Author's Preface" where Boyle assumes that his readers will know the identity of the author.

2 Latin: "Philosophers search for happiness; theologians find it; but only the religious possess it." In view of Boyle's scruples about religion and religious observances, it is interesting that a primary meaning of the Latin term *religiosi* has to do with being scrupulous in religious observances, so a translation more in keeping with Boyle's sentiments might be: "only the religiously scrupulous possess it." On Boyle's scruples, see Hunter 2000.

The Publisher's Advertisement to the Reader

When I shall have told the reader that the following discourse was written in the year 1665 while the author, to avoid the great plague that then raged in London, was reduced with many others to go into the country and frequently to pass from place to place, unaccompanied with most of his books, it will not, I presume, be thought strange that in the mention of some things taken from other writers, as his memory suggested them, he did not annex in the margin[1] the precise places that are referred to. And upon the same score it ought not to seem strange that he has not mentioned some late discoveries and books that might have been pertinently taken notice of and would well have accommodated some parts of his discourse, since things that may thus seem to have been omitted, are of too recent a date to have been known to him when he wrote. But if it be demanded, why then a discourse finished so long ago, did not come abroad much sooner? I must acquaint the reader, that it was chiefly his real concern for the welfare of the study he seems to depreciate, that kept these papers so long by him. For he resisted for several years the desires of persons that have much power with him, and suppressed the following discourse, while he feared it might be misapplied by some enemies to experimental philosophy, that then made a noise against it, without suffering these papers to come abroad, till the addresses and encomiums[2] of many eminent foreign virtuosi, and their desire to be admitted into The Royal Society, had sufficiently manifested, how little its reputation was prejudiced, or like to be endangered, by the attempts of some envious or misinformed persons.[3] And to this reason must be added the author's backwardness to venture abroad a discourse of an unusual nature, on which account, among others, he declined to have his name prefixed to it; though, now the book is printed, he finds cause to fear, that it will not be long concealed; since he meets with some marginal references to other tracts of his, which (these papers having long lain by him) he forgot to have been set down for private use, and which should not have been exposed to public view.

---

1 It was common in seventeenth-century printed works, as well as in manuscripts, to give information in the margin which would now be given in footnotes or endnotes. These notes are referred to as "marginalia."

2 Formal expressions of praise.

3 On the early reception of The Royal Society, see Hunter 1981.

The Author's Preface

I am not so little acquainted with the temper of this age, and of the persons that are likeliest to be perusers of the following tract, as not to foresee it to be probable enough, that some will ask, for what reason a discourse of this nature was written at all; and that others will be displeased that it has been written by me.

Those that would know by what inducements my pen was engaged on this subject may be in great part informed by the epistle itself, in divers[1] places whereof, as especially about the beginning and at the close, the motives that invited me to put pen to paper are sufficiently expressed. And though several of those things are peculiarly applied, and (if I may so speak) appropriated to the person the letter is addressed to; yet that undervaluation I would dissuade him from, of the study of things sacred, is not his fault alone but is grown so rife among many (otherwise ingenious) persons, especially studiers of physics, that I wish the ensuing discourse were much less seasonable than I fear it is. But I doubt that some readers, who would not think a discourse of this nature needless or useless, may yet not be pleased at its being written by one whom they imagine, by the acceptance his endeavours have met with, ought to be obliged to spend his whole time in cultivating that natural philosophy, which in this letter he would persuade to quit the precedency they think it may well challenge before all other sorts of learning.

I am not insensible of the favourable reception that the philosophical papers I have hitherto ventured abroad have had the happiness to receive from the curious, but I hope they will not be displeased if I represent that I am no lecturer or professor of physics, nor have ever engaged myself by any promise made to the public, to confine myself never to write of any other subject. Nor is it reasonable that what I did or may write to gratify other men's curiosity should deprive me of my own liberty and confine me to one subject, especially since there are divers persons, for whom I have a great esteem and kindness, who think they have as much right to solicit me for composures of the nature of this (that they will now have to go abroad) as the virtuosi have to exact of me physiological pieces. And though I be not ignorant, that (in particular) the following discourse, which seems to depreciate the study of nature, may at first sight appear somewhat improper for a person that has purposely written to show the

1 Several.

excellence and usefulness of it, yet I confess that upon a more attentive consideration of the matter I cannot reject, no, nor resist, their reasons who are of a quite differing judgement.

And first, my condition, and my being a secular person[1] (as they speak) are looked upon as circumstances that may advantage an author that is to write upon such a subject as I have handled. I need not tell you that, as to religious books in general, it has been observed that those penned by laymen and especially gentlemen, have (*ceteris paribus*[2]) been better entertained and more effectual than those of ecclesiastics. And indeed it is no great wonder that exhortations to piety and dissuasions from vice and from the lusts and vanities of the world should be the more prevalent for being pressed by those who have, and yet decline, the opportunities to enjoy plentifully themselves the pleasures they dissuade others from. And (to come yet closer to our present purpose) though I will not venture to say with an excellent divine, that whatever comes out of the pulpit, does with many pass but for "the foolishness of preaching,"[3] yet it cannot well be denied, but that if all other circumstances be equal, he is the fittest to commend divinity, whose profession it is not. And it will somewhat add to the reputation of almost any study, and consequently to that of things divine, that it is praised and preferred by those, whose condition and course of life exempting them from being of any particular calling in the commonwealth of learning, frees them from the usual temptations to partiality to this or that sort of study, which others may be engaged to magnify because it is their trade or their interest, or because it is expected from them, whereas these gentlemen are obliged to commend it only because they really love and value it.

But there is another thing that seems to make it yet more fit that a treatise on such a subject should be penned by the author of this. For professed divines are supposed to be busied about studies that, even by their being of a higher, are confessed to be of another nature than those that treat of things corporeal. And since it may be observed that there is scarce any sort of learned men more apt to undervalue those that are versed only in other parts of knowledge than many of our modern naturalists (who are conscious of the excellency of the science they cultivate), it is much to be feared that what would be said of the preeminence of divinity above physiology by preachers—in whom the study of

---

1 I.e., Boyle is a member of the nobility, and not a member of the clergy.

2 Latin: other things being equal.

3 1 Corinthians 1.21.

the latter is thought either but a preparatory thing, or an excursion—would be looked upon as the decision of an incompetent, as well as interested, judge, and their undervaluations of the advantages of the study of the creatures, would be (as their depreciating the enjoyment of the creatures too often is) thought to proceed but from their not having had sufficient opportunities to relish the pleasures of them. But these prejudices will not lie against a person who has made the indagation[1] of nature somewhat more than a parergon,[2] and having by a not-lazy nor short enquiry manifested how much he loves and can relish the delight it affords, has had the good fortune to make some discoveries in it, and the honour to have them publicly, and but too complementally, taken notice of by the virtuosi. And it may be not impertinent to add that those who make natural philosophy their mistress, will probably be the less offended to find it in this tract represented, if not as a handmaid to divinity, yet as a lady of a lower rank; because the inferiority of the study of nature is maintained by a person who, even while he asserts it, continues (if not a passionate) an assiduous courter of nature.[3] So that, as far as his example can reach, it may show that as on the one side a man need not be unacquainted[4] with, nor unfit to relish, the lessons taught us in the book of the creatures, to think them less excellent than those that may be learned in the book of the Scriptures; so on the other side the preference of this last book is very consistent with an high esteem and an assiduous study of the first.

And if any should here object, that there are some passages—which I hope are but very few—that seem a little too unfavourable to the study of natural things, I might allege for my excuse the great difficulty that there must be in comparing two sorts of studies, both of which a man much esteems, so to behave oneself, as to split a hair between them, and never offend either of them. But I will rather represent, that in such kind of discourses as the ensuing it may justly be hoped that equitable readers will consider not only what is said but on what occasion and with what design it is delivered. Now it is plain by the series of the following discourse that the Physeophilus[5] whom it most

1 Investigation.

2 A secondary work, a work apart from one's main occupation.

3 Boyle's imagery flows naturally from the fact that "nature" (Latin: *natura*) and "philosophy" (*philosophia*) are feminine nouns in Latin.

4 Correcting the first edition's "acquainted."

5 Latin: lover of nature.

relates to was by me looked upon as a person both very partial to the study of nature and somewhat prejudiced against that of the Scripture, so that I was not always to treat with him as with an indifferent man but, according to the advice given in such cases by the wise, I was (to use Aristotle's expression) to bend the crooked stick the contrary way in order to the bringing it to be straight,[1] and to depreciate the study of nature much beneath its true value to reduce a great over-valuer to a just estimate of it. And to gain the more upon him, I allowed myself now and then to make use of the contempt he had of the peripatetic and vulgar philosophy, and in some passages to speak of them more slightingly than my usual temper permits, and than I would be forward to do on another occasion; that, by such a complaisance for his opinions, I might have risen[2] to argue with him from them.

But to return to the motives that were alleged to induce me to the publication of these papers, though I have not named them all, yet all of them together would scarce have proved effectual, if they had not been made more prevalent by the just indignation I conceived to see even inquisitive men depreciate that kind of knowledge which does the most elevate, as well as the most bless, mankind, and look upon the noblest and wisest employments of the understanding as signs of weakness in it.

It is not that I expect that whatever can be said, and much less what I have had occasion to say here, will make proselytes[3] of those that are resolved against the being made so, and had

---

1 *Nicomachean Ethics*, Aristotle 1984, 1109 b 2-6.

2 Correcting the first edition "Rises," following Birch 1772.

3 Converts (to a given religion or point of view). Boyle elsewhere remarks, in a similar vein:

> you need not thinke it strange, that I never pretended to convert resolved Atheists. For, besides the difficulty of treating clearly and cogently of such abstruse subjects as are many that relate to Atheism; the Will and Affections have so great an influence upon some mens Understandings, that 'tis almost as difficult to make them *beleive*, as to make them *Love*, against their Will. And it must be a very dazzleing Light, that makes an impression upon those that obstinately shut their Eyes against it. 'Tis not by Gods ordinary workes, but by his Extraordinary Power, that such men must be reclaimd to an acknowledgement of his <Existence>. For they that would find the Truth, especially in matters of Religion, must be diligent Inquirers after it, and *may be* strict Examiners of it, but *must not be* resolved Enemies to it. For to such, if to any, God is a Sun, that is not to be discover'd but by <his> owne Light. (BP 2:64 Boyle 2006, 5, p. 384)

rather deny themselves the most excellent kinds of knowledge, than allow that there can be any more excellent, than what they think themselves masters of. But I despair not, that what is here represented may serve to fortify in a high esteem of divine truths those that have already a just veneration for them, and preserve others from being seduced by injurious, though sometimes witty, insinuations, to undervalue that kind of knowledge that is as well the most excellent in itself, as the most conducive to man's happiness.[1] And for this reason I am the less displeased to see that the following letter is swelled to a bulk far greater than its being but a letter promises and than I first intended. For I confess that when the occasion happened that made me put pen to paper, as I chanced to be in a very unsettled condition (which I fear has had too much influence on what I have written) so I did not design the insisting near so long upon my subject as I have done; but new things springing up (if I may so speak) under my pen, I was content to allow them room in my paper because, writing as well for my own satisfaction as for that of my friend, I thought it would not be useless to lay before my own eyes as well as his those considerations that seemed proper to justify to myself as well as to him the preference I gave divine truths before physiological ones, and to confirm myself in the esteem I had for them. And though I freely confess, that the following discourse does not consist solely of ratiocinations, and consequently is not altogether of an uniform contexture; yet that will, I hope, be thought no more than was fit in a discourse designed not only to convince but to persuade, which if it prove so happy as to do, as I hope the peruser will have no cause to regret the trouble of reading it, so I shall not repent that of writing it.

The Introduction

Sir,

I hoped you had known me better than to doubt in good earnest how I relished the discourse your learned friend entertained us

---

1 Similarly, Boyle's contemporary, Ralph Cudworth, wrote his *True Intellectual System* not to convert atheists ("*they being sunk into so great a degree of Sottishness*"); rather it was intended "*for the Confirmation of* Weak, Staggering, *and* Sceptical Theists" (Cudworth 1678, 741; Preface). See also Appendix G, "Moral Demonstrations."

with yesternight.[1] And I am the more troubled at your question, because your way of inquiring how much your friend's discourse obtained of my approbation gives me cause to fear that you vouchsafe it more of yours then I could wish it. But before I can safely offer you my sense of the discourses about which you desire to know, I must put you in mind that they were not all upon one subject nor of the same nature. And I am enough his servant to acknowledge, without the least reluctance, that he is wont to show a great deal of wit when he speaks like a naturalist only of things purely physical, and when he is in the right seldom wrongs a good cause by his way of managing it. But as for those passages, wherein he gave himself the liberty of disparaging the learned Dr. N only because that doctor cultivates theological as well as physical studies, and does both oftentimes read books of devotion, and sometimes write them, I am not so much a courtier, as to pretend that I liked them. It is true, he did not deny the doctor to be a learned and a witty man, as indeed the wise providence of God has so ordered it to stop the bold mouths of some who would be easily tempted to imagine and more easily to give out, that none are philosophers but such as, like themselves, desire to be nothing else. Our nation is happy in several men who are as eminent for human, as studious of divine, learning. And as great a veneration as they pay to Moses and St. Paul, they are as well versed in the doctrine of Aristotle, and of Euclid, nay, of Epicurus and Descartes too, as those that care not to study anything else.[2] For this reason Mr. N had not the confidence to despise the doctor, and some of his resemblers whom he took occasion to mention. Yet he too plainly disclosed himself to

1 The "learned friend," who becomes "Mr. N" below, is unknown, and may be simply a literary device. Also unidentified is the Dr. N mentioned a few lines later; he too may be a literary device, but though many of Boyle's speakers in various dialogues (particularly in drafts of dialogues) are styled "N" or "NN" Boyle quite likely had real people in mind on this occasion. The characterization is substantial and detailed enough to make that possible, particularly in the case of "your friend," who is clearly identified as a Cartesian, with fairly specific views, opinions, and aspirations.

2 Moses and St. Paul, along with Solomon, St. Peter, and Christ, are the biblical figures to whom Boyle constantly refers, with St. Paul being, after Christ, his most common biblical referent. Among scientific thinkers his references to Aristotle, Bacon, Descartes, Epicurus, Gassendi, Paracelsus, and van Helmont are more frequent by far than references to any other thinkers.

be one of those, who though they will not deny that some who own a value for theology are men of parts, yet they talk as if such persons were so in spite of their being religiously given—that being in their opinion such a blemish, that a man must have very great abilities otherwise to make amends for the disadvantage of valuing sacred studies, and surmount the disparagement it procures him.

Wherefore since this disdainful humour begins to spread much more than I could wish it did among differing sorts of men (among whom I should be glad not to find any naturalists), and since the question you asked me, and the esteem you have for your friend, makes me fear you may look on it with very favourable eyes, I shall not decline the opportunity you put into my hands of giving you, together with a profession of my dislike of this practice, some of my reasons for that dislike. And this the rather, because I may do it without too much exceeding the limits of an epistle, or those which the haste wherewith I must write this does prescribe to me. For your friend does not oppose, but only undervalues theology. He professes to believe the Scriptures (which I so far credit, as to think he believes himself when he says so). We agree upon the principles, so that I am not to dispute with him as against an atheist that denies the author of nature, but only against a naturalist that over-values the study of it. And the truths of theology are things which I need not bring arguments for but am allowed to draw arguments from them.

But though, as I just now intimated, I design brevity yet, for fear the fruitfulness and importance of my subject should suggest things enough to me to make some little method requisite to keep them from appearing confused, I shall divide the following epistle into two distinct parts. In the former of which I shall offer you the chief positive considerations by which I would represent to you the study of divinity as preferable to that of physics; and in the second part I shall consider the allegations that I foresee your friend may interpose in favour of natural philosophy. From which distribution you will easily gather that the motives on the one hand, and the objections on the other, will challenge to themselves distinct sections in the respective parts whereto they belong. So that of the order of the particulars you will meet with, I shall not need to trouble you with any further account.

The Excellency of Theology: or, The Preeminence of the Study of Divinity, above that of Natural Philosophy

The First Part: The Positive Reasons for Studying Theology

To address myself then, without any farther circumstance or preamble, to the things themselves that I mainly intend in this discourse, I consider in general that, as there are scarce any motives accounted fitter to engage a rational man in a study than that the subject is noble, that it is his duty to apply himself to it, and that his proficiency in it will bring him great advantages, so there is not any of these three inducements that does not concur in a very plentiful measure to recommend to us the study of theological truths.

THE FIRST SECTION: THE NOBILITY OF THEOLOGY'S OBJECT

And first, the excellency and sublimity of the object we are invited to contemplate is such that none that does truly acknowledge a deity can deny that there is no speculation whose object is comparable in point of nobleness to the nature and attributes of God. The souls of inquisitive men are commonly so curious to learn the nature and condition of spirits that the over-greedy desire to discover that there are other spiritual substances besides the souls of men, which has prevailed with too many to try forbidden ways of attaining satisfaction. Many have chosen rather to venture the putting themselves within the power of demons than remain ignorant whether or no there are any such beings—as I have learned by the private acknowledgments made me of such unhappy (though not unsuccessful) attempts by divers learned men (both of other professions, and that of physic), who themselves made them in differing places, and were persons neither timorous nor superstitious (but this only upon the by). Certainly that man must have a notion of the Deity as wrong as it is mean, and must but very little consider the nature and attributes of that infinitely perfect being and as little the nature and infirmities of man, who can imagine the divine perfections to be subjects whose investigation a man may (inculpably[1]) despise, or be so much as fully sufficient for. The Scripture tells us that his greatness is incomprehensible[2] and his wisdom inscrutable,[3] that he humbles himself to look into (or

1 Without blame.

2 Psalms 145 [RB's note]. Verse 31.

3 Psalms 147.5 [RB's note].

upon) the heavens and the earth,[1] and that not only this or that man but all the nations of the world are, in comparison of him, but like the small drop of a bucket, or the smaller dust of a balance.[2] Even the heathen philosopher who wrote that eloquent book *De Mundo*, ascribed to Aristotle in his riper years,[3] speaks of the power, and wisdom, and amiableness of God, in terms little less lofty, though necessarily inferior to so infinitely sublime a subject, which they that think they can sufficiently understand, especially without revelation, do very little understand themselves.

But perhaps your friend will object, that to the knowledge of God there needs no other than natural theology? I readily confess, being warranted by an apostle, that the *gnoston tou theou*[4] was not unknown to the heathen philosophers, and that so much knowledge of God is attainable by the light of nature, duly employed, as to encourage men to exercise themselves more than most of them do in that noblest of studies, and render their being no proficients in it injurious to themselves as well as to their maker. But notwithstanding this, as God knows himself infinitely better then purblind man knows him, so the informations he is pleased to vouchsafe us touching his own nature and attributes are exceedingly preferable to any account that we can give ourselves of him, without him.[5] And, methinks, the differing prospects we may have of heaven[6] may not ill adumbrate[7] to us the differing discoveries that may be made of the attributes of its maker. For though a man may with his naked eye see heaven to be a very glorious object, enobled with radiant stars of several sorts, yet when his eye is assisted with a good telescope he can not only discover a number of stars,

1 Psalms 113.6 [RB's note].

2 Isaiah 40.15 [RB's note].

3 Boyle is rightly cautious here about the ascription of *De Mundo* to Aristotle (384-22 BCE). W.D. Ross notes that "*De Mundo* has no claim to be regarded as Aristotle's. It is a work of popular philosophy which combines with much that is genuine Aristotelian doctrine a good deal that is Stoic in origin, and in particular owes much to Posidonius. It may probably be dated between 50 BC and 100 AD" (Ross 1923, 11).

4 Romans 1.19 [RB's note]. "Because that which may be *known of God* [*gnoston tou theou*] is manifest in them; for God hath showed it unto them."

5 See Appendix I, "Coke, Boyle, and Edwards on Testimony," for John Edwards' account, which explicitly follows Boyle on this point.

6 The night sky in this context, not a post-mortem paradise.

7 Indicate faintly, or in outline.

(fixed and wandering),[1] which his naked eye would never have shown him, but those planets which he could see before will appear to him much bigger and more distinct. So, although bare reason well improved will suffice to make a man behold many glorious attributes in the Deity, yet the same reason, when assisted by revelation, may enable a man to discover far more excellencies in God, and perceive them far greater and more distinctly than he contemplated before. And to show how much a dim eye, illuminated by the Scriptures, is able to discover of the divine perfections, and how unobvious they are to the most piercing philosophical eyes that enjoy but the dim light of nature, we need but consider how much more suitable conceptions and expressions concerning God are to be met with in the writings of those fishermen and others that penned the New Testament, and those illiterate Christians that received it, than amongst the most civilized nations of the world (such as anciently the Greeks and Romans, and now the Chinese and East-Indians) and among the eminentest of the wise men and philosophers themselves, (as Aristotle, Homer, Hesiod, Epicurus, and others).

Besides that the book of Scripture discloses to us much more of the attributes of God than the book of nature there is another object of our study for which we must be entirely beholding to theology. For though we may know something of the nature of God by the light of reason, yet we must owe the knowledge of his will, or positive laws, to his own revelation. And we may guess how curious great princes and wise men have been to inform themselves of the constitutions established by wise and eminent legislators, partly by the frequent travels of the ancient sages and philosophers into foreign countries, to observe their laws and government, as well as bring home their learning, and partly by those royal and sumptuous expenses, at which that great and learned monarch Ptolemeus Philadelphus stuck not to procure an authentic copy of the law of Moses, whom he considered but as an eminent legislator.[2] But certainly that, and other laws recorded in the Bible, cannot but appear more noble and worthy objects of curiosity to us Christians, who know them to proceed from an omniscient deity, who being the Author of mankind as well as of the rest of the universe, cannot but have a far perfecter

1 The wandering stars are the planets (Greek *planetes* = wanderer).

2 See further Appendix A, "People Mentioned in the Text"—Ptolemeus Philadelphus.

knowledge of the nature of man than any other of the law-givers, or all of them put together, can be conceived to have had.

But there is a farther discovery of divine matters, wherewith we are also gratified by theology. For besides what the Scripture teaches us of the nature and the will of God, it contains divers historical accounts (if I may so call them) of his thoughts and actions. The great Alexander thought himself nobly employed when he read of the Grecian actions in Homer's verses,[1] and to know the sentiments of great and wise persons upon particular occasions is a curiosity so laudable, and so worthy of an inquisitive soul, that the Southern Queen[2] has been more praised than admired for coming from the remoter parts of the earth to hear the wisdom of Solomon. Now the Scripture does in many places give our curiosity a nobler employment, and thereby a higher satisfaction, than the King of Macedonia[3] or the Queen of Sheba could enjoy. For in many places it does, with great clearness and ingenuity, give us accounts of what God himself has declared of his own thoughts, of divers particular persons and things, and relates what he that knows and commands all things was pleased to say and do upon particular occasions. Of this sort of passages are the things recorded to have been said by God to Noah about the sinful world's ruin, and that just man's preservation,[4] and to Moses in the case of the daughters of Zelophehad.[5] Of this sort are the conferences, mentioned to have passed betwixt God and Abimelech, concerning Abraham's wife;[6]

---

1 Various classical authors mention this (see, e.g., Plutarch, *Life of Alexander* 8.2). In his *History of Philosophy*, Boyle's contemporary Thomas Stanley (1625-78) wrote: "Alexander ... took with him the Iliads of Homer, corrected by Aristotle, and made it his constant companion, insomuch that he put it every night with his dagger, under his pillow" (Stanley 1687, 2:357a).

2 The Queen of Sheba. See note 2, p. 176.

3 That is, Alexander the Great.

4 Genesis 6 [RB's note].

5 Numbers 27.7 [RB's note]. At issue was a question of inheritance: "the LORD spake unto Moses, saying, The daughters of Zelophehad speak right: thou shalt surely give them a possession of an inheritance among their father's brethren; and thou shalt cause the inheritance of their father to pass unto them. And thou shalt speak unto the children of Israel, saying, If a man die, and have no son, then ye shall cause his inheritance to pass unto his daughter" (Numbers 27.7-8). Here and in the other passages mentioned, Boyle (in this context at least) is more interested in the fact of the Lord's speaking to a human than in the content of the speech.

6 Genesis 20 [RB's note].

betwixt God and Abraham touching the destruction of Sodom;[1] betwixt God and Solomon about that king's happy choice;[2] betwixt God and Jonah about the fate of the greatest city of the world;[3] and above all these, those two strange and matchless passages, the one in the first book of Kings, touching the seducing spirit that undertook to seduce Ahab's prophets;[4] and the other, that yet more wonderful relation of what passed betwixt God and Satan, wherein the Deity vouchsafes not only to praise, but (if I may so speak with reverence) to glory in a mortal.[5] Being admitted to the knowledge of these transactions of another world (if I may so call them) wherein God has been pleased to disclose himself so very much is an advantage afforded us by the Scripture of so noble a nature, and so unattainable by the utmost improvement we ourselves can make of our own reason that, did the Scripture contain nothing else that were very considerable, yet that book would highly deserve our curiosity and gratitude.

And on this occasion, I must by no means leave unobserved another advantage that we have from some discourses made us in the Bible, since it too highly concerns us not to be a very great one: and it is, that the Scripture declares to us the judgement that God is pleased to make of some particular men upon the estimate of their life and deportment. Reason alone, and the grounds of religion in general may satisfy us in some measure that God is good and merciful, and therefore it is likely he *may* pardon the sins and frailties of men and accept their imperfect services. Yet we do not know whether he *will* pardon, unless we have his promise of it. And though by virtue of general revelation, such as is pretended to in divers religions, we may be assured that God will accept, forgive, and reward those that sincerely obey him,[6]

---

1 Genesis 18 [RB's note].

2 1 Kings 3 [RB's note].

3 Jonah 4 [RB's note]. The "greatest city" was Nineveh, "wherein are more than sixscore thousand persons that cannot discern between their right hand and their left hand; and also much cattle." As a young man, Boyle referred to this verse when upholding the moral treatment of non-human animals, since God's sparing of Nineveh resulted in part from the presence in it of children ("persons that cannot discern between their right hand and their left") and of many cattle, which he took as showing that the cattle had moral worth independent of their use for humans (BP 37:187). See further Oster 1989 and MacIntosh 1996.

4 1 Kings 22.19-24 [RB's note].

5 Job 1.6,7, etc.; Job 2.3 [RB's note].

6 See Hebrews 5.9 [RB's note].

and perform the conditions of the covenant[1] (whether it be express, or implicit, that he vouchsafes to make with them), yet since it is he that is the judge of the performance of the conditions and of the sincerity of the person, and since he is omniscient, and a "knower of hearts"[2] and so may know more ill of us than even we know of ourselves,[3] a concerned conscience may rationally doubt whether in God's estimate any particular man was so sincere as to be accepted.[4]

But when he himself is pleased to give elogiums[5] (if I may with due respect so style them) to David, Job, Noah, Daniel, etc. while they were alive, and to others after they were dead (and consequently having finished their course, were passed into an irreversible state), we may learn with comfort both that the performance of such an obedience as God will accept is a thing really practicable by men, and that even great sins and misdemeanors are not (if seasonably repented of) certain evidences that a man shall never be happy in the future life. And it seems to be for such a use of consolation to frail men (but not at all to encourage licentious ones) that the lapses of holy persons are so frequently recorded in the Scriptures. Bating[6] those divine writings, I know no books in the world, nor all of them put together, that can give a considering Christian—who has due apprehensions of the inexpressible happiness or misery of an immortal state in heaven or in hell—so great and well grounded a consolation as may be derived from three or four lines in St. John's apocalypse, where he says that he saw in heaven "a great multitude,

---

1 Psalms 103.17-18 [RB's note].

2 Acts 1.24 [RB's note]. Boyle uses the Greek term *kardiognostes*; the first edition had the typographical error "1.21." Aquinas had earlier held that our inmost thoughts cannot be known by other creatures, not even by the angels; they can be known by God alone: "our desires and the thoughts of our hearts (*cogitationes cordium et affectiones voluntatum*) can be known only by God" (ST 1a 57.4 c).

3 1 John 3.20 [RB's note]. This verse is susceptible of a number of interpretations; Boyle's reading of it reveals something of his religious temperament.

4 Pascal, whose theological writings Boyle much admired, wrote "Even the martyrs have reason to fear (Pascal 1952, fr. 921 = Brunschvicg 518)."

5 "Elogium" was used in the seventeenth century as a synonym of "eulogium," itself synonymous with the more modern "eulogy"—a commendatory speech or account.

6 Apart from.

not to be numbered, of all nations, and tribes, and people, and tongues, standing before the throne, and before the Lamb, clothed in white robes, with palms [the ensigns of victory] in their hands," and the praises of God and of the Lamb in their mouths.[1] For from thence we may learn that heaven is not reserved only for prophets, and apostles, and martyrs, and such extraordinary persons, whose sanctity the church admires, but that through God's goodness multitudes of his more imperfect servants have access thither.

Though the infinite perfections and prerogatives of the Deity be such that theology itself can, no more than philosophy, afford us another object for our studies anything near so sublime and excellent as what it discloses to us of God, yet divinity favours us with some other discoveries—about angels, the universe, and our own souls—which though they must needs be inferior to the knowledge of God himself are, for the nobleness of their objects, or for their importance, highly preferable to any that natural philosophy has been able to afford its votaries.

But before I proceed to name any more particulars disclosed to us by revelation, it will be requisite, for the prevention or removal of a prejudice, to remind you that we should not make our estimates of the worth of the things we owe to revelation by the impressions they are wont now to make upon us Christians, who learned divers of them in our catechisms, and perhaps have several times met with most of the rest in sermons or theological books. For it is not to be admired that we should not be strongly affected at the mention of those truths which, how valuable soever in themselves, were for the most part taught us when we were either children, or too youthful to discern and prize their excellency and importance. So that though afterwards they were presented to our riper understanding, yet their being by that time become familiar, and our not remembering that we ignored them, kept them from making any vigorous impressions on us. Whereas if the same things had been (with circumstances evincing their truth) discovered to some heathen philosopher, or some other virtuous and inquisitive man, who valued important truths and had nothing but his own reason to attain them with, he would questionless have received them with wonder and joy. Which to induce us to suppose, we have sundry instances, both in the records of the primitive times, and in the recent relations of the conversion of men to Christianity among the people of

1 Revelation 7.9 [RB's note; RB's bracketed insertion.]

China, Japan, and other literate nations.[1] For though bare reason cannot discover these truths, yet when revelation has once sufficiently proposed them to it, it can readily embrace, and highly value, divers of them, which being here intimated once for all, I now advance to name some of the revelations themselves.

And first, as for angels, I will not now question whether bare reason can so much as assure us, that there are such beings in nature. For though reason may assure us that their existence is not impossible, and perhaps too not improbable, yet I doubt whether it were to mere ratiocination, or clear experience, or any thing else but revelation, conveyed to them by imperfect tradition, that those heathen philosophers who believed that there were separate spirits other than human owed that persuasion. And particularly as to good angels, I doubt whether those ancient sages had any cogent reasons, or any convincing historical proofs or, in short, any one unquestionable evidence of any kind to satisfy a wary person so much as of the being (much less to give a farther account) of those excellent spirits. Whereas theology is enabled by the Scripture to inform us that not only there are such spirits, but a vast multitude of them.[2] That they were made by God and Christ,[3] and are immortal, and propagate not their species.[4] That these spirits have their chief residence in heaven[5] and enjoy the vision of God[6] whom they constantly praise,[7] and punctually obey, without having sinned against him.[8] That also these good angels are very intelligent beings,[9] and of so great power, that one of them was able in a night to destroy a vast army.[10] That they have degrees among themselves,[11] are enemies

---

1 For a view of this issue by Boyle's younger contemporary, Leibniz, see Leibniz 1994.

2 Matthew 26.53; Daniel 7.10 [RB's note]. Boyle's marginal references, here and in the next two pages of the first edition text, occupy the entire outer margin, with some of them out of order. Following Hunter and Davis, I have assigned them to specific places in the text, and have adjusted the misplaced references.

3 John 1.3; Hebrews 1.7; Colossians 1.16 [RB's note].

4 Luke 20.35-36 [RB's note].

5 Matthew 24.36; Mark 13.32 [RB's note].

6 Matthew 18.10 [RB's note].

7 Isaiah 6. 2, 3 [RB's note].

8 Matthew 6.10 [RB's note].

9 2 Sam. 14.20; Mark 13.32 [RB's note].

10 2 Kings 19.35 [RB's note].

11 1 Thessalonians 4.16 [RB's note].

to the devils, and fight against them.[1] That they can assume bodies shaped like ours,[2] and yet disappear in a trice. That they are sometimes employed about human affairs,[3] and that not only for the welfare of empires and kingdoms,[4] but to protect and rescue single good men.[5] And though they are wont to appear in a dazzling splendor, and an astonishing majesty,[6] yet they are all of them ministering spirits, employed for the good of the designed heirs of salvation.[7] And they do not only refuse men's adoration, and admonish them to pay it unto God,[8] but, as they are in a sense made by Jesus Christ, who was true man as well as God, so they do not only worship him, and call him simply, as his own followers were wont to do, "the Lord,"[9] but style themselves fellow servants to his disciples.[10]

And as for the other angels, though the gentiles, as well philosophers as others, were commonly so far mistaken about them as to adore them for true gods, and many of them to doubt whether they were immortal, yet Scripture informs us that they are not self-originated, but created beings.[11] That however a great part of mankind worships them, they are wicked and impure spirits,[12] enemies to mankind,[13] and seducers of our first parents[14] to their ruin.[15] That though they beget and promote confusion among men,[16] yet they have some order among themselves, as having one chief, or leader.[17] That they are evil spirits, not by nature, but apostasy.[18] That their power is very limited, insomuch that a legion of them cannot invade so contemptible a

---

1 Jude 9 [RB's note].
2 Daniel 10.13, 21; Revelation 12.7 [RB's note].
3 Acts 12.7-10 [RB's note].
4 Daniel 10.13 [RB's note].
5 Acts 12.11 [RB's note].
6 2 Kings 6.17; Luke 24.4; Judges 13.6 [RB's note].
7 Hebrews 1.14 [RB's note].
8 Revelation 19.10; Revelation 22.9 [RB's note].
9 Matthew 28.6 [RB's note].
10 Revelation 19.10 [RB's note].
11 John 1.3; Colossians 1.16 [RB's note].
12 Luke 4.33 [RB's note].
13 1 Peter. 5.8 [RB's note].
14 That is, Adam and Eve.
15 2 Corinthians 11.3 [RB's note].
16 Revelation 12.9 [RB's note].
17 Revelation 12.7; Matthew 25.41; 1 John 3.8 [RB's note].
18 Jude 6 [RB's note]. Apostasy is the renouncing of a faith or principle.

thing as a herd of swine, without particular leave from God.[1] That not only good angels, but good men, may, by resisting them, put them to flight,[2] and the sincere Christians that worsted them here, will be among those that shall judge them hereafter.[3] That their being immortal will make their misery so too.[4] That they do themselves believe and tremble at those truths they would persuade men to reject.[5] And that they are so far from being able to confer that happiness which their worshippers expect from them, that they themselves are wretched creatures, reserved in chains of darkness to the judgement of the great day[6] at which they shall be doomed to suffer everlasting torments[7] in the company of those wicked men that they shall have prevailed on.[8]

We may farther consider that as to things corporeal themselves, which the naturalist challenges as his peculiar theme, we may name particulars, and those of the most comprehensive nature, and greatest importance, whose knowledge the naturalist must owe to theology. Of which truths I shall content myself to give a few instances in the world itself, or the universal aggregate of things corporeal—that being looked upon as the noblest and chiefest object that physics affords us to contemplate.

And first, those that admit the truths revealed by theology do generally allow that God is not only the author but creator of the world. I am not ignorant of what Anaxagoras taught, of what he call'd *Mind*[9] (and Tully mentions)[10] in the production of the world, and that what many other Greeks afterwards taught of the world's eternity is peculiarly due to Aristotle, who does little less then brag that all the philosophers that preceded him were of another

---

1 Mark 5.9-10, 13 [RB's note].

2 James 4.7; 1 Peter 5.9 [RB's note].

3 1 Corinthians 6.3 [RB's note].

4 Matthew 25.41 [RB's note].

5 James 2.19 [RB's note].

6 2 Peter 2.4 [RB's note].

7 Jude 6.13 [RB's note].

8 Matthew 25.41 [RB's note].

9 Boyle uses the Greek term *Nous* = Mind.

10 For Anaxagoras and Tully (i.e., Cicero) see Appendix A, "People Mentioned in the Text." In *De Natura Deorum*, I:26, Cicero says of Anaxagoras that he "was the first thinker to hold that the orderly disposition of the universe is designed and perfected by the rational power of an infinite mind," but then goes on to criticize this view of Anaxagoras.

mind.[1] Nor will I here examine (which I elsewhere do) whether, and how far, by arguments merely physical the creation of the world may be evinced. But whether or no mere natural reason can reach so sublime a truth, yet it seems that where it was not excited by revelation-discovery it did not actually do so. For though many of the ancient philosophers believed the world to have had a beginning, yet they all took it for granted that matter had none. Nor does any of them, that I know of, seem to have so much as imagined that any substance could be produced out of nothing. Those that ascribe much more to God than Aristotle does, make him to have given form only, not matter, to the world, and to have but contrived the pre-existent matter into this orderly system we call the universe.[2]

Next, whereas very many of the philosophers that succeeded Aristotle suppose the world to have been eternal, and those that believed it to have been produced had not the confidence to pretend to the knowing how old it was, unless it were some extravagant ambitious people, such as those fabulous Chaldeans, whose fond account reached up to 40,000 or 50,000 years.[3] But

---

1 Boyle gives no reference for his claim that "Aristotle ... does little less then brag that all the philosophers that preceded him were of another mind," but he may have had in mind *On the Heavens*, Book I, 10 (Aristotle 1984, 279b4-280a35), where Aristotle considers and dismisses the views of earlier thinkers on "the question whether the heaven is ungenerated or generated, indestructible or destructible" before going on to consider the general question of whether the world as a whole is eternal. His arguments are both sharper and more subtle than Boyle's dismissive comment suggests. Boyle is also critical of Aristotle's views on the eternity of the world in the *Notion of Nature* (1686), where he writes, "*Aristotle*, by introducing the Opinion of the Eternity of the World (whereof he owns himself to have been the first Broacher) did at least, in almost all Mens Opinion, openly deny God the Production of the World: *So*, by ascribing the admirable Works of God to what he calls *Nature*, he tacitly denies him the Government of the World" (*Works* 10:447).

2 For the views of Presocratic philosophers on this and related issues, see both Hussey 1972 and Kirk, Raven, and Schofield 1983.

3 The view of the Chaldeans is mentioned by Diodorus Siculus (fl. 1st century BCE), *Bibliotheca* ii. 29-31. The current estimate for the age of the earth is just over four and a half billion years; for the universe, current estimates are between thirteen and fourteen billion years. James Ussher, Archbishop of Armagh, who was much admired by Boyle, famously offered a date, based on Old Testament chronology, of 23 October, 4004 BCE for the first day of the world (Ussher 1658, p. 1), which is the probable source for Boyle's confidence that the "fabulous Chaldeans" were guilty of overestimating the matter.

theology teaches us that the world is very far from being so old by 30 or 40 thousand years as they believe, and by very many ages, as divers others have presumed, and gives us, from Scripture, such an account of the age of the world that it has set us certain limits within which so long a duration may be bounded, without mistaking in our reckoning. Whereas philosophy leaves us to the vastness of indeterminate duration, without any certain limits at all.

The time likewise, and the order, and divers other circumstances of the manner wherein the fabric of the world was completed, we owe to revelation, bare reason being evidently unable to inform us of particulars that preceded the origin of the first man.[1] And though I do not think religion so much concerned, as many do, in their opinion and practise, that would deduce particular theorems of natural philosophy from this or that expression of a book that seems rather designed to instruct us about spiritual than corporeal things, I see no just reason to embrace their opinion that would so turn the two first chapters of Genesis into an allegory, so as to overthrow the literal and historical sense of them. And though I take the Scripture to be mainly designed to teach us nobler and better truths than those of philosophy, yet I am not forward to condemn those who think the beginning of Genesis contains divers particulars in reference to the origin of things, which though not unwarily, or alone to be urged in physics, may yet afford very considerable hints to an attentive and inquisitive peruser.

---

1 There was, at the time, a controversy about fossils and their origin. On the one hand, they clearly *appeared* to be the remains of living things. On the other hand, they were made of stone. They were not bones, and for them to have been changed from bone to stone would require transmutation, which was for many a suspect possibility. Robert Plot, who became Professor of Chemistry in Oxford, and who was the first Curator of the Ashmolean Museum, asked "whether the Stones we find in the Forms of Shell-fish, be ... naturally produced by some extraordinary plastic virtue, latent in the Earth or Quarries where they are found? Or, whether they rather owe their Form and Figuration to the Shells of the Fishes they represent, brought to the places where they are now found by a Deluge, Earth-quake, or some other such means, and there being filled with Mud, Clay, and petrifying Juices, have in tract of time been turned into Stones, as we now find them, still retaining the same Shape in the whole, with the same Lineations, Sutures, Eminencies, Cavities, Orifices, Points, that they had whilst they were Shells?" (Plot, 1677, 111).

The duration of the world was by the old philosophers held to be interminable, and the Stoics' opinion, that the world shall be destroyed by fire (which they held from the Jews) was physically precarious.[1] But theology teaches us expressly from divine revelation, that the present *course of nature*[2] shall not last always, and that one day this world (or at least this vortex of ours)[3] shall either be abolished by annihilation, or (which seems far more probable) be innovated and, as it were, transfigured by the intervention of that fire which shall dissolve and destroy the present frame of nature.[4] So that either way, the present state of things (as well natural as political) shall have an end.

And as theology affords us these informations about the creatures in general, so touching the chiefest and noblest of the visible ones, men, revelation discovers very plainly divers very important things, where reason must needs be in the dark.

And first, touching the body of man: the Epicureans attributed its original, as that of all things else, to the casual concourse of atoms, and the Stoics absurdly and injuriously enough (but much more pardonably than their follower herein, Mr. Hobbes) would have men to spring up like mushrooms out of the ground.[5] And

---

1 That is, it cannot be deduced given the accepted truths of physics and nothing more. Boyle's point is not that they were wrong in their belief, for he goes on to agree with it, but that it was inadequately grounded. Laertius (VII.142), noting that Zeno of Citium and other Stoics held that the world would be destroyed, also points out that some, such as Panaetius, held the world to be indestructible. The general Stoic view, however, was that since everything was matter, the divine Mind was also matter in its most subtle form—fire (or aether, or breath)—and that having created the world out of itself, it would ultimately reabsorb it in a universal fiery death of the universe as we know it. This cyclic process of creation and absorption was held to be unending. Boyle's suggestion of a Jewish influence is more pious than probable.

2 Boyle gives the Greek, *Trochos tes geneseos*, and the reference: James 3.6.

3 Boyle's reference is to Descartes' vortex theory. Descartes denied the existence of a vacuum, and as a plenist, offered the view that gravity and planetary motion were to be explained by the tendency of matter to form vortices whose whirling accounted for the observable facts. Our solar system would be such a large vortex (with smaller vortices around the planets), and Boyle is willing to allow that the biblical references to the destruction of the world by fire might refer simply to our solar system.

4 2 Peter 3.7, 10, 13 [RB's note].

5 Boyle is also scornful of this view at BP 2:11(Boyle 2006 4.1, p. 344), and at "Usefulness of Natural Philosophy I," *Works* 3:255. On this topic, see further MacIntosh 1991 and Goodrum 2002.

whereas other philosophers maintain conceits about it, too wild to be here recited, the book of Genesis assures us that the body of man was first formed by God in a peculiar manner, of a terrestrial matter, and it is there described as having been perfected before the soul was united to it.[1] And as theology thus teaches us how the body of man had its first beginning, so it likewise assures us, what shall become of the body after death,[2] though bare natural reason will scarce be pretended to reach to so abstruse and difficult an article as that of a resurrection which, when proposed by St. Paul, produced among the Athenian philosophers nothing else but wonder or laughter.[3]

Theology also teaches us divers other things about the origin and condition of men's bodies as, that all mankind is the offspring of one man and one woman.[4] That the first woman was not made of the same matter, nor after the same manner as the first man, but was afterwards taken from his side.[5] That both Adam and Eve were not, as many Epicureans and other philosophers fancied that the first men were, first infants, whence they did, as we do, grow by degrees to be mature and complete human persons, but were made so all at once. And, that hereafter, as all men's bodies shall rise again, so they shall all (or at least all those of the just) be kept from ever dying a second time.[6]

And as for the human soul, though I willingly grant that much may be deduced from the light of reason only touching its existence, properties, and duration; yet divine revelation teaches it us with more clearness, and with greater authority. For he that made our souls and upholds them can best know what they are, and how long he will have them last. And as the Scripture expressly teaches us that the rational soul is distinct from the body, as not being to be destroyed by those very enemies that kill the body,[7] so about the origin of this immortal soul (about which philosophers can give us but wide and precarious conjectures) theology assures us that the soul of man had not such an origination, as those of other animals, but was God's own immediate workmanship, and was united to the body already formed.[8] Yet the soul is

1 Genesis 2.7 [RB's note].
2 Acts 24.15 [RB's note].
3 Acts 17.20, 32 [RB's note].
4 Genesis 2; Acts 17.26 [RB's note].
5 Genesis 2.21, 32 [RB's note].
6 Luke 20.35, 36 [RB's note].
7 Matthew 10.28 [RB's note].
8 Genesis 2.7; Zechariah 12.1 [RB's note].

not so united to the body but that upon their divorce it will survive, and pass into a state in which death shall have no power over it.[1]

I expect you will here object, that for the knowledge of the perpetual duration of separate souls we need not be beholding to the Scripture since the immortality of the soul may be sufficiently proved by the sole light of nature, and particularly has been demonstrated by your great Descartes. But you must give me leave to tell you, that besides that a matter of that weight and concernment cannot be too well proved, and consequently ought to procure a welcome for all good mediums of probation, besides this, I say, I doubt many Cartesians do, as well as others, mistake both the difficulty under consideration and the scope of Descartes's discourse.[2]

I grant that by natural philosophy alone the immortality of the soul may be proved against its usual enemies, atheists and Epicureans. For the ground upon which these men think it mortal is that it is not a true substance, but only a modification of body, which consequently must perish when the frame or structure of the body whereto it belongs is dissolved. Their ground being this, I say, if we can prove by some intellectual operations of the rational soul (which matter, however modified, cannot reach), that it is a substance distinct from the human body, there is no reason why the dissolution of the latter should imply the destruction of the former, which is a simple substance, and as real a substance as matter itself, which yet the adversaries affirm to be indestructible.

But though by the mental operations of the rational soul and perhaps by other mediums it may, against the Epicureans, and other mere naturalists, who will not allow God to have any thing to do in the case, be proved to be immortal in the sense newly proposed; yet the same proofs will not evince that absolutely it shall never cease to be, if we dispute with philosophers who admit, as the Cartesians and many others do, that God is the sole creator and preserver of all things. For how are we sure but that God may have so ordained that, though the soul of man, by the continuance of his ordinary and upholding concourse, may

1 Luke 20.35-36; Matthew 25.46 [RB's note].

2 In the *Meditations*, Descartes argued that we are, essentially, thinking things, conceptually distinct from our material bodies. Boyle accepts this point, but is concerned to point out, here and elsewhere, that this shows that human immortality is *possible*, not that it is assured.

survive the body, yet, as it is generally believed not to be created till it be just to be infused into the body, so it shall be annihilated when it parts with the body, God withdrawing at death that supporting influence which alone kept it from relapsing to its first nothing. Whence it may appear that, notwithstanding the physical proofs of the spirituality and separableness of the human soul, we are yet much beholding to divine revelation for assuring us that its duration shall be endless.

And now to make good what I was intimating above, concerning the Cartesians, and the scope of Descartes's demonstration, I shall appeal to no other than his own expressions to evince that he considered this matter in the main as we have done, and pretended to demonstrate that the soul is a distinct substance from the body, but not that absolutely speaking it is immortal.

> As to why I wrote nothing concerning the immortality of the soul [answers that excellent author],[1] I did already explain this in the Synopsis of my *Meditations*. And, as I have shown above, I did provide an adequate proof of the fact that the soul is distinct from the body. However, you go on to say that it does not follow from the fact that the soul is distinct from the body that it is immortal, since it could still be claimed that God gave it such a nature that its duration comes to an end simultaneously with the end of the body's life. Here I admit that I cannot refute what you say. For I do not take it upon myself to try to use the power of human reason to settle any of those matters which depend on the free will of God. Our natural knowledge tells us ... (etc.). But if your question concerns the absolute power of God, and you are asking whether he may have decreed that human souls cease to exist precisely when the bodies which he joined to them are destroyed, then it is for God alone to give the answer.[2]

If Descartes would not assume to demonstrate by natural reason so much as the existence of the soul after death, unless upon a supposition, we may well presume that he would still less take upon him to determine what shall be the condition of that soul after it leaves the body. And that you may not doubt of this, I will give you for it his own confession, as he freely wrote it in a private letter to that admirable lady, the princess Elizabeth, first

1 Boyle's interpolation.

2 Descartes, Reply to Objections II [RB's note]. Descartes continues, "And since God himself has revealed to us that this will not occur, there remains not even the slightest room for doubt on this point" (AT 7:153-4, CSMK 2: 108-09).

daughter to Frederick, king of Bohemia, who seems to have desired his opinion on that important question, about which he sends her this answer: "As to the state of the soul after this life, my knowledge of it is far inferior to that of Monsieur (he means Sir Kenelm)[1] Digby. For, setting aside that which religion teaches us of it, I confess, that by mere natural reason we may indeed make many conjectures to our own advantage, and have fair *hopes*, but not *any assurance*," and accordingly in the next clause he gives the imprudence of quitting what is certain for an uncertainty, as the cause why, according to natural reason, we are never to seek death.[2]

Nor do I wonder he should be of that mind. For all that mere reason can demonstrate, may be reduced to these two things: one, that the rational soul, being an incorporeal substance, there is no necessity that it should perish with the body so that, if God have not otherwise appointed, the soul may survive the body and last for ever; the other, that the nature of the soul, according to Descartes, consisting in its being a substance that thinks, we may conclude that though it be by death separate from the body, it will nevertheless retain the power of thinking. But now, whether either of these two things, or both, be sufficient to endear the state of separation after death to a considering man I think may be justly questioned. For immortality, or perseverance in duration, simply considered, is rather a thing presupposed to, or a requisite of, felicity, than a part of it, and being in itself an adiaphorous[3] thing, assumes the nature of the state or condition to which it is joined, and does not make that state happy or miserable, but makes the possessors of it more happy or more miserable than otherwise they would be.

And though some school-men, upon airy metaphysical notions, would have men think it is more eligible to be wretched, than not to be at all, yet we may oppose to their speculative subtleties the sentiments of mankind, and the far more considerable testimony of the Saviour of mankind who, speaking of the disciple that betrayed him, says, that it had been good for that man if he had never been born.[4] And eternity is generally conceived to aggravate no less the miseries of hell than it heightens the joys of heaven. And here we may consider, first, that mere reason cannot

---

1 Boyle's interpolation.

2 Descartes to Princess Elizabeth, 3 November, 1645, AT 4:333, CSMK 3:277.

3 Neutral. Boyle also uses the term "adiaphorous" in chemical contexts, for substances that are neither acidic nor alkaline, for example.

4 Mark 14.21 [RB's note]. See also Matthew 26.24.

so much as assure us absolutely that the soul shall survive the body, for the truth of which we have not only Descartes' confession, lately recited, but a probable argument, drawn from the nature of the thing: as the body and soul were not brought together by any mere physical agents, and since their association and union while they continued together, was made upon conditions that depended solely upon God's free and arbitrary institution, so, for ought reason can secure us of, one of the conditions of that association may be, that the body and soul should not survive each other.

Secondly, supposing that the soul be permitted to outlive the body, mere reason cannot inform us what will become of it in its separate state, whether it will be vitally united to any other kind of body or vehicle, and if to some, of what kind that will be, and upon what terms the union will be made. For possibly it may be united to an unorganized, or very imperfectly organized, body, wherein it cannot exercise the same functions it did in its human body. As we see that even in this life the souls of natural fools are united to bodies wherein they cannot discourse, or at least cannot philosophize. And it is plain that some souls are introduced into bodies which, by reason of paralytical and other diseases, they are unable to move, though that does not always hinder them from being obnoxious[1] to feel pain. So that, for ought we naturally know, a human soul, separated from the body, may be united to such a portion of matter that it may neither have the power to move it, nor the advantage of receiving any agreeable informations by its interventions, having upon the account of that union no other sense than that of pain.[2]

But let us now consider what will follow if I should grant that the soul will not be made miserable by being thus wretchedly matched. We suppose then, that it will be left free to enjoy what belongs to its own nature, but that being only the power of always thinking, it may well be doubted whether the exercise of that power will suffice to make it happy. You will perchance easily believe that I love as well as another to entertain myself with my own thoughts, and to enjoy them undisturbed by visits, and other

---

1 "Obnoxious" is here used in its original and literal sense of "vulnerable."

2 Descartes's disciple Louis de la Forge (1632-66) made a similar point with respect to the punishment of the damned. God can certainly "unite the human soul with some other body [and so it is] relatively easy to conceive ... how fire could burn and torment the souls of those who died in a state of sin" (de la Forge 1666, 214).

avocations. I would, only accompanied by a servant and a book, go to dine at an inn upon a road, to enjoy my thoughts the more freely for that day. But yet, I think, the most contemplative men would, at least in time, grow weary of thinking if they received no supply of objects from without by reading, seeing, or conversing, and if they also lacked the opportunity of executing their thoughts by moving the members of their bodies, or of imparting them, either by discoursing, or writing of books, or by making of experiments.

On this occasion I remember that I knew a gentleman who was, in Spain, for a crime against the state which yet he thought an heroic action, kept close prisoner for a year in a place where though he was allowed a diet not unfit for a person of note (as he was), yet he was not permitted the benefit of any light, either of the day or candles, and was not accosted by any human creature, save at certain times by the jailer that brought him meat and drink, but was strictly forbidden to converse with him. Now though this gentleman by his discourse appeared to be a man of a lively humour, yet being asked by me, what he could do to pass the time in that sad solitude, he confessed to me that though he had the liberty of walking to and fro in his prison, and though by often recalling into his mind all the adventures and other passages of his former life, and by several ways combining and diversifying his thoughts, he endeavoured to give his mind as much variety of employment as he was able, yet that would not serve his turn, and he was often reduced, by drinking large draughts of wine, and then casting himself upon his bed, to endeavour to drown that melancholy which the want of new objects cast him into. And I can easily accept that he found a great deal of difference between the sense he had of thinking when he was at liberty, and that which he had when he was confined to that employment, whose delightfulness, like fire, cannot last long when it is, as his was, denied both fuel and vent. And, in a word, though I most readily grant that thinking interwoven with conversation and action may be a very pleasant way of passing one's time, yet man being by nature a sociable creature, I fear that alone would be a dry and wearisome employment to spend eternity in.

Before I proceed to the next section, I must not omit to take notice, that though the brevity I proposed to myself keeps me from discoursing of any theological subjects save what I have touched upon about the divine attributes, and the things I have mentioned about the universe in general and the human soul, yet there are divers other things, knowable by the help of revelation, and not without it, that are of so noble and sublime a nature that the greatest wits may find their best abilities both fully exercised, and highly gratified, by making enquiries into them. I shall not name for proof of this the adorable mystery of the trinity, wherein it is acknowledged that the most soaring speculators are wont to be posed, or to lose themselves: I shall rather mention the redemption of mankind and the decrees of God concerning men. For though these seem to be less out of the ken of our natural faculties, yet it is into some things that belong to the former of them, that the Scripture tells us, "the angels desire to pry."[1] It was the consideration of the latter of them, that made one that had been caught up into the mansion of the angels[2] amazedly cry out, "O the depth of the riches both of the wisdom and knowledge of God! how unsearchable are his judgements, and his ways past finding out!"[3]

Nor are these the only things that the Scripture itself terms mysteries though, for brevity's sake, instead of specifying any of them I shall content myself to represent to you in general that, since God's wisdom is boundless, it may, sure, have more ways than one to display itself. And though the material world be full of the productions of his wisdom yet that hinders not but that the Scripture may be ennobled with many excellent impresses and, as it were, signatures of the same attribute. For, as I was beginning to say, it cannot but be highly injurious to the Deity, in whom all other true perfections, as well as omniscience, are both united and transcendent, to think that he can contrive no ways to disclose his perfections besides the ordering of matter and motion, and cannot otherwise deserve to be the object of men's studies, and their admiration, than in the capacity of a creator.

And I think I might safely add, that besides these grand and mysterious points I came from mentioning, there are many other noble and important things wherein unassisted reason leaves us in the dark; which, though not so clearly revealed in the Scripture, are yet in an inviting measure discovered there, and consequently deserve the indagation[4] of a curious and philosophical

---

1 1 Peter 1.12 [RB's note].

2 St. Paul.

3 Romans 11.33 [RB's note]. Boyle gives only the first two words of this verse, in Greek: *O bathos*.

4 Investigation.

soul. Shall we not think it worth inquiring whether the satisfaction[1] of Christ was necessary to appease the justice of God, and purchase redemption for mankind? Or whether God, as absolute and supreme governor of the world, might have *freely* remitted the penalties of sin?

Shall we not think it worth the inquiring, upon what account, and upon what terms, the justification[2] of men towards God is transacted, especially considering how much it imports us to know, and how perplexedly a doctrine, not in itself abstruse, is wont to be delivered? Shall we not inquire whether or no the souls of men, before they were united to their bodies, pre-existed in a happier state, as many of the ancient and modern Jews and Platonists, and (besides Origen) some learned men of our times do believe? Shall we not be curious to know whether, when the soul leaves the body, it does immediately pass to heaven or hell (as it is commonly believed), or for want of organs be laid, as it were, asleep in an insensible and inactive state till it recovers the body at the resurrection (as many Socinians and others maintain)?[3] Whether it be conveyed into secret recesses, where, though it be in a good or bad condition, according to what it did in the body, it is yet reprieved from the flames of hell, and restrained from the beatific vision till the day of judgement: (which seems to have been the opinion of many, if not most, of the primitive fathers and Christians)?

Shall we not be curious to know, whether at that great decretory day,[4] this vast fabric of the world, which all confess must have its frame quite shattered, shall be suffered to relapse into its first nothing (as several divines assert), or shall be after its dissolution renewed to a better state and, as it were, transfigured? And shall we not inquire, whether or no in that future state of things which

---

1 "Satisfaction" in the technical sense of Christ's atonement for the world's sins by his suffering.

2 The "justification" of humans is their being freed from the penalty of sin, and being accounted righteous by God.

3 Luke 23.43—"This day shalt thou be with me in paradise"—provides a basis for what was "commonly believed." Berkeley (1685-1753) pointed out that if, as he believed, time was simply the succession of ideas in each individual human, then there was no inconsistency in believing both that the thief who was crucified with Christ would be in paradise in the moment after death *and* that this moment would be at the Last Trump. (For a discussion of Berkeley's views see MacIntosh 1978.)

4 The day of final Judgement.

shall never have an end we shall know one another?[1] (As Adam, when he awaked out of his profound sleep, knew Eve whom he never saw before.[2]) Whether those personal friendships and affections we had for one another here, and the pathetic[3] consideration of the relations (as of father and son, husband and wife, chaste mistress and virtuous lover, prince and subject) on which many of them were grounded, shall continue? Or whether all those things, as antiquated and slight, shall be obliterated and, as it were, swallowed up? (As the former relation of a cousin a great way off is scarce at all considered when the persons come so to change their state as to be united by the strict bonds of marriage.)

But it were tedious to propose all the other points, whereof the divine takes cognizance, that highly merit an inquisitive man's curiosity, and about which all the writings of the old Greek and other heathen philosophers put together will give us far less information than the single volume of canonical Scripture. I foresee indeed that it may nevertheless be objected, that in some of these inquiries revelation encumbers reason by delivering things which reason is obliged to make its hypothesis consistent with. But, besides that this cannot be so much as pretended of all, if you consider how much unassisted reason leaves us in the dark about these matters, wherein it has not been able to frame so much as probable determinations, especially in comparison of those probabilities that reason can deduce from what it finds one way or other delivered in the Scripture—if you consider this, I say, you will, I presume, allow me to say that the revealed truths which reason is obliged to comply with are, if they be burdens to it, but such burdens as feathers are to a hawk, which instead of hindering his flight by their weight enable him to soar toward heaven

---

1 The general seventeenth-century doctrine concerning the memory of particulars, or *event* memory (as opposed to intellectual memory), was that it was a neuro-physiological function: it required a brain. How then were incorporeal entities such as human souls (or angels) able to remember particulars? Would we be able to remember our friends and the events of our past life in a post-mortem existence? In a letter to Constantijn Huygens (10 Oct, 1642, AT 3:796-99, CSMK 3:215-6) Descartes claimed confidently that we would have such post-mortem memories, but postponed any discussion of just *how* that would be possible. See further MacIntosh 1983, and cf. Descartes to Mesland 2 May, 1644, AT 4:114, CSMK 3:233.

2 Genesis 2.21-23 [RB's note].

3 "Pathetic" in the now obsolete sense of producing an effect on the emotions.

and take a larger prospect of things than, if he had not feathers, he could possibly do.

And on this occasion, Sir, the greater reverence I owe to the Scripture itself than to its expositors, prevails upon me to tell you freely that you will not do right either to theology, or (the greatest repository of its truths) the Bible, if you imagine that there are no considerable additions to be made to the theological discoveries we have already, nor no clearer expositions of many texts of Scripture, or better reflections on that matchless book, than are to be met with in the generality of commentators, or of preachers, without excepting the ancient fathers themselves. There are in my opinion two things requisite to qualify a commentator to do right to his theme: a competency of critical knowledge; and a concern for the honour and interest of Christianity in general, assisted by a good judgement to discern and select those things that may most conduce to it. I fear there are not many expositors (as they are called) of the Scripture that are not deficient in the former or the latter of these particulars, and I wish there be not too many that are defective in both.

That the knowledge of at least Greek and Hebrew is requisite to him that takes upon him to expound writings penned originally in those languages you might easily be persuaded to believe, even if the nature of the thing did not manifest it, by considering with what gross mistakes the ignorance of languages has oftentimes blemished not only the interpretations of the schoolmen and others, but even those of the venerable fathers of the church. Generally they were worthy men, and highly to be regarded as the grand witnesses of the doctrines and government of the ancient churches. Most of them were very pious, many of them very eloquent, and some of them (especially the two critics, Origen and Jerome) very learned. Yet so few of the Greek fathers were skilled in Hebrew, and so few of the Latin fathers either in Hebrew or Greek, that many of their homilies, and even comments, leave hard texts as obscure as they found them. And sometimes, misled by bad translations, they give them senses exceeding wide of the true, so that many times in their writings they appear to be far better divines then commentators, and in an excellent discourse upon a text, you shall find but a very poor exposition of it. Many of their eloquent and devout sermons are much better encomiasts[1] of the divine mysteries they treat of, than unveilers. And though some modern translations deserve the praise of being

1 Producers of high-flown praise.

very useful, and less inaccurate than those which the Latin fathers used, yet when I read the Scriptures (especially some books of the Old Testament) in their originals, I confess I cannot but sometimes wonder what came into the mind of some, even of our modern translators, that they should so much mistake, and sometimes injure certain texts as they do. I am prone to think that there is scarce a chapter in the Bible (especially that part of it which is written in Hebrew) that may not be better translated, and consequently more to the credit of the book itself.[1]

This credit it misses of, not only by men's want of sufficient skill in critical learning, but (to come to the second member of our late division) for want of their having judgement enough to observe, and concern enough to propose, those things in the Scripture, and in theology, that tend to the reputation of either. For I fear there are too many, both commentators and other divines, that (though otherwise perhaps pious men) having espoused a church or party, and an aversion from all dissenters, are solicitous when they peruse the Scripture to take notice chiefly if not only (I mean in points speculative) of those things that may either suggest arguments against their adversaries or answers to their objections. But I meet with many fewer than I could wish who make it their business to *search the Scriptures*[2] for those things (such as unheeded prophecies, over-looked mysteries, and strange harmonies) which, being clearly and judiciously proposed, may make that book appear worthy of the high extraction it claims, and consequently of the veneration of considering men—men who are solicitous to discern and make out in the way of governing and of saving men, revealed by God, so excellent an economy, and such deep contrivances and wise dispensations, as may bring credit to religion, not so much as it is *Roman*, or *Protestant*, or *Socinian*, but as it is *Christian*.

But (as I intimated before) these good affections for the repute of religion in general, are to be assisted by a deep judgement. For men that want either that, or a good stock of critical learning, may easily overlook the best observations (which usually are not obvious) or propose as mysteries things that are either not

---

1 Elsewhere Boyle makes the same point: "We find in the Chaldee, Syriac, Arabic, and other eastern tongues, that the Hebrew words and phrases (a little varied, according to the nature of those dialects) have other, and oftentimes very different signification, besides those that the modern interpreters of the Bible have ascribed to them" ("Some Considerations Touching the Style of the Holy Scriptures," *Works* 2:397)."

2 *Ereunantas graphas*, John 5.39 [RB's note].

grounded, or not weighty enough, and so (notwithstanding their good meaning) may bring a disparagement upon what they desire to recommend. And I am willing to grant, that it is rather for want of good skill and good judgement, than good will, that there are so few that have been careful to do right to the reputation of the Scripture, as well as to its sense.

Indeed, when I consider how much more to the advantage of those sacred writings, and of Christian theology in general, divers texts have been explained and discoursed of by the excellent Grotius, by Episcopius, Masius, Mr. Mede, and Sir Francis Bacon, and some other late great wits (to name now no living ones) in their several kinds, than the same places have been handled by vulgar[1] expositors, and other divines, and when I remember too, that one of these newly named worthies was at once a great philosopher, and a great critic (the three first being not so well versed in philosophical learning, and the last being unacquainted with the eastern tongues), I cannot but hope that, when it shall please God to stir up persons of a philosophical genius, well furnished with critical learning and the principles of true philosophy, and shall give them a hearty concern for the advancement of his truths, these men, by exercising upon theological matters that inquisitiveness and sagacity that has made in our age such a happy progress in philosophical ones will make explications and discoveries that will justify more than I have said in praise of the study of our religion and the divine books that contain the articles of it. For these want not excellencies, but only skilful unveilers. And if I do not tell you, that you should no more measure the wisdom of God couched in the Bible by the glosses or systems of common expositors and preachers, than estimate the wisdom he has expressed in the contrivance of the world by Magirus's or Eustachius's physics,[2] yet I shall not scruple to say that you should as little think, that there are no more mysteries in the books of Scripture, besides those that the school-divines and vulgar commentators have taken notice of and unfolded, as that there are no other mysteries in the book of nature than those which the same school-men (who have taken upon them to interpret Aristotle and nature too) have observed and explained. All the fine things that poets, orators, and even lovers have hyperbolically said in praise of the beauty of eyes, will nothing near so much recommend them to a philosopher's esteem as the sight of

1 Common, ordinary.

2 Boyle's point is that these Aristotelian philosophers got "the contrivance of the world" badly wrong.

one eye skillfully dissected,[1] or the unadorned account given of its structure and the admirable uses of its several parts in Scheiner's *Oculus*, and Descartes' excellent *Dioptrics*.[2] And though I do not think myself bound to acquiesce in, and admire every thing that is proposed as mysterious and rare by many interpreters and preachers, yet I think I may safely compare several things in the books we call the Scripture to several others in that of nature in (at least) one regard.

I do not believe all the wonders that Pliny, Ælian, Porta, and other writers of that stamp relate of the generation of animals, yet by perusing such faithful and accurate accounts, as sometimes Galen, *De usu Partium*,[3] sometimes Vesalius, sometimes our Harvey (*de Ovo*)[4] and our later anatomists, and sometimes other true naturalists, give of the generation of animals and of the admirable structure of their bodies, especially those of men, and such other parts of Zoology as Pliny and the other writers I named with him could make nothing considerable of, by perusing these (I say) I receive more pleasure and satisfaction, and am induced more to admire the works of nature, than by all their romantic and superficial narratives. And thus (to apply this to our present subject) a close and critical account of the more veiled and pregnant parts of Scripture and theological matters, with such reflections on them as their nature and collation would suggest to a philosophical, as well as critical, speculator, would far better please a rational considerer, and give him a higher as well as a better grounded veneration for the things explained, than a great many of those slighter or ill-founded remarks, wherewith the expositions and discourses of superficial writers, though never so florid or witty, gain the applause of the less discerning sort of men.

And here, on this occasion, I shall venture to add that I despair not but that a further use may be made of the Scripture than either our divines or philosophers seem to have thought on. Some

---

1 In the "Usefulness of Natural Philosophy I," *Works* 3:265, Boyle writes with enthusiasm about the various methods of dissecting eyes, human, feline, and bovine, and the various aids to such dissections such as boiling or freezing the eyes to aid in bringing out this or that particular feature.

2 AT vol. 6. Translated by P.J. Olscamp in Descartes 1965.

3 On the Usefulness of the Parts of the Body.

4 A reference to Harvey's 1651 work on the generation of animals (*Exercitationes de Generatione Animalium*) which had *ex ovo omnia* (from the egg, everything) as its frontispiece motto.

few theologues indeed have got the name of Supralapsarians, for venturing to look back beyond the fall of Adam for God's decrees of election and reprobation. But, besides that their boldness has been disliked by the generality of divines as well as other Christians, the object of their speculation is much too narrow to be any thing near and adequate to such an hypothesis as I mean. For methinks that the Encyclopedias and Pansophias[1] that even men of an elevated genius have aimed at are not diffused enough to comprehend all that the reason of a man, improved by philosophy, and elevated by the revelations already extant in the Scripture, may, by the help of free ratiocination, and the hints contained in those pregnant writings (with those assistances of God's spirit, which he is still ready to vouchsafe to them that duly seek them) attain unto in this life. The gospel comprises indeed, and unfolds the whole mystery of man's redemption, as far forth as it is necessary to be known for our salvation,[2] and the corpuscularian or mechanical philosophy strives to deduce all the phenomena of nature from adiaphorous matter[3] and local motion. But neither the fundamental doctrine of Christianity, nor that of the powers and effects of matter and motion, seems to be more than an epicycle (if I may so call it) of the great and universal system of God's contrivances, and makes but a part of the more general theory of things knowable by the light of nature and improved by the information of the Scriptures. So that both these doctrines, though very general in respect of the subordinate parts of theology and philosophy, seem to be but members of the universal hypothesis, whose objects I conceive to be the nature, counsels, and works of God, as far as they are discoverable by us (for I say not to us) in this life.[4]

For those to whom God has vouchsafed the privilege of mature reason seem not to enlarge their thoughts enough if they

---

1 A work encompassing "all knowledge."

2 Acts 20.27 [RB's note].

3 Neutral matter, that is, matter not endowed with any qualities but those "primitive and Catholick Affections of Matter, namely, bulk, shape and motion (*Works* 2:21)."

4 "by us ... not to us": Boyle held that there were some truths of nature that could be *understood* by us, if they were revealed to us, but that we could not discover by our own unaided efforts. Boyle seriously considered the possibility that angels might convey such truths to us. Conversely, there might be some truths about God that we could discover even though they had not been revealed to us. On this general issue see Wojcik 1997.

think that the omniscient and almighty God has bounded the operations of his power, and wisdom, and goodness, to the exercise that may be given them for some ages, by the production and government of matter and motion, and of the inhabitants of the terrestrial globe, which we know to be but a physical point in comparison of that portion of universal matter which we have already discovered.

For I account that there are four grand communities of creatures, whereof things merely corporeal make but one. The other three, differing from these, are distinct also from one another. Of the first sort are the race of mankind, where intellectual beings are vitally associated with gross and organical bodies. The second are demons, or evil angels, and the third, good angels. (We know not whether in each of those two kinds of spirits, the rational beings be perfectly free from all union with matter, though never so fine and subtle, or whether they be united to vehicles, not gross, but spirituous, and ordinarily invisible to us.)

Nor may we think, because angels and devils are two names quickly uttered, and those spirits are seldom or never seen by us, there are therefore but few of them and the speculation of them is not considerable. For, as their excellency is great, (as we shall by and by show) so, for their number, they are represented in Scripture as an heavenly host standing on the right and left hand of the throne of God. And of the good angels, our Saviour speaks of having more than twelve legions of them at his command.[1] Nay, the prophet Daniel says, that to the Ancient of days,[2] no less than millions ministered unto him, and hundreds of millions stood before him.[3] And of the evil angels the gospel informs us that enough to call them a legion[4] (which you know is usually reckoned, at a moderate rate, to consist of betwixt six and seven thousand) possessed one single man.

Matter, however vastly extended, and how curiously shaped soever, is but a brute thing that is only capable of local motion and its effects and consequents on other bodies, or the brain of man, without being capable of any true, or at least any intellectual, perception, or true love or hatred. And when I consider the rational soul as an immaterial and immortal being that bears the

1 Matthew 26.53 [RB's note].

2 That is, God.

3 Daniel 7.10 [RB's note] St. Thomas had similar views about the number of angels. They exist "in exceeding great number, far beyond all material multitude" (ST 1a 50.3 c.).

4 Mark 5.9; Luke 8.30 [RB's note].

image of its divine maker, being endowed with a capacious intellect, and a will that no creature can force, I am by these considerations disposed to think the soul of man a nobler and more valuable being, than the whole corporeal world.[1] Though I readily acknowledge the corporeal world to be admirably contrived, and worthy of the almighty and omniscient author, yet it consists but of an aggregate of portions of brute matter, variously shaped and connected by local motion (as dough, and rolls, and loaves, and cakes, and vermicelli, wafers, and pie-crust, are all of them diversified meal), but without any knowledge either of their own nature, or of that of their author, or of that of their fellow-creatures. And as the rational soul is somewhat more noble and wonderful than any thing merely corporeal, how vast soever it can be, and is of a more excellent nature than the most curious piece of mechanism in the world, the human body; so, to enquire what shall become of it and what fates it is like to undergo hereafter does better deserve a man's curiosity than to know what shall befall the corporeal universe. It might justly have been to Nebuchadnezzar a more desirable part of knowledge than that he was so troubled for want of, when it was adumbrated to him in the mysterious dream that contained the characters and fates of the four great monarchies of the world.[2] Man is entrusted with a will of his own, whereas all material things move only as they are moved, and have no self determining power on whose account they can resist the will of God, and as angels, at least some orders of them, are of a higher quality (if I may so speak) than human souls, so it is very probable that in the government of angels that are intellectual voluntary agents, whether good or bad, there is required and employed far greater displays of God's wisdom, power, and goodness, than in the guidance of adiaphorous matter. And the method of God's conduct in the government of these is a far nobler object for men's contemplation than the laws according to which the parts of matter hit against, and justle, one another, and the effects or results of such motions.

And accordingly we find in Scripture that, whereas about the production of the material world, and the setting of the frame of nature God employed only a few commanding words, which

1 Boyle makes a similar point at BP 1:66 (Boyle 2006, 3.5.30, p. 256): "I think that Adam alone, on the account of his immaterial soul endowed with reason & free will, was a more excellent creature than all the beasts and birds & other animals he gave names to, with the whole terraqueous globe that they inhabited, to boot."

2 Daniel 2.31-32, etc. [RB's note].

speedily had their full effects, to govern the race of mankind, even in order to their own happiness, he employed not only laws and commands but revelations, miracles, promises, threats, exhortations, mercies, judgements, and divers other methods and means. Yet oftentimes, when he might well say, as he did once by his prophet, "What could I have done more to my vineyard that I have not done it?"[1] he had just cause to expostulate as he did in the same place, "Wherefore, when I looked that it should bring forth grapes, brought it forth wild grapes?" and to complain of men, as by that very prophet he did even of Israel, "I have spread out my hands all the day to a rebellious people."[2] But not to wander too far in this digression, what we have said of men may render it probable that the grand attributes of God are more signally exercised, and made more conspicuous in the making and governing of each of the three intellectual communities, than in the framing and upholding the community of mere bodily things.

Since all immaterial substances are for that reason naturally immortal, and the universal matter is believed so too, possibly those revolutions that will happen after the day of judgement, wherein though probably not the matter, yet that state and constitution of it, on whose account it is this world, will be destroyed, and make way for quite new frames and sets of things corporeal, and the beings that compose each of these intellectual communities will, in those numberless ages they shall last, travel through I know not how many successive changes and adventures. Perhaps, I say, these things will no less display, and bring glory, to the divine attributes, than the contrivance of the world, and the economy of man's salvation, though these be (and that worthily) the objects of the naturalist's and the divine's contemplation.

There are some passages in the prophetic part of the Scripture, and especially in the book of the apocalypse,[3] which, as they seem to intimate, that as God will perform great and noble things which mechanical philosophy never reached to, and which the generality of divines seem not to have thought of, so divers of those great things may be in some measure discovered by an attentive searcher into the Scriptures—and that so much to the advantage of the devout investigator that St. John, near the beginning of his revelations, pronounces them happy that read the

---

1 Isaiah 5.4 [RB's note]. King James Version gives "What could have been done more to my vineyard, that I have not done in it?"

2 Isaiah 65.2 [RB's note].

3 That is, Revelation.

matters contained in this prophecy and observe[1] the things written therein. Which implies, that by heedfully comparing together the indications couched in those prophetic writings, with events and occurrences in the affairs of the world and the church, we may discover much of the admirable economy of Providence in the governing of both. And I am prone to think the early discoveries of such great and important things to be in God's account no mean vouchsafements, not only because the title of *happy* is here given to him that attains them, but because of the two persons to whom the great discoveries of this kind were made—I mean the prophet Daniel and St. John—the first is by the angel said to be, on that account, a person highly favoured, and the other is in the Gospel represented as our Saviour's beloved disciple. And you will the more easily think the foreknowledge of the divine dispensations gatherable from Scripture to be highly valuable if you consider that, according to St. Paul, those very angels that are called "principalities and powers in heavenly places," learned by the church some abstruse points of "the manifold wisdom of God."[2] But I must no longer indulge speculations that would carry my curiosity beyond the bounds of time itself, and therefore beyond those that ought to be placed to this occasional excursion.

And yet, as on the one side I shall not allow myself the presumption of framing conjectures about those remote dispensations which will not, most of them, have a beginning before this world shall have an end, so on the other side I would not discourage you, or any pious inquirer, from endeavoring to advance in the knowledge of those attributes of God that may successfully be studied, without prying into the secrets of the future.

And here, Sir, let me freely confess to you that I am apt to think that, if men were not wanting to[3] God's glory, and their own satisfaction, there would be far more discoveries made than

1 Revelation 1.3. To render the original word *observe* or *watch*, rather than *keep*, seems more congruous to the sense of the text, and is a criticism suggested to me by an eminent mathematician as well as divine, who took notice, that the word *turei* is used by the Greeks as a term of art, to express the Astronomical Observation of Eclipses, Planetary Conjunctions, Oppositions, and other Celestial Phenomena [RB's note]. Hunter and Davis suggest, plausibly, that Boyle's eminent mathematician and divine may be Seth Ward (*Works* 8:35n).

2 Ephesians 3.10 [RB's note. Boyle notes the Greek version: *Polupoichilos sophia tou theou*].

3 "To fail to help or satisfy (a person or need)" (*OED*).

are yet attained to of the divine attributes. When we consider the most simple or uncompounded essence of God, we may easily be persuaded that what belongs to any of his attributes (some of which thinking men generally admire) must be an object of enquiry exceeding noble, and worthy of our knowledge. And yet the abstruseness of this knowledge is not in all particulars so invincible, but that I strongly hope a philosophical eye, illustrated by the revelations extant in the Scripture, may pierce a great deal farther than has yet been done into those mysterious subjects—subjects which are too often (perhaps out of a mistaken reverence) so poorly handled by divines and schoolmen that not only what they have taught is not worthy of God (for that is a necessary, and therefore excusable, deficiency) but too frequently it is not worthy of men, I mean, of rational creatures, that take upon them to treat of such high points and instruct others about them. And I question not but your friend will the less scruple at this if he call to mind those new and handsome notions about some of the attributes of God that his master Descartes, though but moderately versed in the Scriptures, has presented us with.[1] Nor do I doubt but that a much greater progress might be made in the discovery of subjects where, though we can never know all, we may still know farther, if speculative geniuses would propose to themselves particular doubts and enquiries about particular attributes, and frame and examine hypotheses, establish theorems, draw corollaries and (in short) apply to this study the same sagacity, assiduity, and attention of mind, which they often employ about inquiries of a very much inferior nature—Descartes, for example (how profound a geometrician soever he were), confesses in one of his epistles that he employed no less then six weeks to find the solution of a problem or question of Pappus.[2] And Pythagoras

---

1 Boyle was well read in Descartes, and in various places mentions not only the *Meditations*, but also the *Principles* and Descartes' correspondence when drawing our attention, with approval, to Descartes' comments about God's abilities and the difficulty of our finite minds comprehending the infinite abilities of God.

2 The letter in question is Descartes to Mersenne, 5 April, 1632 (AT 1:244, CSMK 3:37), in which Descartes remarks that it took him "five or six weeks to find the solution," adding, "if anyone else discovers it, I will not believe that he is ignorant of algebra." He mentions his solution of the problem again in a letter to Mersenne at the end of December 1637 (AT 1:478, CSMK 3:78), and gives the solution at the beginning of his *Geometry* (1637, AT 6:377ff, Descartes 1954, 16/17ff). The problem involves finding the locus of the points that result from the

was so addicted to, and concerned for, geometrical speculations, that when he had found that famous proposition which makes the 47th in Euclid's first Book, he is recorded to have offered a hecatomb, to express his joy and gratitude for the discovery: which yet was but of one property of one sort of right-lined triangles.[1]

Certainly if Christian philosophers did rightly estimate how noble and fertile subjects the divine attributes are, they would find in them wherewithal to exercise their best parts, as well as to recompence the employment of them. What I would dissuade does not perhaps proceed only from laziness, but from a mistake: as if there were little to be known of so incomprehensible an object as God, save that in general all his attributes are, like himself, infinite, and consequently not to be fully known by human understandings, because they are finite. This being so, I shall add that though it be true, that by reason of God's infinity, we cannot comprehend him, that is, have a full and adequate knowledge of him, yet we may not only know very many things concerning him but, which is more, may make an endless progress in that knowledge. As, no doubt, Pythagoras (newly mentioned) knew very well what a triangle was, and was acquainted with divers of its properties and affections before he discovered that famous one. And though since him, Euclid,

---

construction of lines from three or more given lines subject to a complicated set of conditions. Descartes' solution generalizes the partial solution given by Pappus (following Euclid and Apollonius), and was thought by him, correctly, to provide a clear case of the advantages offered by his new (algebraic) method. Boyle writes as if "six weeks" were a long time in this context; more accurate is J.F. Scott's remark that Descartes "arrived at a complete solution after spending *only* five or six weeks upon it" (Scott 1952, 97, my emphasis).

1 The theorem to which Boyle refers is the one commonly known as Pythagoras' theorem: in right-angled triangles, the square on the hypotenuse equals the sum of the squares on the other two sides. A hecatomb was originally a sacrifice of one hundred oxen, but the term was also used to mean simply a great public sacrifice. Classical accounts speak simply of a sacrifice of an ox, and as Cicero points out, there is reason to doubt even this, since the Pythagorean ritual forbade sacrifices in which blood was shed (Kirk, Raven, and Schofield 1983, 222); nor is it clear that the theorem referred to in the accounts of the sacrifice *was* Pythagoras' theorem, since the original source, Apollodorus, does not say what the theorem was. None of this affects Boyle's point about the pleasure that mathematical ingenuity bestows on its possessors, however.

Archimedes, and other geometricians have demonstrated I know not how many other affections of the same figure, yet they have not to this day exhausted the subject. And possibly I (who pretend not to be a mathematician) may now and then, in managing certain equations I had occasion for, have lighted upon some theorems about triangles that occurred not to any of them. The divine attributes are such fruitful themes, and so worthy of our admiration, that the whole fabric of the universe and all the phenomena exhibited in it, are but imperfect expressions of God's wisdom, and some few of his other attributes. And I do not much marvel that the angels themselves are represented in Scripture as employed in adoring God and admiring his perfections.[1] For even they, being but finite, can frame but inadequate conceptions of him, and consequently must endeavour by many of them to make amends for the incompleteness of every one of them—which yet they can never but imperfectly do.

And yet God's infinity can but very improperly be made a discouragement of our enquiries into his nature and attributes. For (not now to examine whether infinity, though expressed by a negative word, be not a positive thing in God[2]) we may, notwithstanding his infinity discover as much of him as our nature is capable of knowing. And what harm is it to him that is drinking in a river that he cannot drink up all the water, if he have liberty fully to quench his thirst, and take in as much liquid as his stomach can contain? Infinity therefore should not hinder us from a generous ambition to learn as much as we can of an object, whose being infinite does but make our knowledge of it the more noble and desirable, which indeed it is in such a degree that we need not wonder that the angels are represented as never weary of their employment of contemplating and praising God. For, as I lately intimated, they can have but inadequate ideas of those boundless perfections, and by no number of those ideas can arrive to make amends for the incompleteness of them, so it need

---

1 Isaiah 6.2-3; Luke 2.13-14; Revelation 5.11-12 [RB's note].

2 In *Meditations III* Descartes suggested, in the course of an argument to show that God's properties could not arise from concepts we could obtain by experience, that our concept of infinity could not arise from our notions of finite things; rather, our notion of finitude must be thought of as a restriction on infinity (AT 7:45-6, CSMK 2:31)." Descartes stresses this point, since the etymology of the term "infinity" suggests the opposite. As the readers of his Latin text would have been well aware, "in," in Latin is a negative prefix, so that, on the face of it the infinite (i.e., the unbounded) is (apparently) a negation of the finite.

not seem strange that in fresh discoveries of new parts (if I may so call them) of the same object, it being *such a one*,[1] they should find nobler and happier entertainments than anywhere else variety could afford them.

The second section: Our obligation to study theology

Having thus taken notice of some particulars of those many which may be employed to show how noble the objects are that theology proposes to be contemplated, I now proceed to some considerations that may make us sensible how great an obligation there lies on us to addict ourselves to the study of them.

Of the particulars whereon this obligation may be grounded, I shall now name but two, they being indeed comprehensive ones: *obedience*, and *gratitude*.

And first let me represent that it needs not, I suppose, be solicitously proved that it is the will and command of God that men should learn those truths that he has been pleased to teach, whether concerning his nature or attributes, or the way wherein he will be served and worshipped by man. Even if we had not injunctions of Scripture to that purpose, your friend is too rational a man to believe that God would so solemnly cause his truths to be published to mankind, both by preaching and writing, without intention to oblige those (at least) that have the capacity and opportunity to enquire into some of them. And if it appear to be his will that a person so qualified should search after the most important truths that he has revealed, it cannot but be their duty to do so. For though the nature of the thing itself did not lay any obligation on us, yet the authority of him that commands it would: since being the supreme and absolute lord of all his creatures, he has a full right to make what laws he thinks fit, and enjoin what service he thinks fit, as well as a power to punish those that either violate the one, or deny the other.

Accordingly it is very observable, that before Adam fell, and had forfeited his happy state by his own transgression, he not only had a law imposed upon him,[2] but such a law as, being about a matter itself indifferent (for so it was to eat or not to eat of the tree of life as well as of any other), derived its whole power of obliging from the mere will and pleasure of the law-giver.

1 Genesis 41.38: "And Pharaoh said unto his servants, Can we find such a one as this is, a man in whom the Spirit of God is?"

2 Genesis 2.16-17 [RB's note].

Whence we may learn, that man is subject to the laws of God, not as he is obnoxious[1] to him, but as he is a rational creature; and that the thing that is not a duty in its own nature may become an indispensable one barely by its being commanded. And indeed, if our first parent in the state of innocence and happiness wherein he tasted of God's bounty without, as yet, standing in need of his mercy, was most strictly obliged out of mere obedience to conform to a law, the matter of which was indifferent in itself, sure we, in our lapsed condition, must be under a high obligation to obey the declared will of God, whereby we are enjoined to study his truths, and perform that which has so much of intrinsic goodness in it, that it would be a duty, though it were not commanded, and has such recompences proposed to it that it is not more a duty than it will be an advantage.

But it is not only obedience and interest that should engage us to the study of divine things, but gratitude, and that exacted by so many important motives, that he who said, *if you call someone ungrateful, you have said everything*,[2] could not think ingratitude so much worse than ordinary vices, as a contempt of the duty I am pressing would be worse than an ordinary ingratitude.

It were not difficult on this occasion to manifest that we are extremely great debtors unto God, both as he is the author and the preserver of our very beings, and as he (immediately or mediately) fills up the measure of those continual benefits with all the prerogatives and other favours we do receive from him as men, and the higher blessings, which (if we are not wanting to ourselves) we may receive from him as Christians.

But to show, in how many particulars, and to how high a degree, God is our benefactor, were to launch out into too immense a subject, which it were the less proper for me to do, because I have in other papers discoursed of those matters

1 Vulnerable.

2 This saying, which Boyle quotes in Latin (*ingratum si dixeris, omnia dixeris*) is often mentioned in connection with the Spartan lawgiver, Lycurgus, who is said to have thought it unnecessary to frame a law against ingratitude since the gods themselves would deal with such behaviour. The saying may be a condensation of Pubilius Syrus (*Sententiae* 149), *Dixeris maledicta cuncta cum ingratum hominem dixeris*, "You have pronounced every curse when you pronounce a man ungrateful." John Clarke (*Paroemiologia Anglo-Latina* [London, 1639], 170) offers the translation "You can call a man no worse than unthankful." For a number of manuscript passages in which Boyle emphasizes the fact that we owe gratitude to God, see Boyle 2006, 2.2.1-2.2.26.

already.[1] I will therefore single out a motive of gratitude which will be peculiarly pertinent to our present purpose. For whereas your friend does so highly value himself upon the study of natural philosophy, and despises not only divines, but statesmen, and even the most learned men in other parts of philosophy and knowledge, because they are not versed in physics, he owes to God that very skill, among many other vouchsafements. For it is God who made man "unlike the horse and the mule, who have no understanding,"[2] and endowed him with that noble power of reason, by the exercise of which he attains to whatever knowledge he has of natural things above the beasts that will perish. For that may justly be applied to our other acquisitions which Moses, by God's appointment, told the Israelites concerning the acquists of riches. He bids the people beware that when their herds, and their flocks, and other treasures were multiplied, their heart be not lifted up and prompt them to say: *my* power, and the might of *my* hand, has gotten me this wealth. But, (subjoins that excellent person, as well as matchless law-giver) thou shalt remember the Lord thy God, for it is He that giveth thee power to get wealth.[3]

But to make men rational creatures is not all God has done towards the making them philosophers. For, to the knowledge of particular things, objects are as well requisite as faculties, and if we admit the probable opinion of divines, who teach us that the angels were created before the material world (as being meant by those sons of God, and morning stars, that with glad songs and acclamations celebrated the foundations of the earth[4]) we must allow that there were many creatures endowed with at least as much reason as your friend, who yet were unacquainted with the mysteries of nature, since nature itself had not yet received a being.[5] Wherefore God having as well made the world, as given

1 *Seraphic Love* [RB's note]. That is, "Some Motives and Incentives to the Love of God," usually referred to, as Boyle does here, as "Seraphic Love" (*Works* Vol. 1).

2 Psalms 32.9 [RB's note]

3 Deuteronomy 8.10-14, 18 [RB's note].

4 Job 38.5-7 [RB's note].

5 Earlier, Aquinas had noted that since this opinion concerning the order of creation

> was held by such great doctors as Basil, Gregory Nazianzen and others we must not condemn it as being erroneous: but if we consider carefully yet another opinion held by Augustine and other doctors and

man the faculties whereby he is enabled to contemplate it, naturalists are as much obliged to God for their knowledge, as we are for our intelligence to those that write us secrets in ciphers, and teach us the skill of deciphering things so written, or to those who write what would fill a page in the compass of a single penny, and present us to boot a microscope to enable us to read it. And as the naturalist has peculiar inducements to gratitude for the endowment of knowledge, so ingenuity lays this peculiar obligation on him to express his gratitude in the way I have been recommending. It is one of the most acceptable ways such gratitude can be expressed in, especially since by this way, philosophers may not only exercise their own gratitude towards God, but procure him that of others.

How pleasing men's hearty praises are to God may appear, among other things, by what is said and done by that Royal poet, whom God was pleased to declare a man after his own heart, for he introduces God pronouncing, "whoso offereth praise, glorifieth me,"[1] where the word our interpreters render 'offereth,' in the Hebrew signifies to sacrifice—which agrees with the remark elsewhere that those that pay God their praises, are said to sacrifice "to him the calves of their lips."[2] And that excellent person, to whom God vouchsafed so particular a testimony, was so assiduous in this exercise that the book which we, following the Greek, call *Psalms* is, in the original, from the things it most abounds with, called *Sepher Tehillim*, i.e. *The Book of Praises*. And to let you see, that many of his praises were such as the naturalist may best give, he exclaims in one place, "How manifold are thy works, O Lord?"[3] how wisely hast thou made them, (as Junius and Tremellius render it, and the Hebrew will bear) and elsewhere, "The heavens declare the glory of God, and the firmament sheweth his handiwork,"[4] etc. Again, in another place, "I will praise thee, because I am fearfully and wonderfully made. Marvellous are thy works, and that my soul knoweth right well."[5] And not content with many of the like expressions, he does

now more generally accepted, we shall find that the latter is the more reasonable of the two.... Hence we must conclude that the angels were created together with corporeal creatures, yet without prejudice to the other opinion (*De Potentia Dei* 3.18c).

1 Psalms 50.23 [RB's note].

2 Hosea 14.2 [RB's note].

3 Psalms 104.24 [RB's note].

4 Psalms 19.1 [RB's note].

5 Psalms 139.14 [RB's note].

several times in a devout transport, and poetical strain, invite the heavens, and the stars, and the earth, and the seas, and all the other inanimate creatures, to join with him in the celebration of their common maker. Which though it seem to be merely a poetical scheme, yet in some sort it might become a naturalist who, by making out the power, wisdom, and goodness of the creator, and by reflecting thence on those particulars wherein those attributes shine, may, by such a devout consideration of the creatures, make them in a sense join with him in glorifying their author.

In any other case, I dare say, your friend is not so ill-natured, but that he would think it an unkind piece of ingratitude, if some great and excellent prince, having freely and transcendently obliged him, he should not concern himself to know what manner of man his benefactor is, and should not be solicitous to inform himself of those particulars, relating to the person and affairs of that obliging monarch, which were not only in themselves worthy of any man's curiosity, but about which the prince had solemnly declared he was very desirous to have men inquisitive. And sure it is very disingenious[1] to undervalue or neglect the knowledge of God himself for a knowledge which we cannot attain without him, and by which he designed to bring to us to that study we neglect for it: which is not only not to use him as a benefactor, but as if we meant to punish him (if I may so speak) for having obliged us, since we so abuse some of his favours as to make them inducements to our unthankful disregard of his intentions in the rest. And this ingratitude is the more culpable, because the laws of ingenuity, and of justice itself, charge us to glorify the maker of all things visible, not only upon our own account, but upon that of all his other works. For by God's endowing of none but man here below with a reasonable soul, not only is he the sole visible being that can return thanks and praises in the world, and thereby is obliged to do so, both for himself and for the rest of the creation, but it is for man's advantage that God has left no other visible beings in the world by which he can be studied and celebrated. For reason is such a ray of divinity that, if God had vouchsafed it to other parts of the universe besides man, the absolute empire of man over the rest of the world must have been shared or abridged. So that he to whom it was equally easy to make creatures superior to man (as the Scripture tells us

1 "ingenious" and "ingenuous," and "disingenious" and "disingenuous" were interchangeable in the seventeenth century.

of legions and myriads of angels) as to make them inferior to him, dealt so obligingly with mankind, as rather to trust (if I may so speak) our ingenuity, whether he shall reap any celebrations from the creatures we converse with, than lessen our empire over them or our prerogatives above them.

But I fear that, notwithstanding all the excellency of revealed truths, and consequently of that only authentic repository of them, the Scripture, you, as well as I, have met with some (for I hope there are not many) virtuosi, that think to excuse the neglect of the study of it by alleging that to them who are laymen, not ecclesiastics, there is required to salvation the explicit knowledge but of very few points, which are so plainly summed up in the Apostles' Creed,[1] and are so often and conspicuously set down in the Scripture, that one needs not much search or study it to find them there.

In answer to this allegation, I readily grant that through the great goodness of God, "who is willing to have all men saved, and come to the knowledge of the truth,"[2] that is necessary to be so, there are many fewer articles absolutely necessary to be by all men distinctly believed, than may be met with in divers long confessions of faith, some of which have, I fear, less promoted knowledge than impaired charity. But then it may be also considered;

1. That it is not so easy for a rational man, that will trouble himself to enquire no farther than the Apostles' Creed, to satisfy himself upon good grounds, that all the fundamental articles of Christianity are contained in it.

2. That the creed proposes only the Credenda, not the Agenda of religion, whereas the Scriptures were designed, not only to teach us what truths we are to believe, but by what rules we are

---

1 The Apostles' Creed exists in a variety of closely related formulations. Here is the version given in *The Book of Common Prayer* (1662):

> I Believe in God the Father Almighty, Maker of heaven and earth; And in Jesus Christ his only Son our Lord, Who was conceived by the holy Ghost, Born of the Virgin Mary, Suffered under Pontius Pilate, Was crucified, dead, and buried, he descended into hell; The third day he rose again from the dead, he ascended into heaven, And sitteth on the right hand of God the Father Almighty; From thence he shall come to judge the quick and the dead.
>
> I believe in the holy Ghost; The holy Catholick Church; The Communion of Saints; The forgiveness of sins; The resurrection of the body, And the life everlasting. Amen.

2 1 Timothy 2.4 [RB's note].

to live, the obedience to the laws of Christianity being as necessary to salvation, as the belief of its mysteries.[1]

3. That besides the things which are absolutely necessary, there are several that are highly useful to make us more clearly understand, more rationally and firmly believe, and more steadily practise, the points that are necessary.

4. And since, whether or no those words of our Saviour to the Jews, "Search," or "You search the Scriptures,"[2] be rendered in the imperative or the indicative mode, St. Paul would have the word of Christ to "dwell richly in us,"[3] (by which, whether he meant the holy Scriptures then extant, or the doctrine of Christ, is not here material), thereby teaching us that searching into the matters of religion may become necessary as a duty, though it were not otherwise necessary as a means of attaining salvation. And indeed it is far more pardonable to lack or miss the knowledge of truth, than to despise or neglect it. And the goodness of God to illiterate or mistaken persons is to be supposed meant in pity to our frailties, not to encourage our laziness; nor is it necessary that he that pardons those seekers of his truths that miss them, should excuse those despisers that will not seek them.

But whether or no by this designed neglect of theology the persons I deal with do sufficiently consult their own safety, I doubt they will not much recommend their ingenuity. For to have received from God a greater measure of intellectual abilities than the generality of Christians, and yet willingly to come short of very many of them in the knowledge of the mysteries and other truths of Christianity, which he often invites us—if not expressly commands—to search after, is a course that will not relish of over-much gratitude. Is it a piece of that, and of ingenuity, to receive one's understanding and one's hopes of eternal felicity from the goodness of God, without being solicitous of what may be known of his nature and purposes by so excellent a way as his own revelation of them? To dispute anxiously about the properties of an atom, and be careless about the inquiry into the attributes of the "great God, who formed all things?"[4] To investigate the spontaneous generation of such vile

---

1 John 13.7; Hebrews 5.9 [RB's note].

2 John 5.39 [RB's note]. Boyle gives the original Greek, *ereunate tas graphas*, and notes in a marginal insertion that "Search," or "You search the Scriptures" are both acceptable translations.

3 Colossians 3.16 [RB's note].

4 Proverbs 26.10 [RB's note].

creatures as insects,[1] more than the mysterious generation of the adorable son of God, and, in a word, to be more concerned to know every thing that makes a corporeal part of the world, than the divine and incorporeal author of the whole?

And then, is it not, think you, a great piece of respect, that these men pay to those truths, which God thought fit to send, sometimes prophets and apostles, sometimes angels, and sometimes his only son himself to reveal, that such truths are so little valued by them, that rather than take the pains to study them, they will implicitly, and at adventures believe, what that society of Christians they chance to be born and bred in, have (truly or falsely) delivered concerning them? And does it argue a due regard to points of religion that those who would not believe a proposition in statics, perhaps about a mere point, the centre of gravity, or in geometry, about the properties of some nameless curve line, or some such other things (which to ignore, is usually not a blemish, and about which, to be mistaken, is more usually without danger), should yet take up the articles of faith concerning matters of great and everlasting consequence upon the authority of men fallible as themselves, when satisfaction may be had without them from the infallible word of God? They are in this very unlike those Bereans, whom the evangelist honours with the title of noble, that when the doctrines of the gospel were proposed to them, "they searched the Scriptures daily, whether those things were so."[2]

Again, if a man should refuse to learn to read any more than just as much as may serve his turn by entitling him to the benefit of the clergy, to save him from hanging,[3] would these men think

---

1 At the time it was believed, though not by Boyle, that some insects could be spontaneously generated, and Boyle, despite his remark here, found them fascinating: "as despicable as their Littleness makes the Vulgar apt to think some Creatures, I must confess my wonder dwells not so much on Natures Clocks (if I may so speak) as on her Watches" (Usefulness I, *Works* 3:223)." David Berman points out that Boyle was not alone in this interest in God's minute creations (Berman 1988).

2 Acts 17.11 [RB's note].

3 "Benefit of clergy" was a legal convention dating from the Middle Ages, which allowed certain types of offense to be tried in a clerical court, where there was no death penalty, as opposed to the civil courts, where there was. The range of crimes for which this manoeuvre was allowable was narrowed over time, and restricted to people already convicted in a civil court, but from the fourteenth century on, the right could be claimed by anyone who could read, it being assumed that this was an ability limited to "clerks." See further Greek 1992.

so small a measure of literature, as he had acquired on such an account, could prove that man to be a lover of learning? And yet a neglecter of the study of all not absolutely necessary divine truths during one's life, because of the belief that the articles of the creed may make a shift to keep him from being doomed to hell for ignorance after his death, will not by (what in a learned man must be) so pitiful a degree of knowledge be much better entitled to that ingenuous love of God and his truths, that becomes a rational creature and a Christian.

The ancient prophets, though honoured by God with direct illuminations, were yet very solicitous to find out and learn the very circumstances of the evangelical dispensations, which yet they did not know.[1] And some of the gospel mysteries are of so noble and excellent a nature, that "the angels themselves desire to look into them."[2] And though not all the evangelical truths are precisely necessary to be known, it may be both a duty not to despise the study of them, and a happiness to employ ourselves about it. It was the earnest prayer of a great king, and no less a prophet, that his eyes might be opened to behold (not the obvious and necessary truths, but) "the wondrous things of God's law."[3] He is pronounced happy in the beginning of the Apocalypse that reads and observes[4] the things contained in that dark and obscure part of Scripture. And it is not only those truths that make articles of the creed, but divers other doctrines of the gospel, that Christ himself judged worthy to be concluded with this epiphonema,[5] "He that has ears to hear, let him hear,"[6] on which the excellent Grotius makes this just paraphrase, 'Intelligence was given to us by God above all so that we might contemplate him in the writings that pertain to piety."[7]

---

1 1 Peter 1.10-11 [RB's note].
2 1 Peter 1.12 [RB's note].
3 Psalms 119.18 [RB's note].
4 Revelation 1 [RB's note].
5 A striking sentence which concludes a passage in a discourse.
6 Matthew 11.15; Mark 4.9, 23; Luke 8.8 [RB's note].
7 Boyle quotes Grotius in Latin: *Intellectus nobis à Deo potissimum datus est, ut eum intendamus documentis ad pietatem pertinentibus.* In his commentary on Matthew 11.15, Grotius suggests that "ears" in this context signifies the intellectual faculty (*Aures hic positæ ad significandam intellectivam facultatem*), but I have not found the source of Boyle's quotation in Grotius's *Works*.

The Third Section: The Advantages Accruing from a Study of Theology

I come now to our third and last inducement to the study of divine things which consists in, and comprises, the advantages of that study, which do as much surpass those of all other contemplations as divine things transcend all other objects. And indeed the utility of this study is so pregnant a motive, and contains in it so many invitations, that your friend must have as little sense of interest as of gratitude if he can neglect such powerful and such engaging invitations.

For, in the first place, theological studies ought to be highly endeared to us by the delightfulness of considering such noble and worthy objects as are therein proposed.

The famous answer given by an excellent philosopher,[1] who being asked what he was born for, replied, "To contemplate the sun," may justly recommend their choice, who spend their time in contemplating the maker of the sun, to whom that glorious planet itself is but a shadow.[2] And perhaps that philosopher failed more in the instance than in the notion: for his answer implies that man's end and happiness consists in the exercise of his noblest faculties on the noblest objects. And surely the seat of formal happiness is the soul, and that happiness consequently consists in the operations of the soul's faculties; similarly, as the supreme faculty of the mind is the understanding, so the highest pleasures may be expected from the due exercise of it upon the most sublime and worthiest objects. And therefore I wonder not, that though some of the school-men would assign the will a larger share in man's felicity than they will allow the intellect, yet the generality of them are quite of another mind, and ascribe the preeminence in point of felicity to the superior faculty of the soul. But, whether or no this opinion be true in all cases, it may at least be admitted in ours: for the chief objects of a Christian philoso-

1 Anaxagoras. The story is told by Diogenes Laertius (2.10), and was well known in Boyle's day. The seventeenth-century historian of philosophy, Stanley, recounts it, mentioning Laertius as the source. As noted in Appendix A, "People Mentioned in the Text," Aristotle provides an earlier source.

2 Boyle does not believe that the sun is a planet, but he here keeps the older terminology that referred to the sun and moon as planets, along with Mercury, Venus, Mars, Jupiter and Saturn—the moving, or apparently moving (as opposed to the "fixed stars"), heavenly bodies available to naked-eye observation.

pher's contemplation, being as well the infinite goodness, as the other boundless perfections of God, they are naturally fitted to excite in his mind an ardent love of that adorable being, and of those other joyous affections and virtuous dispositions, that have made some men think happiness chiefly seated in the will.

But having intimated thus much by the way, I pass on to add that the contentment afforded by the assiduous discovery of God and divine mysteries has so much of the affinity with the pleasures that shall make up men's blessedness in heaven itself, that they seem rather to differ in degree than in kind. For the happy state even of angels is by our Saviour represented by this employment, that "they continually see the face of his father who is in heaven."[1] And the same infallible teacher, intending elsewhere to express the celestial joys that are reserved for those, who for their sake denied themselves sensual pleasures, employs the vision of God as an emphatic periphrase of felicity: "Blessed," said he, "are the pure in heart, for they shall see God."[2] And as Aristotle teaches that the soul does after a sort become that which it speculates,[3] St. Paul and St. John assure us, that God is a transforming object, and that in heaven "we shall be like him, for (or, *because*[4]) we shall see him as he is."[5] And though I readily admit that this beatific vision of God, wherein the understanding is the proper instrument, includes divers other things which will concur to the complete felicity of the future life, yet I think we may be allowed to argue, that that ravishing contemplation of divine objects will make no small part of that happy estate which in these texts takes its denomination from it.

I have above intimated, that the Scripture attributes to the angels themselves transports of wonder and joy upon the contemplation of God, and the exercises they consider of his wisdom, justice, or some other of his Attributes. But lest, in referring you to the angels, you should say that I do in this discourse lay aside the person of a naturalist, in favour of divines, I will refer

---

1 Matthew 18.10.

2 Matthew 5.8 [RB's note].

3 Observes mentally. Boyle's reference is to the Aristotelian/scholastic doctrine that perception involves the form of the object being transferred to the perceiving entity, which takes upon itself the form it perceives. The percipient "is made like it and is such as that thing is" (*On the Soul*, Aristotle 1984, 418a3-6).

4 *oti* [RB's note]. Boyle's point is that the Greek *oti* can also be the "for" of causality.

5 2 John 3.2 [RB's note].

you to Descartes himself, whom I am sure your friend will allow to have been a rigid philosopher if ever there were any. Thus then he speaks in that treatise, where he thinks he employs a more than mathematical rigour, and where he was obliged to utter those (I had almost said passionate) words I am going to cite from him, only by the impressions made on him by the transcendent excellency of the object he contemplated:

> But before examining this point[1] more carefully and investigating other truths which may be derived from it, I should like to pause here and spend some time in the contemplation of God; to reflect on his attributes, and to gaze with wonder and adoration on the beauty of this immense light, so far as the eye of my darkened intellect can bear it. For just as we believe through faith that the supreme happiness of the next life consists solely in the contemplation of the divine majesty, so experience tells us that this same contemplation, albeit much less perfect, enables us to know the greatest joy of which we are capable in this life.[2]

But as high a satisfaction as the study of divine things affords us by the nobleness of its object, the contentment is not much inferior that accrues from the same study upon the score of the sense of a man's having in it performed his duty. To make actions of this nature satisfactory to us there is no need that the things we are employed about should in themselves be excellent or delightful: the inward gratulations of conscience for having done our duties is able to gild the bitterest pills and, like the wood that grew by the waters of Marah,[3] to correct and sweeten that liquor which before was the most distasteful. Those ancient pagan

---

1 The previous paragraph concludes:

> The whole force of the argument lies in this: I recognize that it would be impossible for me to exist with the kind of nature I have—that is, having within me the idea of God—were it not the case that God really existed. By "God" I mean the very being the idea of whom is within me, that is, the possessor of all the perfections which I cannot grasp, but can somehow reach in my thought, who is subject to no defects whatsoever. It is clear enough from this that he cannot be a deceiver, since it is manifest by the natural light that all fraud and deception depend on some defect. (AT 7:51-52, CSMK 2:35).

2 Descartes, *Meditations* III [RB's note]. The reference is to AT 7:52, CSMK 2:35-6. Boyle quotes the Latin version.

3 Exodus 15.25 [RB's note].

heroes, whose virtues may make us blush, being guided but by natural reason and innate principles of moral virtues, could find the most difficult and most troublesome duties, upon the bare account of their being duties, not only tolerable but pleasant. And though to deny some lusts be, in our Saviour's esteem, no less uneasy than for a man to pluck out his right eye or cut off his right hand,[1] yet even ladies have with satisfaction chosen, not only to deny themselves the greatest pleasures of the senses, but to sacrifice the seat of them, the body itself, to preserve the satisfaction of being chaste.[2] Nor are they only the dictates of obedience that we comply with in this study, but those of gratitude, and that is a virtue that has so powerful an ascendant upon ingenuous minds, that those whose principles and aims were not elevated by religion, have, in acknowledgment to their parents and their country, courted the greatest hardships, and hazards, and sufferings, as if they were as great delights and advantages. And a grateful person spends no part of his life to his greater satisfaction, than that which he ventures or employs for those to whom he is obliged for it, and oftentimes finds a greater contentment even in the difficultest acknowledgments of a favour than he did in receiving of it.

Another advantage, and that no mean one, that may accrue from the contemplation of theological truths, is the improvement of the contemplator himself in point of piety and virtue. For, as the gospel is styled "The mystery of godliness,"[3] and St. Paul elsewhere calls what it teaches, "the truth which is according to godliness,"[4] that is, a doctrine framed and fitted to promote the interest of piety and virtue in the world: so this character and encomium belongs (though perhaps not equally) to the more retired truths discovered by speculation, as well as to those more

---

1 Matthew 5.29-30 [RB's note].

2 In 1687, shortly before his death Boyle published the second part of a piece (the first part having been lost) entitled *The Martyrdom of Theodora and Didymus* (*Works* 11, V), in which Theodora does indeed choose death before giving up either her religion or her chastity. The work was begun in the 1640s, but was extensively rewritten. An earlier version of the same work was seen by John Mallet who kept a copy which is now available in *Works* 13. Michael Hunter and Edward Davis note Lawrence Principe's very plausible suggestion that Boyle's piece is based on Pierre Corneille's *Théodore, vierge et martyre* of 1646 (*Works* 13:xxii). Boyle's version gave rise in turn to Handel's oratorio *Theodora*.

3 1 Timothy 3.16 [RB's note].

4 Titus 1.1 [RB's note].

obvious ones that are familiarly taught in catechisms and confessions of faith. I would by no means lessen the excellency and prerogatives of fundamentals, but since the grand and noblest engagements to piety and virtue are a high veneration for God and his Christ, and an ardent love of them, I cannot but think that those particular inquiries that tend to make greater discoveries of the attributes of God, of the nature, and offices, and life of our Saviour, and of the wisdom and goodness they have displayed in the contrivance and effecting of man's redemption, do likewise tend to increase our admiration and inflame our love for the possessors of such divine excellencies, and the authors of such invaluable benefits. And as the brazen serpent,[1] that was but a type of one of the gospel mysteries, brought recovery to those that looked up to it, so the mysteries themselves, being duly considered, have had a very sanative[2] influence on many that contemplated them. Nor is it likely that he that discerns more of the depth of God's wisdom and goodness, should not, other things being equal, be more disposed than others to admire him, to love him, to trust him, and so to resign up himself to be governed by him—which frame of mind both is itself a great part of the worship of God, and does directly tend to the production and increase of those virtues, without the practise of which, the Scripture plainly tells us, that we can neither obey God nor express our love to him. And from this bettering of the mind by the study of theology will flow (to add that upon the by) another benefit, namely, that by giving us a higher value for God and his truths, it will endear heaven to us, and so not only assist us to come thither, but heighten our felicity there.

I know it may be said, that the melioration[3] of the mind is but a moral advantage. But give me leave to answer that, besides that it is such a moral advantage as supposes an intellectual improvement whose fruit it is, a moral benefit may be great enough, even in the judgement of a mere philosopher, and an Epicurean, to deserve as much study as natural philosophy itself. And that you may not think that I speak this only, because I write in this epistle as a friend to divines, I will tell you that Epicurus himself, who has nowadays so numerous a sect of naturalists to follow him, studied physics and wrote so many treatises about physical matters for this end: that by knowing the natural causes of

---

1 Numbers 21.9 [RB's note].

2 Healthy.

3 Improvement.

thunder, lightning, and other dreadful phenomena, the mind might be freed from the disquieting apprehensions men commonly had, that such strange and formidable things proceeded from some incensed deity, and so might trouble the mind as well as the air. This account I have been giving of Epicurus his design is but what seems plainly enough intimated by his own words, preserved us by Laertius, near the end of his physiological epistle[1] to Herodotus where, recommending to him the consideration of what he had delivered about physical principles in general, and meteors in particular, he subjoins, "if we attend to these things, we will give a correct and complete causal account of the source of our disturbance and fear, and so dissolve them."[2] And to this in the close of his meteorological epistle to Pythocles, his best interpreter, Gassendi, makes him speak consonantly, in these words, "Most important, devote yourself to the contemplation of the basic principles, from which everything follows, and the nature of the infinite, and things related to them;[3] attend also to the criteria and the feelings and the purpose for the sake of which we reason about these things: tranquility and an unperturbed mind." But this is not all the testimony I can give you from Epicurus himself to the same purpose, for among his *Principle Doctrines*,[4] preserved us by Laertius (himself reputed an Epicurean[5]), I find one that goes further, "If our suspicions about heavenly phenomena and about death did not trouble us at all and were never anything to us, and, moreover, if not knowing the limits of pains and desires did not trouble us, then we would have no need of natural science." Thus far the testimony of Epicurus,

1 "Physiological epistle," that is, a letter concerning matters we would now style physics.

2 Diogenis Laertii *libr.* 10 [RB's note]. In the original text, Boyle here, and in the next two quotations, uses Gassendi's Latin translation of Laertius' Greek. For the English translation I have used Epicurus 1994, with slight modifications.

3 Gassendi's version of Epicurus here is fairly loose. The basic principles from which everything follows are atoms, and the term Gassendi translates (reasonably) as infinity, *apeirias*, in this context is more accurately rendered (as Inwood and Gerson do) as the *unlimited*, or, in an Epicurean context, the *void*.

4 Boyle uses the Latin title *Ratæ Sententiæ*.

5 In the seventeenth century, the fact that Laertius speaks well of Epicurus would be enough to lead to this conclusion. However, as R.D. Hicks notes (Laertius 1925, 1:xiii-xiv) there is no good reason to think that Laertius was an Epicurean.

of whose mind though I am not at all, as to what he would intimate,[1] "That physiology is either proper to free the mind from the belief of a provident deity and the soul's immortality, or fit for no other considerable purposes," yet this use we may well make of these declarations: that, in Epicurus's opinion, a moral advantage that relates to the government of the affections may deserve the pains of making inquiries into nature.

And since it hence appears that a mere philosopher, who admitted no providence, may think it worth his pains to search into the most abstruse parts of physics and the difficultest phenomena of nature, only to ease himself of one troublesome affection, fear, it need not be thought unphilosophical to prosecute a study that will not only restrain one undue passion, but advance all virtues, free us from all servile fears of the Deity, and tend to give us a strong and well-grounded hope in him, and make us look upon God's greatest power, not with terror, but with joy.

There is yet another advantage belonging to the study of divine truths which is too great to be here pretermitted. For whereas there is scarce any thing more incident to[2] us while we inhabit our (*Battę Chómer*) "cottages of clay,"[3] and dwell in this "vale of tears"[4] than afflictions, it ought not a little to endear to us the newly mentioned study that it may be easily made to afford us very powerful consolations in that otherwise uneasy state.

I know it may be said that the speculations about which the naturalist is busied are pleasing diversions, as well as noble employments of the mind. And I deny not that they are often so, when the mind is not hindered from applying itself attentively to them, so that afflictions slight and short may well be weathered out by these philosophical avocations. But the greater and sharper sort of afflictions, and the approaches of death, require more powerful remedies than these diversions can afford us. For in such cases, the mind is wont to be too much discomposed to apply the attention requisite to the finding a pleasure in physical speculations. And in sicknesses, the soul is oftentimes as indisposed to relish the pleasures of merely human studies, as the languishing body is to relish those meats which at other times were

1 That is, Boyle does not agree with Epicurus' claim.

2 Liable to befall or occur to.

3 Job 4.19 [RB's note].

4 That the world is a valley of sorrow, of trouble, of misery, of tears has a long history, with the phrase "vale of tears" found as early as the mid-sixteenth century (OED, entry "vale").

delightful. And there are but few that can take any great pleasure to study the world when they apprehend themselves to be upon the point of being driven out of it, and in danger of losing all their share in the objects of their contemplation. It will not much qualify our sense of the burning heat of a fever, or the painful gripes of the colic, to know that the three angles of a triangle are equal to two right ones, or that heat is not a real quality (as the schools would have it) but a modification of the motion of the insensible parts of matter, and pain not a distinct, inherent quality in the things that produce it, but an affection of the sentiment.[1] The naturalist's speculations afford him no consolations that are extraordinary in, or peculiar to, the state of affliction, and the avocations they present him with do rather amuse the mind from an attention to lesser evils, than bring it any advantages to remove or compensate them, and so work rather in the nature of opiates, than of true cordials.

But now, if such a person as Dr. N[2] falls into adversity the case is much otherwise. For we must consider that when the study of divine things is such as it ought to be, though that in itself, or in the nature of the employment, be an act or exercise of reason, yet being applied, out of obedience, and gratitude, and love to God, it is upon the account of its motives, and its aim, an act of religion, and as it proceeds from obedience, and thankfulness, and love to God, so it is most acceptable to him, and upon the account of his own appointment, as well as goodness, is a most proper and effectual means of obtaining his favour. And then, I presume, it will easily be granted that he who is so happy as to enjoy that, can scarce be made miserable by affliction. For not now to enter upon the commonplace of the benefits of afflictions[3] to them that love God, and to them that are loved by him, it may suffice that he who (as the Scripture speaks) "knows our

---

1 A property of sensation.

2 We should remember that Dr. N "cultivates theological as well as physical studies."

3 There are a variety of texts that set out the benefits of afflictions, the most straightforward being Psalms 34.19, "Many are the afflictions of the righteous: but the Lord delivereth him out of them all." Isaac Penington (1616-79) refers to Hebrews 12.11 ("no chastening for the present seemeth to be joyous, but grievous: nevertheless afterward it yieldeth the peaceable fruit of righteousness unto them which are exercised thereby") for "The proper nature, and sweet benefits of afflictions" (Part 3, "A basket of fragments," Penington 1656).

frame,"[1] and has promised those that are his that they shall not be "over-burdened,"[2] is disposed and wont to give his afflicted servants both extraordinary comforts in afflictions, and comforts appropriate to that state.

For though natural philosophy be like its brightest object, the stars, which, however the astronomer can with pleasure contemplate them, are unable, being mere natural agents, to afford him a kinder influence than usual in case he be cast upon his bed of languishing[3] or into prison, yet the almighty and compassionate maker of the stars, being not only a voluntary, but the most free agent, can suit and proportion his reliefs to our necessities, and alleviate our heaviest afflictions by such supporting consolations, that not only can such afflictions never surmount our patience, but are oftentimes unable so much as to hinder our joy. And when death, that "king of terrors,"[4] presents itself, whereas the mere naturalist sadly expects to be deprived of the pleasure of his knowledge by losing those senses and that world, which are the instruments and the objects of it, and perhaps (discovering beyond the grave nothing but either a state of eternal destruction, or of eternal misery), fears either to be confined for ever to the sepulchre, or exposed to torments that will make even such a condition desirable, the pious student of divine truths is not only freed from the wracking apprehensions of having his soul reduced to a state of annihilation, or cast into hell, but enjoys a comfortable expectation of finding far greater satisfaction than ever in the study he now rejoices to have pursued, since the change, that is so justly formidable to others, will but bring him much nearer to the divine objects of his devout curiosity, and strangely elevate and enlarge his faculties to apprehend them.

And this leads me to the mention of the last advantage belonging to the study I would persuade you to, and indeed, the highest advantage that can recommend any study, or invite men to any undertaking, for this is no less than the everlasting fruition of the divine objects of our studies hereafter, and the comfortable expectation of it here. For the employing of one's time and parts to admire the nature and providence of God and contemplate the divine mysteries of religion, as it is one of the chief of those

---

1 Psalms 103.14 [RB's note].

2 1 Corinthians 10.13 [RB's note].

3 Psalms 41.3.

4 Job 18.14 [RB's note]. On Boyle's fear of death, see Michael Hunter's comments referred to in Boyle's Life, p. 17 above.

homages and services, whereby we venerate and obey God, so it is one of those to which he has been pleased to apportion no less a recompence than that which can have no greater—the enjoyment of himself. The saints and angels in heaven have divers of them been employed to convey the truths of theology[1] and are solicitous "to look into those sacred mysteries,"[2] and God has been pleased to appoint that those men who study the same lessons that they do here, shall study them in their company hereafter. And doubtless, though heaven abound with inexpressible joys, yet it will be none of the least that shall make up the happiness even of that place, that the knowledge of divine things that was here so zealously pursued shall there be completely attained. For those things that do here most excite our desires, and quicken the curiosity and industry of our searches, will not only there continue, but be improved to a far greater measure of attractiveness and influence. For all those interests, and passions, and lusts, that here below either hinder us from clearly discerning, or keep us from sufficiently valuing, or divert us from attentively enough considering, the beauty and harmony of divine truths, will there be either abolished, or transfigured. And as the object will be unveiled, so our eye will be enlightened, that is, as God will there disclose those worthy objects of the angels' curiosity, so he will enlarge our faculties to enable us to gaze without being dazzled upon those sublime and radiant truths, whose harmony as well as splendor we shall be then qualified to discover, and consequently with transports to admire. And this enlargement and elevation of our faculties will, proportionably to its own measure, increase our satisfaction at the discoveries it will enable us to make. For theology is like a heaven, which wants not[3] more stars than appear in it, but we want[4] eyes, quick-sighted and piercing enough to reach them. And as the milky way, and other whiter parts of the firmament, have been full of immortal lights from the beginning, and our new telescopes have not placed, but found them there, so when our Saviour, after his glorious resurrection, instructed his apostles to teach the gospel, it is not said that he altered any thing in the Scriptures of Moses and the prophets, but only "opened" and "enlarged their intellects, that they might understand the Scriptures."[5] And the royal prophet makes it his prayer, "that God

1 Daniel 9.21-2; Luke 1.11, 26; Acts 10.4-6 [RB's note].

2 1 Peter 1.12 [RB's note].

3 Does not lack.

4 Lack.

5 Luke 24.45 [RB's note].

would be pleased to open his eyes, that he might see wonderful things out of the law,"[1] being (as was above intimated) so well satisfied, that the word of God wanted not admirable things, that he is only solicitous for the improvement of his own eyes, that they might be qualified to discern them.

I had almost forgotten one particular about the advantages of theological studies that is too considerable to be left unmentioned, for as great as I have represented the benefits accruing from the knowledge of divine truths, yet, to endear them to us, it may be safely added that, to procure us these benefits, the actual attainment of that knowledge is not always absolutely necessary, but a hearty endeavour after it may suffice to entitle us to them. The patient chemist,[2] that consumes himself and his estate in seeking after the philosophers stone, if he miss of his idolized elixir, had as good, nay better, have never sought it, and remains as poor in effect, as he was rich in expectation. The husbandman that employs his seed and time to obtain from the ground a plentiful harvest if, after all, an unkind season happen, must see his toil made fruitless, "the long labours of the year are vain."[3]

Too many patients, that have punctually done and suffered for recovery all that physicians could prescribe, meet at last with death instead of health. You know what entertainment has been given by skilful geometricians to the laborious endeavours even of such famous writers as Scaliger, Longomontanus, and other Tetragonists,[4] and that their successor Mr. Hobbes, after all the ways he has taken, and those he has proposed to square the circle, and double the cube, by missing of his end has, after his various attempts, come off not only with disappointment but with disgrace.[5] And (to give an instance even in things celestial) how many pains have been taken to find out longitudes, and make astrological predictions with some certainty which, for want of coming up to what they aimed at, have been useless, if not prej-

---

1 Psalms 119.18 [RB's note].

2 I.e., alchemist.

3 Ovid, *Metamorphoses*, 1.273, John Dryden's translation. Boyle quotes the original: *longique perit labor irritus Anni.*

4 Tetragonist: one who attempts to square the circle, that is, to produce, using only a straight edge and compass, a square having the same area as a given circle. Boyle's use of the term is one of its earliest appearances in English.

5 Boyle's great dislike of Hobbes left him willing to believe the worst of Hobbes on every occasion, but in this case his summing up is simply, if devastatingly, accurate. For full details, see Jesseph 1999.

udicial, to the attempters. But God (to speak with St. Paul on another occasion) "that made the world, and all things therein, and is Lord of heaven and earth, seeks not our services, as though he needed any thing, seeing he giveth life, and breath, and all things."[1] His self-sufficiency and bounty are such that he seeks in our obedience the occasions of rewarding it, and prescribes us services because the practise of them is not only suitable to our rational nature but such as will prevail with his justice, to let his goodness make our persons happy. Agreeably to this doctrine we find in the Scripture, that Abraham is said to have been "justified by faith, when he offered his son Isaac upon the altar"[2] (though he did not actually sacrifice him) because he endeavoured to do so—God, graciously accepting the will for the deed, accepted also of the blood of a ram instead of Isaac's.[3] And thus we know, that it was not David but Solomon that built the temple of Jerusalem, and yet God says to the former of those kings (as we are told by the latter) "For as much as it was in thine heart to build an house for my name, thou didst well in that it was in thine heart: notwithstanding thou shalt not build the house," etc.[4]

And if we look to the other circumstances of this story, as they are delivered in the second book of Samuel, we shall find that upon David's declaration of a design to build God a house, God himself vouchsafes to honour him, as he once did Moses, with the peculiar title of "His servant," and commands the prophet to say to him, "Also the lord tells thee, that he will make thee an house," to which is added one of the most gracious messages that God ever sent to any particular man, by which we may learn that God approves and accepts even those endeavours of his servants, if they be real and sincere, that never come to be actually accomplished. Good designs and endeavours are our part, but the events of those, as of all other things, are in the all-disposing hand of God who, if we be not wanting to what lies in us, will not suffer us to be losers by the defeating dispositions of his providence, but crown our endeavours either with success, or with some other recompence, that will keep us from being losers by missing of that.

And indeed, if we consider the great elogies[5] that the Scrip-

1 Acts 17.24-5 [RB's note].

2 James 2.21 [RB's note].

3 Genesis 22.

4 2 Chronicles 6.8-9 [RB's note].

5 "Elogies" was often used in the seventeenth century as a synonym of "eulogies."

ture, frequently as well as justly, gives God's goodness (which it represents as over, or as above, all his works[1]) and that his "purer eyes"[2] punish, as well as see, the murder and adultery of the heart, when those intentional sins are hindered from advancing into actual ones, we can scarce doubt but he, whose justice punishes sinful aims, will allow his infinite goodness to recompense pious attempts. And therefore our Saviour pronounces them blessed, that "hunger and thirst after righteousness,"[3] assuring them that they shall be satisfied, and thereby sufficiently intimating to us that an earnest desire after a spiritual grace (and such is the knowledge of divine things) may entitle a man to the complete possession of it, if not in this life, yet in the next, where we shall not any more "walk by faith, but by sight,"[4] and obtain a knowledge as well as other endowments befitting that glorious state, wherein the purchaser of it for us, assures us, that we shall be [*isaggeloi*] equal, or like to the angels.[5]

The considerations, Sir, I have hitherto laid before you, to recommend the study of divine truths have I hope persuaded you that it is on many accounts both noble and eligible in itself, and therefore I shall here conclude the first part of this discourse. And in regard that the undervaluation Physeophilus expresses for that excellent employment seems to flow (chiefly at least) from his fondness and partiality for natural philosophy, it will next concern us to compare the study of theology with that of physics, and show that the advantages which your friend alleges in favour of the latter are partly much lessened by disadvantageous circumstances, and partly much outweighed by the transcendent excellencies of theological contemplations, the study whereof will thereby appear to be not only eligible in itself, but preferable to its rival. And I must give you warning to expect to find the second part, which the making this comparison challenges to itself, a good deal more prolix[6] than the first, not only because it often requires more trouble, and more words, to detect and disprove an

---

1 Psalms 145.9.

2 Habakkuk. 1.13 [RB's note].

3 Matthew 5.6 [RB's note].

4 2 Corinthians 5.7 [RB's note].

5 Luke 20.36 [RB's note, and his bracketing of the Greek.]

6 Boyle underestimates his prolixity in the first part. The two sections are of almost equal length, with the first section being just over 20,000 words and the second, just over 22,000.

error, than to make out a truth, but also because that divers things tending to the credit of divinity (which consequently might have been brought into the first part of this discourse), were thought more fit to be interwoven with other things in the answers made to the objections examined in the second.

The Excellency of Theology: or, The Preeminence of the Study of Divinity, above that of Natural Philosophy

The Second Part: A Comparison of the Advantages of Natural Philosophy and Theology

THE FIRST SECTION: THE DELIGHTS AND DRAWBACKS OF NATURAL PHILOSOPHY[1]

I shall without preamble, begin this discourse, by considering the delightfulness of physics, as the main thing that inveigles your friend and divers other virtuosi, from relishing, as they ought, and otherwise would, the pleasantness of theological discoveries. And to deal ingenuously with you, I shall not scruple to acknowledge, that though the address I have made to nature has lasted several years, and has been toilsome enough, and not inexpensive, yet I have been pleased enough with the favours, such as they are, that it has from time to time accorded me, not to complain of having been unpleasantly employed. But though I readily allow the attainments of naturalists to be able to give philosophical souls sincerer pleasures than those that the more undiscerning part of mankind is so fond of, yet I must not therefore allow them to surpass, or even equal, the contentment that may accrue to a soul qualified by religion, to relish the best things most from some kind of theological contemplations.

This, I presume, will sufficiently appear, if I show you that the study of physiology is not unattended with considerable inconveniences, and that the pleasantness of it may be, by a person studious of divinity, enjoyed with endearing circumstances.

But before I name any of the particular reasons that I am to represent, I fear it may be requisite to interpose a few words to obviate a mistake which, if not prevented, may have an ill aspect, not only upon the first section, but upon a great part of the following discourse. For I know that it may be said, that whereas I allege divers things to lessen the lately mentioned delightfulness of the study of physic, and to depreciate some other advantages by which the following sections would recommend it, some of the same things may be objected against the delightfulness of the study of divinity. But this objection will not, I presume, much move you, if you consider the argument and scope of the two parts of this letter. For in the former I have shown by positive

1 An earlier version of this first section, with omissions, occurs at BP 8:153-9.

proofs that the study of theology is attended with divers advantages which belong to it, either *only* as some of them do, or *principally* as others. And now in the second part I come to consider whether what is alleged in behalf of the study of philosophy deserves to counter-balance those prerogatives or advantages. And therefore it neither need be, nor is it my design, to compare, for instance, the delightfulness of the two studies, theology and physics; but by showing the inconveniences that allay[1] the latter, to weaken the argument that is drawn from that delightfulness, to conclude it preferable to the study of theology. So that my work in this and the following sections is not so much to institute comparisons, as to obviate or answer allegations. For since I have in the past discourse grounded the excellency of the study of divinity chiefly upon those great advantages that are peculiar to it, my reasonings would not be frustrated, even though it should appear that, in point of delightfulness, certainty, etc. that study should, in many cases, be liable to the same objections with the study of nature, since it is not mainly for these qualities but, as I was saying, for other and peculiar excellencies that I recommended divinity. And therefore, supposing the delightfulness, etc. of that and of physics, to be allayed by the same or equal inconveniences or imperfections, that supposition would not hinder the scales to be swayed in favour of divinity, upon the score of those advantages that are unquestioned and peculiarly belong to it.

I know not whether I need add that, notwithstanding this, you are not to expect that I should give philosophy the wounds of an enemy. For my design being not to discourage you, nor any ingenious man, from courting it at all, nor from courting it much, but from courting it too much, and despising divinity for it, I employ against it not a sword to wound, but a balance, to show that its excellencies, though solid and weighty, are less so than the preponderating ones of theology. And this temper and purpose of mine renders my task difficult enough to have, perhaps, some right to your pardon as well as some need of it, if I do not everywhere steer so exactly, as equally to avoid injuring the cause I am to plead for, and disparaging a study, which I would so little depreciate that I allow it a great part of my inclinations, and not a little share of my time. And having said this, to keep the design of this discourse from being misunderstood, I hope we may now proceed to the particulars whose scope we have been declaring.

---

1 allayed = mixed, or modified; often used in the seventeenth century, metaphorically or literally, to mean mixed with an inferior metal.

Returning then to what I was about to say before this long but needful advertisement interrupted me, I shall resume my discourse of the delightfulness of the study of physics—about which I was going in the first place to tell you, that I know you and your friend will freely grant me, that the knowledge of the empty and barren physiology that is taught in the schools, as it exacts not much pains to be acquired, so it affords but little satisfaction when attained. And as I know you will give me leave to say this, so, being warranted by no slight experience of my own, I shall take leave to say also that the study of that experimental philosophy, which is that whereof your friend is so much enamoured is, if it be duly prosecuted, a very troublesome and laborious employment. For, to mention at present but this, that great variety of objects the naturalist is not only by his curiosity, but by their secret dependances upon one another, engaged to consider, and several ways to handle, will put him upon needing, and consequently upon applying himself to such a variety of mechanic people (as distillers, drugsters, smiths, turners, etc.) that a great part of his time, and perhaps all his patience, shall be spent in waiting upon tradesmen, and repairing the losses he sustains by their disappointments, which is a drudgery greater than any who has not tried it will imagine, and which yet, being as inevitable as unwelcome, does very much counter-balance and allay the delightfulness of the study we are treating of, in which so great a part of a man's care and time must be laid out in providing the apparatuses necessary for the trying of experiments.

But this is not all. For when you have brought an experiment to an issue, though the event may often prove such as you will be pleased with, yet it will seldom prove such as you can acquiesce in. For it fares not with an inquisitive mind in studying the book of nature, as in reading of Aesop's *Fables*, or some other collection of apologues of differing sorts, and independent one upon another, where when you have read over as many at one time as you think fit, you may leave off when you please, and go away with the pleasure of understanding those you have perused, without being solicited by any troublesome itch of curiosity to look after the rest, as those which are needful to the better understanding of those you have already gone over, or that will be explicated by them, and scarce without them. But in the book of nature, as in a well contrived Romance,[1] the parts have such a connection and relation to one another, and the things we would

1 That is, a work of fiction.

discover are so darkly or incompletely knowable by those that precede them, that the mind is never satisfied till it comes to the end of the book, till when all that is discovered in the progress, is unable to keep the mind from being molested with impatience to find that yet concealed, which will not be known till one does at least make a further progress. And yet the full discovery of nature's mysteries is so unlikely to fall to any man's share in this life, that the case of the pursuers of them is at best like theirs, that light upon some excellent Romance, of which they shall never see the latter parts.

For indeed (to speak now without a simile) there is such a relation between natural bodies, and they may in so many ways (and divers of them unobserved) work upon, or suffer from, one another,[1] that he who makes a new experiment, or discovers a new phenomenon, must not presently[2] think that he has discovered a new truth, or detected an old error. For, at least if he be a considering man, he will oftentimes find reason to doubt, whether the experiment or observation has been so skillfully and warily made in all circumstances, as to afford him such an account of the matter of fact, as a severe naturalist would desire. And then, supposing the historical part no way defective, there are far more cases than are taken notice of, wherein so many differing agents may produce the exhibited phenomenon, or have a great influence upon the experiment or observation, that he must be less jealous[3] than becomes a philosopher, to whom experiments do not oftentimes as well suggest new doubts, as present new phaenomena.

And even those trials that end in real discoveries do, by reason of the connection of physical truths and the relations that natural bodies have to one another, give such hopes and such desires of improving the acquisitions we have already made to the explicating of other difficulties, or the making of further discoveries, that an inquisitive naturalist finds his work to increase daily upon his hands. The event of his past toils, whether it be good or bad, does but engage him into new ones, either to free himself from his scruples, or improve his successes. So that though the pleasure of making physical discoveries is, considered in itself, very great, yet this does not a little impair it: that the same attempts which afford that delight do so frequently beget both anxious doubts

---

1 To affect, or be affected by, one another.

2 Immediately.

3 Vigilant in scrutinizing.

and a disquieting curiosity. So that if knowledge be, as some philosophers have styled it, the aliment of the rational soul, I fear I may too truly say, that the naturalist is usually fain to live upon salads and sauces which, though they yield some nourishment, excite more appetite than they satisfy, and give us indeed the pleasure of eating with a good stomach, but then reduce us to an unwelcome necessity of always rising hungry from the table.[1]

Of divers things that lessen the delightfulness of physiological studies I do so amply discourse in other papers that I might well remit you thither, but indeed it is not necessary that I should insist on this argument any further. It is true that such a reference might be very proper if the mysteries of theology and physic were like those of necromancy (or some other part of unlawful magic), whereof the former could not be well relished without an abhorrence of the latter.[2] But as the two great books—of nature and of Scripture—have the same author, so the study of the latter does not at all hinder an inquisitive man's delight in the study of the former. The doctor I am pleading for may as much relish a physical discovery as Physeophilus; nay, by being addicted to theology and religion he is so far from being incapable of the contentments accruing from the study of nature that, beside those things that recommend it to others, there are several things that peculiarly endear it to him.

---

1 This is an interesting analogy from the abstemious Boyle, of whom the Rev. John Ward said, about 1673: "Mr. Boyl never drinks any strong drink: hee every morning eats bread and butter, with powder of eye-bright spread on the butter. His supper is water-gruel and a couple of eggs: his dinner is mutton, or veal, or a pullet, or walking henne, (as hee calls them,) which goe to the barne door when they will" (quoted Maddison 1969, 187n). Eyebright is the popular name of the plant *Euphrasia officinalis*. Although tinctures of this herb are astringent and if applied to the eye can cause redness, itching, and swelling, it was believed at the time that "Eye bright ... strengthens the head, eyes, and memory, [and] clears the sight" (Salmon 1671, 399-400). Boyle suffered from bad eyesight throughout his life. At the very beginning of his scientific career, he tells us that he suffered from a "distemper" in his eyes that prevented him "not onely to write my self so much as one Experiment, but even to read over my self what I dictated to others" (*Works* 1:145).

2 Boyle was both fascinated by, and fearful of, "unlawful" investigations. Here he is concerned to point out that a discovery of such secrets as physical experiments reveal is consistent with a love of theology, while a discovery of such secrets as "unlawful magic" may reveal is not. His attitude is discussed in interesting and informative detail by Larry Principe in Principe 1998.

For first, he has the contentment to look upon the wonders of nature not only as the productions of an admirably wise author of things, but of such a one as he entirely honours and loves, and to whom he is related. He that reads an excellent book, or sees some rare engine, will be otherwise affected with the sight or the perusal, if he knows it to have been made by a friend, or a parent, than if he considers it but as made by a stranger whom he has no particular reason to be concerned for. And if Rehoboam did not as well degenerate from the sentiments of mankind, as from his family, he could not but look upon that magnificent temple of Solomon with another eye than did the throngs of strangers that came only to gaze at it as an admirable piece of architecture, while he considered that it was his father that built it.[1] And if (as we see) the same heroic actions which we read in history of some great monarch that strangers barely and unconcernedly admire, the natives of his country do not only venerate but affectionately interest themselves therein, because they are his countrymen, and their ancestors were his subjects: how much more may we suppose the same actions would affect them if they had the honour to be that prince's children?

We may well, therefore, presume that it is not without a singular satisfaction that the contemplator we are speaking of does, in all the wonders of nature, discover how wise, and potent, and bountiful that author of nature is, in whom he has a great interest: and that so great a one, as both to be admitted into the number of his friends, and adopted into the number of his sons, and is thereby in some measure concerned in all the admiration and praises that are paid either by himself or others to those adorable attributes that God has displayed in the great masterpiece of power and wisdom, the world. And when he makes greater discoveries in these expressions and adumbrations of the divine perfections, the delightfulness of his contemplation is proportionally increased upon such an account, as that which endears to the passionate lover of some charming beauty an excellent, above an ordinary, picture of her; because the same things that make him, as it does other gazers, look upon it as a finer piece, make him look upon it as the more like his mistress,

---

1 The life of Rehoboam, the son of Solomon, may be found in 1 Kings 12-14 and 2 Chronicles 10-12. While Boyle's views about the effects of Rehoboam's awareness of his father's involvement in the building of the temple may be correct, there is no specific scriptural mention of his attitude to the temple.

and thereby entertain him with the sublimer ideas of the beloved original, to whose transcendent excellencies he supposes that the noblest representations must be the most resembling.

And there is a farther reason why our contemplator should find a great deal of contentment in these discoveries. For we have in our nature so much of imperfection, and withal so much of inclination to self-love, that we do too confidently proportion our ideas of what God can do for us to what we have already the knowledge or the possession of. And though, when we make it our business, we are able with much ado somewhat to enlarge our apprehensions and raise our expectations beyond their wonted[1] pitch, yet still they will be but scantly promoted and heightened if those things themselves be but mean and ordinary, which we think we have done enough if we make them surpass. A country villager, born and bred in a homely cottage, cannot have any suitable apprehensions of the pleasures and magnificence of a great monarch's court, and if he should be bid to screw up his imagination to frame ideas of them, they would be borrowed from the best tiled house he had seen in the market towns where he had sold his turnips or corn, and the wedding feast of some neighbouring farmer's daughter. And though a child in the mother's womb had the perfect use of reason, yet could it not in that dark cell have any ideas of the sun or moon, or beauties or banquets, or algebra or chemistry, and many other things which his elder brothers, that breath fresh air and freely behold the light, and are in a more mature estate, are capable of knowing and enjoying.

Now among thinking men, whose thoughts run much upon that future state which they must shortly enter into but shall never pass out of, there will frequently and naturally arise a distrust which, though seldom owned, proves oftentimes disquieting enough. For such men are apt to question how the future condition which the gospel promises can afford them so much happiness as it pretends to, since they shall in heaven but contemplate the works of God, and praise him, and converse with him, all which they think may, though not immediately, be done by men here below, without being happy: but he that by telescopes and microscopes, dexterous dissections, and well employed furnaces, etc., discovers the wondrous power and skill of him that contrived so vast and immense a mass of matter into so curious a piece of workmanship as this world, will pleasingly be convinced of the boundless power and goodness of the great Architect. And when

1 Usual.

he sees how admirably every animal is furnished with parts requisite to its respective nature, and that there is particular care taken that the same animal, as for example, man, should have differing provisions made for him according to his differing states within the womb and out of it—a human egg, and an embryo, being much otherwise nourished and fitted for action, than is a (complete) man—he, I say, who considers this, and observes the stupendious[1] providence and excellent contrivances that the curious priers into nature (and none but they) can discover, will be as well enabled as invited to reason thus within himself: that sure God, who has with such admirable artifice framed silkworms, butterflies, and other meaner insects, and with such wonderful providence taken care that the nobler animals should as little want any of all the things requisite to the completing of their respective natures, and who, when he pleases, can furnish some things with qualifications quite differing from those which the knowledge of his other works could have made us imagine, (as is evident in the loadstone and in quicksilver among minerals,[2] and the sensitive plant among vegetables, the chameleon among animals, etc.), this God, I say, must needs be fully able to furnish those he delights to honour with objects suitable to their

---

1 The common spelling until the late seventeenth century. Boyle finds many of God's works stupendous: Christ's resurrection is a "stupendious miracle" (BP 7:101; [Boyle 2006, 3.6.29, p. 291); God controls and regulates "the stupendiously swift motions of the great globes" (CV1, *Works* 11:300); his power is "stupendious" (BP 5:46; Boyle 2006, 3.4.4, p. 234); the world is "a great and stupendious automaton" (BP 7:187v), an "immense and stupendious fabrick" (BP 4:77; Boyle 2006, 2.2.67, p. 161). Others shared Boyle's view. "The Wisdom and goodness of the Maker," said Locke, "plainly appears in all the Parts of this stupendious Fabrick, and all the several degrees and ranks of Creatures in it" (*Essay* 2.9.12), and cf. Willis 1683, 1.5, p. 29.

2 The very beginning of the seventeenth century saw the publication of Gilbert's *De Magnete* (1600), and interest in magnetism remained strong throughout the century, with the loadstone and the compass needle providing both scientific and theological interest. In *High Veneration to God* (1685), Boyle, in the course of a discussion in which he suggests that in other parts of the universe God might have instantiated different laws of nature, offers as an example of this possibility, the fact that "the Loadstone is a Mineral so differing in divers affections, not onely from all other Stones, but from all other bodies, that are not Magnetical, that this Heteroclite Mineral scarce seems to be Originary of this World of ours, but to have come into it, by a remove from some other World or Systeme" ("High Veneration to God," *Works* 10: 173).

improved faculties, and with all that is requisite to the happiness he intends them in their glorified state, and is able to bring this to pass by such amazing contrivances as perhaps will be quite differing from any that the things we have yet seen suggest to us any ideas of.

And sure he, that has in so immense, so curious, and so magnificent a fabric, made such provision for men, who are either desperately wicked or but very imperfectly good, and in a state where they are not to enjoy happiness but by obedience and sufferings to fit themselves for it, may safely be trusted with finding them in heaven employments and delights becoming the felicity he designs them there: as we see that here below, he provides as well for the soaring eagle, as for the creeping caterpillar, (and is able to keep the ocean as fully supplied with rivers, as lakes or ponds are with springs and brooks). And as a state of celestial happiness is so great a blessing, that those things that afford us either greater assurances, or greater foretastes of it, are of the number of the greatest contentments and advantages that short of it we can enjoy, so it is hard for any divine to receive so much of this kind of satisfaction as he who, by skillfully looking into the wonders of nature, has his apprehensions of God's power and manifold wisdom (as an apostle calls it[1]) elevated and enlarged. As when the Queen of Sheba had particularly surveyed the astonishing prudence that Solomon displayed in the ordering of his magnificent court, she transportedly concluded that those servants of his that were allowed the honour and privilege of a constant and immediate attendance on him to be happy enough to deserve a monarch's envy.[2]

---

1 Ephesians 3.10 [RB's note].

2 And when the queen of Sheba had seen all Solomon's wisdom, and the house that he had built, and the meat of his table, and the sitting of his servants, and the attendance of his ministers, and their apparel, and his cupbearers, and his ascent by which he went up unto the house of the LORD; there was no more spirit in her. And she said to the king, It was a true report that I heard in mine own land of thy acts and of thy wisdom. Howbeit I believed not the words, until I came, and mine eyes had seen it: and, behold, the half was not told me: thy wisdom and prosperity exceedeth the fame which I heard. Happy are thy men, happy are these thy servants, which stand continually before thee, and that hear thy wisdom. (1 Kings 10.4-8)

The Second Section: The Practical Goods Resulting from Natural Philosophy and from Theology

I doubt not but you have too good an opinion of your friend, not to think that you may allege in his favour, that the chief thing which makes him prefer physiology to all other kind of knowledge, is that it enables those who are proficients in it to do a great deal of good, both by improving of trades and by promoting of physic itself. And I am too mindful of what I wrote to Pyrophilus[1] to deny, either that it can assist a man to advance physic and trades, or that by so doing, he may highly advantage mankind. And this I, who would not lessen your friends esteem for physics, but only his partiality, willingly acknowledge to be so allowable an endearment of experimental philosophy, that I do not know anything, that to men of a humane, as well as ingenious, disposition, ought more to recommend the study of nature, except the opportunity it affords men to be just and grateful to the author both of nature and of man. I do not then deny that the true naturalist may very much benefit mankind, but I affirm that, if men be not wanting to themselves, the divine may benefit them much more.

It were not perchance either unseasonable or impertinent to tell you on this occasion that he who effectually teaches men to subdue their lusts and passions does as much as the physician contribute to the preservation of their bodies by exempting them from those vices, whose no less usual than destructive effects are wars, and duels, and rapines, and desolations, and the pox,[2] and surfeits, and all the train of other diseases that attend gluttony and drunkenness, idleness and lust, which are not enemies to man's life and health barely upon a physical account, but upon a moral one, as they provoke God to punish them with temporal as well as spiritual judgements, such as plagues,[3] wars, famines, and

1 In some of his writings the name "Pyrophilus" was used by Boyle to refer to his nephew, Richard Jones (1641-1712), son of his sister Katherine. However it also appears in his works as, in effect, a generic name. (See "The Author's Advertisement" to "Usefulness I," *Works* 3:195.)

2 The pox: any of a number of diseases but most usually, especially in derogatory contexts, syphilis.

3 Plague struck in Geneva three years before Boyle's arrival there as a boy. About that time a woman had been arraigned for adultery and it was decided that God had sent the plague to Geneva as a chastisement for her "immorality." It was therefore further decided to put the woman to death, and despite a plea for mercy from her husband (who had initially

other public calamities, that sweep away a great part of mankind, besides those personal afflictions of bodily sickness, and disquiets of conscience, that do both shorten men's lives, and embitter them. Whereas piety having (as the Scripture assures us) promises both of this life, and of that which is to come, those teachers that make men virtuous and religious, by making them temperate, and chaste, and inoffensive, and calm, and contented, do not only procure them great and excellent dispositions to those blessings, both of the right hand and of the left,[1] which God's goodness makes him forward to bestow on those who by grace and virtue are made fit to receive them, but do help them to those qualifications that, by preserving the mind in a calm and cheerful temper, as well as by affording the body all that temperance can confer, do both lengthen their lives and sweeten them. These things, I say, it were not impertinent to insist on, but I will rather choose to represent to you that the benefits which men may receive from the divine surpass those which they receive from the naturalist both in the nobleness of the advantages and in the duration of them.

Be it granted then, that the naturalist may much improve both physic and trades. Yet since these themselves were devised for the service of the body, the one to preserve or restore his health, and the other to furnish it with accommodations or delights, the boasted use of natural philosophy, by its advancing trades and

---

denounced her), the sentence was carried out (Vaucher 1951, 350). The plague struck London in 1665 and the House of Commons felt that Hobbes's atheism (and that of his friend, the Catholic priest, Thomas White) was a probable cause of both the Great Fire and the plague of London, and ordered an investigation of their works (Mintz 1969, 62).

1 In Proverbs 8.11-20 we are urged to

> despise not the chastening of the LORD; neither be weary of his correction: For whom the LORD loveth he correcteth; even as a father the son in whom he delighteth." Moreover, "Happy is the man that findeth wisdom, and the man that getteth understanding. For the merchandise of it is better than the merchandise of silver, and the gain thereof than fine gold. She is more precious than rubies: and all the things thou canst desire are not to be compared unto her. Length of days is in her right hand; and in her left hand riches and honour. Her ways are ways of pleasantness, and all her paths are peace. She is a tree of life to them that lay hold upon her: and happy is every one that retaineth her. The LORD by wisdom has founded the earth; by understanding has he established the heavens. By his knowledge the depths are broken up, and the clouds drop down the dew.

physic, will still be to serve the body, which is but the lodging and instrument of the soul, and which, I presume, your friend, and which I am sure yourself, will be far from thinking the noblest part of man. I know it may be said, nor do I deny it, that divers mechanical arts are highly beneficial, not only to the inventors, but to those places and perhaps those states, where such improvements are found out and cherished.

But though I most willingly grant that this consideration ought to recommend experimental philosophy, as well to states as to private persons, yet many of these improvements do rather transfer than increase mankind's goods, and prejudice one sort of men as much as they advantage another, (as in the case of the eastern spices, of whose trade the Portuguese and Dutch by their later navigations did, by appropriating it to themselves, deprive the Venetians) or else do but increase that which, though very beneficial to the producers, is not really so to mankind in general: of which we have an example in the invention of extracting gold and silver out of the ore, with mercury. For though it has vastly enriched the Spaniards in the West Indies, yet it is not of any solid advantage to the world, no more than the discovery of the Peruvian and other American mines, by which (especially reckoning the multitudes of unhappy men that are made miserable, and destroyed in working them), mankind is not put into a better condition than it was before.

And if the philosopher's stone itself, (supposing there be such a thing) were not an incomparable medicine, but were only capable of transmuting other metals into gold, I should perhaps doubt, whether the discoverer of it would much advantage mankind, there being already gold and silver enough to maintain trade and commerce among men. And for all other purposes, I know not why a plenty of iron, and brass, and quick-silver, which are far more useful metals, should not be more desirable. But not to urge this, we may consider that these advancements of enriching trades do still bring advantages but to the outward man, and those many arts and inventions that aim at the heightening the pleasures of the senses belong but to the body, and even in point of gratifying that are not so requisite and important as many suppose,[1] education, custom, etc., having a greater interest than most imagine in the relish men have even of sensitive pleasures.

1 See examples of this in my Notes about Sensation and Sensible Qualities [RB's note]. For an excellent account of Boyle's views on sensible qualities see Anstey 2000, especially chapters 3 and 4.

And as for physic, not to mind you, that it has been loudly (how justly, I here examine not,) complained of, that the new philosophy has made far greater promises than have yet been performed, I shall only take notice that, since all that physic is wont to pretend to, is to preserve health, or restore it, there are multitudes in the world that have no need of the assistance the naturalist would give the physician, and a healthy man, as such, is already in a better condition than the philosopher can hope to place him in, and is no more advantaged by the naturalist's contribution to physic than a sound man that sleeps in a whole skin is by all the fine tools of a surgeon's case of instruments and the various compositions of his chest.

And as the benefits that may be derived from theology much surpass those that accrue from physics in the nobleness of the subject they relate to, so have they a great advantage in point of duration. For all the service that medicines, and engines, and improvements can do a man, as they relate but to this life, so they determine[1] with it. Physic indeed and chemistry do, the one more faintly, and the other more boldly, pretend sometimes not only to the cure of diseases, but the prolongation of life: but since none will suspect, but that the masters of those parts of knowledge would employ their utmost skill to protract their own lives, those that remember that Solomon and Helmont lived no longer than millions that were strangers to philosophy, and that even Paracelsus himself, for all his boasted arcana, is by Helmont and other chemists confessed to have died some years short of 50,[2] we may

---

1 Terminate.

2 In the early *Usefulness of Experimental Natural Philosophy* (1663), Boyle had noted, with respect to the somewhat premature death of Paracelsus (1493-1541), that

> on the one side I think the Arguments, which *Helmont* and others draw from the Providence of God, for the curableness of all Diseases are not very cogent, and somewhat irreverent (For God being not oblig'd any more to continue Life or Health to sinful Man then to Beasts that never offended Him, we ought humbly to thank Him, if He hath, among his Creatures, dispers'd Remedies for every Disease, but hath no right to accuse Him if He have not); so on the other side, I am not much convinc'd by the grand Argument alleadg'd against *Paracelsus*, and the Chymists, that hold all Diseases to be in their own Nature curable, namely, That they themselves, many of them (no, nor even their very Master) lived not to the Age attain'd by many Strangers to Chymistry.
>
> For this, That many of them ... died young enough, and ... by Sick-

very justly fear, that nature will not be so kind to its greatest votaries, as to give them much more time than other men, for the payment of the last debt all men owe to it. And if a few years respite could by a scrupulous and troublesome use of diet and remedies be obtained, yet that, in comparison of the eternity that is to follow, is not at all considerable. But, whereas within no great number of years (a little sooner, or a little later) all the remedies, and reliefs, and pleasures, and accommodations, that philosophical improvements can afford a man will not keep him from the grave, (which within very few days will make the body of the greatest virtuoso as hideous and as loathsome a carcass as that of any ordinary man), the benefits that may accrue to us by divinity, as they relate chiefly, though not only, to the other world, so they will follow us out of this, and prove then incomparably greater than ever, when they alone shall be capable of being enjoyed. So that philosophy, in the capacity we here consider it, does but as it were provide us some little conveniences for our passage, like some accommodations for a cabin, which outlasts not the voyage; but religion provides us a vast and durable estate or, as the Scripture styles it, an unshaken kingdom,[1] when we are arrived at our journey's end. And therefore the benefits accruing from religion, may well be concluded preferable to their competitors, since they not only reach to the mind of man, but reach beyond the end of time itself, whereas all the variety of inventions that philosophy so much boasts of, as while they were in season they were devised for the service of the body, so they make us busy, and pride ourselves about things that within a short time will not (so much as upon its score) at all concern us.

> ness ... is a much stronger Objection against the Men, then against their Opinion; for it infers indeed plausibly, that they had not such Remedies as they boasted of ... but concludes not that no such Remedies can be prepar'd by any other. (*Works* 3:345-6).

See also the note on Paracelsus in Appendix A "People Mentioned in the Text."

1 See Hebrews 12.25-29.

The third section: The supposed certainty and clearness of physics as opposed to the darkness and uncertainty of theological matters

I expect you should here urge on your friends behalf, that the study of physics has one prerogative (above that of divinity) which, as it is otherwise a great excellency, so does much add to the delightfulness of it. I mean, the certainty and clearness, and the thence resulting satisfactoriness of our knowledge of physical in comparison of any we can have of theological matters, whose being dark and uncertain, the nature of the things themselves, and the numerous controversies of differing sects about them, sufficiently manifest.

But upon this subject, divers things are to be considered.

For first, as to the fundamental and necessary articles of religion, I do not admit the allegation, but take those articles to be both evident, and capable of a moral demonstration. And if there be any articles of religion for which a rational and cogent proof cannot be brought, I shall for that very reason conclude that such articles are not absolutely necessary to be believed, since it seems no way reasonable to imagine, that God having been pleased to send not only his prophets and his apostles, but his only son into the world, to promulgate to mankind the Christian religion, and both to cause it to be consigned to writing, that it may be known, and to alter the course of nature by numerous miracles, that it might be believed, it seems not reasonable, I say, to imagine, that he should not propose those truths, which he in so wonderful and so solemn a manner recommended, with at least so much clearness, as that studious and well-disposed readers may certainly understand such as are necessary for them to believe.[1]

Secondly, though I will not here engage myself in a disquisition of the several kinds or, if you please, degrees, of demonstration (which yet is a subject that I judge far more considerable than cultivated), yet I must tell you, that as a moral certainty

1 This view of Boyle's was a standard one. Defending Protestantism earlier in the century Chillingworth wrote: "nothing is necessary to be believed, but what is plainly revealed. For to say, that when a place of Scripture, by reason of ambiguous termes, lies indifferent between divers senses, whereof one is true, and the other is false, that God obliges men under pain of damnation, not to mistake through error and humane frailty, is to make God a Tyrant, and to say that he requires us certainly to attain that end, for the attaining whereof we have no certain meanes. (Chillingworth 1638, 92).

(such as we may attain about the fundamentals of religion) is enough in many cases for a wise man, and even a philosopher to acquiesce in, so that physical certainty, which is pretended for the truths demonstrated by naturalists, is, even where it is rightfully claimed, but an inferior kind or degree of certainty, as moral certainty also is. For even physical demonstrations can beget but a physical certainty, (that is, a certainty upon supposition that the principles of physics be true,) not a metaphysical certainty, wherein it is absolutely impossible, that the thing believed should be other than true. For instance, all the physical demonstrations of the ancients about the causes of particular phenomena of bodies, suppose, that *ex nihilo nihil fit*,[1] and this may readily be admitted in a physical sense, because according to the course of nature, no body can be produced out of nothing, but speaking universally it may be false, as Christians generally, and even the Cartesian naturalists, asserting the creation of the world, must believe that *de facto* it is.[2]

And so whereas Epicurus does, I remember, prove that a body once dead cannot be made alive again, by reason of the dissipation and dispersion of the atoms it was, when alive, composed of;[3] though all men will allow this assertion to be physically

1 From nothing, nothing comes.

2 Descartes says explicitly that God created the world from nothing as a going concern, complete with "not just the seeds of plants but the plants themselves," etc. (*Principles of Philosophy*, 3.45, AT 8A:100, CSMK 1:256; cf. *Discourse on Method*, Part 5, AT 6:45, CSMK 1:133-4.)

3 Boyle mentions earlier in the *Excellency of Theology* that he read Epicurus's "Letter to Herodotus" in Diogenes Laertius, and may here be thinking of the passage (*Lives*, 2:X.65, p. 597) where Epicurus remarks that "when the whole frame [of the body] is broken up, the soul is scattered." Justin Martyr (c. 100-c. 165) argued that Epicurus, given his materialistic views, was committed to the possibility of resurrection:

> since the atoms remain indestructible, it is not at all impossible, that by coming together again, and receiving the same arrangement and position, they should make a body of like nature to what was formerly produced by them; as if a jeweller should make in mosaic the form of an animal, and the stones should be scattered by time or by the man himself who made them, he having still in his possession the scattered stones, may gather them together again, and having gathered, may dispose them in the same way, and make the same form of an animal. And shall not God be able to collect again the decomposed members of the flesh, and make the same body as was formerly produced by Him? (Chapter 6 of the fragmentary lost work "On the Resurrection.")

demonstrable, yet the contrary may be true, if God's omnipotence intervenes, as all the philosophers that acknowledge the authority of the New Testament, where Lazarus and others are recorded to have been raised from the dead,[1] must believe, that it actually did appear, and even all unprejudiced reasoners must allow it to be possible, there being no contradiction implied in the nature of the thing. But now to affirm, that such things as are indeed contradictories cannot be both true, or, that *factum infectum reddi non potest*,[2] are metaphysical truths, which cannot possibly be other than true, and consequently beget a metaphysical and absolute certainty. And your master Descartes was so sensible of a dependence of physical demonstrations upon metaphysical truths, that he would not allow any certainty not only to them, but even to geometrical demonstrations, till he had evinced, that there is a God, and that he cannot deceive men that make use of their faculties aright.[3]

To which I may add, that even in many things that are looked upon as physical demonstrations, there is really but a moral certainty. For when, for instance, Descartes and other modern philosophers, take upon them to demonstrate, that there are divers comets that are not meteors, because they have a parallax lesser than that of the moon, and are of such a bigness, and some of them move in such a line, etc. it is plain, that divers of these learned men had never the opportunity to observe a comet in their lives, but take these circumstances upon the credit of those astronomers that had such opportunities. And though the inferences, as such, may have a demonstrable certainty, yet the prem-

---

Boyle made the same point in his short work "Some Physico-Theological Considerations About the Possibility of the Resurrection," annexed to "The Reconcileableness of Reason and Religion," *Works* 8:295-313. See also "Forms and Qualities," *Works* 5:353-54.

1 John 11, 12.

2 What is done cannot be undone. It is worth noting here that Boyle considers this to be a truth which "cannot possibly be other than true." He agrees with both Aristotle and Aquinas: not even God can change the past.

3 Following up on the points made in *Meditation IV* concerning truth and error, Descartes points out in *Meditation VI* that we cannot be mistaken if we are careful in our judgements but notes that although "God is not a deceiver ... the pressure of things to be done does not always allow us to stop and make ... a meticulous check; [hence] it must be admitted that in this human life we are often liable to make mistakes about particular things (AT 7:90, CSMK 2:62)."

ises they are drawn from having but an historical one, the presumed physico-mathematical demonstration can produce in a wary mind but a moral certainty, and not the greatest neither of that kind that is possible to be attained, as he will not scruple to acknowledge, that knows by experience how much more difficult it is than most men imagine to make observations about such nice[1] subjects, with the exactness that is requisite for the building of an undoubted theory upon them.

There are I know not how many things in physics, that men presume they believe upon physical and cogent arguments, wherein they really have but a moral assurance. This is a truth heeded by so few that I have been invited to take the more particular notice of them in other papers,[2] written purposely to show the doubtfulness and incompleteness of natural philosophy; of which discourse, since you may command a sight, I shall not scruple to refer you thither for the reasons of my affirming here, that the most even of the modern virtuosi are wont to fancy more of clearness and certainty in their physical theories than a critical examiner will find. However, that you may not look upon this as a put off, rather than a reference, I will here touch upon a couple of subjects which men are wont to believe to be, and which indeed ought to be, the most thoroughly understood: I mean the nature of body in general, and the nature of sensation.

And for the first of these, since we can turn ourselves no way, but we are every where environed and incessantly touched by corporeal substances, one would think that so familiar an object that does so assiduously, and so many ways affect our senses, and for the knowledge of which we need not inquire into the distinct nature of particular bodies, nor the properties of any one of them, should be very perfectly known unto us. And yet the notion of body in general, or *what it is that makes a thing to be a corporeal substance, and discriminates it from all other things*, has been very hotly disputed of, even among the modern philosophers, & *adhuc sub judice lis est.*[3] And though your favourite Descartes, in making the nature of a body to consist in extension every

---

1 "Nice," in this context = "requiring or involving great precision, accuracy, or minuteness (OED)."

2 Boyle makes a similar point in *Reason and Religion, Works* 8:281, a work which was also written in the early 1660s (for dating see *Works* 8:xxi).

3 It is still *sub judice*—still under discussion. For an excellent discussion of this question from a seventeenth-century perspective (concentrating on Leibniz and Newton) see Bennett and Remnant 1978.

way,[1] has a notion of it which it is more easy to find fault with than to substitute a better, yet I fear it will appear to be attended not only with this inconvenience, that God cannot, within the compass of this world, wherein if any body vanish into nothing, the place or space left behind it must have the three dimensions, and so be a true body, *annihilate* the least particle of matter,[2] at least without, at the same instant and place, creating as much, (which agrees very ill with that necessary and continual dependence, which he asserts matter itself to have on God for its very being[3]) but with such other inconveniences, that some friends of yours, otherwise very inclinable to the Cartesian philosophy, know not how to acquiesce in it. And yet I need not tell you, how fundamental a notion the deviser of it asserts it to be.

Neither do I see, how this notion of a corporeal substance will any more than any of the formerly received definitions of it extricate us out of the difficulties of that no less perplexed than famous controversy, *de compositione continui*.[4] And though some ingenious men, who perhaps perceive better than others how intricate it is, have of late endeavoured to show that men need not

---

1 As a plenist Descartes made extension the essential character of material things, and equated the presence of spatial dimensions with the presence of body. Accepting the infinity of the universe, the Cartesian Arnold Geulincx (1624-69) suggested that beyond our portion of the universe lies infinite space, "completely solid, completely dark, [and] harder than any adamant" (Geulincx 1965, 2:493, quoted Ruestow 1973, 82).

2 Locke makes a similar point in the *Essay*, 2:13.21 [*bis*] / 22. Newton pointed out a further problem for the plenist: assuming that there is a single matter of which all material objects are composed, the result is that everything will be equally dense, a point used by Bentley and Clarke in their Boyle Lectures. Newton's compressed but clear argument is in Definition I and in Book III, Proposition VI, Corollaries III and IV of the *Principia* (Newton 1972, 1:39-41, 2:575). For Bentley and Clarke see Bentley 1699, 205-06 and Clarke 1738, 2:531-32.

3 *Meditation III*, AT 7:49, CSMK 2:33.

4 Latin: on the composition of the continuum. Concerning continuity Aristotle noted that it was a mathematical commonplace that between any two points on a line there is a third and hence an infinite number (*Physics*, Aristotle 1984, 200b19), a fact which gives rise to the situation that puzzled many seventeenth thinkers including Boyle: is matter infinitely divisible (in principle), or not? Either possible answer seems to give rise to problems which leave us in intellectual difficulties, and Boyle often makes use of this case to highlight the weakness of our intellects. For a discussion of the issues involved see Leibniz 1672; Russell 1937, chapter 9, "The Labyrinth of the Continuum"; and Mancosu 1996, chapter 5, "Paradoxes of the Infinite."

be solicitous to determine this controversy, it not being rightly proposed by the schoolmen that have started it, and though I perhaps think that natural philosophy may be daily advanced without the decision of it, because there is a multitude of considerable things to be discovered and performed in nature, without so much as dreaming of this controversy, yet still, as I would propose the question, the difficulties, till removed, will spread a thick night over the notion of body in general.

For, either a corporeal and extended substance is (either really or mentally) divisible into parts endowed with extension, and each of these parts is divisible also into other corporeal parts, lesser and lesser, *in infinitum*, or else this subdivision must stop somewhere (for there is no mean between the two members of the distinction) and in either case the opinion pitched upon will be liable to those inconveniences, not to say absurdities, that are rationally urged against it by the maintainers of the opposite, the objections on both sides being so strong, that some of the more candid, even of the modern metaphysicians, after having tired themselves and their readers with arguing pro and con, have confessed the objections on both sides to be insoluble.

But though we do not clearly understand the nature of body in general, yet sure we cannot but be perfectly acquainted with what passes within our selves in reference to the particular bodies we daily see, and hear, and smell, and taste, and touch. But alas, though we know but little, save by the informations of our senses, yet we know very little of the manner by which our senses inform us. And to avoid prolixity, I will at present suppose with you that the ingenious Descartes and his followers have given the fairest account of sensation that is yet extant. Now according to him, a man's body being but a well organized statue, that which is truly called sensation is not performed by the organ, but by the mind, which perceives the motion produced in the organ (for which reason he will not allow brutes to have sense properly so called), so that if you ask a Cartesian, how it comes to pass that the soul of man, which he justly asserts to be an immaterial substance, comes to be wrought upon, and that in such various manners, by those external bodies that are the objects of our senses, he will tell you, that by their impressions on the sensories they variously move the fibres or threads of the nerves wherewith those parts are endowed, and by which the motion is propagated to that little kernel in the brain, call'd by many writers the *conarion*, where these differing motions being perceived by the there residing soul, become sensations, because of the intimate union, and, as it were, permistion[1] (as Descartes himself expresses it) of the soul with the body.

But now, Sir, give me leave to take notice that this union of an incorporeal with a corporeal substance (and that without a medium) is a thing so unexampled in nature, and so difficult to comprehend, that I somewhat question whether the profound secrets of theology, not to say the adorable mystery itself of the incarnation, be more abstruse than this. For how can I conceive that a substance purely immaterial should be united without a physical medium (for in this case there can be none) with the body, which cannot possibly lay hold on it, and which it can pervade and fly away from at pleasure, as Descartes must confess the soul actually does in death? And it is almost as difficult to conceive how any part of the body, without excepting the animal spirits, or the conarion, (for these are as truly corporeal as other parts of the human statue) can make impressions upon a substance perfectly incorporeal, and which is not immediately affected by the motions of any other parts, besides the *genus nervosum*.[2] Nor is it a small difficulty to a mere naturalist (who, as such, does not in physical matters take notice of revelations about angels) to conceive how a finite spirit can either move or, which is much the same thing, regulate and determine the motion of a body.

But that which I would on this occasion invite you to consider is this: that supposing the soul does in the brain perceive the differing motions communicated to the outward senses, yet this, however it may give some account of sensation in general, will not at all show us a satisfactory reason of particular and distinct sensations. For if I demand why for instance when I look upon a bell that is ringing, such a motion or impression in the conarion produces in the mind that peculiar sort of perception, seeing, and not hearing, and another motion, though coming from the same bell at the same time, produces that quite differing sort of perception that we call sound, but not vision, what can be answered,

1 A thorough mixing or intermingling. "The mind is united to the body," Descartes wrote in *Meditation VI*, "and is, as it were, intermingled [*permixtione*] with it" (AT 7:81). Princess Elizabeth was one of Descartes' most resolute questioners on this issue. See further Brown 2006.

2 The group of bodily organs supplied by nerves: muscles, tendons and other organs. The standard seventeenth-century view was that the nerves were the conduits for the "animal spirits," though Boyle (without dissenting from the received view) noted "that prying Anatomists have not been able in dissected Nerves to discern so much as the channels through which they pass" (*Works* 10:265).

but that it was the good pleasure of the author of human nature to have it so? And if the question be asked about the differing objects of any one particular sense, as, why the great plenty of unperturbed light that is reflected from snow, milk, etc, does produce a sensation of whiteness, rather than redness or yellowness? Or why the smell of castor, or asafoetida,[1] produces in most persons that which they call a stink, rather than a perfume? (Especially since we know some hysterical women that think it not only a wholesome, but a pleasing smell.) And if also you further ask, why melody and sweet things do generally delight us, and discords and bitter things do generally displease us, nay, why a little more than enough of some objects that produce pleasure will produce pain (as may be exemplified in a cold hand, as it happens to be held out at a just, or at too near a distance, from the fire)? If, I say, these, and a thousand other questions of the like kind, be asked, the answer will be but the general one, that is already given: that such is the nature of man. For to say that moderate motions are agreeable to the nature of the sensory they are excited in, but violent and disorderly ones (as jarring sounds, and scorching heat) do put it into too violent a motion for its texture, will by no means satisfy. For, besides that this answer gives no account of the variety of sensations of the same kind, as of differing colours, tastes, etc., but reaches only to pleasure and pain, even as to these, it will reach but a very little way, unless the givers of it can show how an immaterial substance should be more harmed by the brisker motion of a body than by the more languid.

And as you and your friend think you may justly smile at the Aristotelians for imagining that they have given a tolerable account of the qualities of bodies when they have told us that they spring from certain substantial forms, though when they are asked particular questions about these incomprehensible forms, they do in effect but tell us in general, that they have such and such faculties, or effects, because nature, or the author of nature, endowed them therewith, so I hope you will give me leave to think, that it may keep us from boasting of the clearness and certainty of our knowledge about the operations of sensible objects. For, as the Aristotelians cannot particularly show how their qualities are produced, so we cannot particularly explicate how they

---

1 Castor is an oily substance obtained from beavers. Asafoetida is a resinous gum, with an unpleasant ammoniac smell. Both were used in medicines in Boyle's time.

are perceived; the principal thing that we can say, being in substance this: that our sensations depend upon such a union or permistion of the soul and body as we can give no example of in all nature, nor no more distinct account of, than that it pleased God so to couple them together.

But I beg your pardon for having detained you so long upon one subject, though perhaps it will not prove time misspent if it has made you take notice that, in spite of the clearness and certainty for which your friend so much prefers physics before theology, we are yet to seek (I say yet, because I know not what time may hereafter discover) both for the definition of a corporeal substance, and a satisfactory account of the manner of sensation. Without the true notion of a body we cannot understand that object of physics in general, and without knowing the nature of sensation, we cannot know that from whence we derive almost all that we know of any body in particular.

If after all this your friend shall say that Descartes's account of body and other things in physics being the best that men can give, if they be not satisfactory it must be imputed to human nature not to the Cartesian doctrine, I shall not stay to dispute how far the allegation is true, especially since, though it be admitted, it will not prejudice my discourse. For whatsoever the cause of the imperfection of our knowledge about physical matters be, that there is an imperfection in that knowledge is manifest, and that ought to be enough to keep us from being puffed up by such an imperfect knowledge, and from undervaluing upon its account the study of those mysteries of divinity which, by reason of the nobleness and remoteness of the objects, may much better than the nature of corporeal things (which we see, and feel, and continually converse with) have their obscurity attributed to the weakness of our human understandings. And if it be a necessary imperfection of human nature that, while we remain in this mortal condition the soul, being confined to the dark prison of the body,[1] is capable (as even Aristotle somewhere confesses) of

---

1 "The Christian virtuoso," said Boyle, "considers the rational soul [as] a kind of imprisoned angel" ("Christian Virtuoso II," *Works* 12:504), and makes a similar point in the manuscripts: "I freely confess that I much applaud those elevated souls that not content with the speculation of Bodys, & things corporeal, which are the subjects of the curiosity & studies of other Philosophers; generously aspire to the knowledge & conversation of incorporeal spirits; & <of> that angelical Community (if I may so call it) that consists of Rational & Immortal beings not clog'd with visible Bodys" (BP 1:66v; Boyle 2006, 3.5.20, p. 256). In the frag-

but a dim knowledge, so much the greater value we ought to have for Christian religion, since by its means (and by no other without it) we may attain a condition wherein, as our nature will otherwise be highly blessed and advanced, so our faculties will be elevated and enlarged, and probably made thereby capable of attaining degrees and kinds of knowledge, to which we are here but strangers. In favour of which I will not urge the received opinion of divines, that before the fall (which yet is a less noble condition than is reserved for us in heaven) Adam's knowledge was such that he was able at first sight of them to give each of the beasts a name expressive of its nature,[1] because that in spite of some skill (which my curiosity for divinity, not philosophy, gave me) in the holy tongue, I could never find, that the Hebrew names of animals, mentioned in the beginning of Genesis, argued a (much) clearer insight into their natures, than did the names of the same or some other animals in Greek or other languages, wherefore, (as I said) I will not urge Adam's knowledge in paradise for that of the saints in heaven, though the notice he took of Eve at his first seeing of her, (if it were not conveyed to him by secret revelation) may be far more probably urged, than his naming of the beasts: but I will rather mind you, that the protomartyr's sight was strengthened so, as to see the heavens opened and Jesus standing at the right hand of God.[2] And when the prophet had prayed that his servant's eyes might be opened he immediately saw the mountain, where they were, all covered with chariots and horsemen, which, though mentioned to be of fire, were altogether invisible to him before.[3] To which, as a higher argument, I shall only add a couple of passages of Scripture which seem to allow us even vast expectations as to the knowledge our glorified nature may be advanced to. The one is that which St. Paul says to the Corinthians, "For now we see through a glass darkly, but then face to face: now I know in part, but then

mentary "A Dialogue between the Soul and Body," Boyle's contemporary Andrew Marvell agreed: the soul is "hung up, as 'twere, in chains / Of nerves, and arteries, and veins," but Marvell nicely allows the body a similar plaint: "O who shall me deliver whole / From bonds of this tyrannic soul?" (Marvell 1681, 13.)

1 That Adam gave "each of the beasts a name expressive of its nature" was generally accepted in the seventeenth century, but the claim seems to go beyond the textual remark at Genesis 2.19-20 that "whatsoever Adam called every living creature, that was the name thereof."

2 Acts 7.56 [RB's note].

3 2 Kings 6.17 [RB's note].

shall I know even as also I am known."[1] And the other, where Christ's favourite disciple tells believers, "Beloved, now we are the sons of God, and it does not yet appear what we shall be, but we know, that when he shall appear, we shall be like him: for we shall see him as he is."[2]

What has hitherto been discoursed contains the first consideration that I told you might be proposed about the certainty ascribed to the knowledge we are said to have of natural things, but this is not all I have to represent to you on this subject. For I consider further that it is not only by the certainty we have of them that the knowledge of things is endeared to us, but also by the worthiness of the object, the number of those that are unacquainted with it, the remoteness of it from common apprehensions, the difficulty of acquiring it without peculiar advantages, the usefulness of it when attained, and other particulars which it is not here necessary to enumerate.

I presume you doubt not but your friend does very much prefer the knowledge he has of the mysteries of nature (at many of which we have as yet but ingenious conjectures) to the knowledge of one that understands the elements of arithmetic, though he be demonstratively sure of the truth of most of his rules and operations. And questionless Copernicus received a much higher satisfaction in his notion about the stability of the sun and the motion of the earth, though it were not so clear but that Tycho, Ricciolus, and other eminent astronomers have rejected it, than in the knowledge of divers of the theorems about the sphere that have been demonstrated by Euclid, Theodosius, and other geometricians.[3] Our discovering that some comets are not, as the schools would have them, sublunary meteors, but celestial bodies, and the conjectural theory, which is all that hitherto we have been able to attain of them, do much better please both your friend, and you, and me, than the more certain knowledge we have of the time of the rising and setting of the fixed stars. And

---

1 1 Corinthians 13.12 [RB's note].

2 1 John 3.2 [RB's note].

3 Classically, spherical geometry was considered a branch of astronomy, so Boyle's contrast here between the heliocentric hypothesis of Copernicus and "the theorems about the sphere" would have seemed a natural one. (The Pythagoreans had made a fourfold distinction between the study of quantity [arithmetic], of the relation between quantities [music], of magnitude at rest [geometry], and magnitude inherently moving [spherics or astronomy]).

the estimates we can make, by the help of parallaxes of the heights of those comets, and of some of the planets, though they are uncertain enough (as may appear by the vastly different distances that are assigned to those bodies by eminent astronomers), yet these uncertain measures of such elevated and celestial lights do far more please us than that we can, by the help of a geometrical quadrant or some such instrument, take with far greater certainty the height of a tower or a steeple. And so a mathematician, when he probably conjectures at the compass of the terrestrial globe and divides, though but inaccurately, its surface, first, into proportions of sea and land, and then into regions of such extents and bounds and, in a word, skillfully plays the cosmographer, thinks himself much more nobly and pleasantly employed than when, being reduced to play the surveyor, he does with far more certainty measure how many acres a field contains and set out with what hedges and ditches it is bounded.

Now, that the knowledge of God and of those mysteries of theology that are ignored by far the greatest part of mankind, has more sublime and excellent objects, and is unattained to by much the greatest part even of learned men, and nevertheless is of invaluable importance and of no less advantage towards the purifying and improving us here, and the making us perfect and happy hereafter, the past discourse has very much miscarried if it has not evinced. Wherefore, as to be admitted into the privy-council of some great monarch (and thereby be enabled to give a probable guess at those thoughts and designs of his that govern kingdoms and make the fates of nations) is judged preferable to that clearer knowledge that a notary can have of the dying thoughts and intentions of an ordinary person whose will he makes; and as the knowledge of a skilful physician, whose art is yet conjectural, is preferable to that of a cutler that makes his dissecting knives, though this man can more certainly perform what he designs in his own profession than the physician can in his; and (in fine) as the skill of a jeweler, that is conversant about diamonds, rubies, sapphires, and some other sorts of small stones, which being for the most part brought us out of the Indies, we must take many things about them upon report, is, because of the nobleness of the object, preferred to that of a mason that deals in whole quarries of common stones, and may be sure upon his own experience of divers things concerning them, which as to jewels we are allowed to know but upon tradition; so a more dim and imperfect knowledge of God and the mysteries of religion may be more desirable, and upon that account more delightful, than a clearer knowledge of those inferior truths that physics is wont to teach.

I must now mention one particular more which may well be added to those that peculiarly endear physics to the divine that is studious of them. For, as he contemplates the works of nature not barely for themselves, but to be the better qualified and excited to admire and praise the Author of nature, so his contemplations are delightful to him, not barely as they afford a pleasing exercise to his reason, but as they procure him a more welcome approbation from his conscience—these distinct satisfactions being not at all inconsistent. And questionless, though Esau did at length miss of his aim, yet, while he was hunting venison for the good old patriarch that desired it of him, besides the pleasure he was used to take in pursuing the deer he chased, he took a great one in considering, that now he hunted to please his father, and in order to obtain of him an inestimable blessing.[1] So, when David employed his skilful hand and voice in praising God with vocal and instrumental music, he received in one act a double satisfaction, by exercising his skill and his devotion, and was no less pleased with those melodious sounds, as they were hymns, than as they were songs. And this example prompts me to add, that as the devout student of nature we were speaking of does intentionally refer the knowledge he seeks of the creatures to the glory of the creator, so in his discoveries, that which most contents him is that the wonders he observes in nature heighten that admiration he would fain raise to a less disproportion to the wisdom of God, and furnish him with a nobler holocaust[2] for those sacrifices of praise he is justly ambitious to offer up to the Deity. And as there is no doubt to be made but that when David invented (as the Scripture intimates that he did) new instruments of music,[3] there was nothing in that invention that pleased him so much, as that they could assist him to praise God the more melodiously. So the pious student of nature finds nothing more welcome in the discoveries he makes of its wonders than the rises and helps they may afford him, the more worthily to celebrate and glorify the divine attributes adumbrated[4] in the creatures. And as a huntsman

---

1 Genesis 27 [RB's note]. The first edition had "37."

2 Originally, a wholly-consumed burnt offering to a god. By extension, and in Boyle's usage, simply an offering to the Deity.

3 Amos 6.5 [RB's note]. See also: 2 Chronicles 7.6, "And the priests waited on their offices: the Levites also with instruments of music of the Lord, which David the king had made to praise the Lord."

4 Shown faintly.

or a fowler, if he meets with some strange bird or beast, or other natural rarity, thinks himself much the more fortunate if it happen to be near the court where he may have the king to present it to than if he were to keep it but for himself or some of his companions, so our devout naturalist has his discoveries of nature's wonders endeared to him, by having the Deity to present them to, in the veneration they excite in the finder, and which they enable him to engage others to join in.

THE FOURTH SECTION: THE NATURAL PHILOSOPHER'S UNJUSTIFIED PRIDE OF ACHIEVEMENT

But I confess Sir, I much fear that that which makes your friend have such detracting thoughts of theology is a certain secret pride, grounded upon a conceit that the attainments of natural philosophers are of so noble a kind, and argue so transcendent an excellency of parts in the attainer, that he may justly undervalue all other learning without excepting theology itself.

You will not, I suppose, expect that a person who has written so much in praise of physics, and laboured so much for a little skill in it, should now here endeavour to depreciate that so useful part of philosophy. But I do not conceive that it will be at all injurious to it to prefer the knowledge of supernatural to that of mere natural things, and to think that the truths which God indiscriminately exposes to the whole race of mankind, to the bad as well as to the good, are inferior to those mysterious ones whose disclosure he reckons among his peculiar favours, and whose contemplation employs the curiosity and, in some points, exacts the wonder of the very angels.[1] That I may therefore repress a little the overweening opinion your friend has of his physical attainments, give me leave to represent a few particulars conducive to that purpose.

And first, as for the nobleness of the truths taught by theology and physics, those of the former sort have manifestly the advantage, being not only conversant about far nobler objects, but discovering things that human reason of itself can by no means reach unto, as has been sufficiently declared in the foregoing part of this letter.

Next, we may consider, that whatever may be said to excuse pride (if there were any) in Moscus the Phoenician, who is affirmed to have first invented the atomical hypothesis, and in

1 See 1 Peter 1.12.

Democritus and Leucippus (for Epicurus scarce deserves to be named with them), that highly advanced that philosophy, and in Monsieur Descartes, who either improved or at least much innovated the corpuscularian hypothesis; whatever (I say) may be alleged on the behalf of these men's pride, I see no great reason why it should be allowed in such as your friend who, though ingenious men, are neither inventors, nor eminent promoters of the philosophy they would be admired for, but content themselves to learn what others have taught, or at least to make some little further application of the principles that others have established and the discoveries they have made. And whereas your friend is not a little proud of being able to confute several errors of Aristotle and the ancients, it were not amiss if he considered that many of the chief truths that overthrow those errors were the productions of time and chance,[1] and not of his daring ratiocinations. For there needs no great wit to disprove those that maintain the uninhabitableness of the torrid Zone or deny the antipodes, since navigators have found many parts of the former well peopled, and sailing round the earth have found men living in countries diametrically opposite to ours. Nor will it warrant a man's pride that he believes not the moon to be the only planet that shines with a borrowed light, or the galaxy to be a meteor, since that now the telescope shows us that Venus has its full and wane like the moon,[2] and that the milky way is made up of a vast multitude of little stars inconspicuous to the naked eye. And indeed of those other discoveries that overthrow the astronomy of the ancients and much of their philosophy about the celestial

---

1 Ecclesiastes 9.11: "I returned, and saw under the sun, that the race is not to the swift, nor the battle to the strong, neither yet bread to the wise, nor yet riches to men of understanding, nor yet favour to men of skill; but time and chance happeneth to them all."

2 That Venus waxes and wanes like the moon is not observable to the naked eye. This apparent lack of phases was one of the pieces of empirical evidence against the Copernican view that the earth and other planets orbited the sun, for such phases should occur if the sun and not the earth is the centre of the solar system. Despite this and other conflicting empirical evidence Copernicus (and even earlier, Aristarchus [310-250 BCE]) opted for a heliocentric cosmos, prompting Galileo to remark, "I cannot find any bounds for my admiration, how that reason was able in Aristarchus and Copernicus, to commit such a rape on their senses as in despite thereof to make herself mistress of their credulity" (Galileo 1967, III; this passage translated by E.A. Burtt, quoted in Kemp Smith 1952, 220).

bodies, few or none have any cause to boast but the excellent Galileo, who pretends to have been the inventor of the telescope: for that instrument once discovered, to be able to reject the septenary number of the planets[1] by the detection of the four satellites of Jupiter, or talk of the mountains and valleys in the moon, requires not much more excellency in your friend than it would to descry in a ship, where the naked eye could discern but the body of the vessel, (to descry, I say) by the help of a prospective glass, the masts, and sails, and deck, and perceive a boat towed at her stern. Though indeed Galileo himself had no great cause to boast of the invention, though we are much obliged to him for the improvement of the telescope, since no less a master of dioptrics than Descartes does acknowledge with other writers that perspective-glasses were not first found out by mathematicians or philosophers, but casually by one Metius, a Dutch spectacle-maker. On which occasion I shall mind you, that to hide pride from man, divers others of the chief discoveries that have been made in physics have been the productions, not of philosophy, but chance, by which gunpowder, glass, and, for ought we know, the verticity[2] of the load-stone, (to which we owe both the Indies[3]) came to be found in these later ages, as (more recently) the milky vessels of the mesentery, the new receptacles of the chyle, and that other sort of vessels which most men call the lymph-ducts, were lighted on but by chance, according to the ingenious confession of the discoverers themselves.[4]

---

1 The "septenary number of the planets" refers to the view that there were seven planets. Traditionally, the seven heavenly bodies treated as planets were the sun, the moon, Mercury, Venus, Mars, Jupiter, and Saturn. The discovery by Galileo of the four moons, now known as the Galilean moons (announced in *Siderius Nuncius*, 1610), Io, Europa, Callisto, and Ganymede (so named by Marius, following a suggestion of Kepler's), showed that there were additional extraterrestrial bodies. Galileo referred to the moons as Medicean, and gave them numbers rather than names.

2 Tendency to turn towards a vertex or pole.

3 The compass was being used in navigation in China in the eleventh century; it was developed in the west in Amalfi, in what is now Italy, about 1300.

4 As noted in the introductory section, "Boyle's Life and Works" (p. 27), the "receptacles of the chyle" were discovered by Jean Pecquet. The "milky vessels" are the vessels that carry the chyle (lymph given a milky look from the absorption of emulsified fats) from the small intestine to the thoracic, or left lymph, duct. A mesentery is a fold of tissue that attaches organs to the body wall, particularly that which anchors the small intestine to the back of the abdominal wall, and through which the lymph passes.

We may farther consider that those very things which are justly alleged in the praise of the corpuscularian philosophy itself ought to lessen the pride of those that but make use of it. For that hypothesis, supposing the whole universe (the soul of man excepted) to be but a great automaton, or self-moving engine, wherein all things are performed by the bare motion (or rest), the size, the shape, and the situation or texture of the parts of the universal matter it consists of, all the phenomena result from those few principles, single or combined, (as the several tunes or chimes that are rung on five bells), and these fertile principles being already established by the inventors and promoters of the particularian hypothesis, all that such persons as your friend are wont farther to do, is but to investigate or guess by what kind of motions the three or four other principles are varied. So that the world being but, as it were, a great piece of clock-work, the naturalist as such is but a mechanic, however the parts of the engine he considers be some of them much larger, and others much minuter, than those of clocks or watches. And for an ordinary naturalist to despise those that study the mysteries of religion as much inferior to physical truths, is no less unreasonable than it were for a watch-maker, because he understands his own trade, to despise privy-counselors who are acquainted with the secrets of monarchs and mysteries of state, or than it were for a ship-carpenter, because he understands more of the fabric of the vessel, to despise the admiral that is acquainted with the secret designs of the prince and employed about his most important affairs.

That great restorer of physics, the illustrious Verulam,[1] who has traced out a most useful way to make discoveries in the intellectual globe, as he calls it, confesses that his work was (to speak in his own terms) *partus temporis potius quám ingenii*.[2] And though I am not of his opinion where he says, in another place, that his way of philosophizing does *exaequare ingenia*,[3] yet I am apt to think that the fertile principles of the mechanical philosophy being once settled, the methods of inquiring and experimenting being found out, and the physico-mechanical instruments of

1 Francis Bacon, Baron Verulam.

2 Latin: "a child of time rather than of wit" (Francis Bacon, "Epistle Dedicatory" to the *Instauratio Magna* [1620]).

3 Latin: "equalize the talents," or "level the wits." In the *New Organon*, Book I, Aphorism lxi, Bacon says, "the course I propose for the discovery of sciences is such as leaves but little to the acuteness and strength of wits, but places all wits and understandings nearly on a level."

working on nature's and art's productions being happily invented, the making of several lesser improvements, especially by rectifying some almost obvious or supine[1] errors of the schools, by the assistance of such facilitating helps, may fall to the lot of persons not endowed with any extraordinary sagacity or acuteness of parts.

And though the investigation and clear establishment of the true principles of philosophy, and the devising the instruments of knowledge, be things that may be allowed to be the proper work of sublimer wits, yet, if a man be furnished with such assistances, it is not every discourse that he makes, or thing which he does by the help of them, that is difficult enough to raise him to that illustrious rank. And indeed, divers of the vulgar errors, as well as of scholars as other men, being mainly grounded upon the mere and often mistaken authority of Aristotle, and perhaps some frivolous reasons of his scholastic interpreters or such precarious and ungrounded things, that to ruin them does oftentimes require more of boldness than skill. It may perhaps be said of your friend, in relation to his philosophical successes against such vulgar errors as I am speaking of, what a Roman said of Alexander's triumph over the effeminate Asiatics, *quod nihil aliud quam bene ausus sit vana contemnere.*[2] And in some cases it happens that, when once a grand truth or a happy way of experimenting has been found, divers phenomena of nature that had been left unexplained, or were left mis-explained by the schools did, in my opinion, require a far less straining exercise of the mind to unriddle and explain them, than must have been requisite to dispel the darkness that attended divers theological truths that are now cleared up, and perhaps than I have myself now and then employed in some of those attempts to illustrate theological matters that you may have met in some papers that I have presumed to write on such subjects. And it will perhaps be said that the improvements that such virtuosi as your friend are wont to make of the fertile theorems and hints that have been presented them by the founders or prime benefactors of true natural philosophy, are so poor and slender, and do so much more often proceed from industry and chance than they argue a transcen-

1 Lazy or indolent.

2 Livy (*Ab urbe condita* [*The history of Rome*] 9.17) is contrasting Alexander's bloodless victory over Darius, where he needed to do "nothing more daring than to show a just contempt for [Darius'] empty show [of power]," with what would have happened had he taken on someone *really* formidable, such as the Romans.

dent sagacity or a sublimity of reason that, though such persons may have cause enough to be delighted with what they have done, yet they have none to be proud of it. Their performances may deserve our thanks and perhaps some of our praise, but reach not so high as to merit our admiration, which is to be reserved for those that have been either framers, or grand promoters, of true and comprehensive hypotheses, or else the authors of other noble and useful discoveries, in many ways applicable.

It will not perhaps be improper to add on this occasion that, as our knowledge is not very deep, not reaching with any certainty to the bottom of things, nor penetrating to their intimate or innermost natures, so its extent is not very large, not being able to give us with any clearness and particularity an account of the celestial and deeply subterranean parts of the world, of which all the others make but a very small (not to say contemptible) portion.[1]

For, as to the very globe that we inhabit, not to mention how many plants, animals, and minerals we are as yet wholly ignorant of, and how many others we are but slenderly acquainted with, I consider, that the objects about which our experiments and inquiries are conversant do all belong to the superficial parts of the terrestrial globe, of which the earth, known to us, seems to be but as it were the crust or scurf. But what the internal part of this globe is made up of is no less disputable than of what substance the remotest stars we can descry consist. For even among the modern philosophers some think the internal portion of the earth to be pure and elementary earth which, say they, must be found there, or no where. Others imagine it to be fiery and the receptacle either of natural or hellish flames. Others will have the body of the terrestrial globe to be a great and solid magnet. And the Cartesians on the other side (though they all admit store of subterranean loadstones) teach that the same globe was once a fixed star and that, though it have since degenerated into a planet, yet the internal part of it is still of the same nature that it was before, the change it has received proceeding only from having had its

1 Such pessimism was common. Writing about the same time, Locke remarked that our "narrow weake facultys [can] reach noe farther then the observation and memory of some few effects produced by visible and externall causes but in a way utterly out of reach of [our] apprehension" (*De arte medica*, Locke 1669, 82), a point repeated twenty years later in the *Essay Concerning Humane Understanding* (4.3.16). (Thanks to Peter Anstey for drawing *De arte medica* to my attention.)

outward parts quite covered over with thick spots (like those to be often observed about the sun), by whose condensation the firm earth we inhabit was formed. And the mischief is, that each of these jarring opinions is almost as difficult to be demonstratively proved false as true. For, whereas to the centre of the earth there is, according to the most modest account of our late cosmographers, above three thousand and five hundred miles,[1] my inquiries among navigators and miners have not yet satisfied me that men's curiosity has actually reached above one mile or two at most downwards (and that not in above three or four places) either into the earth or into the sea. So that as yet our experience has scarce grated any thing deep upon the husk (if I may so speak) without at all reaching the kernel of the terraqueous globe.

And alas! what is this globe of ours, of which itself we know so little, in comparison of those vast and luminous globes that we call the fixed stars, of which we know much less? For though former astronomers have been pleased to give us, with a seeming accurateness, their distances and bignesses, as if they had had certain ways of measuring them, yet later and better mathematicians will (I know) allow me to doubt of what those have delivered. For since it is confessed that we can observe no parallax in the fixed stars (nor perhaps in the highest planets) men must be yet to seek for a method to measure the distance of those bodies. And not only the Copernicans make it to be I know not how many hundred thousands of miles greater than the Ptolemeans, and very much greater than even Tycho, but Ricciolus himself, though a great anti-Copernican, makes the distance of the fixed stars vastly greater than not only Tycho, but (if I mis-remember not) than some of the Copernicans themselves. Nor do I wonder at these so great discrepancies (though some amount perhaps to some millions of miles), when I consider that astronomers do not measure the distance of the fixed stars by their instruments but accommodate it to their particular hypotheses. And by this uncertainty of the remoteness of the fixed stars you will easily gather that we are not very sure of their bulk, no not so much as in reference to one another, since it remains doubtful whether the differing sizes they appear to us to be of, proceed from a real

1 As Boyle says, this is a "modest" estimate. In the *Excellency ... of the Mechanical Hypothesis* Boyle remarks that "the terraqueous globe is ... seven or eight thousand miles in diameter," [235] and his upper figure there is a more accurate estimate (Earth's diameter is approximately 12,800 km.). His main point, about our lack of certain and detailed knowledge concerning the centre, still holds.

inequality of bulk or only from an inequality of distance, or partly from one of those causes and partly from the other.

But it is not my design to take notice of those things which the famous disputes among the modern astronomers manifest to be dubious. For I consider that there are divers things relating to the stars, which are so remote from our knowledge, that the causes of them are not so much as disputed of, or inquired into, such as may be among others, why the number of the stars is neither greater nor lesser than it is? Why so many of those celestial lights are so placed as not to be visible to our naked eyes, nor even when they are helped by ordinary telescopes? (which extraordinary good ones have assured me of); why among the familiarly visible stars, there are so many in some parts of the sky, and so few in others? Why their sizes are so differing, and yet not more differing? Why they are not more orderly placed, so as to make up constellations of regular or handsome figures (of which the triangle is, perhaps, the single example) but seem to be scattered in the sky as it were by chance, and have as confused configurations as the drops that fall upon one's hat in a shower of rain? To which divers other questions might be added, as about the stars, so about the interstellar part of heaven, which several of the modern Epicureans would have to be empty, save where the beams of light (and perhaps some other celestial effluvia) pass through it, and the Cartesians on the contrary think to be full of an ethereal matter, which some, that are otherwise favourers of their philosophy, confess they are reduced to take up but as an hypothesis. So that our knowledge is much short of what many think, not only if it be considered intensively, but extensively (as a schoolman would express it). For there being so great a disproportion between the heavens and the earth, that some moderns think the earth to be little better than a point in comparison even of the orb of the sun, and the Cartesians, with other Copernicans, think the great orb itself (which is equal to what the Ptolemeans call'd the sun's orb) to be but a point in respect of the firmament. And all our astronomers agree that at least the earth is but a physical point in comparison of the starry heaven.

Of how little extent must our knowledge be which leaves us ignorant of so many things, touching the vast bodies that are above us, and penetrates so little a way even into the earth that is beneath us, that it seems confined to but a small share of the superficial part of a physical point! Of which consideration the natural result will be, that though what we call our knowledge may be allowed to pass for a high gratification to our minds, it ought not to puff them up, and what we know of the system, and the nature of things corporeal, is not so perfect and satisfactory as to justify our despising the discoveries of spiritual things.

One of the former parts of this letter may furnish me with one thing more to evince the excellencies and prerogatives of the knowledge of the mysteries of religion, and that one thing is such that I hope I shall need to add nothing more, because it is not possible to add any thing higher. And that is, the preeminence above other knowledge, adjudged to that of divine truths by a judge above all exception and above all comparison, namely, by God himself.

This having been but lately shown, I shall not now repeat it, but rather apply what has been there evinced by representing, that if he who determines in favour of divine truths were such a one as was less acquainted than our overweening naturalists with the secrets of their idolized physics, or if he were, though an intelligent, yet (like an angel) a bare *contemplator* of what we call the works of nature, without having any interest in their productions, your friends not acquiescing in his estimate of things might have, though not a fair excuse, yet a stronger temptation.

But when he by whose direction we prefer the higher truths revealed in the Scripture before those which reason alone teaches us concerning those comparatively mean subjects—corporeal things—is the same God that not only understands the whole universe and all its parts far more perfectly than a watch-maker can understand one of his own watches (in which he can given an account only of the contrivance, and not of the cause of the spring, nor the nature of the gold, steel, and other bodies his watch consists of) but did make both this great automaton, the world, and man in it, we have no colour to imagine that he should either be ignorant of, or injuriously disparage, his own workmanship, or impose upon his favourite creature, man, in directing him what sort of knowledge he ought most to covet and prize. So that since it is he who framed the world and all those things in it we most admire that would have us prefer the knowledge he has vouchsafed us in his word, before that which he has allowed us of his works, sure it is very unreasonable and unkind to make the excellencies of the workmanship a disparagement to the author, and the effects of his wisdom a motive against acquiescing in the decisions of his judgement, as if, because he is to be admired for his visible productions, he were not to be believed, when he tells us, that there are discoveries that contain truths more valuable than those which relate but to the objects, that he has exposed to all men's eyes.

The fifth section: The value of the fame that scientific attainments bring

I doubt not but that I should be guilty of a most important omission if I should here forget to consider one thing which I fear has a main stroke in the partiality your friend expresses in his preference of physics to theology And that is, that he supposes he shall by the former acquire a fame, both more certain and more durable, than can be hoped for from the latter.

And I acknowledge, not only with readiness, but with somewhat of gratulation[1] of the felicity of this age, that there is scarce any sort of knowledge more in request than that which natural philosophy pretends to teach, and that among the awakened and inquisitive part of mankind as much reputation and esteem may be gained by an insight into the secrets of nature as by being entrusted with those of princes, or dignified with the most splendid marks of their favour.

But though I readily confess thus much, and though perhaps I may be thought to have had, I know not by what fate, as great a share of that perfumed smoke, applause, as (at least) some of those, which among the writers that are now alive your friend seems most to envy for it, yet I shall not scruple to tell you, partly from observation of what has happened to others, and partly too upon some little experience of my own, that neither is it so easy as your friend seems to believe it, to get by the study of nature a sure and lasting reputation, neither ought the expectation of it, in reason, make men undervalue the study of divinity. Nor would it here avail to object (by way of prevention) that the difficulties and impediments of acquiring and securing reputation lie as well in the way of divines as philosophers, since this objection has been already considered at the beginning of this second part of our present tract. Besides that, the progress of our discourse will show that the naturalist, aspiring to fame, is liable to some inconveniences which are either not at all, or not near equally, incident to[2] the divine. Wherefore without staying to take any further notice of this preventive allegation I shall proceed to make good the first part of the assertion that preceded it. Which that I may the more fully do, give me leave (after having premised, that a man must either be a writer, or forbear to print what he knows) to propose to you the following considerations.

---

1 A feeling of pleasure or joy.

2 Liable to befall or occur to.

And first, if your Physeophilus should think to secure a great reputation by forbearing to couch any of his thoughts or experiments in writing, he may thereby find himself not a little mistaken. For if once he have gained a repute (upon what account soever) of knowing some things that may be useful to others, or of which studious men are wont to be very desirous, he will not avoid the visits and questions of the curious. Or, if he should affect a solitude, and be content to hide himself, that he may hide the things he knows, yet he will not escape the solicitations that will be made him by letters. And if these ways of tempting him to disclose himself prevail not at all with him to do so, he will provoke the persons that have employed them, who finding themselves disobliged by being defeated of their desires, if not also their expectations, will for the most part endeavour to revenge themselves on him, by giving him the character of an uncourteous and ill-natured person and will endeavour, perhaps successfully enough, to decry his parts, by suggesting that his affected concealments proceed but from a conscientiousness[1] that the things he is presumed to possess, are but such as, if they should begin to be known, would cease to be valued.

You will say, perchance, that so much reservedness is a fault, nor shall I dispute it with you, whether it be or not. But if he be open and communicative in discourse to those strangers that come to pump him, such is the disingenious temper of too, too many, that he will be in great danger of having his notions or experiments arrogated by those to whom he imparts them, or at least by others, to whom those may (though perchance designlessly) happen to discourse of them. And then, if either Physeophilus or any of his friends that know him to be author of what is thus usurped, should mention him as such, the usurpers and their friends would presently become his enemies and, to secure their own reputation, will be solicitous to lessen and blemish his. And if you should now tell me that your friend might here take a middle way, as that which in most cases is thought to be the best, by discoursing at such a rate of his discoveries as may somewhat gratify those that have a curiosity to learn them, and yet not speak so clearly as divest himself of his propriety[2] in them, I should reply that neither is this expedient a sure one, nor free from inconveniences. For most men are so self-opinionated that they will easily believe themselves masters of things if they do but half

1 In the now obsolete sense of "consciousness."

2 Ownership, property.

understand them. And though the persons to whom the discourse was immediately made should not have too great an opinion of themselves, no more than too great a sagacity, yet they may easily, by repeating what they heard and observed, give some more piercing wit a hint sufficient to enable him to make out the whole notion, or the discovery, which he will then without scruple and without almost any possibility of being disproved, assume for his own. But if it happen (as it often will in extemporaneous discourse), that a philosopher be not rightly understood, either because he has not the leisure, no more than a design, to explain himself fully, or because the persons he converses with bring not a competent capacity and attention, he then runs a greater danger than before. For the vanity most men take in being known to have conversed with eminent philosophers, makes them very forward to repeat what they heard such a famous wit say and oftentimes, being secure of not being contradicted, ignorantly to misrecite it, or wittingly to wrest it in favour of the opinion they would countenance by it. So that, whereas by the formerly mentioned frankness of discourse he is only in danger to have the truths he discovered arrogated by others, this reservedness exposes him to have opinions and errors that he never dreamt of, fathered on him. And when a man's opinions or discoveries come once to be publicly discoursed of, without being proposed by himself, or some friend well instructed by him, he knows not what errors or extravagancies may be imputed to him (and that without a moral possibility left to most men to discern them) by the mistake of the weak, or the disingenuity of the partial, or the artifices of the malicious. And even the greatness of a man's reputation does sometimes give such countenance to vain reports and surmises, as by degrees to shake, if not ruin, it. As we see, that Friar Bacon,[1] and Trithemius, and Paracelsus, who for their times were knowing as well as famous men, had such feats ascribed to them, as by appearing fabulous to most of the judicious, have tempted many to think that all the great things that were said of them were so too.

These are some of the inconveniences that a naturalist may be liable to, if he forbear the communicating of his thoughts and discoveries himself. But if Physeophilus should, to shun these, aspire to fame by the usual way of writing books, he may indeed avoid these, but perhaps not without running into other inconveniences and hazards very little inferior to them.

---

1 I.e., Roger Bacon.

First then, we may consider, that whether a man writes in a systematical way, as they have done who have published entire bodies of natural philosophy, or methodical treatises of some considerable part of it, or whether he write in a more loose and unconfined way of any particular subject that belongs to physics, whichsoever, I say, of these two ways of writing books he shall make choice of he will find it liable to inconvenience enough.

For if he write systematically, first, he will be obliged (that he may leave nothing necessary undelivered) to say divers things that have been said (perhaps many times) by others already, which cannot but be unpleasant, not only to the reader but (if he be ingenious) to the writer. Next, there are so many things in nature, whereof we know little or nothing, and so many more of which we do not know enough, that our systematical writer, though we should grant him to be very learned, must needs either leave divers things that belong to his theme untreated of, or discourse of them slightly and oftentimes (in likelihood) erroneously. So that in this kind of books there is always much said that the reader *did* know, and commonly not a little that the writer *does not* know. And to this I must add in the third place, that natural philosophy, being so vast and pregnant a subject that (especially in so inquisitive an age as this) almost every day discovers some new thing or other about it, it is scarce possible for a method that is adapted but to what is already known, to continue long the most proper, as the same clothes will not long fit a child whose age will make him quickly outgrow them. And therefore succeeding writers will have a fair pretence to compile new systems that may be more adequate to philosophy improved since the publication of the former. And though there were little of new to be added, and it were more easy to alter than to mend the method of our supposed author, yet novelty itself is a thing so pleasing and inviting to the generality of men, that it often recommends things that have nothing else to recommend them, and we may apply to a great many other things, what I remember a famous courtier of my acquaintance used to say of mistresses, that another was preferable to a better, (the better being but the same).

But now if, declining the systematical way, one shall choose the other of writing loose tracts and discourses, he may indeed avoid some of the lately mentioned inconveniences, but will scarce avoid the being plundered by systematical writers. For these will be apt to cull out those things that they like best, and insert them in their methodical books (perhaps much curtailed, or otherwise injured in the repeating), and will place them, not as their own author did, where they may best confirm or adorn his discourse and be illustrated or upheld by it, but where it may best serve the turn of the compiler. And these methodical books promise so much more compendious a way than others to the attainment of the sciences they treat of, that though really for the most part they prove greater helps to the memory than the understanding, yet most readers being for want of judgement or of patience of another mind, they are willing to take it for granted that in former writers, if there have been any thing considerable, it has been all carefully extracted as well as orderly digested by the later compilers. And though I take this to be a very erroneous and prejudicial conceit, yet it obtains so much, that as goldsmiths that only give shape and lustre to gold are far more esteemed, and in a better condition, than miners who find the ore in the bowels of the earth, and with great pains and industry dig it up and refine it into metal, so those that with great study and toil successfully penetrate into the hidden recesses of nature, and discover latent truths, are usually less regarded or taken notice of by the generality of men than those who by plausible methods and a neat style reduce the truths that others have found out into systems of a taking order and a convenient bulk.

I consider in the second place that, as the method of the books one writes, so the bulk of them may prove prejudicial to the naturalist that aspires to fame. For if he write large books it is odds but that he will write in them many things inaccurate, if not impertinent,[1] or that he will be obliged to repeat many things that others have said before. And if he writes but small tracts, as is the custom of the most judicious authors, who have no mind to publish but what is new and considerable, as their excellency will make them to be the sooner dispersed so the smallness of the bulk will endanger them to be quickly lost, as experience shows us of divers excellent little tracts which, though published not many years ago, are already out of print (as they speak)[2] and not to be met with save by chance in stationers' shops. So that these writings (which deserve a better fate) come, after a while, either to be lost (which

1 Irrelevant.

2 The first reference the OED gives to "out of print" is 1668, but the phrase also occurs in earlier works. In a bookseller's advertisement appended to Isaac Penington's *Divine Essays* (1654), we find a list of "Books extant," and books "out of print," so Boyle's "as they speak" seems correct. Indeed, Boyle himself uses the phrase in the Preface to his earlier "New Experiments Touching Cold" of 1665 (*Works* 4:218).

is the case of divers) or to have their memory preserved only in the larger volume of some compiler, whose industry is only preferable to his judgement, it being observable that (by I know not what unlucky fate) very few (for I do not say, none) that addict themselves to make collections out of others, have the judgement to cull out the choicest things in them, and the small tracts we are speaking of, being preserved but in such a quoter or abridger, will run a very great danger of being conveyed to posterity but under such a representation as it pleases the compiler.

And this (that I may proceed to my third consideration) may make the naturalist's fame very uncertain, not only because of the want of judgement that (as I newly said) is too often observable in compilers, whereby they frequently leave far better things than they take, but for the want of skill to understand the author they cite and epitomize, or candour to do him right. For sometimes men's physical opinions, and several passages of their writings, are so misrepresented by mistake or design, especially if those that recite their opinions be not of them, that men are made to teach or deliver things quite differing from their sense, and perhaps quite contrary to it; of which I myself have had some unwelcome experience, a learned writer pretending, I know not how often, that I asserted an opinion which I did expressly reject. And another noted writer having (not out of design, but unacquaintedness with mechanics, and the subject I wrote of) given me commendations for having by a new experiment proved a thing, the quite contrary whereof I intended thereby to evince, and am not alone mistaken, if I did not do it.

Other naturalists I have met with whose writings compilers have traduced out of hatred to their persons or their religion, as if truth could in nothing be a friend to one that is the traducer's enemy, or as if a man that falls into an error in religion, could not light upon a good notion in philosophy, in spite of all the truths we owe to Aristotle, Epicurus, and the other heathen philosophers. Nay, some there are that will set themselves to decry a man's writings not because they are directly his enemies, but because he is esteemed by theirs, as you may remember an instance in a servant of yours, who had divers things written against him upon this very account. Nor is it only by the citations of professed adversaries or opponents that a worthy writer's reputation may be prejudiced, since it is not infrequently so by those that mention him with an encomium, and seem disposed to honour him. For I have observed it to be the trick of certain writers, to name an author with much compliment, only for some one or few of the least considerable things they borrow of him, by which artifice they endeavour to conceal their being plagiaries of more and better, which yet is more excusable than the practise of some who proceed to that pitch of disingenuity, that they will rail at an author to whom indeed they owe too much, that they may not be thought to be beholden to him.

But fourthly, I must add that, besides these dangers that a naturalist's reputation with posterity may run through the ignorance or perverseness of men, it is liable to divers other hazards from the very nature both of men, of opinions, and of things.

For, as men's geniuses and inclinations are naturally various in reference to studies, one man passionately affecting one sort of them, and another being fond of quite differing ones, so those inclinations are oftentimes variously and generally determined by external and accidental causes. As, when some great monarch happens to be a great patron, or a despiser, and perhaps adversary, of this or that kind of learning; and when some one man has gained much applause for this or that kind of study, limitation or emulation oftentimes makes many others addict themselves to it. Thus though Rome under the consuls was inconsiderable for learning, yet the reputation of Cicero, and favour of Augustus, brought learning into request there, where the small countenance it met with among most of the succeeding emperors kept it far inferior to what it had been among the Greeks about Alexander's age. And the age of the same Augustus was ennobled with store of poets, not only by the countenance which he and Maecenas afforded them, but probably also by the examples they gave to, and the emulation they excited in, one another. And after the decay of the Roman empire, in the fourth century, natural philosophy and mathematics being very little valued and less understood, by reason that men's studies were, by the genius of those ages, applied to other subjects, every hundred years scarce produced one improver (not to say one eminent cultivator) either of mathematics or of physics. By which you may see how little certainty there is that, because a man is skilled in natural philosophy, and that science is now in request, his reputation shall be as great as now, when perhaps the science itself will be grown out of repute.

But besides the contingencies that may happen to a naturalist's fame upon this account—that the science he cultivates is, as well as others, subject to wanes and eclipses in the general esteem of men—there is another uncertainty arising from the vicissitudes that are to be met with in the estimates men make of differing hypotheses, sects, and ways of philosophizing about the same science, and particularly about natural philosophy. For during those learned times when physics first and most flourished among the Greeks, Democritus, Leucippus, Epicurus, Anaxagoras, Plato, and almost all the naturalists that preceded Aristotle, were corpuscularians, endeavoring, though not all by the same way, to give an account of the phenomena of nature, and even of qualities themselves, by the bigness, shape, motion, etc. of corpuscles, or the minutest active parts of matter. Whereas Aristotle, having attempted to deduce the phenomena from the four first qualities, the four elements, and some few other barren hypotheses, ascribing what could not be explicated by them, (and consequently far the greatest part of nature's phenomena) to substantial forms and occult qualities (principles that are readily named, but scarce so much as pretended to be understood), and having upon these slight and narrow principles reduced physics into a kind of system, which the judicious modesty of the corpuscularians had made them backward to do, the reputation that his great pupil Alexander as well as his learning gave him, the easiness of the way he proposed to the attainment of natural philosophy, the good luck his writings had to survive those of Democritus and almost all the rest of the corpuscularians when Charles the Great began to establish learning in Europe; these, I say, and some other lucky accidents that concurred, did for about seven or eight hundred years together make the corpuscularian philosophy not only be *jostled*, but even *exploded* out of the schools by the peripatetic,[1] which in our times is, by very many, upon the revival of the corpuscularian philosophy, rejected, and by more than a few derided as precarious, unintelligible, and useless. And to give an instance in a particular thing (which, though formerly named, deserves to be again mentioned to our present purpose) Aristotle himself somewhere confesses (not to say brags) that the Greek philosophers, his predecessors, did unanimously teach that the world was (I say not created, but) made,[2] and yet he, almost by his single authority, and the subtle arguments (as some have been pleased to think them) that he employed, (though divers of them were borrowed of Ocellus Lucanus[3]) was able for many ages to introduce into the schools of philosophers that irreligious and ill-grounded

1 Aristotelian.

2 See note to p. 121.

3 For Ocellus see Appendix A, "People Mentioned in the Text." The work which Boyle here suggests as influencing Aristotle is in fact subsequent to, and heavily influenced by, Aristotle.

opinion of the eternity of the world which afterwards the Christian doctrine made men begin to question and which now both that and right reason have persuaded most men to reject.

And this invites me to consider farther that the present success of the opinions that your Physeophilus befriends ought not to make him so sure as he thinks he is, that the same opinions will be always in the same or greater vogue, and have the same advantages in point of general esteem that they now have over their corrivals.[1] For opinions seem to have their fatal seasons and vicissitudes as well as other things, as may appear not only by the examples of it newly given, but also by the hypothesis of the earth's motion, which having been in great request before Pythagoras (who yet is commonly thought the inventor of it), had its reputation much increased by the suffrage of the famous sect of the Pythagoreans (whom Aristotle himself takes notice of as the patrons of that opinion[2]), and yet afterwards for near 2000 years it was laughed at, as not only false, but ridiculous. After all which time, this so long antiquated opinion being revived by Copernicus, has in a little time made so great a progress among the modern astronomers and philosophers, that if it go on to prevail at the same rate the motion of the earth will be acknowledged by all its mathematical inhabitants. But though it be often the fate of an oppressed truth to have at length a resurrection, yet it is not always its peculiar privilege, for obsolete errors are sometimes revived, as well as discredited truths, so that the general disrepute of an opinion in one age will not give us an absolute security, that it will not be in as general request in another, in which it may perhaps not only revive, but reign.

Nor is it only in the credit of men's opinions about philosophical matters that we may observe an inconstancy and vicissitude, but in the very way and method of philosophizing. Democritus, Plato, Pythagoras, and others, who were of the more sincere and ingenious cultivators of physics among the Greeks, exercised themselves chiefly either in making particular experiments and observations, as Democritus did in his manifold dissections of animals, or else applied mathematics to the explicating of a particular phenomenon of nature, as may appear (not to mention what Hero teaches in his *Pneumatics*) by the accounts, Democritus, Plato, and others give of fire and other elements, from the figure and motion of the corpuscles they consist of. And although this way of philos-

1 A corrival is a rival having an equal claim to acceptability.

2 Aristotle 1984, "On the Heavens," 293a20ff.

ophizing was so much in request before Aristotle that (albeit he unluckily brought in another, yet) there are manifest and considerable footsteps of it to be met with in some of his writings (and particularly in his books of *Animals*, and his *Mechanical Questions*),[1] yet the scholastic followers of Aristotle did for many ages neglect the way of philosophizing of the ancients, and (to the great prejudice of learning) introduced everywhere instead of it a quite contrary way of writing. For they not only laid aside the mathematics, (of which they were for the most part very ignorant), but instead of giving us intelligible and explicit (if not accurate) accounts of particular subjects, grounded upon a distinct and heedful consideration of them, they contented themselves with hotly disputing, in general, certain unnecessary, or at least unimportant, questions about the objects of physics, about *materia prima*, substantial forms, privation, place, generation, corruption, and other such general things with which, when they had quite tired themselves and their readers, they usually remained utter strangers to the particular productions of that nature about which they had so much wrangled, and were not able to give a man so much true and useful information about particular bodies as even the meanest mechanics, such as mine-diggers, butchers, smiths, and even dairymaids, could do. Which made their philosophy appear so imperfect and useless, not only to the generality of men, but to the more elevated and philosophical wits, that our great Verulam attempted with much skill and industry (and not without some indignation) to restore the more modest and useful way practiced by the ancients of inquiring into particular bodies without hastening to make systems, into the request it formerly had, wherein the admirable industry of two of our London physicians, Gilbert and Harvey, has not a little assisted him. And I need not tell you that since him, Descartes, Gassendi, and others, having taken in the application of geometrical theorems for the explication of physical problems, he, and they, and other restorers of natural philosophy, have brought the experimental and mathematical way of inquiring into nature into at least as high and growing an esteem as ever it possessed when it was most in vogue among the naturalists that preceded Aristotle.

To the considerations I have hitherto deduced,[2] which

---

1 The books on animals are *The History of Animals* and *The Parts of Animals.* The *Mechanics* is not Aristotle's but may predate Archimedes. All three may be found in Aristotle 1984.

2 That is, adduced.

perhaps might alone suffice for my purpose, I shall yet subjoin one that I take to be of greater weight than any of them, for the manifesting how difficult it is to be sure that the physical opinions which at present procure a champion or promoter of them veneration, shall be still in request. For besides that inconstant fate of applauded opinions, which may be imputed to the inconstancy of men, there is a greater danger that threatens the aspirer's reputation from the very nature of things. For the most general principles of all, viz., the figure, bigness, motion, and other mechanical affections of the small parts of matter being (as your friend believes) sufficiently and clearly established already, he must expect to raise his reputation from subordinate hypotheses and theories, and in these I shall not scruple to say that it is extremely difficult, even for those that are more exercised than he, in framing them and in making of experiments to have so reaching and attentive a prospect of all things fit to be known, as not to be liable to have their doctrine made doubtful, or disproved by something that he did not discover, or that after-times may. I doubt not but you would easily be prevailed with to allow this if I had leisure and conveniency to transmit to you my *Sceptical Naturalist.*[1] And without having recourse to that tract, it may possibly suffice that we consider that one of the conditions of a good hypothesis is,[2] that it fairly comport not only with all other truths, but with all other phenomena of nature, as well as those it is framed to explicate. For this being granted (which cannot be denied), he that establishes a theory which he expects shall be acquiesced in by all succeeding times, and make him famous in them, must not only have a care that none of the phenomena of nature that are already taken notice of do contradict his hypothesis at the present, but that no phenomena that may be hereafter discovered shall do it for the future. And I very much question whether Physeophilus *does* or, upon no greater a number and variety of experiments than most men build upon,

1 An early work of Boyle's, now lost, listed in inventories in the 1660s. See *Works* 14:331, 335.

2 See the Requisites of a good Hypothesis [RB's note]. This work of Boyle's, cast in dialogue form (listed in "A Catalogue of the Honble Mr. Boyles Writings unpublish'd taken the 7th of July *1684*," BP 36:59-60, and also mentioned in "The Publisher's Advertisement" for *Of the Excellency and Grounds of the Corpuscular or Mechanical Philosophy*) is now lost, though some fragments remain. See Appendix D, "The Requisites of a Good Hypothesis," for a short fragment listing the points of good, and excellent, hypotheses.

can know how incomplete the history of nature we yet have is, and how difficult it is to build an accurate hypothesis upon an incomplete history of the phenomena it is to be fitted to, especially considering that (as I was saying) many things may be discovered in after-times by industry or chance, which are not now so much as dreamed of, and which may yet overthrow doctrines speciously[1] enough accommodated to the observations that have been hitherto made.

Those ancient philosophers, that thought the torrid Zone to be uninhabitable did not establish their opinion upon wild reasonings, and as it continued uncontrolled for many ages, so perhaps it would have always done, if the discoveries made by modern navigations had not manifested it to be erroneous. The solidity of the celestial orbs was, for divers centuries above 1000 years, the general opinion of astronomers and philosophers, and yet in the last age and in ours, the free trajectory that has been observed in the motion of some comets from one of the supposed orbs to another, and the intricate motions in the planet Mars, (observed by Kepler and others, to be sometimes nearer, as well as sometimes remoter from the earth than is the sun), these, I say, and other phenomena undiscovered by the ancients have made even Tycho, as well as most of the recent astronomers, exchange the too long received opinion of solid orbs for the more warrantable belief of a fluid ether. And though the celestial part of the world, by reason of its remoteness from us, be the most unlikely of any other to afford us the means of overthrowing old theories by new discoveries, yet even in that we may take notice of divers instances to our present purpose, though I shall here name but this one, viz., that after the Ptolemaic number and order of the planets had passed uncontradicted for very many ages, and even the Tychonians and Copernicans (however they did by their differing hypotheses dissent from the Ptolemaic system (as to the order) did yet acquiesce in it as to the number of the planets), by the happy discoveries made by Galileo of the satellites of Jupiter, and by the excellent Huygens, of the new planet about Saturn,[2] (which I think I had the luck to be the first that observed and showed disbelievers of it in England,) the astronomers of all persuasions are brought to add to the old septenary number of the

---

1 "Specious" is always used by Boyle in the sense of "beautiful" or "nice" and not in our sense of "plausible but mistaken," or "misleadingly attractive."

2 I.e., Saturn's moon Titan.

planets, and take in five others that their predecessors did not dream of. That the chyle prepared in the stomach passed through the mesaraic veins to the liver, and so to the heart, was for many ages the unanimous opinion not only of physicians but anatomists, whose numerous dissections did not tempt them to question it, and yet, since the casual, though lucky, discoveries made of the milky vessels in the thorax by the dexterous Pecquet, those that have had with you and I the curiosity to make the requisite experiments are generally convinced, that (at least) a good part of the chyle goes from the stomach to the heart without passing through the mesaraic veins, or coming at all to the liver.[1]

It were easy to multiply instances of this kind, but I rather choose to add that it is not only about the qualities, and other attributes of things, but about their causes also, that new and oftentimes accidental discoveries may destroy the credit of long and generally approved opinions. That quicklime exceedingly heats the water that is poured on to quench it, on the account of antiperistasis,[2] has been very long and universally received by the school-philosophers, where it is the grand and usual argument, urged to establish antiperistasis, and yet I presume you have taken notice, that this proof is made wholly ineffectual in the judgement of many of the virtuosi, by some contrary experiments of mine, and particularly that of exciting in quicklime full as great an effervescence by the affusion of hot water instead of cold.[3] So it has been generally believed that in the congelation of water, that liquor is condensed into a narrower room, whereas our late experiments[4] have satisfied most of the curious, that ice is water expanded, or (if you please) that ice takes up more room than the water did, while it remained unfrozen. And whereas the notion of nature's abhorrence of a vacuum, has not only ever since Aristotle's time made a great noise in the schools, but seems to be con-

---

1 See note to p. 27.

2 The doctrine of antiperistasis involves the claim that "Nature ... furnish[es] cold and heat, with that self-invigorating power, which each of them may put forth, when 'tis environ'd with its contrary" (*Works* 4:463). An example which Boyle considers is the coolness of air in a cellar when surrounded in summer by hotter areas (*Works* 4:464).

3 See this subject handled at large in an appendix to the author's Examen of antiperistasis [RB's note]. See *Works* 4:469-70.

4 In the History of Cold [RB's note]. See *Works* vol. 4, esp. 301-5. With falling temperatures water condenses until 4°C and then begins to expand, which allows ice to be "water expanded," and thereby to form on the surface.

firmable by a multitude of phenomena, the experiments of Torricelli, and some of ours,[1] evidencing that the air has a great weight and a strong spring, have, I think, persuaded almost all that have impartially considered them that, whether there be or be not such a thing as they call *fuga vacui*,[2] yet suction, and the ascension of water in pumps, and those other phenomena that are generally ascribed to it, may be very well explicated without it, and are indeed caused by the weight of the atmosphere, and the elastic power of the air.

And this puts me in mind to take notice that even practical inventions, where one would think the matter of fact to be evident, may by undreamed of discoveries be brought to lose the general reputation they had for completeness in their kind. For to endear the invention of sucking pumps and of siphons, it has been generally presumed, that by means of either of these, water and any other liquor may, *ob fugam vacui*,[3] be raised to what height one pleases, and accordingly ways have been proposed by famous authors to convey water from one side of an high mountain to the other. Whereas first the unexpected disappointments that were met with by some pump-makers, and afterwards experiments purposely made, sufficiently evince that neither a pump nor a siphon will raise water to above 35 foot or thereabouts, nor quicksilver to so many inches.

And as to the invention of weather-glasses, which has been so much and justly applauded and used, as it has been generally received for the truest standard of the heat and cold of the weather, so it seems to be liable to no suspicion of deceiving us. For not only is it evident that in winter when the air is very cold the water rises much higher than in summer and other seasons, when it is not so. But if you but apply your warm hand to the bubble at the top, the water will be visibly depressed by the rarified air, which upon the removal of the hand returning to its former coldness, the water will forthwith as manifestly ascend again.[4] And yet by finding that, as the atmosphere has a considerable weight, so this weight is not always the same, but varies much, and that, as far as I can yet discover, uncertainly enough, I have had the luck to satisfy many of the curious that these open

1 Now published in the book of New Physico-mechanical Experiments [RB's note]. See *Works* 1:141ff.

2 Latin: avoidance of a vacuum.

3 Latin: to avoid a vacuum.

4 See a tract on this subject premised by the author to his Book of Cold [RB's note]. See *Works* 4:229ff.

thermometers are not to be safely relied on, since in them the liquor is made to rise and fall, not only as men have hitherto supposed, by the cold and heat of the ambient air, but (as I have shown by divers new experiments) according to the varying gravity of the atmosphere, which variation has not only a sensible, but a very considerable influence upon the weather-glass. To these instances I shall annex only one more, from which we may learn that notwithstanding a very heedful survey of all that at present a man can take notice of, or well suspect that he ought to take into his consideration, the case may be such that, having devised an instrument, he may use it many years with good success, and yet, unless he were able to live very many more, he shall not be sure to out-live the danger of finding the same instrument (though to sense as well conditioned as ever) fallacious. As he that first applied a magnetic needle to the finding of the meridian line, might very probably conclude that his needle pointing directly N and S or declining from it just two or three, or some other determinate number of degrees, he had discovered a certain and ready way, without the help of sun or stars or astronomical instruments, to describe a meridian line, and if he lived but an ordinary number of years after his observation, he might probably have found his instrument not deceitful, which yet it may now be, the magnetic needle not only declining in many places from the true points of N and S but (as later discoveries inform us) varying in tract of time its declination in the self same place.

The considerations hitherto proposed might easily enough be increased by more of the same tendency, especially if I thought fit to borrow from a discourse of mine purposely written *About the partiality and uncertainty of fame*,[1] but instead of adding to their number, I should think myself obliged to excuse my having already mentioned so many, and insisted so much upon them, if I did not vehemently[2] suspect that in your Physeophilus (as well as in many other modern naturalists), scarce anything does more contribute to an undervaluation of the study of divinity, than that being eagerly ambitious of a certain, as well as a posthumous fame, he is confident that physiology will help to it, and therefore the design of his discourse made me think it expedient to spend some time to manifest, *That it is far less easy than he thinks, to be*

1 This tract is lost, but see Appendix E, "Boyle on Fame," for a short fragment containing Boyle's views on the unimportance of fame.

2 Strongly.

as sure that he shall have the praises of future ages, as that (though he have them) he shall not hear them.[1]

The past considerations have, I presume, convinced you that it is no such easy matter for a naturalist to acquire a great reputation and be sure it will prove a lasting one. Wherefore, that I may also confirm the second part of what formerly I proposed, I now proceed to show that, though the case were otherwise, yet he would have no reason to slight the study of divinity.

I. For, in the first place, nothing hinders but that a man who values and inquires into the mysteries of religion may attain to an eminent degree in the knowledge of those of nature. For frequently men of great parts may successfully apply themselves to more than one study, and few of them have their thoughts and hours so much engrossed by that one subject or employment but that, if they have great inclinations as well as fitness for the study of nature, they will find time not only to cultivate it but to excel in it. You need not be told that Copernicus, to whom our late philosophers owe so much, was a churchman, that his champion Lansbergius was a minister, and that Gassendi himself was a doctor of divinity. Among the Jesuits you know that Clavius and divers others have as prosperously addicted themselves to mathematics as divinity. And as to physics, not only Scheiner, Aquilonius, Kircher, Schottus, Zucchius, and others have very laudably cultivated the optical and some other parts of philosophy, but Ricciolus himself, the learned compiler of that voluminous and judicious work of the *Almagestum Novum*, wherein he has inserted divers accurate observations of his own, is not only a divine but a professor of divinity. And without going out of our own country, I could, if I dared for fear of offending the modesty of those I should name, or injuring the merit of those I should omit, I could (I say) if it were not for this, among our English ecclesiastics name you divers who, though they apply themselves so much to the

---

1 Just over a century later we find Kant making a similar point:

> Man's natural endowments—not merely his talents and the impulses to enjoy them, but above all else the moral law within him—go so far beyond all the utility and advantage which he may derive from them in this present life, that he learns thereby to prize the mere consciousness of a righteous will as being, apart from the shadowy reward of posthumous fame, supreme over all other values; and so feels an inner call to fit himself, by his conduct in this world, and by the sacrifice of many of its advantages, for citizenship in a better world upon which he lays hold in idea. (Kant 1787, B425-6).

study of the Scripture as to be not only solid divines but excellent preachers, have yet been so happily conversant with nature that, if they had lived in the learned times of the Greeks, they would have rivaled, if not eclipsed, some of them, Pythagoras and Euclid, others of them, Anaxagoras and Epicurus, and some of them, even Archimedes and Democritus themselves.[1]

And certainly, provided there be curiosity and industry enough employed in the study of nature, it is not necessary that the knowledge of nature should be the ultimate end of that study, a fondness of the object being required only in order to the engaging the mind to such a serious application as a higher aim may sufficiently invite us to, and will rather promote than discourage. David became no less skilful in music, than those that were addicted to it only to please themselves in it,[2] though we may reasonably suppose, that so pious an author of psalms and instruments aspired to an excellency in that delightful science that he might apply and prefer it to the service of the temple, and promote the celebration of God's praises with it. And as experience has manifested that the heathen philosophers, that courted moral virtue for itself, did not raise it to that pitch to which it was advanced by the heroic practises of those true Christians, that in the highest exercise of virtue had a religious aim at the pleasing and enjoying of God, so I see not why natural knowledge must be more prosperously cultivated by those selfish naturalists, that aim but at the pleasing of themselves in the attainment of that knowledge, than those religious naturalists, who are invited to attention

---

1 For notes on the thinkers Boyle lists see Appendix A, "People Mentioned in the Text." It is not clear which "English ecclesiastics" he has in mind, though the divisions are interesting. Clearly Pythagoras and Euclid are seen as mathematicians (in our sense, not in the far-reaching seventeenth-century sense), and one clear clerical candidate as a rival for them mathematically would have been Boyle's friend John Wallis, the Savilian Professor of Geometry at Oxford, a founder of the Royal Society, and (mathematically) a destroyer of Hobbes (see Jesseph 1999 for details). Another candidate may be another of Hobbes's opponents, the Savilian Professor of Astronomy, Seth Ward. (The date of the composition of *The Excellency of Theology* is too early for Boyle to have had Newton in mind.) Boyle's placing of Anaxagoras and Epicurus in a separate category from Archimedes and Democritus may be the result of his opinion of the comparative abilities of the two pairs. Earlier in the *Excellency of Theology* he suggested that "Epicurus scarce deserves to be named with" [196] Democritus and Leucippus.

2 Amos 6. 5 [RB's note].

and industry not only by the pleasantness of the knowledge itself but by a higher and more engaging consideration, namely, that by the discoveries they make in the book of nature both themselves and others may be excited and qualified the better to admire and praise the Author, whose goodness does so well match the wisdom they celebrate, that he declares in his word, that those that honour him, he will honour.[1]

And as a man that is not in love with a fair lady, but has only a respect for her, may have as true and perfect, though not as discomposing, an idea of her face as the most passionate *inamorato*, so I see not, why a religious and inquisitive contemplator of nature may not be able to give a good account of it, without preferring nature so far to all other objects of his study, as to make it his mistress, and perhaps too his idol.

II. And now I proceed to consider in the second place, that matters of divinity may, as well as those of philosophy, afford a reputation to him that discovers or illustrates them. For though the fundamental articles of Christian religion be, as I have formerly declared, little less evident than important, yet there are many other points in divinity, and passages in the Scripture, which (for reasons that I have elsewhere mentioned[2]) are exceeding hard to be cleared, and do not only pose ordinary readers, and the common sort of scholars, but will sufficiently exercise the abilities of a great wit, and give him opportunity enough to manifest that he is one. For divers of the points I speak of are much benighted[3] upon the score of the sublimity of the things they treat of, such as are the nature, attributes, and decrees of God, which cannot be easy to the dim understandings of us that are but men. And many other particulars that are not abstruse in their own nature are yet made obscure to us by our ignorance (or at least imperfect knowledge), of the disused languages wherein they are delivered, and the great remoteness of the ages when, and the countries where, the things recorded were done or said. So that oftentimes a man may need and show as great learning and judgement to dispel the darkness wherein time has involved things, as that which nature has cast on them. And in effect we see that St. Augustine, St. Jerome, Origen, and others of the fathers, have acquired no less a reputation, than Empedocles,

---

1 1 Samuel 2.30 [RB's note].

2 See "The Style of the Scripture" (*Works* vol. 2) where Boyle discusses this matter at length.

3 Obscured or darkened.

Anaxagoras, or Zeno.[1] And Grotius, Salmasius, Mr. Mede, Dr. Hamond, and some other critical expounders of difficult texts of Scripture have thereby got as much credit, as Fracastorius by his book *De sympathia & antipathia*, Levinus Lemnius by his *De occultis rerum miraculis*, or Cardanus (and his adversary Scaliger) by what they wrote *De subtilitate*, or even Fernelius himself by his book *De abditis rerum causis*.[2]

And it will contribute to the credit which theological discoveries and illustrations may procure a man, that the importance of the subjects and the earnestness wherewith men are wont to busy themselves about them, some upon the score of piety and others upon that of interest, some to learn truths and others to defend what they have long or publicly taught for truth, does make greater numbers of men take notice of such matters and concern themselves far more about them than about almost any other things, and especially far more than about matters purely philosophical, which but few are wont to think themselves fit to judge of and concerned to trouble themselves about. And accordingly we see, that the writings of Socinus, Calvin, Bellarmine, Padre Paulo, Arminius, etc. are more famous and more studied than those of Telesius, Campanella, Severinus Danus, Magnenus, and divers other innovators in natural philosophy. And Erastus, though a very learned physician, is much less famous for all his elaborate disputations against Paracelsus, than for the little tract against particular forms of church-government. And I presume you have taken notice, as well as I, that there are scarce any five new controversies in all physics, that are known to, and hotly contended for, by so many as are the five articles of the Remonstrants.[3]

---

1 Given the conjunction with Empedocles and Anaxagoras, Boyle probably has Zeno of Elea in mind, but in his works he also refers to Zeno of Citium.

2 Latin: *On the Hidden Causes of Things*.

3 The five articles of the Remonstrants say in sum (1) that God's eternal and unchangeable purpose allows that believers may be saved through grace, that is, that predestination is conditional, not absolute; (2) that Christ died for everyone so that Atonement is, in intention, universal; (3) that humans are in a state of apostasy and sin, and cannot save themselves; (4) that though without the help of God's grace, humans cannot be saved, this grace is not irresistible; and (5) that those who are "incorporated into Christ by true faith" cannot be "misled or plucked out of Christ's hands" by any power of Satan, but whether they can turn away from faith "must be more particularly determined out of the Holy Scripture, before we ourselves can teach it with the full confidence of our mind."

III. My second consideration being thus dispatched, it remains that I tell you in the third place, that supposing, but not granting, that to prosecute the study of divinity one must of necessity neglect the acquisition of reputation, yet this inconvenience itself ought not to deter us from the duty it would dissuade. For in all deliberations, wherein any thing is proposed to be quitted or declined to obey or please God, methinks we may fitly apply that of the prophet to the Jewish king, who being persuaded (to express his concern for God's glory) to decline the assistance of an idolatrous army of Israelites, and objecting, that by complying with the advice given him he should lose a sum of money amounting to no less than the hire of a potent army, received from the prophet this brisk, but rational, answer, "The Lord is able to give thee far more than this."[1]

The apostle Paul, who had been traduced, reviled, buffeted, scourged, imprisoned, shipwrecked, and stoned for his zeal to propagate the truths whose study I plead for, after he had once had a glimpse of that great recompense of reward that is reserved for us in heaven, scruples not to pronounce that he finds upon casting up the account (for he uses the arithmetical term *logizomai*[2]) "that the sufferings of this present time are not worthy to be compared with the glory that is to be revealed in us."[3] And if all that the persecuted Christians of his time could suffer were not suitable (for so I remember the same Greek word to signify elsewhere)[4] or proportionable to that glory, it will sure far outweigh what we can now forego or decline for it. The loss of an advantage, and much more the bare missing of it, being usually but a negative affliction in comparison of the actual sufferance of evil. Christ did not only tell his disciples that he who should give the least of his followers so much as a cup of cold water upon the score of their relation to him, should not be unrewarded, but when the same persons asked him, what should be done to them who had left all to follow him, he presently allots them thrones, as much outvaluing that all they had lost as an ordinary recompense may exceed a cup of cold water. And indeed God's goodness is so great and his treasures so unexhausted that, as he is forward to recompence even the least services that can be done him, so he is able to give the greatest a proportionable reward.

---

1 2 Chronicles 25.9 [RB's note].

2 Greek: "I reckon" or "I calculate."

3 Romans 8.18 [RB's note].

4 Luke 23.15 [RB's note].

Solomon had an opportunity such as never any mortal had (that we know of) either before or since, of satisfying his desires, whether of fame, or any other thing that he could wish. "Ask what I shall give thee,"[1] was the proffer made him by Him, that could give all things worth receiving, and yet the wisdom even of Solomon's choice, approved by God himself, consisted in declining the most ambitioned things of this life for those things that might the better qualify him to serve and please God. And to give you an example in a greater than Solomon, we may consider that he "who, being in the form of God, thought it not robbery to be equal with God,"[2] and who by leaving heaven did, to dwell on earth, quit more than any inhabitant of the earth can to gain heaven, and denied more to become capable of being tempted, than he did when he was tempted with an offer of "All the kingdoms of the world, and the glory of them."[3] This Saviour, I say, is said in Scripture to have, "For the joy that was set before him, endured the cross, and despised the shame,"[4] as if heaven had been a sufficient recompense for even his renouncing honours, and embracing torments.

He that declines the acquisition of the applause of men for the contemplation of the truths of God, does but forbear to gather that while it is immature, which by waiting God's time he will more seasonably gather when it is full ripe, and wholesome, and sweet. That "immarcescible[5] crown" (as St. Peter calls it[6]) which the gospel promises to them, "who by patient continuance in well doing seek for glory and honour,"[7] will make a rich amends for the declining of a fading wreath here upon earth, where reputation is oftentimes as undeservedly acquired, as lost, whereas in heaven, the very having celestial honours argues a title to them. And since it is our Saviour's reasoning, that his disciples ought to rejoice when their reputation is pursued by calumny, as well as their lives by persecution, "because their reward is great in heaven,"[8] we may justly infer that the grounded expectation of so illustrious a condition may bring us more content, even when it is not attended with a present applause, than this applause can

---

1 1 Kings 3.5 [RB's note].

2 Philippians 2.6 [RB's note].

3 Matthew 4, 8-10; Luke 4, 5-8.

4 Romans 2.7 [RB's note].

5 Incorruptible, unfading.

6 1 Peter 5.4.

7 Hebrews 12.2 [RB's note].

8 Matthew 5.11-12.

give those who want[1] that comfortable expectation. So that, upon the whole matter, we have no reason to despond, or to complain of the study of theology, for but making us decline an empty and transitory fame for a solid and eternal glory.

The Conclusion

By this time, Sir, I have said as much as I think fit (and therefore, I hope, more than upon your single account was necessary) to manifest that Physeophilus had no just cause to undervalue the study of divinity, nor our friend the doctor, for addicting himself to it. I hope you have not forgotten what I expressly enough declared at the beginning of this letter, that both your friend and your admitting the holy Scriptures, I knew myself thereby to be warranted to draw proofs from their authority. And if I need not remind you of this, perhaps I need not tell you by way of apology that I am not so unacquainted with the laws of discoursing but that, if I had been to argue with atheists or sceptics, I should have forborne to make use of divers of the arguments I have employed, as fetched from unconceded topics, and substituted others for such as yet I think it very allowable for me to urge when I deal with a person such as your friend, who does only undervalue the study of the Scriptures, not reject their authority. And if the prolixity I have been guilty of already did [not][2] forbid me to increase it by apologies not absolutely necessary, I should perchance rather think myself obliged to excuse the plainness of the style of this discourse, which both upon the subject's score, and yours, may seem to challenge a richer dress. But the matter is very serious, and you are a philosopher, and when the things we treat of are highly important, I think truths clearly made out to be the most persuasive pieces of oratory.

A discourse of this nature is more likely to prove effectual on intelligent perusers, by having the reasons it presents perspicuously proposed, and unprejudicedly entertained, than by their being pathetically urged, or curiously adorned. And I have the rather forborne expressions that might seem more proper to move than to convince, because I foresee I may very shortly have occasion to employ some of the former sort in another letter to a friend of yours and mine, who will, I doubt, make you a sharer in

---

1 Lack.

2 Following Hunter and Davis, *Works* 8:98, "not" is inserted here as required by the sense of the statement.

the trouble of reading it. But writing this for you and Physeophilus, I was far more solicitous to give the arguments I employ a good temper than a bright gloss. For even when we would excite devotion, if it be in rational men, the most effectual pieces of oratory are those which like burning-glasses inflame by nothing but numerous and united beams of light. If this letter prove so happy as to give you any satisfaction, it will thereby bring me a great one, for prizing you as I do, I cannot but wish to see you esteem those things now, which I am confident we shall always have cause to esteem, and then most, when the light of glory shall have made us better judges of the true worth of things. And it would extremely trouble me to see you a disesteemer of those divine things which, as long as a man undervalues, the possession of heaven itself would not make him happy. And therefore, if the blessing of him whose glory is aimed at in it, make the success of this paper answerable to the wishes, the importance of the subject will make the service done you by it suitable to the desires of,

Sir,

Your most faithful, most affectionate, and most humble servant.

ABOUT THE

EXCELLENCY

AND

GROUNDS

Of the

MECHANICAL HYPOTHESIS,

Some Conſiderations,

Occaſionally propos'd to a Friend.

By T. H. *R. B.* E.[1]

Fellow of the *Royal Society*.

LONDON,

Printed by *T. N.* for *Henry Herringman*, at the *Anchor* in the *Lower Walk* of the *New Exchange*. 1674.

---

1 The Honourable Robert Boyle, Esquire.

The Publisher's Advertisement

The following paper having been but occasionally and hastily penned, long after what the author had written (by way of Dialogue) about *The Requisites of a Good Hypothesis*,[1] it was intended that if it came forth at all, it should do so as an appendix to that discourse, because though one part of it does little more than name some of the heads treated of in the Dialogue, yet, according to the exigency of the occasion, the other part contains several things, either pretermitted or but more lightly touched on in the discourse. But, although the author's design were to reserve these thoughts as a kind of paralipomena[2] to his Dialogue, yet, since he is not willing to let that, at least quickly, come abroad, and these are fallen into my hands, I will make bold, with his good leave, to annex them to the foregoing treatise, not only to complete the bulk of the book, but because of some affinity between them, since both aim at manifesting the excellency of the studies they would recommend. And perhaps it will not be unwelcome to some of the curious to find that our noble author, in the same book wherein he prefers the study of divine things to that of natural ones, does himself prefer the mechanical principles before all other hypotheses about natural things, they being in their own nature so accommodating as to make considering men understand, rather than dispute of, the effects of nature.

---

1 As noted above in *The Excellency of Theology*, this work of Boyle's is now lost, though some fragments remain. See Appendix D, "The Requisites of a Good Hypothesis," for a short fragment listing the points of good, and excellent, hypotheses, and see MacIntosh 1992 for an account of Boyle on hypotheses.

2 Supplement.

Of the Excellency and Grounds of the Corpuscular or Mechanical Philosophy

The importance of the question you[1] propose would oblige me to refer you to *The Dialogue About a Good Hypothesis*, and some other papers of that kind, where you may find my thoughts about the advantages of the mechanical hypothesis somewhat amply set down and discoursed of. But since your desires confine me to deliver in few words, not what I believe resolvedly, but what I think may be probably said for the preference or the preeminence of the corpuscular philosophy above Aristotle's, or that of the chemists,[2] you must be content to receive from me, without any preamble, or exact method, or ample discourses, or any other thing that may cost many words, a succinct mention of some of the chief advantages of the hypothesis we incline to. And I the rather comply on this occasion with your curiosity, because I have often observed you to be alarmed and disquieted when you hear of any book that pretends to uphold or repair the decaying philosophy of the schools, or when some bold chemist that arrogates to those of his sect the title of philosophers, and pretends to build wholly upon experience, to which he would have all other naturalists thought strangers.

That therefore you may not be so tempted to despair by the confidence or reputation of those writers, that do some of them applaud, and others censure what, I fear, they do not understand (as when the Peripatetics cry up substantial forms, and the chemists mechanical explications of nature's phenomena), I will propose some considerations that will, I hope, not only keep you kind to the philosophy you have embraced, but perhaps (by some considerations which you have not yet met with), make you think it probable that the new attempts you hear of from time to time will not overthrow the corpuscularian philosophy, but either be foiled by it, or found reconcilable to it.

But when I speak of the corpuscular or mechanical philosophy, I am far from meaning with the Epicureans that atoms, meeting together by chance in an infinite vacuum, are able of themselves to produce the world and all its phenomena, nor with some modern philosophers that, supposing God to have put into the whole mass of matter such an invariable quantity of motion,

---

1 As with the intended recipient of the *Excellency of Theology*, the intended recipient (if any) of this *Excellency* is unidentified.

2 That is, the followers of Paracelsus.

he needed do no more to make the world, the material parts being able by their own unguided motions, to cast themselves into such a system (as we call by that name).

I plead only for such a philosophy as reaches but to things purely corporeal, and distinguishing between the first original of things, and the subsequent course of nature, teaches, concerning the former, not only that God gave motion to matter, but that in the beginning he so guided the various motions of the parts of it, as to contrive them into the world he designed they should compose (furnished with the seminal principles and structures or models of living creatures), and established those rules of motion and that order amongst things corporeal, which we are wont to call the laws of nature. And having told this as to the former, it may be allowed as to the latter to teach, that the universe being once framed by God, and the laws of motion being settled and all upheld by his incessant concourse and general providence, the phenomena of the world thus constituted are physically produced by the mechanical affections of the parts of matter, and how they operate upon one another according to mechanical laws. And now having shown what kind of corpuscular philosophy it is that I speak of I proceed to the particulars that I thought the most proper to recommend it.

I. The first thing that I shall mention to this purpose is the intelligibility or clarity of mechanical principles and explications. I need not tell you, that among the Peripatetics, the disputes are many and intricate about matter, privation, substantial forms, and their eduction,[1] etc. And the chemists are sufficiently puzzled (as I have elsewhere shown[2]) to give such definitions and accounts of their hypostatical principles[3] as are reconcilable to one another, and even to some obvious phenomena. And much more dark and intricate are their doctrines about the archeus, astral beings, gas, blass,[4] and other odd notions, which perhaps have in part occasioned the darkness and ambiguity of their

---

1 Drawing forth, eliciting.

2 In "The Sceptical Chymist," *Works* vol. 2.

3 Elemental principles, i.e., the principles of salt, sulphur and mercury.

4 The Paracelsans held that there were *archei* that, functioning as, in effect, internal alchemists, controlled the various physiological activities of the body. The most important was the archeus of the stomach, which separated pure from impure parts of food and distributed the useful portions to other parts of the body. *Gas* and *blas* are two of the three new explanatory concepts invoked by van Helmont, the other being *magnal*, an emanation which filled the pores of air. (Helmont held that air was composed of particles which were *minima naturalia*: particles

expressions, that could not be very clear when their conceptions were far from being so. And if the principles of the Aristotelians and Spagyrists are thus obscure, it is not to be expected that the explications made by the help only of such principles should be clear. And indeed many of them are either so general and slight, or otherwise so unsatisfactory that, granting their principles, it is very hard to understand or admit their applications of them to particular phenomena. And even in some of the more ingenious and subtle of the Peripatetic discourses upon their superficial and narrow theories, methinks the authors have better played the part of painters than philosophers, and have only had the skin, like drawers of landscapes, to make men fancy they see castles and towns and other structures that appear solid and magnificent, and to reach to a large extent, when the whole piece is superficial, and made up of colours and art, and comprised within a frame perhaps scarce a yard long.

But to come now to the corpuscular philosophy, men do so easily understand one another's meaning, when they talk of local motion, rest, bigness, shape, order, situation, and contexture of material substances, and these principles do afford such clear accounts of those things that are rightly deduced from them only,[1] that even those Peripatetics or chemists that maintain other principles, acquiesce in the explications made by these when they can be had, and seek not any further, though perhaps the effect be so admirable as would make it pass for that of a hidden form, or occult quality. Those very Aristotelians, that believe the celestial bodies to be moved by intelligences, have no recourse to any peculiar agency of theirs to account for eclipses. And we laugh at those East Indians that to this day go out in multitudes with some instruments that may relieve the distressed luminary, whose loss of light they fancy to proceed from some fainting fit out of which it must be roused. For no intelligent man, whether chemist or Peripatetic, flies to his peculiar principles, after he is informed that the moon is eclipsed by the interposition of the earth between it and the

---

that were the smallest particles in nature, indivisible in fact, even if one could *conceive* of their being divided.) The other two emanations, blas (which comes from the stars), and gas (which seems to have been thought of as mainly water vapour) are used to explain meteorological phenomena. For further details, see Chapters 15-17 of *Ortus medicinae* (van Helmont 1648).

1 Leibniz, who was explicitly *not* a corpuscularian, nonetheless agreed with Boyle about this, as noted in the Introduction.

sun, and the sun by that of the moon between it and the earth. And when we see the image of a man cast into the air by a concave spherical looking glass, though most men are amazed at it, and some suspect it to be no less than an effect of witchcraft, yet he that is skilled enough in catoptrics[1] will, without consulting Aristotle, or Paracelsus, or flying to hypostatical principles and substantial forms, be satisfied that the phenomenon is produced by the beams of light reflected and thereby made convergent according to optical, and consequently mathematical, laws.

But I must not now repeat what I elsewhere say, to show that the corpuscular principles have been declined by philosophers of different sects, not because they think not our explications as clear, if not much more so, than their own, but because they imagine that the applications of them can be made but to few things and consequently are insufficient.

II. In the next place I observe that there cannot be fewer principles than the two grand ones of mechanical philosophy, matter and motion. For matter alone, unless it be moved, is altogether inactive, and while all the parts of a body continue in one state without any motion at all, that body will not exercise any action, nor suffer any alteration itself, though it may perhaps modify the action of other bodies that move against it.

III. Nor can we conceive any principles more primary than matter and motion. For either both of them were immediately created by God or (to add that for their sakes that would have matter to be unproduced), if matter be eternal, motion must either be produced by some immaterial supernatural agent, or it must immediately flow by way of emanation from the nature of the matter it appertains to.

IV. Neither can there be any physical principles more simple than matter and motion, neither of them being resoluble into any things whereof it may truly, or so much as tolerably, be said to be compounded.

V. The next thing I shall name to recommend the corpuscular principles is their great comprehensiveness. I consider then, that the genuine and necessary effect of the sufficiently strong motion of one part of matter against another is either to drive it on in its entire bulk, or else to break or divide it into particles of determi-

1 From the Greek, "of or in a mirror"; hence, the part of Optics that deals with reflections.

nate motion, figure, size, posture, rest, order, or texture.[1] The two first of these, for instance, are each of them capable of numerous varieties. For the figure of a portion of matter may either be one of the five regular figures treated of by geometricians, or some determinate species of solid figures, as that of a cone, cylinder, etc. Or irregular, though not perhaps anonymous, as the grains of sand, hoops, feathers, branches, forks, files, etc. And as the figure, so the motion of one of these particles may be exceedingly diversified, not only by the determination to this or that part of the world, but by several other things, as particularly by the almost infinitely varying degrees of celerity, by the manner of its progression with, or without, rotation, and other modifying circumstances, and more yet by the line wherein it moves as (besides straight) circular, elliptical, parabolical, hyperbolical, spiral, and I know not how many others. For, as later geometricians have shown that those crooked lines may be compounded of several motions (that is, traced by a body whose motion is mixed of, and results from, two or more simpler motions), so how many more curves may, or rather may not be made by new compositions and decompositions of motion, is no easy task to determine.

Now, since a single particle of matter, by virtue of two only of the mechanical affections that belong to it, be diversifiable so many ways, how vast a number of variations may we suppose capable of being produced by the compositions and decompositions of myriads of single invisible corpuscles that may be contained and contexted in one small body, and each of them be imbued with more than two or three of the fertile catholic[2] principles above mentioned? Especially since the aggregate of those corpuscles may be farther diversified by the texture resulting from their convention into a body which, as so made up, has its own bigness, and shape, and pores (perhaps very many, and various), and has also many capacities of acting and suffering upon the score of the place it holds among other bodies in a world constituted as ours is. So that, when I consider the almost

1 Boyle stresses the *determinate* motion, figure, etc. because, while it is analytic that a particle of matter should have *some* motion (or be at rest), and *some* shape, etc., it is by no means clear why it should have just this precise shape. So Boyle elsewhere argues, either its *precise* shape (etc.) is an unsolvable mystery, or we must look to God for the explanation. And, he argues, it is explanatorily more satisfactory to have one unexplained entity which explains all the rest than an almost innumerable number of mysteries (see BP 2.1-36; Boyle 2006 4.1, p. 341).

2 Universal.

innumerable diversifications that compositions and decompositions may make of a small number, not perhaps exceeding twenty of distinct things, I am apt to look upon those who think the mechanical principles may serve indeed to give an account of the phenomena of this or that particular part of natural philosophy, as statics, hydrostatics, the theory of the planetary motions, etc., but can never be applied to all the phenomena of things corporeal, I am apt, I say, to look upon those otherwise learned men, as I would do upon him, that should affirm that by putting together the letters of the alphabet one may indeed make up all the words to be found in one book, as in Euclid, or Virgil, or in one language, as Latin, or English, but that they can by no means suffice to supply words to all the books of a great library, much less to all the languages in the world.

And whereas there is another sort of philosopher that, observing the great efficacy of the bigness, and shape, and situation, and motion, and connection in engines, are willing to allow that those mechanical principles may have a great stroke in the operations of bodies of a sensible bulk, and manifest mechanism, and therefore may be usefully employed in accounting for the effects and phenomena of such bodies, who yet will not admit that these principles can be applied to the hidden transactions that pass among the minute particles of bodies, and therefore think it necessary to refer these to what they call nature, substantial forms, real qualities, and the like unmechanical principles and agents.[1]

But this is not necessary, for both the mechanical affections of matter are to be found, and the laws of motion take place, not only in the great masses and the middle-sized lumps, but in the smallest fragments of matter. And a lesser portion of it, being as well a body as a greater, must as necessarily as it, have its determinate bulk and figure. He that looks upon sand in a good microscope will easily perceive that each minute grain of it has as well its own size and shape as a rock or mountain. And when we let fall a great stone and a pebble from the top of a high building, we find not but that the latter as well as the former moves conformably to the laws of acceleration in heavy bodies descending. And the rules of motion are observed, not only in cannon bullets, but in small shot, and the one strikes down a bird according to

---

1 This somewhat blithely ignores the problem corpuscularians had with cohesion. As noted above (p. 65n1) Newton, in the year following Boyle's death, considered the possibility that cohesion might be the result of certain "attractive virtues," that is, powers, that elementary particles have—powers quite distinct from those observable in macroscopic objects.

the same laws, that the other batters down a wall. And though nature (or rather its Divine Author) be wont to work with much finer materials, and employ more curious contrivances than art (whence the structure even of the rarest watch is incomparably inferior to that of a human body), yet an artist himself, according to the quantity of the matter he employs, the exigency of the design he undertakes, and the bigness and shape of the instruments he makes use of, is able to make pieces of work of the same nature or kind of extremely differing bulk, where yet the like, though not equal, art and contrivance, and oftentimes motion too, may be observed: as a smith, who with a hammer and other large instruments can, out of masses of iron, forge great bars or wedges, and make those strong and heavy chains that were employed to load malefactors, and even to secure streets and gates may, with lesser instruments, make smaller nails and filings, almost as minute as dust, and may yet, with finer tools, make links of a strange slenderness and lightness, insomuch that good authors tell us of a chain of divers links that was fastened to a flea, and could be moved by it. If I misremember not, I saw something like this, besides other instances that I beheld with pleasure of the littleness that art can give to such pieces of work, as are usually made of a considerable bigness. And therefore to say that, though in natural bodies, whose bulk is manifest and their structure visible, the mechanical principles may be usefully admitted, that are not to be extended to such portions of matter, whose parts and texture are invisible, may perhaps look to some, as if a man should allow, that the laws of mechanism may take place in a town-clock, but cannot in a pocket-watch. Or to give you an instance mixed of natural and artificial, as if, because the terraqueous globe is a vast magnetic body of seven or eight thousand miles in diameter, one should affirm that magnetic laws are not to be expected to be of force in a spherical piece of loadstone that is not perhaps an inch long. Yet experience shows us that, notwithstanding the inestimable disproportion between these two globes, the terrella[1] as well as the earth has its poles, equator, and meridians, and in divers other magnetic properties emulates the terrestrial globe.

They that, to solve the phenomena of nature, have recourse to agents which, though they involve no self-repugnancy in their very notions, as many of the judicious think substantial forms and real qualities do, yet they are such that we conceive not how they

---

1 A spherical (and hence earth-shaped) magnet.

operate to bring effects to pass. These, I say, when they tell us of such indeterminate agents as the soul of the world, the universal spirit, the plastic power, and the like, though they may in certain cases tell us some things, yet they tell us nothing that will satisfy the curiosity of an inquisitive person, who seeks not so much to know, what is the general agent, that produces a phenomenon as, by what means, and after what manner, the phenomenon is produced. The famous Sennertus and some other learned physicians tell us of diseases which proceed from incantation. But sure it is but a very slight account that a sober physician, that comes to visit a patient reported to be bewitched, receives of the strange symptoms he meets with, and would have an account of, if he be coldly answered, that it is a witch or the devil that produces them, and he will never sit down with so short an account, if he can by any means reduce those extravagant symptoms to any more known and stated diseases, as epilepsy, convulsions, hysterical fits, etc.[1] And, if he can not, he will confess his knowledge of this distemper to come far short of what might be expected and attained in other diseases, wherein he thinks himself bound to search into the nature of the morbific matter, and will not be satisfied till he can, probably at least, deduce from that and the structure of a human body, and other concurring physical causes, the phenomena of the malady. And it would be but little satisfaction to one that desires to understand the causes of what occurs to observation in a watch, and how it comes to point at, and strike, the hours, to be told that it was such a watch-maker that so contrived it, or to him that would know the true cause of an echo, to be answered, that it is a man, a vault, or a wood that makes it.

And now at length I come to consider that which I observe the most to alienate other sects from the mechanical philosophy, namely, that they think it pretends to have principles so universal and so mathematical, that no other physical hypothesis can comport with it, or be tolerated by it.

But this I look upon as an easy indeed, but an important, mistake, because by this very thing, that the mechanical princi-

1 Boyle makes a similar point in *The Notion of Nature*, where he writes, "I shall scarce think him an Inquisitive or a Judicious Doctor, who should imagine, that he explains [or] gives an intelligible and particular Account of the astonishing Symptoms of those strange Diseases, that divers very Learned and sober Physitians impute to Witchcraft, when he says, that those strange Distortions and convulsive Motions, for Instance, and other Prodigious Effects, were produc'd by a wicked immaterial spirit, call'd a Devil" (*Works* 10:554).

ples are so universal, and therefore applicable to so many things, they are rather fitted to include, than necessitated to exclude, any other hypothesis that is founded in nature, as far as it is so. And such hypotheses, if prudently considered by a skilful and moderate person, who is rather disposed to unite sects than multiply them, will be found, as far as they have truth in them, to be either legitimately (though perhaps not immediately), deducible from the mechanical principles, or fairly reconcilable to them. For such hypotheses will probably attempt to account for the phenomena of nature, either by the help of a determinate number of material ingredients, such as the *tria prima*[1] of the chemists, by participation whereof other bodies obtain their qualities, or else by introducing some general agents, as the Platonic soul of the world, or the universal spirit, asserted by some Spagyrists, or by both these ways together.

Now to dispatch first those that I named in the second place, I consider that the chief thing that inquisitive naturalists should look after in the explicating of difficult phenomena is not so much what the agent is or does, as what changes are made in the patient, to bring it to exhibit the phenomena that are proposed, and by what means, and after what manner, those changes are effected. So that the mechanical philosopher being satisfied that one part of matter can act upon another but by virtue of local motion, or the effects and consequences of local motion, he considers that as, if the proposed agent be not intelligible and physical, it can never physically explain the phenomena, so, if it be intelligible and physical, it will be reducible to matter, and some or other of those catholic affections of matter, already often mentioned. And the indefinite divisibility of matter, the wonderful efficacy of motion, and the almost infinite variety of coalitions and structures, that may be made of minute and insensible corpuscles being duly weighed, I see not why a philosopher should think it impossible to make out by their help the mechanical possibility of a corporeal agent, how subtle, or diffused, or active soever it be, that can be solidly proved to be really existent in nature, by what name soever it be called or disguised. And though the Cartesians be mechanical philosophers yet according to them their *materia subtilis*, which the very name declares to be a corporeal substance is, for ought I know, little (if it be at all) less diffused through the universe, or less active in it, than the universal spirit of some Spagyrists, not to say, the *world*

1 The principles of salt, sulphur and mercury.

soul[1] of the Platonists. But this upon the by, after which I proceed, and shall venture to add, that whatever be the physical agent, whether it be inanimate or living, purely corporeal, or united to an intellectual substance,[2] the above mentioned changes that are wrought in the body that is made to exhibit the phenomena may be effected by the same or the like means, or after the same or the like manner as, for instance, if corn be reduced to meal, the materials and shape of the millstones, and their peculiar motion and adaptation, will be much of the same kind, and (even though they were not, the grains of corn will suffer a various contrition and comminution[3] in their passage to the form of meal whether the corn be ground by a water mill, or a windmill, or a horse mill, or a hand mill, that is, by a mill whose stones are turned by inanimate, by brute, or by rational, agents. And if an angel himself should work a real change in the nature of a body, it is scarce conceivable to us men how he could do it without the assistance of local motion since, if nothing were displaced or otherwise moved than before (the like happening also to all external bodies to which it related), it is hardly conceivable, how it should be in itself other than just what it was before.

But to come now to the other sort of hypotheses formerly mentioned, if the chemists, or others that would deduce a complete natural philosophy from salt, sulphur, and mercury, or any other set number of ingredients of things, would well consider what they undertake, they might easily discover that the material parts of bodies, as such, can reach but to a small part of the phenomena of nature while these ingredients are considered but as quiescent things, and therefore they would find themselves necessitated to suppose them to be active, and that things purely corporeal cannot be but by means of local motion, and the effects that may result from that, accompanying variously shaped, sized, and aggregated parts of matter. So that the chemists and other materialists (if I may so call them), must (as indeed they are wont to do) leave the greatest part of the phenomena of the universe unexplicated by the help of the ingredients, (be they fewer or more than three) of bodies, without taking in the mechanical and more comprehensive

---

1 Boyle has the Latin *anima mundi.*

2 For Boyle, a human action is the result of a "physical agent ... united to an intellectual substance." That is, Boyle is a straightforward Cartesian dualist.

3 Breaking up into fragments, pulverizing.

affections of matter, especially local motion. I willingly grant that salt, sulphur, and mercury, or some substances analogous to them, are to be obtained by the action of the fire from a very great many dissipable[1] bodies here below. Nor would I deny that in explicating divers of the phenomena of such bodies it may be of use to a skilful naturalist to know and consider, that this or that ingredient, as sulphur, for instance, does abound in the body proposed, whence it may be probably argued that the qualities, that usually accompany that principle when predominant, may be also, upon its score, found in the body that so plentifully partakes of it. But not to mention, what I have elsewhere shown,[2] that there are many phenomena to whose explication this knowledge will contribute very little or nothing at all, I shall here only observe that, though chemical explications be sometimes the most obvious and ready, yet they are not the most fundamental and satisfactory.[3]

For the chemical ingredient itself, whether sulphur or any other, must owe its nature and other qualities to the union of insensible particles in a convenient size, shape, motion or rest, and contexture, all which are but mechanical affections of convening corpuscles. And this may be illustrated by what happens in artificial fireworks. For, though in most of those many differing sorts that are made either for the use of war, or for recreation, gunpowder be a main ingredient, and divers of the phenomena may be derived from the greater or lesser measure, wherein the compositions partake of it, yet, besides that there may be fireworks made without gunpowder (as appears by those made of old by the Greeks and Romans), gun-powder itself owes its aptness to be fired and exploded to the mechanical contexture of more simple portions of matter, nitre, charcoal, and sulphur. And sulphur itself, though it be by many chemists mistaken for a hypostatical principle, owes its inflammability to the convention of yet more simple and primary corpuscles, since chemists confess that it has an inflammable ingredient, and experience shows that it very much abounds with an acid and uninflammable salt, and is not quite devoid of terrestreity.[4] I know it may be

1 That is, bodies that can be dissipated or dispersed.

2 "The Sceptical Chymist," *Works* vol. 2.

3 Though Boyle and other chemists before Lavoisier did not really develop a theory of chemical elements, it is interesting to note that Boyle felt that any such theory would need to be supplemented by an account from physics.

4 The property of containing earthy matter.

here alleged, that the productions of chemical analyses are simple bodies, and upon that account irresoluble. But, that divers substances, which chemists are pleased to call the salts, or sulphurs, or mercuries of the bodies that afforded them, are not simple and homogeneous has elsewhere been sufficiently proved,[1] nor is their not being easily dissipable or resoluble a clear proof of their not being made up of more primitive portions of matter. For compounded and even decompounded[2] bodies may be as difficultly resoluble as most of those that chemists obtain by what they call their analysis by the fire: witness common green glass, which is far more durable and irresoluble than many of those that pass for hypostatical[3] substances. And we see that some enamels will be several times even vitrified[4] in the fire, without losing their nature, or oftentimes so much as their colour, and yet enamel is manifestly not only a compounded, but a decompounded body, consisting of salt and powder or pebbles or sand, and calcined tin and, if the enamel be not white, usually of some tingeing metal or mineral. But how indestructible soever the chemical principles be supposed, divers of the operations ascribed to them will never be well made out, without the help of local motion (and that diversified too), without which we can little better give an account of the phenomena of many bodies, by knowing what ingredients compose them, than we can explain the operations of a watch, by knowing of how many and of what metals the balance, the wheels, the chain, and other parts, are made, or than we can derive the operations of a windmill from the bare knowledge that it is made up of wood, and stone, and canvas, and iron.

And here let me add, that it would not at all overthrow the corpuscularian hypothesis, though it should be made appear, either by more exquisite purifications, or by some other operations than the usual analysis of the fire, that the material principles of elements of mixed bodies should not be the *tria prima* of the vulgar chemists, but either substances of another nature, or else fewer, or more in number, as would be, if that were true (which some Spagyrists affirm, but I could never find) that from all sorts of mixed bodies, five, and but five, differing similar substances can

---

1 In "The Sceptical Chymist," *Works* vol. 2.

2 Compounded of parts which are themselves compounded; originally, as Boyle elsewhere notes, a grammarian's term.

3 Elemental.

4 To vitrify is to turn into glass or a glass-like substance, usually by the application of heat.

be separated. Nor, if it were true, that the Helmontians had such a resolving menstruum[1] as the alkahest[2] of their master, by which he affirms, that he could reduce stones into salt of the same weight with the mineral, and bring both that salt and all other kind of mixed and tangible bodies into insipid water. For what ever be the number or qualities of the chemical principles, if they be really existent in nature it may very possibly be shown that they may be made up of insensible corpuscles of the determinate bulks and shapes, and by the various coalitions and contextures of such corpuscles, not only three or five, but many more material ingredients may be composed or made to result, and, though the alkahestical reductions newly mentioned should be admitted, yet the mechanical principles might well be accommodated even to them. For the solidity, taste, etc. of salt may be fairly accounted for by the stiffness, sharpness, and other mechanical affections of the minute particles, whereof salts consist, and if by a farther action of the alkahest, the salt or any other solid body, be reduced into insipid water, this also may be explicated by the same principles, supposing a further comminution of the parts, and such an attrition as wears off the edges and points that enabled them to strike briskly the organ of taste.

As to fluidity and firmness, those mainly depend upon two of our grand principles, motion and rest. And I have elsewhere shown,[3] by several proofs, that the agitation or rest, and the looser contact or closer cohesion of the particles is able to make the same portion of matter, at one time a firm, and at another time, a fluid body, so that, though the further sagacity and industry of chemists (which I would by no means discourage) should be able to obtain from mixed bodies homogeneous substances differing in number, or nature, or both, from their vulgar salt, sulphur, and mercury, yet the corpuscular philosophy[4] is so general and fertile, as to be fairly reconcilable to such a discovery. It is also so useful that these new material principles will, as well as the old *tria prima*, stand in need of the more catholic prin-

---

1 A solvent.

2 The alkahest of the Helmontians was intended to be a universal solvent. However the recipe for it was, as Clericuzio remarks, "a matter of contention." See further Clericuzio 2000, 112-13 for discussion and further references.

3 "The History of Fluidity and Firmness," *Works* vol. 2.

4 The Latin version of the text has "*Mechanica philosophia*"—mechanical philosophy.

ciples of the corpuscularians,[1] especially local motion. And indeed, whatever elements or ingredients men have (that I know of) pitched upon, yet if they take not in the mechanical affections of matter, their principles have been so deficient, that I have usually observed that the materialists without at all excepting the chemists, do not only, as I was saying, leave many things unexplained to which their narrow principles will not extend but, even in the particulars they presume to give an account of, they either content themselves to assign such common and indefinite causes as are too general to signify much towards an inquisitive man's satisfaction. Or, if they venture to give particular causes, they assign precarious or false ones which are liable to be easily disproved by circumstances, or instances, whereto their doctrine will not agree, as I have often elsewhere had occasion to show.

The chemists need not be frightened from acknowledging the prerogative of the mechanical philosophy, since that may be reconcilable with the truth of their own principles, as far as these agree with the phenomena they are applied to. For these more confined hypotheses may be subordinated to those more general and fertile principles, and there can be no ingredient assigned, that has a real existence in nature, that may not be derived either immediately, or by a row of decompositions, from the universal matter, modified by its mechanical affections. For if with the same bricks, diversely put together and ranged, several walls, houses, furnaces, and other structures, as vaults, bridges, pyramids, etc. may be built, merely by a various contrivance of parts of the same kind, how much more may great variety of ingredients be produced by, or, according to the institution of nature, result from, the various coalitions and contextures of corpuscles, that need not be supposed, like bricks, all of the same or near the same size and shape, but may have amongst them, both of the one and the other, as great a variety as need be wished for, and indeed a greater than can easily be so much as imagined. And the primary and minute concretions that belong to these ingredients may, without opposition from the mechanical philosophy, be supposed to have their particles so minute and strongly coherent, that nature of itself does scarce ever tear them asunder; as we see that mercury and gold may be successively made to put on a multitude of disguises, and yet so retain their nature as to be reducible to their pristine forms. And you know, I lately told you

1 The Latin text has "*principiis Mechanicorum*"—the principles of the mechanical philosophers.

that common glass and good enamels, though both of them are factitious[1] bodies, and not only mixed but decompounded concretions, have yet their component parts so strictly united by the skill of illiterate tradesmen, as to maintain their union in the vitrifying violence of the fire. Nor do we find, that common glass will be wrought upon by *aqua fortis*, or *aqua regis*,[2] though the former of them will dissolve mercury, and the latter gold.

From the fore-going discourse it may (probably at least) result, that if, besides rational souls, there are any immaterial substances (such as the heavenly intelligences, and the substantial forms of the Aristotelians) that regularly are to be numbered among natural agents, their way of working being unknown to us, they can but help to constitute and effect things but will very little help us to conceive how things are effected, so that by what ever principles natural things be constituted, it is by the mechanical principles that their phenomena must be clearly explicated.[3] As for instance, though we should grant the Aristotelians that the

---

1 Artificial.

2 Latin: *aqua fortis* (literally "strong water") is nitric acid; Latin: *aqua regis* (royal water) is a mixture of hydrochloric and nitric acid, so called because it will dissolve the "noble" metals, gold and platinum. (Platinum, though discovered and used by pre-Columbian people in South America, was not known to Europeans until the second quarter of the eighteenth century, so from Boyle's point of view *aqua regis* was "noble" because it dissolved gold.)

3 Boyle makes the same point with particular reference to human minds in the *Notion of Nature*:

> The *Rational Soul* or *Mind* of Man, as it is distinct from the sensitive Soul, being an immaterial Spirit; is a substance of so Heteroclite a kind, in reference to things so vastly differing from it as mere *Bodies* are, that since I could neither, without injuring it, treat of it promiscuously with the Corporeal Works of God, nor speak worthily of it, without frequently interrupting and disordering my Discourse by Exceptions, that would either make it appear intricate, or would be very troublesome to you or any other that you may think fit to make my Reader; I thought I might, for others ease and my own, be allow'd to set aside the considerations of it in the present Treatise: And the rather, because all other parts of the Universe being, according to the receiv'd Opinion, the Works of *Nature*, we shall not want in them Subjects more than sufficiently numerous, whereon to make our *Examen*. Though I shall here consider the World but as the great System of things Corporeal, as it once really was, towards the close of the sixth day of the Creation, when God had finish'd all his material Works, but had not yet Created *Man*. [*Works* 10:452]

planets are made of a quintessential matter, and moved by angels or immaterial intelligences, yet, to explain the stations, progressions, and retrogradations, and other phenomena of the planets, we must have recourse either to eccentrics, epicycles, etc., or to motions made in elliptical or other peculiar lines and, in a word, to theories wherein the motion, and figure, situation, and other mathematical or mechanical affections of bodies are mainly employed. But if the principles proposed be corporeal things, they will be then fairly reducible or reconcilable to the mechanical principles, these being so general and pregnant that, among things corporeal, there is nothing real (and I meddle not with chimerical beings,[1] such as some of Paracelsus's) that may not be derived from, or be brought to, a subordination to such comprehensive principles. And when the chemists shall show that mixed bodies owe their qualities to the predominance of this or that of their three grand ingredients, the corpuscularians will show that the very qualities of this or that ingredient flow from its peculiar texture, and the mechanical affections of the corpuscles it is made up of. And to affirm, that because the furnaces of chemists afford a great number of uncommon productions and phenomena, there are bodies or operations amongst things purely corporeal that cannot be derived from or reconciled to the comprehensive and pregnant principles of the mechanical philosophy is as if, because there are a great number and variety of anthems, hymns, pavins, threnodies, courants, gavots, branles, sarabands, jigs, and other (grave and sprightly) tunes[2] to be met with in the books and practises of musicians, one should maintain that there

---

1 In Greek mythology, the chimera had a lion's head, a goat's body, and a serpent's tail—hence a paradigm case of something impossible.

2 A pavane was a slow and dignified processional dance, associated in Boyle's day with the Spanish court; a threnody was a lament or a dirge, particularly for the dead; the courante, favoured by Louis XIV (1638-1715), was a couples' dance, whose popularity was displaced by the minuet; a gavotte was originally a peasant dance from the region about Gap in the French Alps, which became popular in the French court in the seventeenth century; branles (also brangles) were Renaissance circle dances, sometimes involving miming or various facial expressions; a saraband is a dance whose origins are obscure, but in Boyle's time it had arrived at the French court via Spain, and had changed from a dance whose sensual movements caused it to be banned in places to something more like a slow minuet. It is found incorporated in the works of Bach, Handel, and others. Later Satie wrote three sarabands for piano, and Debussy and others made use of the form.

are in them a great many tunes, or at least notes, that have no dependence on the scale of music. Or, as if because, besides rhombusses, rhomboids, trapeziums, squares, pentagons, chiliagons, myriagons, and innumerable other polygons, regular and irregular, one should presume to affirm, that there are among them some rectilinear figures, that are not reducible to triangles, or have affections that will overthrow what Euclid has taught of triangles and polygons.

To what has been said I shall add but one thing more: that as, according to what I formerly intimated, mechanical principles and explications are for their clearness preserved even by materialists themselves and others in the cases where they can be had, so the sagacity and industry of modern naturalists and mathematicians, having happily applied them on several of those difficult phenomena (in hydrostatics, the practical part of optics, gunnery, etc.) that before were, or might be, referred to occult qualities, it is probable that when this philosophy is more deeply searched into and farther improved, it will be found applicable to the solution of more and more of the phenomena of nature. And on this occasion let me observe, that it is not always necessary—though it be always desirable—that he that propounds an hypothesis in astronomy, chemistry, anatomy, or other part of physics, be able, *a priori*, to prove his hypothesis to be true, or demonstratively to show that the other hypotheses proposed about the same subject must be false. For as, if I mistake not, Plato said that the world was God's epistle written to mankind,[1] and might have added, consonantly to another saying of his, it was written in mathematical letters, so, in the physical explications of the parts and system of the world, methinks, there is somewhat like what happens when men conjecturally frame several keys to enable us to understand a letter written in ciphers. For though one man by his sagacity have found out the right key, it will be very difficult for him either to prove otherwise than by trial, that this or that word is not such as it is guessed to be by others according to their

1 O theos aei geometrei [RB's note]. That is, "God always geometrizes," also attributed to Plato by Boyle in "Usefulness II," *Works* 6:463. This saying, though consistent with Plato's views, does not appear in Plato's writings. A character in one of the dialogues of Plutarch (c. 46-after 119 CE) suggests that Plato "asserted that God is always doing geometry," but adds, "if indeed this statement is to be attributed to Plato." Plutarch replies, "I remarked that while this statement is not made explicitly in any of Plato's writings, it is well enough attested and is in harmony with his character" (Plutarch 1961, Vol. 9, Book 8, Q. 2, p. 119.)

keys, or to evince, *a priori*, that theirs are to be rejected, and his to be preferred, yet, if due trial being made, the key he proposes shall be found so agreeable to the characters of the letter as to enable one to understand them and make a coherent sense of them, its suitableness to what it should decipher is, without either confutations, or extraneous positive proofs, sufficient to make it be accepted as the right key of that cipher. And so, in physical hypotheses there are some that, without noise, or falling foul upon others, peaceably obtain discerning men's approbation only by their fitness to solve the phenomena for which they were devised, without crossing any known observation or law of nature. And therefore, if the mechanical philosophy go on to explicate things corporeal at the rate it has of late years proceeded at, it is scarce to be doubted, but that in time unprejudiced persons will think it sufficiently recommended by its consistency with itself, and its applicableness to so many phenomena of nature.

A recapitulation.

Perceiving, upon a review of the foregoing paper, that the difficulty and importance of the subject, has seduced me to spend many more words about it than I at first designed, it will not now be amiss to give you this short summary of what came into my mind to recommend to you the mechanical philosophy, and obviate your fears of seeing it supplanted, having first premised once for all, that presupposing the creation and general providence of God, I pretend to treat but of things corporeal, and do abstract in this paper from immaterial beings (which otherwise I very willingly admit) and all agents and operations miraculous or supernatural.

I. Of the principles of things corporeal, none can be fewer without being insufficient, and none can be more primary than matter and motion.

II. The natural and genuine effect of variously determined motion in portions of matter is to divide it into parts of differing sizes, and shapes, and to put them into different motions. And in a world framed as ours is, the consequences that flow from these are, as to the separate fragments: posture, order, and situation; and, as to the conventions of many of them: peculiar compositions and contextures.

III. The parts of matter endowed with these catholic affections are by various affectations reduced to natural bodies of several kinds, according to the abundance of the matter, and the various compositions and decompositions of the principles, which all suppose the common matter they diversify. And these several kinds of bodies, by virtue of their motion, rest, and other mechanical affectations, which fit them to act on, and suffer from, one another, become endowed with several kinds of qualities (whereof some are called manifest, and some occult), and those that act upon the peculiarly framed organs of sense, whose perceptions by the animadversive[1] faculty[2] of the soul are sensations.

IV. These principles, matter, motion (to which rest is related) bigness, shape, posture, order, texture, being so simple, clear, and comprehensive, are applicable to all the real phenomena of nature, which seem not explicable by any other not consistent with ours. For, if recourse be had to an immaterial principle or agent, it may be such a one, as is not intelligible, and however it will not enable us to explain the phenomena, because its way of working upon things material would probably be more difficult to be physically made out, than a mechanical account of the phenomena. And notwithstanding the immateriality of a created agent, we cannot conceive how it should produce changes in a body, without the help of mechanical principles, especially local motion, and accordingly we find not, that the reasonable soul in man is able to produce what changes it pleases in the body, but is confined to such, as it may produce by determining or guiding the motions of the spirits, and other parts of the body, subservient to voluntary motion.

V. And if the agents or active principles resorted to, be not immaterial, but of a corporeal nature, they must either in effect be the same with the corporeal principles above-named or, because of the great universality and simplicity of our principles, the new ones proposed must be less general than they. Consequently they must be capable of being subordinated or reduced to ours, which by various compositions may afford matter to several hypotheses, and by several coalitions afford minute concretions exceedingly numerous and durable, and consequently fit to become the elementary ingredients of more compounded bodies, being in most trials similar, and as it were the radical parts, which may, after several manners, be diversified, as in Latin the themes are by prepositions, terminations, etc., and in Hebrew, the roots by the haeemantic[3] letters. So that the fear,

---

1 Attending or noticing.

2 The faculty of attending or noticing.

3 A mnemonic word which, in the original Hebrew, contains the letters used in derivative words and inflected forms.

that so much of a new physical hypothesis as is true will overthrow or make useless the mechanical principles, is as if one should fear, that there will be a language proposed, that is discordant from, or not reducible to, the letters of the alphabet.

THE END.

Appendix A: People Mentioned in the Text

Abimelech: The interchange that Boyle mentions between God and Abimelech, the King of Gerar, is chronicled at Genesis 20. Abraham had journeyed to Gerar after the destruction of the cities of the plain, and since "Abraham said of Sarah his wife, She is my sister ... Abimelech king of Gerar sent, and took Sarah."[1] This led to a nocturnal interchange between God and Abimelech in which Abimelech pleaded his innocence in the matter and since "Abimelech had not come near her"[2] the incident was smoothed over. God revoked various punishments he had already instigated, and Abimelech gave Abraham sheep and cattle, male and female slaves, and a large amount of money. Boyle's primary interest in the account lies in the fact that it provides a clear case in which God lets humans know of his interests, intents, and desires. The incident provided logicians with a clear-cut example of the distinction between relational and other properties. In 1654 Zachary Coke noted, "Relation by it self is not perceived by the senses.... Abimelech saw Sarah to be a fair woman, but could not see her to be Abrahams wife."[3]

Abraham: As well as providing Boyle with yet another case of God's interaction with humans, Boyle also notes Abraham's willingness to sacrifice Isaac as an example of extreme faith. At MS 189:100, where Boyle is discussing the differing strengths of faith, Abraham's is noted as being "of the 1st magnitude." In the next century, Kant, comparing the uncertainty of supposed revelation against the certainty of moral imperatives, notes that even if such a revelation "appears to have come to him from God Himself (like the command delivered to Abraham to slaughter his own son like a sheep) it is at least possible that in this instance a mistake has prevailed," and that therefore the supposed command should not be obeyed.[4]

Ælian (c. 170-c. 230 CE): Claudius Ælianus taught rhetoric in Rome and wrote a number of works, including *Varia Historia*

1 Genesis 20.2.

2 Genesis 20.4.

3 Coke 1654, 45.

4 Kant 1793, 175.

(Historical Miscellanies) and *De Natura Animalium* (On the Characteristics of Animals), in which there is the first recorded mention of fly fishing. Boyle objected to his view that generation could occur spontaneously. Running counter to the views of many of his contemporaries, Boyle explicitly denied spontaneous generation even in insects (CV1, *Works* 11:300).

Ahab and Ahab's prophets: Ahab was a king of Israel who "did more to provoke the LORD God of Israel to anger than all the kings of Israel that were before him." He married Jezebel; he worshipped Baal, and he refused to heed Micaiah, of whom he said "he doth not prophesy good concerning me, but evil." In one of what Boyle calls "two strange and matchless passages"[1] we discover that after about four hundred of Ahab's prophets had told him he would be successful in a forthcoming battle Micaiah told Ahab that he had seen

> the LORD sitting on his throne, and all the host of heaven standing by him on his right hand and on his left. And the LORD said, Who shall persuade Ahab, that he may go up and fall at Ramothgilead? And one said on this manner, and another said on that manner. And there came forth a spirit, and stood before the LORD, and said, I will persuade him. And the LORD said unto him, Wherewith? And he said, I will go forth, and I will be a lying spirit in the mouth of all his prophets. And he said, Thou shalt persuade him, and prevail also: go forth, and do so. Now therefore, behold, the LORD hath put a lying spirit in the mouth of all these thy prophets, and the LORD hath spoken evil concerning thee.[2]

Ahab, however, refused to listen, and after commanding that Micaiah be put in prison and given the "bread of affliction and ... water of affliction,"[3] duly went off to be killed in battle.

Alexander the Great (356-23 BCE): Alexander, the son of Philip of Macedon, and pupil of Aristotle, conquered much of the then known world. Boyle tells us that as a child "at Eton he (Boyle, not Alexander) became a passionate ... Friend to Reading" as a result of "the accidentall Persusall of [*The History*

1 *Works* 8:16 [115].

2 1 Kings 22.19-23.

3 1 Kings 22.27.

of Alexander the Great by] Quintus Curtius which first made him in Love with other then Pedanticke Bookes, & conjur'd up in [him] that unsatisfy'd Curiosity <Appetite> of Knowledge, that is yet as greedy, as when it first was rays'd."[1]

Anaxagoras (500-428 BCE): Anaxagoras taught that there were infinite kinds of matter, all present, in varying degrees, in every individual object, and indeed in every portion of space. There is "a portion of everything in everything," with the nature of the individual item being explained by the preponderance of one sort over the others. Anaxagoras held that "The Greeks are wrong to recognize coming into being and perishing; for nothing comes into being nor perishes, but is rather compounded or dissolved from things that are,"[2] which makes him suspect from Boyle's Christian point of view. However, the ordering currently present in the universe was a result of the activity of Mind which brought about the changes in the world, and accounted for the existence of living things. Anaxagoras was expelled from Athens for reasons that are no longer clear. Traditionally it was held that the basis for his expulsion was his impiety, a charge supposedly based on his view that the sun was a large hot lump of metal. The charge may have been an indirect attack on Pericles who, like Euripides, had been a pupil of his. Like Boyle, Anaxagoras, though stressing the need for Mind as an explanatory device for the system as a whole, nonetheless seems to have insisted on strictly mechanistic explanations for goings-on within the system. Aristotle reports that "when somebody asked Anaxagoras for what reason one might choose to come into being and live, they say he replied to the question by saying, 'To observe the things in the heavens, the stars in it, the moon, and sun,' because indeed nothing else is worth anything." (Aristotle 2002; Aristotle has a similar account in the *Eudemian Ethics*, Aristotle 1984, 1216a 11-14.)

Aquilonius (1546-1617): François D'Aguilon (Aquilonius) was the author of *Opticorum libri sex philosophis juxta ac mathematicis utiles* (Anvers, 1613), or *Six Books of Optics, useful for philosophers and mathematicians alike*, a work illustrated by Rubens. D'Aguilon (the Opticomathematician as Boyle's slightly older contemporary, Walter Charleton, called him), was widely respected in the seventeenth century. Both Christiaan Huygens and his father,

1 BP 37:175; Hunter 1994, 7.

2 Kirk, Raven, and Schofield 1983, 358, fr 469.

Constantijn, found D'Aguilon's *Opticorum* important and helpful. Boyle mentions Aquilonius as someone who successfully combined an interest in theology and natural philosophy: "Among the Jesuits you know that Clavius and divers others have as prosperously addicted themselves to mathematics as divinity. And as to physics, not only Scheiner, Aquilonius, Kircher, Schottus, Zucchius, and others have very laudably cultivated the optical and some other parts of philosophy."[1]

Archimedes (c. 287-12 BCE): Archimedes, to whom Boyle constantly refers in manuscript and in his published works, was the world's greatest pre-Newtonian mathematician and physicist. Many stories have gathered around him, including the one that Boyle recounts while making the point that the pleasures of the understanding are the highest that humans "can naturally receive": "I cannot much wonder [Boyle wrote] that the famous Archimedes lighting in a Bath upon an Experiment to resolve a perplexing difficultie in Naturall Philosophy, should leap out of the Bath, and run unclothed like a madman, crying nothing but *Eureka, Eureka, I have found it, I have found it*."[2] Archimedes' work on the lever gave rise to his remark, "Give me a place to stand, and I can move the earth," and his work on pulleys allowed him to move on land, by himself, a fully loaded ship that had been dragged ashore by many men with great difficulty. His work on finding the areas and volumes of a number of plane and solid figures anticipates much of what we now think of as integration in calculus. "His work," Thomas Heath said, "represents a sum of mathematical achievements unsurpassed by any one man in the world's history."[3] He was killed by a Roman soldier during the sack of Syracuse in the second Punic War.

Aristarchus (c. 310-250 BCE): Aristarchus of Samos was an early proponent of the heliocentric view of the universe. Consonant with this, he held that the earth rotates daily on its axis, and that the universe is much larger than was then imagined. Aristarchus, who was a very fine mathematician as well as an astronomer, applied geometric methods to calculating astronomical distances. Mathematically his methods were excellent, but since his prior assumptions were mistaken, his accurate calculations led to erroneous results.

---

1 *Works* 8:93 [219].

2 *Works* 3:201.

3 Heath 1921, 2:20.

Aristotle (c. 384-22 BCE): see the Introductory section, "Predecessors and Influences."

Arminius (1560-1609): Jakob Hermandszoon Arminius (and his followers, the Arminians or Remonstrants) held, against more orthodox Calvinists, that predestination was conditional, not absolute. God gives forgiveness of sins and eternal life to all who repent and believe in Jesus Christ; it is his *will* that all should be saved, but he has foreseen the belief or unbelief of each human and thus has, from eternity, decided the fate of each individual. See also the entries for Grotius and Episcopius.

Augustine (354-430): As recorded in his *Confessions* Augustine—Boyle's "St. Austin"—was converted to Christianity from Manichaeism as a young man. His Neoplatonic views were highly influential throughout the Middle Ages. Epistemologically, he was far removed from Boyle, but Boyle always speaks of him with respect, though it is fairly clear that it is his theological rather than his philosophical or scientific views that Boyle admires. His abhorrence of lying was shared by Boyle. Augustine is firm on the matter: lying, he tells a correspondent (in *Contra Mendacium*), is always wrong, even if it is the only way to catch a heretic.

Augustus (63 BCE-14 CE): Gaius Julius Caesar Octavianus Augustus is commended by Boyle for his patronage of intellectual matters, and it was under his rule that Horace (65 BCE-8 CE), Virgil (70-19 BCE), Ovid (43 BCE-17 CE), Propertius (48-15 BCE) and Livy (59 BCE-17 CE) flourished. Augustus claimed his inheritance from Caesar after Caesar's assassination in 43 BCE, and, after a variety of internal disputes, was effectively in sole control of Rome (which he "found made of brick, and left made of marble"[1]) from 29 BCE, in which year he proclaimed universal peace. His counsellor, Gaius Maecenas (c. 70-8 BCE) was equally a patron of the arts. Virgil's *Georgics* was written in honour of Augustus.

Bacon, Francis (1561-1626): see the Introductory section, "Predecessors and Influences."

Bacon, Roger (Friar Bacon, c. 1214-92/4): In his *Opus Maius*, Bacon stressed the importance of studying mathematics, since

1 Suetonius, *Divus Augustus, De Vita Caesarum*, XXIX.

"every science requires mathematics."[1] In the same work he argued for light's having a finite velocity (something still found dubious by Boyle's friend and assistant Robert Hooke in the seventeenth century) and, strongly influenced by his Arabic predecessors such as Al Hazen and Al Kindi, and his older near contemporary Grosseteste, made a number of other important points concerning optics and vision. His other interests included magnetism and alchemy, where again he was influenced by his Arabic predecessors, in this case Ibn Sina (Avicenna). He gives a recipe for gunpowder which is somewhat deficient in saltpetre. His interest in experimentation is clear, as is his breadth, and it is not surprising that Boyle found that legends attached themselves to him. His *Opus Tertium* includes, as do the *Opus Maius* and the *Opus Minus*, sections on alchemy. Apparently as a result of his criticisms of various leading Dominicans, and of senior members of his own Franciscan order, he was imprisoned from 1277 until 1292. It is not clear whether he died in 1292, or two years later in 1294.

Bellarmine, St. Robert (1542-1621): In the controversy concerning the Copernican hypothesis (declared heretical in 1616 and suspended "until it can be corrected") Bellarmine held that *if* the Copernican hypothesis could be "strictly demonstrated" it could be accepted, and scriptural language apparently at odds with it could be interpreted as metaphorical. Until such a *strict* demonstration was offered, however, the heliocentric system (including Galileo's version of it) was to be rejected. Boyle often points out the inappropriateness of requiring "strict demonstration" in empirical matters. The young Boyle summed up the situation: Galileo's "ingenious Bookes, perhaps because they could not be so otherwise were confuted by a Decree from Rome."[2] Bellarmine was canonized in 1930.

Brahe, Tycho (1546-1601): Tycho Brahe was the most accurate naked-eye astronomical observer ever known. Even after the invention of the telescope his observations, which corrected many earlier errors, continued to be both useful and, in many cases, more accurate than later results. His observations were used by Kepler (his assistant at the very end of Brahe's life) to test and eliminate a number of hypotheses concerning planetary

1 Bacon 1733, Part IV, chapter 2, p. 58.

2 BP 37:183v-184, Hunter 1994, 19.

orbits before he settled on the correct elliptical result. Boyle notes Tycho's observation and report of a supernova in 1572 as a paradigm case of our ability to recognize reliable testimony and learn from it. He rejected both the Copernican and the Ptolemaic accounts of the solar system and offered a compromise: the then known five non-terrestrial planets revolve about the sun making up a system which in turn revolves about the stationary earth. Mathematically all three systems "save the appearances," but the subsequent work of Kepler, Galileo and Newton made the heliocentric system the preferred option.

Calvin, Jean (1509-64): Jean Calvin, the French theologian and reformer, is mentioned by Boyle in *The Excellency of Theology* merely as one of a number of thinkers whose theological works have had as much influence as those of natural philosophers. However in *Seraphic Love*, while remarking that he will not discuss the controversies involved, he makes it clear that Calvin's major doctrinal thesis, that of predestination, is unacceptable and should not be adopted by practising Christians (*Works* 1: 108-09). Calvin's control of Geneva from 1541 onward shaped that city into the form it still had when Boyle visited it as a boy.

Campanella, Tommaso (1568-1639): Tommaso Campanella's life reveals an ability to upset and antagonize colleagues, acquaintances and superiors unmatched since Abailard's time. As a student he argued with his instructors and urged the same behaviour on his classmates. He was strongly influenced by the works of Telesio. Defending Telesio with the tact that seems to have marked his life, Campanella remarked that pure Peripatetics "are heretics, whereas Telesio is a Christian philosopher." Eventually, after a number of charges of immorality (sometimes but not always successfully defended against), seizure of his manuscripts, accusations of being a follower of Democritus (whose views he had in fact attacked), at least six occasions of physical torture (twice saving himself from confessing under torture by feigning madness, later using this experience as proof of the freedom of the will), various charges of heresy and conspiracy (he felt himself to be a plausible reformer of the century, and was not shy in making this known), and a number of earlier incarcerations, on 13 November, 1602 the Holy See sentenced him to be imprisoned "with no hope for liberation." This imprisonment in fact lasted until 1626. Released in 1626, he was rearrested a month later and not freed again until 1629. His life continued stormy, and he fled to France in disguise in 1634, where he was received with favour by Richelieu. Even then, however, his disagreement with Gassendi over atomism brought him fresh hostility. Finally, when dying, he turned to astrological practices in an attempt to lengthen his life. Boyle admired "the subtill Campanella," but felt that his "excellent parts deserv'd to have been instructed by Experiments."[1]

Cardanus (1501-76): Girolamo Cardano lacked social but not mathematical graces. He produced the first general solution to cubic equations. He is said to have been addicted to gambling and chess. Cardano was aware of the possibility of negative and complex roots for equations, and pointed out that if we multiply $5 + \sqrt{-15}$ by $5 - \sqrt{-15}$ we get 40, but added "thus far does arithmetical subtlety go, of which this, the extreme, is ... so subtle that it is useless."[2] (As late as Descartes negative numbers were regarded as "false numbers." Complex numbers were even further beyond the pale.) Cardano was a system-maker—an activity Boyle found dubious. He published a scientific encyclopaedia in which he treated both alchemy (lowering the four elements to three by omitting fire, which he regarded as a form of motion) and electromagnetism. His mathematical ability is clear, but his originality is cast in doubt by the suggestion that the cubic solution was given to him by Tartaglia who may, however, have been anticipated in turn by Scipione del Ferro. An English translation of his interesting autobiography is available (Cardano 2002).

Chaldeans: Chaldea is the region of ancient Babylonia formed by the Mesopotamian plain, and bordered on the south by the Persian Gulf. The Chaldeans ultimately gained control of the Babylonian empire, which was conquered by Cyrus in 539 BCE However, "Chaldean" was also a term generally applied to those Babylonian priests who were trained in the arts and in astronomy and astrology, so the "fabulous Chaldeans" who, in Boyle's opinion, underestimated the age of the earth were early Babylonian astronomers. (See also p. 121, note.)

Charlemagne (Charles the Great, 747-814): After a series of conquests in which he vastly extended his realm, Charlemagne turned to more peaceful pursuits and founded an academy at

---

1 *Works* 13:166, 231.

2 *Ars Magna*, Chapter 37, Cardano 1663, 4:287.

Aachen (Aix-la-Chapelle) to which many scholars, of whom Alcuin of York was perhaps the most notable, were invited. His attempts, aided by Alcuin, to foster education and the arts, along with his concern for agriculture, a stable legal system and an acceptable system of administration, gave rise to the "Carolingian renaissance" that did not, however, long survive his death. His grandson Charles the Bald also encouraged learning and supported the work of the Irish Neoplatonist John Scottus Eriugena, despite the fact (which he may not have noticed) that Eriugena's views skated along the edge of heresy.

Cicero (106-43 BCE): Marcus Tullius Cicero was a soldier, an orator, a statesman, and in philosophy, an academic sceptic. Although Boyle admired him as a rhetorician (Cicero, says Boyle, is "reputed (and that Deservedly) an Eloquent man"), and refers to his views on rhetoric at length in the *Style of the Scriptures*, it is Cicero's *On the Nature of God* that he most frequently cites. Cicero was killed as a result of his published attacks on Antony after the assassination of Caesar. In addition to his views on religion Boyle was interested in Cicero's negative views on the doctrines of the classical atomists.

Clavius (1538-1612): Christopher Clavius devised the reform that led to the present Gregorian—after Gregory XIII—calendar. There were two parts to the reform. One was moving ahead ten days in terms of the old calendar, while the other involved moving the beginning of the year from March 25 to January 1 and introducing our present system of leap years. Catholic, but not Protestant, states accepted the reform at once (in 1582). Defending the reform against attacks, Clavius wrote *Novi calendarii romani apologia* (1595). The reform was adopted late, and at various dates, by the non-Catholic states. Britain adopted the new style calendar in 1752; countries whose national religion was Eastern Orthodox were much later. For example, Russia (or the USSR) made the switch in 1918, after the revolution. Boyle's interest in Clavius was as someone versed in mathematics as well as in divinity.

Copernicus (1473-1543): Nicolas Copernicus studied mathematics and optics at the University of Kracow and, subsequently, canon law at the University of Bologna. He then studied medicine at the University of Padua. *De Revolutionibus*, in which he argued for a heliocentric solar system, was completed by 1530, but an earlier version was circulated among friends in 1514. *De Revolutionibus* was published just before his death, in large part due to his student Georg Rheticus, who persuaded Copernicus that it was sufficiently revised. *De Revolutionibus* was placed on the Index in 1616 (and removed in 1835). As first published it contained a preface suggesting that the sun-centred system was simply a mathematical convenience; Kepler, a firm believer in the actuality of the heliocentric system, showed subsequently that the preface was by Osiander, not Copernicus. In *The Excellency of Theology* Boyle points out that Copernicus, "to whom our late philosophers owe so much,"[1] was a churchman. Copernicus was canon of Frauenburg, though he never became a priest, and he was also bailiff, military governor, judge, tax collector, vicar-general, physician and reformer of the coinage (though his proposals were not acted upon). "Of all discoveries and opinions, none may have exerted a greater effect on the human spirit than the doctrine of Copernicus," said Goethe.[2]

Daniel: For Boyle, Daniel is important as one praised by God, along with David, Job, and Noah. Daniel himself reports (Daniel 10) that after three weeks in which "I ate no pleasant bread, neither came flesh nor wine in my mouth," he had a vision in which, as Boyle notes, an angel told him that he was "a man greatly beloved." The episode is also important for Boyle elsewhere in a way not mentioned in this text since the angel also provided Daniel with knowledge of the future, and knowledge of future contingents by God was a standing puzzle for believers.[3] (For discussion see Appendix F, "Future Contingents.")

David: David is popularly known for his killing of Goliath; Boyle's interest in him is manifold, but chiefly as one praised by God, and one to whom God spoke directly. He became King, and was also, he tells us, a prophet (2 Samuel, 23.2, a claim substantiated by St. Peter at Acts 2.30). Boyle does not dwell upon David's adultery with Bathsheba and his involvement in her husband's death. To punish David (and Bathsheba) God

---

1 *Works* 8:92 [219].

2 Goethe 1948, 16:395.

3 The Book of Daniel was also standardly cited in support of the goals of the new philosophy: "Many shall run to and fro and knowledge shall be increased" (Daniel 12.4). On this topic see further Webster 1975. (Thanks to Colleen Franklin for drawing this to my attention.)

arranged that their son should die. Subsequently however they had another son, Solomon, who was allowed to live and flourish.

Democritus (c. 460-c. 370 BCE): Democritus is, with Leucippus, one of the two earliest known atomists. Democritus held that there were physically indivisible atoms and, to allow for motion, the void. Boyle's knowledge of him comes mainly via Epicurus and Lucretius. In an early paper Boyle wrote:

> The Atomicall Philosophy invented or brought into request by Democritus, Leucippus, Epicurus, & their Contemporaries, though since the inundation of Barbarians & Barbarisme expelled out of the Roman world all but the casually escaping Peripatetic Philosophy, it has been either wholly ignored in the European Schools or mentioned there but as an exploded System of Absurdities yet in our less partial & more inquisitive times it is so luckily revived & so skillfully celebrated in divers parts of Europe by the learned pens of Gassendus, Magnenus, Descartes & his disciples, our deservedly famous Countryman Sir Kenelme Digby & many other writers especially those that handle magneticall & electricall operations that it is now grown too considerable to be any longer laughed at, & considerable enough to deserve a serious enquiry (BP 26:162, *Works* 13:227).

Later he remarked, "In the controversy between Aristotle and Democritus ... I take not upon me to determine here anything about the Truth of the Opinions, but only about the goodnes of the Argumentations. And thô I fear that neither has opin'd well, yet Democritus seems to have Philosophis'd the better of the two."[1] For Aristotle's arguments against Democritus see Appendix C, "Aristotle's Arguments against the Void."

Descartes (1596-1650): see the Introductory section, "Predecessors and Influences."

Digby, Kenelm (1603-65): Boyle describes "the eminently-learned Sir Kenelme Digby,"[2] who was related to Boyle by marriage, as "my Noble Friend,"[3] and elsewhere calls him "our

---

1 BP 9:106r; Boyle 2006, p. 327.

2 *Works* 3:165.

3 *Works* 3:348.

deservedly famous Countryman."[1] Digby wrote a lengthy treatise on the body as a preliminary to his much shorter one on the soul, explaining that before writing on the soul one should see how much could be explained purely in terms of the body:

> my desire and intent ... is onely, to shew from what principles, all kindes of corporeall operations do proceed; and what kind of operations all these must be, which may issue out of these principles: to the end, that I may from thence, make a steppe to raise my discourse to the contemplation of the soule; and shew, that her operations are such, as cannot proceed from those principles; which being adequate and common to all bodies, we may rest assured, that what cannot issue from them, cannot haue a body for its source.[2]

In view of his acceptance of atoms (though of an unusual kind), and his belief that all operations of bodies are the result of local motion, Boyle regarded Digby as a corpuscularian, as, subsequently, did Leibniz.

Diogenes Laertius: Laertius probably wrote his *Lives of Eminent Philosophers* in the early third century CE. Apart from the *Lives*, it is not known who he was, or where and when he was born. Laertius is not a critical historian—he happily retells anecdotes which vary from the unlikely to the impossible. Nonetheless, he is highly readable and, having preserved a great deal of information about earlier philosophers, he was a standard source of knowledge about the classical thinkers for Boyle and Boyle's contemporaries.

Elizabeth of Bohemia (1618-80): Princess Elizabeth of Bohemia, the granddaughter of James I on her mother's side, had, due to the political and religious crises of the time, a very disjointed upbringing. As a child she was separated from her parents for eight years from 1619 to 1627. Rejoining them in their exile in the Netherlands, she studied a wide variety of subjects with a tutor. In 1642 she read Descartes's *Meditations*, and in 1643 she wrote to Descartes, beginning a correspondence about his philosophical views in the course of which she revealed herself as being an extremely competent philosopher. In June of 1643, for example, she wrote to Descartes as follows:

---

1 BP 26:162, *Works*, 13:227.

2 Digby 1644, preface.

> [I]t would be easier for me to concede matter and extension to the soul, than the capacity of moving a body and of being moved, to an immaterial being. For, if the first occurred through the soul's informing the body; the spirits that perform the movement would have to be intelligent, which you do not allow to anything corporeal. And although in your Metaphysical Meditations you show the possibility of the second, it is nonetheless very difficult to see how a soul, such as you have described, after having had the power and the habit of reasoning well, can lose all that because of some vapours, and that, although the soul can subsist without the body and has nothing in common with it, it is so governed by it. [AT 3:685.]

The correspondence lasted until Descartes's death in 1650, with Descartes still unable to provide satisfactory answers to Elizabeth's probing questions. In 1667 she entered a Protestant convent in Westphalia, ultimately becoming abbess. She died in 1680 after a long and painful illness. For a detailed discussion of Elizabeth's philosophical importance see Brown 2006.

Empedocles (c. 492-c. 432 BCE): Empedocles of Acragas (in Sicily) is mentioned by Boyle only as one of a number of naturalists who are not more respected than various members of a group of theologians. Empedocles was the originator of the four element theory of matter, holding that things are composed, basically, of earth, water, air, and fire. He also held, for conceptual reasons, that light had a finite velocity, a claim that Boyle's assistant Robert Hooke still found dubious even after the Danish astronomer Ole Rømer had produced an accurate estimate of its speed.

Epicurus (c. 341-270 BCE): see the Introductory section, "Predecessors and Influences."

Episcopius (1583-1643): Simon Bischop (Episcopius), an exact contemporary of Grotius, was a Dutch leader of the Arminians (Remonstrants) in the fight against the Calvinist doctrine of predestination. He defended his views, unsuccessfully, at the Synod of Dort (1618), and subsequently Remonstrant church services were banned and Episcopius was banished. He found refuge in the Spanish Netherlands and was allowed back into the Netherlands in 1625 when the ban was removed. His *Institutiones theologicae* (1650) sets out the Remonstrant views in clear detail.

Erastus (1524-83): Thomas Erastus wrote, as Boyle notes, a work against Paracelsus, *Disputationes de Medicina Nova Paracelsi* (1572), in which he denies that worms are generated by decaying bodies. Erastus noted that the degree of decomposition of a body is proportional to the degree of heat involved. Erastus was a believer in witches and advocated burning them. In the *Anatomy of Melancholy* Burton remarks that "Many deny witches at all, or if there be any, they can doe no harme," but classes Erastus with "most Lawyers, Divines, Physitians, Philosophers" as being of the opposite opinion.[1]

Euclid (fl. 300 BCE): Little is known of the life of Euclid, the great Greek geometer. He taught in Alexandria, and probably studied in Athens. The first complete English translation of the *Elements*—by John Billingsly, with a preface by John Dee—appeared in 1570, but the version most likely used by Boyle as an adult is the translation by Isaac Barrow (Latin 1655, English 1660). Aubrey suggests that Boyle required Hooke's help to understand Euclid, but Boyle would undoubtedly have had an earlier acquaintance with Euclidean geometry.

Eustachius (c. 1573-1640): Eustachius de Sancto Paulo, here in company with Magirus dismissed by Boyle (and not mentioned elsewhere in his works), wrote an Aristotelian textbook on natural philosophy that Descartes felt to be a paradigmatic account of Scholastic physics.

Fabricius (1537-1619): Hieronymus Fabricius was a pupil of Fallopius, and Harvey in turn was one of his students. Harvey credits him with the discovery of a system of valves in the veins that made Harvey's discovery of the circulation of the blood possible. He was only twenty-five when Fallopius died, but was nonetheless appointed to be his successor at the University of Padua. He wrote on a number of topics as well as on anatomy, but it is his work on generation that chiefly interested Boyle. As a medical doctor he refused fees and only accepted presents from wealthy patients under pressure. After his death a statue was erected to his memory in Padua.

Fernelius (1497-1558): Jean François Fernel was a leading Renaissance physician. *De naturali parte medicinae* (On the Natural

1 Burton 1638, 54-5.

Parts of Medicine) appeared in 1542 and was followed in 1554 by *Medicina*, a systematic survey of what was then known about human disease. *De abdilis rerunt causis* (On the Hidden Causes of Things), mentioned by Boyle, was published in 1548.

Fracastorius (1478-1553): Boyle mentions the *De Sympathia & Antipathia* (1546) of Girolamo Fracastoro in which Fracastoro offers, among other things, an explanation of magnetism in terms of the "sympathy" that the loadstone and iron have for each other.

Galen (c. 129-c. 199 are the traditional dates, but his death may have been considerably later**):** Galen of Pergamum was a follower of Hippocrates. He accepted the theory of the four humours. He was a dedicated medical experimenter, whose dissections of animals (mostly Barbary apes) occasionally led to mistakes when the results were extrapolated to humans. His *De usu Partium* (On the Usefulness of the Parts [of the human body]) is praised by Boyle for its "faithful and accurate accounts."[1]

Galileo (1564-1642): Galileo Galilei used the newly discovered telescope to reveal the fact that matter beyond the moon was changeable just as terrestrial matter was, thereby calling into doubt one of the pillars of Aristotelian physics. He also produced a nice thought experiment to show that the peripatetic notion that heavier bodies fall faster than lighter bodies could not be correct: suppose that heavy bodies do fall faster than lighter ones. Join a heavy body and a lighter one. The two together should fall more slowly than the heavy body alone (since the lighter one will slow the descent of the heavier one), and since the two have a greater combined weight than the heavier one alone, they should fall more swiftly. Thus the conjoined system should fall both more and less quickly than the heavy body. That is impossible. Therefore each body must fall at the same speed as the other. Boyle was familiar with Galileo's two major works, *Dialogue Concerning the Two World Systems* and *Dialogues Concerning Two New Sciences*, which he also read in Mersenne's French translation. The young Boyle admired "the greate Star-gazer Galileo"[2] and the mature Boyle did not change his opinion in this matter.

---

1 *Works* 8:32 [136].

2 BP 37:183v-184, Hunter 1994, 19.

Gassendi (1592-1655): see the Introductory section "Predecessors and Influences."

Gilbert (c. 1544-1603): William Gilbert practised as a physician in London for more than thirty years, and served as Royal Physician to Elizabeth I and, shortly before his death, to James I of England. Gilbert was as suspicious of theologians as he was of the Aristotelians, believing that both hindered the development of natural philosophy. Gilbert is chiefly known for his *De Magnete* of 1600, in which he treats the earth as a giant loadstone or magnet, and offers a number of experiments on magnetic bodies and conjectures concerning magnetism.

Grotius (Hugo de Groot, 1583-1645): Perhaps best known today for his *On the Law of War and Peace* (1625), Grotius impressed Boyle with his defence of Christianity, and Protestantism in particular, in *On the Truth of the Christian Religion* (1627), and with his annotations of the Bible, written in the last five years of his life. Grotius' support for the Remonstrant cause led to his imprisonment in Holland. Convicted of treason, he was sentenced to death but, with the aid of his wife, escaped, initially to Antwerp and subsequently to France, where eventually he served Sweden as an ambassador at the French court. In *On the Truth of the Christian Religion* Grotius effectively notices the importance of the notion of *moral demonstration*,[1] which Boyle found of considerable importance.

Hamond (1605-60): Henry Hammond, the "father of English Biblical criticism," is mentioned by Boyle in *The Excellency of Theology* as one of the "expounders of difficult texts of Scripture [who] have thereby got ... much credit."[2] One of the works of which Boyle was thinking was undoubtedly *Paraphrase and Annotations on the New Testament* (1653). Besides his *Practical Catechism* (1644), Hammond also began, but did not complete, an annotation of the Old Testament. As a Royalist Hammond was briefly imprisoned during the Interregnum. His preaching, said his biographer John Fell, was not, as the ordinary preaching of the times too often was, "an unpremeditated, undigested effusion

---

1 See Appendix G, "Moral Demonstrations," and Appendix I, "Coke, Boyle, and Edwards on Testimony," as well as the section on Demonstration in the Introduction.

2 *Works* 8:95 [222].

of shallow and crude conceptions; but a rational and just discourse, that was to teach the Priest as well as the Lay-hearer."[1]

Harvey (1578-1657): William Harvey, discoverer of the circulation of the blood, is always mentioned with admiration by Boyle. In *The Excellency of Theology* and in a number of other works, Boyle refers approvingly to Harvey's 1651 work *On the Generation of Animals*. *Ex ovo omnia*, everything from the egg, said Harvey, and Boyle found Harvey to be a "true naturalist" in virtue of his careful observation.

Helmont (c. 1579-1644): Johannes Baptista van Helmont was an alchemical writer whose many works Boyle read with the same care that he devoted to those of Descartes or Aristotle. Van Helmont was a careful experimenter; he used a chemical balance for weighing materials in his experiments. One of his best known experiments involved growing a willow tree for five years, during which time it showed an increase in weight of over 74 kg. while the earth in which it grew showed scarcely any decrease. Since he had given it only rainwater, he concluded that it was composed of water. This neglects the interaction with the carbon dioxide in the air, but in fact willows do have a large percentage of water in their makeup. Boyle mentions the experiment in *The Sceptical Chymist* and in *Forms and Qualities*. Van Helmont coined the word "gas" (from "chaos") to describe matter in its gaseous state. His son Franciscus Mercurius van Helmont (c. 1614-99) transcribed most of Anne Finch Conway's notebook, thereby saving what might otherwise have been lost, her important philosophical work, *The Principles of the Most Ancient and Modern Philosophy*, much admired by Leibniz.

Hero (Hiero, Heron, dates highly uncertain; various authors offer dates ranging from the first century BCE to the early third century CE)**:** Hero of Alexandria was, as Boyle suggests, strongly interested in practical applications of mathematics, he "applied mathematics to the explicating of [particular phenomena] of nature."[2] In the work that Boyle specifically singles out, the *Pneumatica*, Hero is particularly concerned with the ways in which compressed air, steam, and water may be employed.

---

1 Fell 1661, 10.
2 Works 8:87 [212].

Hobbes (1588-1679): see the Introductory section, "Predecessors and Influences."

Homer (9th-8th cent. BCE?) and Hesiod (fl. 800 BCE): The dates of Homer are highly uncertain. Both the *Iliad* and the *Odyssey* detail various interactions between gods and humans. Hesiod was the author of *Works and Days* and of *Theogony*, an account of the gods and the beginning of the world. Boyle mentions them both as being among "the eminentest of the wise men," but notes that "those fishermen and others that penned the New Testament" give us "much more suitable conceptions and expressions concerning God."[1]

Huygens (1629-95): The Dutch physicist and astronomer Christiaan Huygens was one the greatest of seventeenth-century natural philosophers, and a considerable admirer of Boyle, whose works he found, approvingly, "full of experiments."[2] Like Boyle and Newton, Huygens held that the matter of the universe was a single matter; unlike Newton he held that light was wavelike, not particulate (*Traité de la lumiere*, 1678). In *Cosmotheoros* (published posthumously 1698, Englished as *The Celestial Worlds Discover'd: or, Conjectures concerning the Inhabitants, Plants and Productions of the Worlds in the Planets*) Huygens speculated on the possibility of life on other planets in the solar system. Huygens was the first to discover the true shape of Saturn's ring; he also discovered the inclination of its plane to the ecliptic (for details, see Alexander 1962). Huygens invented the first truly accurate pendulum clock. In 1659 he produced the first drawing of Mars. By assuming that Sirius had the same brightness as the sun, Huygens calculated its distance. (His approximation was considerably too small, but was the best estimate then available.)

Jerome (c. 341-420): St. Jerome, who produced the standard translation of the Bible into Latin (the Vulgate version), was very aware of the ways in which translators might get things wrong and held, consistently, that only the original text should be treated as inspired. He was also aware that the original writers, though inspired, might choose their language in accordance with the common views of their times. He was continually aware of the difficulties that a literal reading of the Bible poses, and in general does not attempt to gloss over them.

---

1 *Works* 8:15 [113].

2 Huygens 1888, 10:239.

Job: There is no agreement among theologians as to whether Job actually existed, the alternative to accepting him as a historical figure being to view the Book of Job as a spiritually edifying parable in poetic form. As portrayed in that work, Job is an upright and wealthy man. As a result of a jibe by Satan, God allows Satan to kill Job's children and the members of his household and, eventually, cause him bodily harm in order to test his steadfastness. Job remains upright, but does remark that he has been hard done by. God then—the feature that particularly interests Boyle in *The Excellency of Theology*—responded to Job "out of the whirlwind," pointing out that He was extremely powerful and knowledgeable which led Job to reply, "I know that thou canst do every thing, and that no thought can be withholden from thee. [I have] uttered that I understood not; things too wonderful for me, which I knew not.... I have heard of thee by the hearing of the ear: but now mine eye seeth thee. Wherefore I abhor myself, and repent in dust and ashes." Subsequently Job lived another 140 years and once again had a number of children and became eminent. Opinions vary on precisely how edifying this tale is.

John: "Our Saviour's beloved disciple," St. John the Evangelist, was one of the original twelve apostles along with his brother James. Although there is some question about the authorship of the fourth gospel, Boyle would have been in no doubt that the son of Zebedee was the author, and that St. John was referring to himself as "the disciple whom Jesus loved" in John 19, 20, and 21. He also considered Revelation to have been written by St. John, though again, modern scholars find this unlikely.

Jonah: Both before and after his three days and three nights sojourn in the belly of a "great fish," God and Jonah conversed regarding the fate of Nineveh, the aspect of the story that particularly interests Boyle in *The Excellency of Theology*. Since God predicted, through Jonah, that Nineveh would be destroyed, and then, upon the repentance of the king and inhabitants, God "repented of the evil, that he had said that he would do unto them; and he did it not,"[1] the Book of Jonah presents something of a theological puzzle, given (a) the certainty of divine prophesy, and (b) the unchangeableness of God, both of which seem here to be denied.

---

1 Jonah 3.10.

Junius (1545-1602): see Tremillius.

Kepler (1571-1639): Kepler studied theology at Tübingen, intending to become a cleric, but while there he read the work of Copernicus, which turned him in a different, though also heavenly, direction. He became a teacher of mathematics at Graz and, when he was forced to leave because of his Protestantism, he was given a position as an assistant to Tycho Brahe in Prague. Kepler is famous for his three laws of planetary motion (that the planets have elliptical orbits, with the sun at one focus; that in equal times equal areas are swept out by a line joining the planet and the sun; and that the squares of the planet's orbital periods are proportional to the cubes of their mean distance from the sun). Unlike Brahe, Kepler was a firm believer in the Copernican view of the solar system, and it is to Kepler that we owe the discovery that the preface to *De Revolutionibus* was by Osiander, not Copernicus. Kepler also did influential work in optics and in mathematics.

Kircher (1602-80): Athanasius Kircher, the German Jesuit and Renaissance polymath, was, among many other things, the designer of the magic lantern, which Locke used as a model for the way in which ideas in the mind follow one upon another (Locke 1975, 2.14.9). He was the founder of the Museum Kircherianum in Rome. He wrote extensively on a wide variety of topics, including archaeology, linguistics, magnetism, volcanic eruptions, and optics, the topic mentioned by Boyle in *The Excellency of Theology*, publishing in 1646 his *Ars magna lucis et umbrae in mundo*, a work to which Boyle refers in a number of his works.

Lansbergius (1561-1632): Johannes Phillipus Lansbergius, or Philip van Lansbergen, was a minister and, as Boyle remarks, a defender of the views of Copernicus. In the *Anatomy of Melancholy*, Burton tells us that "*Philippus Lansbergius* hath lately vindicated [the Copernican hypothesis], and demonstrated [it] with solid arguments in a just volume.... The said *Johannes Lansbergius* ... hath since defended his assertion against all the cavills and calumnies of *Fromundus* his *Anti-Aristarchus*, *Baptista Morinus*, and *Petrus Bartholinus*: *Fromundus* ... hath written against him againe."[1]

Leucippus (5th century BCE): Beyond his being the originator of atomism (postulating not only atoms, but a void between

1 Burton 1638, 256.

them), and the teacher of Democritus, almost nothing is known of Leucippus, though he is held to have written a treatise *On the Mind*. Aristotle suggested, plausibly, that Leucippus was reacting against the views of the Eleatics who, somewhat paradoxically, denied both plurality in matter and the reality of motion.

Lemnius (1505-68): The Flemish physician and astrologer, Levinus Lemnius, a student of Vesalius, was the author of *De occultis rerum miraculis*, published in two books in 1559, expanded to four books in 1564. He was, he says, a life-long student of anything unknown, mysterious or curious. *De occultis* was a popular collection of strange phenomena. It has been suggested that Lemnius' aim was to combat what he saw as the naturalizing tendency of his contemporaries in order to continue to guarantee God a place in nature.

Longomontanus (1562-1647), or Severin Sorensen ("Longomontanus" after his birthplace, Longberg in Jutland; "Severin" was his given name, Soren his father)**:** Longomontanus was Tycho Brahe's assistant, and published *Astronomia Danica* in 1622, presenting Brahe's results in a systematic form for the first time. It was effectively replaced by Kepler's *Tabulae Rudolphinae* (1627), but was nonetheless reprinted in 1640 and 1663. His attempted squaring of the circle, *Inventio quadraturae circuli* (1634), was followed by a number of other works of similar intent. On seeing the twelfth of these, *Rotundi in plano ...*, the mathematician John Pell (1611-85, elected a member of the Royal Society 1663), persuaded the publisher to let him add a two-page refutation to the printed version, which the publisher, rather surprisingly, did. This resulted in an acrimonious dispute that went on for some years.[1]

Maecenas: see Augustus

Magirus (1615-97): Johannes Magirus is mentioned disparagingly by Boyle as an Aristotelian physicist in *The Excellency of Theology* and in *Forms and Qualities*. His *Physiologiæ peripateticæ* (1647) was the textbook from which Newton became acquainted with Aristotelian physics at Cambridge.

---

1 For an account of the controversy with Pell, see Malcolm and Stedall 2005, pp. 110-21; see also van Maanen 1986.

Magnenus (1590-1679, some dating suggests c. 1600-c. 1669): In his *Democritus reviviscens* (1646), Johann Chrysostom Magnenus speculated about the size and shape of atoms. He allowed only three types of atom, those of earth, air and fire. As a physician he used tobacco syrup as a medicine and wrote a treatise on tobacco (1648). He considered astrology to be "the queen of the sciences."

Masius (1516-73): Andreas Masius was a Flemish scholar whose commentary on Joshua (1574) was an early work in what came to be seen as "Higher Criticism," the critical study of the historic origins, dates, and authorship of the various books of the Bible. Masius wrote a number of other Biblical commentaries and was, like Grotius and Episcopius, seen by Boyle and others as a leading Biblical commentator.

Mede (1586-1638): Joseph Mede was professor of Greek at Cambridge, where he was a Fellow of Christ's College. George Herbert, his contemporary at Cambridge, was influenced by his writings. He was noted for his piety, and his *Clavis Apocalyptica* (*The Key to Revelation*, 1627) was an extensive commentary on the Book of Revelation. His complete works were published in the same year as *The Excellency of Theology*, and were viewed by Newton as the greatest influence on his interpretation of Biblical prophecy.

Metius (died between 1624 and 1631): Jacob Metius, "a Dutch spectacle-maker,"[1] as Boyle calls him, was thought by Descartes to be the inventor of the telescope, though Hans Lippershey, apparently independently and almost simultaneously, also aligned a concave eyepiece lens and a convex objective lens in a tube to make a telescope. Metius' brother Adriaan (1571-1635) was a mathematician and astronomer interested in alchemy. Their father suggested 355/113 as an approximation of π, and after their father's death, Adriaan published his conjecture (1625). Although this approximation was in fact known to the Chinese much earlier, it is now generally referred to as Metius's number.

Mochus, or Moschus: "Learned men," said Boyle, attribute "the devising of the atomical hypothesis ... to one Moschus a

1 *Works* 8:75 [197].

Phoenician.[1] The learned men were relying chiefly on Sextus Empiricus and Strabo, who were in turn reporting Posidonius' belief that "the ancient doctrine about atoms originated with Mochus, a Sidonian, born before the Trojan times."[2]

Moses: Found by Pharaoh's daughter by the riverside, Moses grew up destined to be the saviour of the Israelites from the Egyptians and lead them to a land flowing with milk and honey. On the way Moses led the people across the bed of the Red Sea, which God had parted by means of "a strong east wind" that divided the water long enough to allow the fleeing Israelites, but not the pursuing Egyptians, to cross.[3] Moses spoke frequently with God, as when, for example, a man was found gathering sticks on the Sabbath and God told Moses to have him stoned to death (which was done, Numbers 15.32-36), or when he went up a mountain and received tablets of stone replete with God's commandments (Exodus 24.12).

Nebuchadnezzar (d. 562 BCE): In the course of restoring the empire of Babylon, Nebuchadnezzar conquered (597 BCE) and then destroyed (586 BCE) Jerusalem. Boyle's interest in him in the current work lies in the report in Daniel 2. Nebuchadnezzar had a dream which he then forgot. He called together his wise men and demanded that they should tell him what his dream had been, and what the correct interpretation of it was. The various "magicians ... astrologers ... sorcerers, and ... Chaldeans" said (not without reason), "it is a rare thing that the king requireth, and there is none other that can show it before the king, except the gods, whose dwelling is not with flesh." The king did not like

---

1 "Sceptical Chymist," *Works* 2:260.

2 Strabo, *Geography* 7:271. See also Sextus Empiricus, *Against the Mathematicians*, 1.363.

3 Boyle points out that "God has been pleas'd to express a manifest regard to the stated Lawes, and usual course of things: and seems as it were to husband his omnipotence, by suffering naturall causes to performe some part of the work (and perhaps as much of it as they are able) and forbearing to display his Almighty power, save in those parts of it, that must necessarily be miraculous, because they require a power surpassing that of ordinary nature.... Thus when God divided the Red Sea to make it afford passage to his people, he employ'd a stronge East wind that blew all that night to divide the waters. (BP 7:114r-v, MS 199:145r-144v; Boyle 2006, 3.6.3, p. 266).

this reply, and had them all killed. Luckily, "the secret [was] revealed unto Daniel in a night vision," and Daniel duly reported the dream to Nebuchadnezzar and interpreted it for him (it concerned, Daniel said, the rise and prospects of four kingdoms).[1] Boyle suggests that the future fate of our souls is "a more desirable part of knowledge"[2] than Nebuchadnezzar's dream-given knowledge which was concerned merely with the material world.

Noah: Noah's well-known story is told in Genesis 6-9. God decided that since humans were evil he would wipe out all life on earth. Relenting slightly, he had Noah build an Ark, and take on board seven pairs of every species of bird and of ritually clean animals, and for ritually unclean animals a single pair. The record is unclear in regard to the logistics of assembling and dealing with this group. In *The Excellency of Theology*, Boyle's interest in Noah is as someone to whom God has spoken directly, thus giving us empirical evidence of such an occurrence.

Ocellus Lucanus (fl. c. 150 BCE): Iamblichus, in his *Life of Pythagoras* (Iamblichus 1965), mentions two brothers "of the Lucani, Ocellus and Occillus" as Pythagoreans. However the work *On the Nature of the Universe* to which Boyle refers is not by the Pythagorean Ocellus, and shows clear signs of Aristotelian influence. In *The Excellency of Theology*, Boyle suggests that many of Aristotle's "subtle arguments [for] that irreligious and ill-grounded opinion of the eternity of the world"[3] originated with Lucanus, but this is putting the influenced cart before the originating horse.

Origen (c. 185-254): Origen of Alexandria was a prolific and highly influential writer. He held that scripture must be interpreted in a manner worthy of God, and so if a literal interpretation led to anything impossible or unworthy of God, it should be rejected in favour of a metaphorical one. He was a pupil of the Neoplatonist Ammonius Saccas, and his *On First Principles* is a work of Christian Neoplatonism. Holding that God created from eternity, the revealed truth of the finite nature of this world leads him to postulate the existence of a series of worlds before (and after) this one. These views, and a number of other somewhat

---

1 Daniel 2.

2 *Works* 8:34 [139].

3 *Works*, 8:86 [212].

unorthodox views led to crises in the Church in the fourth and fifth centuries. Some orthodox theologians still hold that Origen's willingness to look for allegorical interpretations goes too far; others find his views unexceptional.

Padre Paulo (1552-1623): Paolo Sarpi, mentioned by Boyle as one of a number of influential theological writers, was a Catholic priest who stood against Rome and the Pope when the Republic of Venice was put under a Papal interdict in 1606. He survived an attempted assassination the following year, which many felt was instigated by Rome. His *History of the Council of Trent*, published under a pseudonym, was strongly anti-papal. Sarpi was a friend and supporter of Galileo.

Pappus (fl. near the end of the third century CE): Pappus of Alexandria wrote several commentaries on earlier mathematical works, all of which are now lost save for fragments. However, his *Synagoge* (*Collection*), a survey of earlier works, with incisive additions by Pappus himself, has survived in a complete form and reveals "an accomplished and versatile mathematician, a worthy representative of the classical Greek geometry."[1]

Paracelsus (1493-1541): Theophrastus Bombast von Hohenheim was born in Switzerland of German parents. Paracelsus took the degree of MD at Ferrara in Italy, and in 1527-28 was appointed professor of medicine at Basel. Boerhaave says that, in his introductory lecture, he burnt the works of Galen and Ibn Sina (Avicenna) with sulphur and nitre, while expressing his hope that they were both in a situation similar to that of their works. As a result of a legal battle concerning his fee for some prescribed medication, he was forced to leave Basel, and spent the rest of his life in various places in Europe. He was a heavy drinker, and is said to have dictated many of his works when drunk. He accepted the theory of the four elements but held that in practice they appeared as three *principles*, two standard alchemical principles, mercury (the principle of fusibility and volatility), and sulphur (the principle of inflammability), to which Paracelsus added salt (the principle of fixity and incombustibility). In *The Excellency and Grounds of the Mechanical Hypothesis* Boyle points out that even if "the chemists ... show that mixed bodies owe their qualities to the predominance of this or that of their three grand ingre-

1 Heath 1921, 2:358.

dients, the corpuscularians will show that the very qualities of this or that ingredient flow from its peculiar texture, and the mechanical affections of the corpuscles it is made up of."[1]

Paul, St.: St. Paul (Saul of Tarsus), originally a persecutor of the Christians, recounts in Acts 22 his conversion experience on the road to Damascus:

> as I made my journey, and was come nigh unto Damascus about noon, suddenly there shone from heaven a great light round about me. And I fell unto the ground, and heard a voice saying unto me, Saul, Saul, why persecutest thou me? And I answered, Who art thou, Lord? And he said unto me, I am Jesus of Nazareth, whom thou persecutest. And they that were with me saw indeed the light, and were afraid; but they heard not the voice of him that spake to me. And I said, What shall I do, Lord? And the Lord said unto me, Arise, and go into Damascus; and there it shall be told thee of all things which are appointed for thee to do.

As a result St. Paul began to spread the Gospel, along with his own interpretation and views. Some theologians suggest that St. Paul subverted Christ's teaching, offering a kind of misogynist asceticism in place of Christ's doctrine of love. Such a view is far from Boyle's, whose frequent citations attest to his intimate knowledge of, and respect for, the writings of St. Paul.

Pecquet (1624-74): Jean Pecquet was the "casual, though lucky" discoverer "of the milky vessels in the thorax."[2] Pecquet announced his discovery of what is now called the thoracic duct in 1651 in his *Experimenta nova anatomica*, noting that he had discovered it some time previously. The "milky vessels" are the vessels that carry the chyle (lymph given a milky look from the absorption of emulsified fats) from the small intestine to the thoracic duct.

Peter, St.: "When Jesus beheld him, he said, Thou art Simon the son of Jona: thou shalt be called Cephas, which is by interpretation, a stone,"[3] that is, *Peter*. Subsequently, Matthew tells us,

1 *Works* 8:114 [244].

2 *Works* 8:90 [216].

3 John 1.42.

Christ asked the disciples, "But whom say ye that I am? And Simon Peter answered and said, Thou art the Christ, the Son of the living God. And Jesus answered and said unto him, Blessed art thou, Simon Barjona: for flesh and blood hath not revealed it unto thee, but my Father which is in heaven. And I say also unto thee, That thou art Peter, and upon this rock I will build my church; and the gates of hell shall not prevail against it. And I will give unto thee the keys of the kingdom of heaven."[1] St. Peter provided mediaeval logicians with a clear cut case of knowledge of future contingents[2] when, as Mark reports, Christ told him, "Before the cock crow twice, thou shalt deny me thrice."[3] St. Peter died in Rome, presumably martyred in Nero's persecution. A later account (end of the second century) says that he was crucified upside down, but there is no clear historical evidence for this.

Plato (c. 428-348 BCE): "The European philosophical tradition," said Alfred North Whitehead, "consists of a series of footnotes to Plato,"[4] and while that may be an overstatement there is no denying the importance and impact of Plato's views on subsequent, particularly Christian, philosophy. Plato was a disciple of Socrates, and a teacher of Aristotle. He stressed the importance of mathematics and, impressed by the fact that various conceptual and mathematical propositions are timelessly or eternally true, he postulated the non-spatio-temporal existence of mathematical objects and of Forms to explain this feature of our knowledge. He wrote extensively on ethical and political matters and on epistemology but, unlike Aristotle, clearly felt that truths revealed by empirical investigation were comparatively trivial and unimportant. When Boyle mentions him it is—as it is in *The Excellency of Theology*—simply as one of a group of people named to exemplify some point.

Pliny the Elder (23-79): In his *Historia Naturalis*, to which Boyle often refers, Gaius Plinius Secundus provided a detailed, if

---

1 Matthew 16.15-19.

2 See Appendix F, "Future Contingents."

3 Mark 14.30, 72.

4 Whitehead 1929, 63. Whitehead continues, "I do not mean the systematic scheme of thought which scholars have doubtfully extracted from his writings. I allude to the wealth of general ideas scattered through them."

somewhat uncritical, account of the views on natural philosophy that were accepted in his time. Studying an eruption of Vesuvius, his curiosity led to him going too near the eruption and staying too long, which resulted in his death (mentioned by Boyle in the "Usefulness of Natural Philosophy," *Works* 3:201).

Porta (1535-1615): Giambattista della Porta published a work on optics, *De refractione, optices parte* (1593), and claimed to have invented the telescope, a claim that appears to be unsubstantiated. He started a society for the study of natural philosophy, the Accademia dei Segreti, which was closed down by the Inquisition. His major work was *Magia naturalis* (1558) in which he discussed a wide range of subjects and stressed the value of experiments. Towards the end of his life he published *De distillatione* (1609).

Ptolemy Philadelphus (308-246BCE): Ptolemy II of Egypt had a basically peaceful reign that saw Egypt in control of the Mediterranean and the Red Sea (he had a canal built from the Nile to the Red Sea). He encouraged literature and the arts, continued supporting the acquisition of texts by the Library founded by his father, and completed the building of the lighthouse at Pharos, one of the seven wonders of the ancient world. Boyle is interested in him because he had the law of Moses translated into Greek (a claim which some scholars now find dubious). Philo Judaeus reports:

> Ptolemy, surnamed Philadelphus, was ... in all virtues which can be displayed in government, the most excellent sovereign, not only of all those of his time, but of all that ever lived; so that even now, after the lapse of so many generations, his fame is still celebrated.... [B]eing a sovereign of this character, and having conceived a great admiration for and love of the legislation of Moses, [he] conceived the idea of having our laws translated into the Greek language.... [He called together a band of translators, who chose Pharos as a tranquil place for their task and] there they remained, and having taken the sacred scriptures, they lifted up them and their hands also to heaven, entreating of God that they might not fail in their object. And he assented to their prayers, that the greater part, or indeed the universal race of mankind might be benefited, by using these philosophical and entirely beautiful commandments for the correction of their lives.[1]

1 Philo Judaeus, *Life of Moses, II*, V-VI.

Ptolemy (c. 90-170 CE): Ptolemy of Alexandria offered, in his *Almagest*, a geocentric version of the solar system, showing the planets and the sun revolving around the earth in circular orbits. Since the actual orbits are ellipses of small eccentricity this meant that various "epicycles" had to be introduced into the model in order to "save the appearances"—to make the theory and the observations match. The circularity of the orbits (probably a result of Aristotle's views on circular motion) was something that lingered on, with Galileo clinging to circular orbits even after Kepler had communicated his new calculations (revealing that the actual orbits were elliptical) to him. Ptolemy drew heavily on previous Greek astronomers, particularly to the now lost work of Hipparchus (c. 170-c. 125 BCE). Ptolemy also wrote on trigonometry and on optics. He also (Proclus reports) attempted a proof of Euclid's parallel postulate.

Pyrophilus: As mentioned in the notes, the name "Pyrophilus" was often used by Boyle to refer to his nephew, Katherine's son Richard Jones (1641-1712). However, he tells us in "The Author's Advertisement" to "Usefulness I" (*Works* 3:195), that it was there used to refer to someone other than Richard Jones. The name also appears as a generic name (see, for example "The Degredation of Gold," *Works*, vol. 9.)

Pythagoras (c. 580-500 BCE): Pythagoras of Samos was a charismatic figure who founded what was effectively a religious order, whose members produced important results in mathematics and physics. The Pythagoreans, Proclus said, looked upon mathematical results as providing both the result itself and a platform from which even higher results could be obtained, thereby lifting "the soul on high instead of allowing it to go down among sensible objects and so become subservient to the common needs of this mortal life." Although "Pythagoras' Theorem," that in right-angled triangles the sum of the squares on the other two sides equals the square on the hypotenuse, is traditionally (and by Boyle) attributed to Pythagoras, there is no good evidence for this. The earliest sources attributing it to him are considerably later than Pythagoras' lifetime. However he was clearly a gifted mathematician, and the theorem may very well be his. Philosophically, Pythagoras and his school had a strong influence on Plato.

Rehoboam: The son of Solomon who, Boyle suggests, would be even more impressed than the rest of us by the magnificence of

Solomon's temple in virtue of his relation to the builder. Accounts of Rehoboam's life may be found at 1 Kings 12-14, and 2 Chronicles 10-12.

Remonstrants: see Arminius

Ricciolus (1598-1671): Giambattista Riccioli, a Jesuit astronomer frequently mentioned by Boyle, wrote *Almagestrum Novum Astronomicum* (1651) in which he gave the first lunar map on which craters are named after people.

Salmasius (1588–1653): Claude de Saumaise (Claudius Salmasius), mentioned by Boyle as "a critical expounder of difficult texts of Scripture,"[1] wrote a treatise in favour of the divine right of monarchy (*Defensio regia pro Carlo I*, 1649), which provoked Milton's reply, (*Defensio pro populo anglicano*, 1651). Among his many works were a commentary on Pliny (1629), a work against astrology (*De anni climactericis et antiqua astrologia diatribe*, 1648), a work in favour of usury, and a pair of anti-papal tracts.

Sarpi: see Padre Paulo.

Scaliger (1540-1609): Joseph Justus Scaliger was the son of Julius Caesar Scaliger (1484-1558), the Renaissance scholar and polymath. J. J. Scaliger is known for his work on textual criticism and on the correct methods of dating ancient chronology. In 1594 he published the small work *Cyclometria elementa duo*, in which he proposed a solution to the problem of squaring the circle. This produced a response (and refutation) by various mathematicians including Clavius and Viète. In his *Appendix ad Cyclometrica sua* of 1595, Scaliger attempted, unsuccessfully, to meet their objections.

Scheiner (1575-1650): Christoph Scheiner, a German Jesuit natural philosopher, noted the existence of sunspots independently of Galileo and entered into a controversy on their nature suggesting, in order to retain the incorruptibility of supralunar matter, that they were the shadows of otherwise unobservable satellites of the sun. (Galileo noted that the fact that sunspots changed their shape made this claim implausible.) Scheiner held a geocentric view of the solar system. Boyle's reference in *The*

---

1 *Works* 8:95 [222].

Excellency of Theology is to Scheiner's work on optics, *Oculus, hoc est fundamentum opticum* (1619), which provided a detailed study of the nature and working of the eye.

Schottus (1608-66): Gaspar Schott, a Jesuit mentioned by Boyle as one who combined divinity and physics, wrote a number of popular treatises on mathematics, physics, and magic. His *Magia universalis naturæ et artis* (4 vols., 1657-59) contains accounts of experiments in optics and acoustics. His *Mechanicahydraulica-pneumatica* (1657) has a description of von Guericke's air-pump.

Sennertus (1572-1627): Daniel Sennert was an early seventeenth-century atomist. He combined the views of Aristotle, atomism (in the form of *minima naturalia*) and alchemy. He was, as William Newman has demonstrated, strongly influenced by the late thirteenth-century alchemist (pseudo-) Geber. As Boyle notes, he accepted (*Practica medicinae*, 1636) the possibility of some diseases being caused by incantation. He rejected, however, a commonly accepted cure: the weapon salve. The weapon salve was a cure that involved treating not the wound (which was simply wrapped in a clean cloth and cleaned regularly with white wine or with urine), but the weapon, with the weapon salve, which had human blood as a main ingredient. Then, claimed Paracelsus' disciple, Oswald Crollius (c. 1560-1609), "This *Cure* is done by the magnetique attractive power of this *Salve*, caused by the Starres, which by the mediation of the ayre, is carried and adjoyned to the Wound, that so the Spirituall operation thereof may bee effected." Sennert, however, was unconvinced: "those Wounds, which are thought to bee Cured by the *Weapon-salve*, I think to bee cured by the help of Nature onely."[1]

Severinus Danus (1542-1602): Peder Severin was a Paracelsan, and court physician to the Danish king. In his *Idea medicinae philosophicae* he waxed lyrical on the importance of empirical knowledge. You should, he told his readers,

> sell your lands, your houses, your clothes and your jewelry; burn up your books. On the other hand, buy yourselves stout shoes, travel to the mountains, search the valleys, the deserts, the shores of the sea, and the deepest depressions of the earth; note with care the distinctions between animals, the differences

1 Sennert 1637, pp. 4, 2.

of plants, the various kinds of minerals, the properties and mode of origin of everything that exists. Be not ashamed to study diligently the astronomy and terrestrial philosophy of the peasantry. Lastly, purchase coal, build furnaces, watch and operate with the fire without wearying. In this way and no other, you will arrive at a knowledge of things and their properties.[1]

Socinus and Socinians: The Socinians, followers of Laelius Socinus (Lelio Sozzini, 1525-62) and his nephew, Faustus Socinus (Fausto Paolo Sozzini, 1539-1604), rejected the Trinity and the divinity of Christ, and influenced the growth of Unitarianism. Orthodox seventeenth-century writers tended to lump them in with atheists as The Enemy, but Boyle, interestingly, considers them under the general label of *Christian* (*Works* 8:30 [134]), along with Protestants and Roman Catholics.

Solomon: Boyle often refers to Solomon simply as the wise man, and his wisdom is shown, Boyle thinks, by (among other things) his choosing an understanding heart and the ability to distinguish good from evil when offered a gift by God.[2] Boyle also refers in *The Excellency of Theology* to the magnificent temple constructed by Solomon who seemed, in addition to his wisdom, to have had an interest in aesthetic and related pleasures. He is reported as having had 700 wives and 300 concubines, though some authorities have suggested that 700 wives is a textual error and that the actual figure is quite likely a mere 70.

Spagyrists: A term apparently invented by Paracelsus to describe practitioners of alchemy; in Boyle's use, the term refers to Paracelsus' followers as well as to Paracelsus, as people who used *chemical* principles in their explanations of material phenomena, and particularly in their attempts to cure various diseases.

Stoics: see Zeno of Citium.

Telesius (1509-88): Bernardino Telesio was an anti-Aristotelian who wanted natural knowledge to rely on the senses, not on reason. The natural philosopher should start "in the dust." His

---

1 Petrus Severinus, *Idea Medicinæ Philosophicæ* (3rd ed., Hagae Comitis, 1660 [1571]), p 39, quoted Debus 1965, 20.

2 1 Kings 3.9.

major work, *De rerum natura juxta propria principia* (*On the Nature of Things according to their Own Principles*) was published in two segments, the first in 1565, the augmented final version in 1586. Subsequent philosophers clearly influenced by Telesio include Campanella, Bruno, Gassendi, and Bacon, who called Telesio "the first of the moderns."

Theodosius (2nd century BCE): Theodosius' *Sphaerica*, to which Boyle refers, was used in classical times as a textbook to supplement Euclid. It does not contain much that is original, but it was a valuable compilation of the results of others. See further Heath 1921, 2:252, Jesseph 1999, 17, and Proclus 1970, 29-30.

Torricelli (1608-47): Shortly before his early death from typhoid fever Evangelista Torricelli, in his *Opera geometrica* (1644), further developed the work on parabolic projectile motion in Galileo's *Discourses Concerning Two New Sciences*. Torricelli worked as Galileo's assistant in the last few months of Galileo's life. By inverting a tube filled with mercury in a vessel of mercury, Torricelli produced a vacuum, and recognized that the cause of the empty space was the weight of the atmosphere not completely balancing the weight of the mercury. This also led to his suggestion on how to "make an instrument which will exhibit changes in the atmosphere," that is, a barometer. He also derived experimentally what is now called Torricelli's theorem: that the flow of liquid through an opening is proportional to the square root of the height of the liquid.[1] (This is now seen as a special case of a more general theorem formulated by Daniel Bernoulli in 1738.) For a variety of reasons his completed works were not published until the twentieth century, and much original material was lost when the Torricelli Museum in Faenza was destroyed in 1944.

Tremellius (c. 1510-80): John Immanuel Tremellius, a Jewish convert to Calvinism, produced, in conjunction with François du Jon, or Junius (1545-1602), a heavily-annotated translation from Hebrew into Latin of the Old Testament, mentioned by Boyle in *The Excellency of Theology* (*Works* 8:41 [148]). Tremellius' translation, seen as a Protestant alternative to Jerome's Vulgate, was

1 Ignoring friction, and the area of the opening, we have $v = \sqrt{2gh}$; where v is the velocity, g is the gravitational constant, and h is the height of the liquid.

published along with the translation of the New Testament by Calvin's successor Theodore Beza (1519-1605) in the late 1570s.

Trithemius (1462-1516): Johannes Trithemius became the Abbot of Sponheim at a very young age, and succeeded in making it world-famous for its collection of books and for the academic prowess of its abbot. As Boyle says, various legends collected around him, and he was held to have considerable knowledge of magic and the art of dealing with spirits. In *De Laude Scriptorium* (1492), he defended manuscript copying against the new technology of movable type.

Tully: see Cicero.

Tycho: see Brahe.

Verulam: see Francis Bacon.

Vesalius (1514-64): Andreas Vesalius broke with traditional academia by performing many dissections himself (instead of having them done by an assistant while he lectured from a text). His *De humani corporis fabrica libri septem* (*The Seven Books on the Structure of the Human Body*, 1543) contained his description, accompanied by detailed woodcuts, of his results, based on his dissections. Boyle mentions him as one who has produced an admirable account of the structure of human bodies.

Ward (1617-89): Seth Ward was Savilian Professor of Astronomy at Oxford from 1649 to 1660, after which he became first Bishop of Exeter (until 1667) and then Bishop of Salisbury. In *Spring of the Air* (*Works* 1:194) Boyle says that he "justly count[s] it an Honor to be known to" Ward, Wren and Wallis.

Zeno of Citium (c. 333/44-262 BCE): Zeno of Citium was the founder of Stoicism, so called because he lectured from a porch (Greek *stoa*). Diogenes Laertius reports that the Athenians passed the following decree:

> Whereas Zeno of Citium, son of Mnaseas, has for many years been devoted to philosophy in the city and has continued to be a man of worth in all other respects, exhorting to virtue and temperance those of the youth who came to him to be taught, directing them to what is best, affording to all in his own

conduct a pattern for imitation in perfect consistency with his teaching, it has seemed good to the people—and may it turn out well—to bestow praise upon Zeno of Citium ... and to crown him with a golden crown according to the law, for his goodness and temperance, and to build him a tomb in the Cerambicus at the public cost. [Diogenes Laertius, 1:VI.10-11, p. 121]

Zeno of Elea (c. 490/485-430? BCE): Zeno of Elea, the follower (with some significant differences of opinion) of Parmenides, is well known as the author of a number of paradoxes, of which four in particular fascinate philosophers: The Stadium, Achilles and the tortoise, the Arrow, and the moving rows, or half the time equals twice the time.

(1) The stadium paradox points out that to cover a given distance, half that distance must first be traversed, then half of that half and so ad infinitum. However, an infinite series of traversals cannot be accomplished in a finite time.

(2) For the Achilles, suppose that "Achilles, swift of foot," as Homer calls him, gives the tortoise a head start in a race. To catch the tortoise, Achilles must first reach the tortoise's starting point, by which time the tortoise will have moved on. This will be constantly true. so Achilles can never catch the tortoise.

(3) At any given moment of its flight, an arrow, supposedly in motion, occupies its own length. But something occupying its own length is at rest, not in motion, and a set of moments of the arrow at rest do not constitute an arrow in motion.

(4) The fourth assumes the dictum that "time is the measure of motion" and considers two objects moving in opposite directions past a stationary third, which provides a reference point. Starting like this:

```
⇐[a1][a2][a3]
  [b1][b2][b3]
  [c1][c2][c3] ⇒
```

After one unit of movement we have:

```
⇐[a1][a2][a3]
        [b1][b2][b3]
             [c1][c2][c3] ⇒
```

Object A has moved one unit relative to B, but two units relative to C. But if "time is the measure of motion" it has taken A twice the time to pass B that it took to pass C: "twice the time is equal to half the time." Some writers have suggested that the first two of these paradoxes tell, or are intended to tell, against the assumption that time is continuous, the second two against the assumption that time is discrete. On Zeno's paradoxes see further Salmon 1970.

Zucchius, Nicholaus (1586-1670): Niccolo Zucchi, an Italian Jesuit who developed one of the earliest reflecting telescopes, which he described in his *Optica Philosophia experimentalis et ratione a fundamentis constituta* (2 vols., 1652-56). The *Optica* was read by both Gregory and Newton before their construction of similar though improved telescopes. Boyle remarks that Zucchius "is wont to be far more industrious then other *Aristotelians* (and on some subjects is careful to propose Experiments, though he [is] not so clear and happy in expressing his thoughts)." (*Works* 4:494.)

Appendix B: Boyle's "Corpuscularianism" [see text pp. 211-13, 229-48]

In the *Origine of Forms and Qualities*, published in 1666, Boyle mentions "that Philosophy, which, I find, I have been much imitated in calling *Corpuscularian*,"[1] and three years later, Leibniz also attributed the term to Boyle:

> At the beginning I readily admitted that we must agree with those contemporary philosophers who have revived Democritus and Epicurus and whom Robert Boyle aptly calls corpuscular philosophers, such as Galileo, Bacon, Gassendi, Descartes, Hobbes, and Digby, that, in explaining corporeal phenomena, we must not unnecessarily resort to God or to any other incorporeal thing, form or quality (*Nec Deus intersit, nisi dignus vindice nodus inciderit*[2]), but that, so far as can be done, everything should be derived from the nature of body and its primary qualities—magnitude, figure, and motion."[3]

In *The Excellency of Theology*, Boyle tells us that "The gospel comprises indeed, and unfolds the whole mystery of man's redemption, as far forth as it is necessary to be known for our salvation, and the corpuscularian or mechanical philosophy strives to deduce all the phenomena of nature from adiaphorous matter[4] and local motion,"[5] and the point is further stressed in *The Excellency and Grounds of the Mechanical Hypothesis*. In *Certain Physiological Essays*, Boyle tells us something of his intention in coining the term:

> I consider'd, that the Atomical & Cartesian Hypotheses,

1 "Proemial Discourse," *Works* 5:289.

2 Latin: "Neither should a god intervene, unless there is a knot worthy of his cutting" (Horace, *Ars Poetica*, 191).

3 "The Confession of Nature against Atheists," Gerhardt 4:106; Loemker 1969, 169.

4 Neutral matter, that is, matter not endowed with any qualities but those "primitive and Catholick Affections of Matter, namely, bulk, shape and motion" (*Works* 2:21).

5 *Works* 8:32 [137]. The following year, Thomas Smith, in a work heavily influenced by *The Excellency of Theology* and dedicated to Boyle, made a number of similar points. See Appendix G, "Moral Demonstrations."

though they differ'd in some material points from one another, yet in opposition to the Peripatetick and other vulgar Doctrines they might be look'd upon as one Philosophy: For they agree with one another, and differ from the Schools in this grand & fundamental point, that not only they take care to explicate things intelligibly; but that whereas those other Philosophers give only a general and superficial account of the Phænomena of Nature from certain *substantial Forms*, which the most ingenious among themselves confess to be Incomprehensible, and certain *real Qualities*, which knowing men of other Perswasions think to be likewise Unintelligible; both the Cartesians and the Atomists explicate the same Phænomena by *little Bodies* variously figur'd and mov'd. I know that these two Sects of Modern Naturalists disagree about the Notion of Body in general, and consequently about the Possibility of a true Vacuum, as also about the Origine of Motion, the indefinite Divisibleness of Matter, and some other points of less Importance than these: But in regard that some of them seem to be rather Metaphysical than Physiological Notions, and that some others seem rather to be requisite to the Explication of the first Origine of the Universe, than of the Phænomena of it in the state wherein we now find it; in regard of these, I say, and some other Considerations, and especially for this Reason, That both parties agree in deducing all the Phænomena of Nature from Matter and local Motion; I esteem'd that notwithstanding these things wherein the Atomists and the Cartesians differ'd, they might be thought to agree in the main, and their Hypotheses might by a Person of a reconciling Disposition be look'd on as, upon the matter, one Philosophy. Which because it explicates things by Corpuscles, or minute Bodies, may (not very unfitly) be call'd Corpuscular; though I sometimes style it the Phœnician Philosophy, because some ancient Writers inform us, that not only before *Epicurus* and *Democritus*, but ev'n before *Leucippus* taught in *Greece*, a Phœnician Naturalist[1] was wont to give an account of the Phænomena of Nature by the Motion and other Affections of the minute Particles of Matter. Which because they are obvious and very powerful in Mechanical Engines, I sometimes also term it the Mechanical Hypothesis or Philosophy.[2]

1 Moschus. See Appendix A, "People Mentioned in the Text."

2 "Certain Physiological Essays," *Works* 2:87.

Appendix C: Aristotle's Arguments against the Void [see text pp. 63, 216–17]

In Book IV of the *Physics* Aristotle offers a number of arguments against the notion of a vacuum, and thereby against the claim that matter is composed of discrete atoms. His arguments are valid, and his premises are empirically plausible.[1] Aristotle felt that the principles specific to any given science were to be empirically derived: "it is the business of experience to give the principles which belong to each subject."[2] Of course, as with any valid argument, all these arguments can do is demonstrate that either their conclusions are correct or that one or more of the premises is false.

Let us begin with a point of background: time seems to have a fixed direction. Aristotle wanted, similarly, a preferred direction for one of the spatial dimensions. Right and left, front and back, are relative to us but, empirically, up and down are not. Turning around alters the first two, but even standing on one's head doesn't alter up and down. So Aristotle's answer to the question: "why do some things fall and others not?" and, indeed, to the question, "why are some things heavier than others?" is given in terms of a system of natural places and motions. It is, said Aristotle, *natural* (i.e., in their nature) for heavy things to move downward, and lighter things such as smoke to move upwards.

Given this, if we imagine a Democritean void, we are, Aristotle thought, imagining a situation in which there would be no natural places. So, for Leibnizian Sufficient-Reason-like reasons (*Physics* 214b30-35), if there *is* a void, there will be no reason for things to move to *here* rather than *there*, in this direction rather than that: so they *won't* move. (In passing, we should note that this result was accepted by Boyle, who explicitly invoked God both for the initial push and for the sustaining of the laws of nature that accounted for all subsequent motion, apart from that initiated by rational agents.[3]) However, if things *were* to move in

---

1 Interestingly, Newton's dismissal of Aristotle's position depended not on an empirical, but on a theoretical point, that things in the universe are composed of a single matter. For Newton's argument see the note to p. 186 of the text.

2 Aristotle 1984, 46a17-21.

3 A similar point is used by the Cartesian Louis de la Forge to argue for occasionalism (de la Forge 1666, 146).

such a void, they would move at random. Aristotle sums up, explicitly and correctly at *Physics* 215a12, "Either ... nothing has a natural locomotion, or else there is no void." But experience, he felt, daily revealed the negation of the left disjunct. The whole argument to this disjunctive conclusion would have been accepted as both valid and sound by Aristotle's seventeenth-century opponents. Further, the choice of disjuncts is made on empirical, not on conceptual, grounds. This is worth stressing, for E.J. Dijksterhuis in his influential work *The Mechanization of the World Picture* has suggested that

> Aristotle's opinion is based not on his establishment either of an internal contradiction in the atomistic doctrine or of the fact that its consequences are contrary to experience, but solely on the incompatibility of the opposed view with his own fundamentally different theories. The only exception is formed by the argument on the impossibility of any absolute determination of place and direction in an infinite homogeneous space. For the rest, the whole argument is emotional rather than logical in character, an expression of self-assertion rather than a refutation.[1]

However, Aristotle often, as in this case, assumes our acquiescence in what he takes to be obvious empirical facts without dwelling on them particularly. Here he is, for example, reminding us of the implausibility of light travelling:

> Empedocles (and with him all others who used the same forms of expression) was wrong in speaking of light as "travelling" or being at a given moment between the earth and its envelope, its movement being unobservable by us; that view is contrary both to the clear evidence of argument and to the observed facts; if the distance traversed were short, the movement might have been unobservable, but where the distance is from extreme East to extreme West, the strain upon our powers of belief is too great.[2]

The fact that he was wrong empirically in this case should not blind us to the fact that he believed his argument to be driven by facts. It is also worth noting that Robert Hooke, in 1675, agreed that light was transmitted instantaneously and felt that the

1 Dijksterhuis 1961, 40.

2 Aristotle 1984, 418b 21-6.

attempt by the "ingenious *Monsieur Romer*" to measure its speed was a failure.[1]

Aristotle does not merely assume that there is no void. He invites us to assume that there is a void, and further assume the possibility of motion in a void. We would then, says Aristotle, absolutely correctly, be faced with the following conclusion: that "a thing will either be at rest or must be moved *ad infinitum*, unless something more powerful gets in its way."[2] In a hypothetical void, bodies would obey inertial laws, in short. Again, there is the implicit, empirically backed, assumption that this is not how the world is: both terrestrial and celestial motions tell against it.

Finally, Aristotle offers two interesting arguments that depend on an empirically tempting hypothesis: that velocity through a medium is inversely proportional to the density of that medium (215b 1-11). Given this assumption, Aristotle points out that, for a given propelling force, the velocity will approach infinity as the resistance approaches zero, and would, he thought, be undefined in the limit: "the void," he says, "can bear no ratio to the full," that is, the required division by zero is not meaningful (215b 20).

Aristotle's final argument is ingenious but somewhat complex in the original. Here it is in modern terms. Suppose, as above, that velocity through a medium is inversely proportional to the density of that medium, and that we do have a void. Now suppose further a body with a constant propelling force traversing a given portion of the void in a finite time, say T_v. Let the time taken to move through the same distance in air be T_a, and let the density of air be D_a. Now consider a substance whose density is $D_a \times \frac{T_v}{T_a}$.

This substance will have non-zero density since D_a, T_a, and T_v are all positive quantities, and since by hypothesis the time of traversal is proportional to the density, the time taken for our body to move the same distance through this new medium, T_n, say, is given by

$$\frac{T_n}{D_a \times \frac{T_v}{T_a}} = \frac{T_a}{D_a}$$

i.e., $T_n = T_v$

1 Hooke 1705, 77, 99, 108, 130.

2 Aristotle 1984, 215a 20.

But that is to say that it will take the same time to traverse a filled space as it will to traverse an empty one, which Aristotle thinks is impossible, since it would mean either that a resisting medium had zero resistance, or else that a void had finite resistance (215b24-216a8).

Appendix D: The Requisites of a Good Hypothesis [see text pp. 214 and 228-29]

At BP 37:121 there are two parallel columns, consisting of points concerning a good, and an excellent, hypothesis, respectively:

The Requisites of a good Hypothesis are:
1 That it be Intelligible.
2 That it neither Assume nor Suppose anything Impossible, Unintelligible, absurd, or demonstrably False.
3 That it be consistent with itself.
4 That it be fit and sufficient to Explicate the *Phænomena*, especially the Chief.
5 That it be at least consistent with the rest of the *Phænomena* it particularly relates to; and do not contradict any other known *Phænomena* of Nature, or manifest *Physical Truth*.

The Qualities & Conditions of an *Excellent Hypothesis* are:
1 That it be *not Precarious*, but have sufficient Grounds in the Nature of the thing itself: or at least be well recommended by some Auxiliary proofs.
2 That it be the *Simplest* of all the Good ones we are able to frame, at least containing nothing that is superfluous or Impertinent.
3 That it be the *only* Hypothesis that can Explicate the *Phænomena*, or at least, that dos Explicate them so well.
4 That it enable a skilful Naturalist to foretell future Phænomena by their Congruity or Incongruity to it; and especially the events of such Experiments as are aptly devis'd to examine it, as things that ought or ought not, to be consequent to it.

There is a similar listing at BP 35:202. See also *Works* 1:xxxiii-iv.

Appendix E: Boyle on Fame [see text, pp. 204–19]

Boyle's "discourse ... *About the partiality and uncertainty of fame*" is now lost, but BP 5:38 contains a short fragment on the topic:

> He that is in any degree a skilfull estimator of the value of things, will easily grant that Titles, Preferments, and those other outward Advantages that are but accessary to a man are far les commendable then Piety Vertue, and those other Attributes that are as it were constituent parts of himselfe; and give him an Intrinsick worth or preheminence. For what real change doth it make in a man, that others make him low legs, and In speaking to him call him *your Lordship*, or *your Highness*: for such Tryfles as these, not only doe not evidence that a man is truly esteemable, but they are not soe much as probable signes that he is really esteem'd: such kind of superficiall and customary respects, being not paid to the man consider'd in himselfe, but to his quallity and station, whether he deserve that eminence or not. 'Tis true, that a High Birth and a Larg fortune, lay great obligations upon men to noble and vertuous actions; and are excellent instruments in the hands of those whom they prevaile <with> to comply with such obligations. But we may too often observe, that these externall advantages doe in effect prove stronger temptations to vice then ingagements to vertue; and they are Instruments of desireable qualitys without being certaine signes, much less necessary Causes of them. And the Examples of Gallant Ancestors, will noe more make one of their degenerate off-spring, a brave man; Than the Inheriting a cuttlers shop,[1] will make a Coward Valiant.

1 A cutler's shop is one in which cutting implements such as knives and daggers are sold.

Appendix F: Future Contingents [see text pp. 54, 258, 267, 275]

Future contingents pose a problem for all philosophers, but a special problem for philosophical believers such as Boyle. There is a straightforward, and common, sense of *necessity* and *possibility* in which the necessary is the now-irrevocable. In this sense of *necessity* and *possibility*, the two notions are time dependent. It *was*, for example, possible for you never to have read a word of this sentence, but that is *now* no longer possible. In this sense of possibility and necessity, past and present truths are now necessary, as are *some* future truths—just those, St. Thomas Aquinas noted, that are "already present in their causes."[1] But there are also statements about the future which are *contingent*. That you will (or won't) have a slice of toast tomorrow morning is, it seems, not yet settled. It is also, to put it no higher, tempting to believe that every indicative assertion is either true or false (and not both). This is, said Leibniz, "the first and greatest principle of the truths of reason."[2] But, as Aristotle noted, combining this belief with the notion of *necessity* just outlined seems to lead to an unacceptable conclusion:

> What is, necessarily is, when it is; and what is not, necessarily is not, when it is not. But not everything that is, necessarily is; and not everything that is not, necessarily is not. For to say that everything that is, is of necessity, when it is, is not the same as saying unconditionally that it is of necessity. Similarly with what is not. And the same account holds for contradictories: everything necessarily is or is not, and will be or will not be; but one cannot divide and say that one or the other is necessary. I mean, for example: it is necessary for there to be or not to be a sea-battle tomorrow; but it is not necessary for a sea-battle to take place tomorrow, nor for one not to take place—though it is necessary for one to take place or not to take place. So, since statements are true according to how the

---

1 Even in the "state of innocence, man did not know future contingent events except in their causes or in the Word, just as the angels know them" (*De Veritate* 8.12 ad 9).

2 *Theodicy* 169, Gerhardt 6:211.

> actual things are, it is clear that wherever these are such as to allow of contraries as chance has it, the same necessarily holds for the contradictories also. This happens with things that are not always so or are not always not so. With these it is necessary for one or the other of the contradictories to be true or false—not, however, this one or that one, but as chance has it; or for one to be true *rather* than the other, yet not *already* true or false.[1]

That every indicative sentence has precisely one of two truth values is the doctrine of bivalence. As Aristotle points out, it should not be confused with its near neighbour, the doctrine of excluded middle, which holds that, for every indicative sentence, *s*, the sentence "either *s* is the case or it is not the case that *s*" is a necessary truth. It is possible, and consistent, to hold that the sentence "Either you will have a slice of toast tomorrow morning, or you won't," is true, and indeed necessarily true, while at the same time denying that its components ("you will have a slice of toast tomorrow morning"; "you will not have a slice of toast tomorrow morning") have a truth value—are either true or false.

Most commentators take Aristotle to be suggesting a "truth-gap" solution[2] to the problem: genuine future tense sentences do not now have a truth value.[3] They will *acquire* a truth value, but they do not have one yet.[4] Moreover, as Prior noted, for such sentences "their 'wait and see' character so infects whatever compounds they enter into that the present-tense assertion that such a proposition is now true has itself this 'wait and see' character and must just lie on the table until the verifying event occurs; and

---

1 Aristotle 1984, *De Interpretatione*, 19a23-19a39.

2 Proponents of paraconsistent logics such as Graham Priest and Bryson Brown have pointed out the possibility of a "truth glut" solution: rather than denying future contingents (and certain self-referring paradoxical sentences such as "This sentence is false") any truth value, we can, they suggest, let them have *both* truth values. This heroic stance is not one which would have commended itself to Boyle.

3 "*Genuine* future tense sentences," because, as Ockham noted, it is necessary to eliminate sentences such as "It will be the case tomorrow that two days ago I had toast for breakfast," which is actually about the past even though it begins with a future tense operator.

4 See further Ryle's discussion of predictions, and our use of "correct," "fulfilled," and "true," in connection with them. ("'It was to be'," in Ryle 1954, 19-20.)

ditto statements before now that the thing would happen after now."[1]

However, the problem is exacerbated for believers who hold (as seventeenth-century writers did) that God has present knowledge of future events. For, in that case, God *now* knows what will happen tomorrow, and indeed knew it even before his creation of the world. God, says Boyle, "lov'd us even before we had a beeing; And our Felicity, in his Decrees, preceded our Existence in this world. God lov'd you numerous ages before you were; and his Goodnesse is so entirely its own Motive, that even your Creation (since when alone, you can pretend to merit his love) is the Effect of it."[2] But if that is the case, if everything we do was foreseen by God, who created precisely the world in which we would do these things, how can we claim to be acting freely? The problem was not solved by the great mediaeval thinkers such as Aquinas and Ockham, and seventeenth-century thinkers such as Descartes, Boyle and Locke admitted themselves equally perplexed by it. Here are three representative texts:

Descartes[3]

39. That the freedom of the will is self-evident.

That there is freedom in our will, and that there are many things which we can choose either to believe or not to believe, is so evident that it must be numbered among the primary and absolutely common notions which are innate to us. This was made especially obvious above, when we tried to doubt everything, and got as far as imagining that some very powerful author of our being was trying to deceive us in every way. Even so, we were still aware that we had this freedom to withhold our belief in anything which was not obviously certain and established. And

1 Prior 1967, 123. Prior's "whatever compounds they enter into" is a little strong, since logically true sentences such as "$Fp \rightarrow F(q \vee \neg q)$" are necessarily true now, but if we narrow the claim in the obvious way to compounds that are neither necessarily true nor necessarily false, Prior's point remains.

2 "Seraphic Love," *Works* 1:91. Boyle may have been influenced in his view by Jeremiah 1.5: "Before I formed thee in the belly I knew thee; and before thou camest forth out of the womb I sanctified thee, and I ordained thee a prophet unto the nations."

3 Descartes, *Principles* 1.39-41 (AT 8:20). This translation is by G. MacDonald Ross in Descartes 1998.

nothing can be more self-evident and transparently obvious than whatever still seemed indubitable at that stage in the argument.

40. That it is also certain that everything has been predetermined by God.

Now that we acknowledge the existence of God, we can see that his power is so immense, that we consider it blasphemous to believe that we could ever do anything without its already having been preordained by him. But we can easily involve ourselves in major difficulties if we try to bring this predetermination together[1] with the freedom of our will, and to understand both of them simultaneously.

41. How the freedom of our will and the predetermination of God are to be brought together at the same time.

We shall get ourselves out of these difficulties if we remember that our mind is finite, whereas God has infinite power, by which he not merely foresaw from eternity, but also willed and predetermined everything that exists or could possibly exist. So we have made sufficient contact with this power to perceive clearly and distinctly that it is in God; but we have not grasped it fully enough to see how it leaves free human actions undetermined. On the other hand, we are so aware of the freedom and indifference which is within us, that there is nothing we can grasp more evidently or more completely. It would be absurd to doubt something which we are intimately familiar with and which we experience within ourselves, simply because there is something else which we do not understand, and which we know from its very nature must be incomprehensible to us.

---

1 GMR's note: "The Latin is *concilio*, which has a number of meanings, including 'bring together,' 'unite,' 'have sex with,' 'win the favour of,' and 'obtain.' I have no evidence of its meaning 'reconcile' or 'harmonise,' which is how other translators render it here. In fact, Descartes' message in this and the next paragraph is that freedom and preordination *cannot* be reconciled — at least not by our feeble understanding — and that we should not even attempt to reconcile them. He is telling us how to cope with their irreconcilability. As with the union of the soul and the body, it is something we mortals cannot begin to understand, and the best we can hope for is that the mystery will be revealed to us in the afterlife."

Boyle

The Generality of our Philosophers as well as Divines beleive that God has a foreknowledge of <all> future contingencys: <& yet how> a Certaine Prescience <can consist with> the free will of Man (which yet is generally granted him, in things meerely morall or Civill) is soe difficult to discerne that the Socinians are wont to deny such things as depend upon the Will of Free Agents to be the proper objects of Omniscience, & the Head of the Remonstrants <thô a very subtle writer> confesses he knows not how <clearly> to make out the Consistency of <Gods> Prescience & mans freedome: both which he yet confesses to be Truths, being compelld to acknowledge the former, (for the latter is Evident,) <as well> by the infinitenes that must be ascribd to Gods Perfections as by the Prophetick Predictions, whereby such contingent Events have been actually foretold. And the reconsilement of these Truths is not a difficulty peculiar to the Christian Religion, but concernes speculative men in all Religions, who acknowledge the Diety to be infinitely perfect, & allow man, as they doe, to be a Free Agent.[1]

Locke

I own freely to you the weakness of my understanding, that though it be unquestionable that there is omnipotence and omniscience in God our maker, and I cannot have a clearer perception of any thing than that I am free, yet I cannot make freedom in man consistent with omnipotence and omniscience in God, though I am as fully perswaded of both as of any truths I most firmly assent to. And therefore I have long since given off the consideration of that question, resolving all into this short conclusion, that if it be possible for God to make a free agent, then man is free, though I see not the way of it.[2]

1 BP 2:49-50; printed in "Reason and Religion," *Works* 8:272-73.

2 Locke to William Molyneux, 20 January, 1693 (Locke 1979, 4:625-26).

Appendix G: Moral Demonstrations: Boyle, Smith, and "A Person of Honour" [see text pp. 59-60, 182-85)]

For a discussion of Boyle's view of "moral demonstrations," as opposed to demonstrations proper, see the relevant section of the Introduction. Here is a further piece from Boyle's manuscript remains in which he argues, interestingly, that though, in general, strong arguments are necessary in intellectual discussion, there may be a place in theological discussion for somewhat weaker arguments, where what is at issue is confirmation rather than conversion:

> I know it may be objected that tis a disservice to Religion to pretend to demonstrate it by weak or insufficient Arguments since they do but harden Atheists & other Infidels in their unbelief by giveing them a Rise to presume that the arguments whereon our Religion is founded are but weak & such as they are able to answer.[1] But thô I readily grant that he who writing professedly against Atheists & Libertines shal scarce imploy any Arguments save weak ones or shal lay so much stress upon these as to propound them as demonstrations is much to blame in point of discretion: yet when a man writes not barely to confute professed infidels & obstinate Cavilers but partly to confirm those that are true thô not wel instructed & setled belivers & shal propose divers solid & wel weighd Arguments to evince the Truth such a writer I say may be allowed to add now & then to his more weighty Arguments some of less force provided he lay not too much stress upon them & declare he dos not. For by this precaution he wil leave the adversaries no

---

1 Boyle is here acknowledging a standard worry. Noting that the temporal finitude of the world was undemonstrable, Aquinas said, "And it is useful to consider this, lest anyone, presuming to demonstrate what is of faith, should bring forward reasons that are not cogent, so as to give occasion to unbelievers to laugh, thinking that on such grounds we believe things that are of faith" (ST 1a 46.2c). In the previous century Maimonides had made the same point in the same context (*Guide for the Perplexed* II.16).

just ground of rejecting or undervalueing the grand proofs of our Religion. And then this inconvenience being obviated the capacitys & the dispositions wether natural or acquird of the minds of men are so various & some of them may be much more impresst on by arguments in themselves weaker than they would be by stronger ones as some patients wil not take the best physick in the form of a potion thô they wil readily swallow it when presented in pills or many refuse or relish the same meat as tis cookt more or less agreable to their palats & stomachs & wil be nourisht by herbs or fruit then Beaf or Mutton And this being so I see not why it may not be allowable to mingle with the more solid Arguments some that are more proportionate to such mens capacitys in writings which are intended not onely to confute infidels but to establish the Faith of believers, many of which are not so fit to understand the more learned sort of Arguments as disposd to be confirmd by some of an inferior but more proportionate to their capacity or more congruous to their personal constitutions of mind. And for ought I know it may be both just & prudent to have regard in our writings less to the resolved infidel then to the weaker believer since we cannot hope to convert the former how cogent soever our reasons be without an extraordinary divine assistance[1] as may appear by the obstinacy of the Jews against the miracles as wel as discourses of our Saviour whereas we may Reasonabley hope to remove the doubts & strengthen the faith & consequently encrease the happiness & piety of those that are in the temper of him that said to the Messias Lord I believe help thou my unbelief & those disciples that prayd that he would encreas their faith.[2]

In the year after the publication of *The Excellency of Theology*, Thomas Smith dedicated *The Credibility of the Mysteries of the Christian Religion* (Smith 1675), a work strongly influenced by *The Excellency of Theology*, to Boyle. In it he argued that

Religion ... must be allowed to have its mysteries; there being such a vast disproportion between things relating to *God* and

1 See note 3, p. 106.

2 BP 7:118-9, Boyle 2006, 2.1.17, pp. 107-8; MS 185:25v-28 has an earlier draft. Boyle's references are to Mark 9.24, "And straightway the father of the child cried out, and said with tears, Lord, I believe; help thou mine unbelief" and to Luke 17.5, "And the apostles said unto the Lord, Increase our faith."

his nature, and the things of the world. The contemplation of nature is curious and useful; it is part of the service and worship we owe to God the Creatour, to admire his wisdom and power in the beautiful frame and order of things, which is best done by enquiring into their natures and properties, into their powers and operations and qualities, by examining the curious contexture and the fitness and usefulness of their parts, and there is nothing in the whole universe, but deserves to be considered, and very much conduces to this end.

This is the business of *Philosophy*, and what contemplative minds labour in the search of, to discover and make out how things were at first made, and are still continued in their being, and to find out their peculiar virtues, whereby they produce such a variety of effects, and how they may be altered or improved for the farther use and benefit of mankind. Nothing of which can be effected, at least but very imperfectly, and in a way scarce tolerable, by acquiescing in general observations, derived from weak and slight notices, without descending to severe trials and experiments, or by relying upon the principles of *ordinary Philosophy*, that are confessedly unintelligible, and which instead of explaining nature, do but perplex and confound the understanding, and which have nothing to maintain and keep up their credit, but the authority of a name and the immoderate love of antiquity.

...

It is utterly false, that nothing is credible, but what can be proved and made out by reason. There are indeed several degrees of credibility, according to which the mind does admit some things with a greater ease and freeness than others. But however be the matter proposed never so unlikely or unusual, if the authority be just and good, it must not therefore be pronounced incredible, because perchance it is not fully agreeable to the present state of affairs and practice of the World, or because I have some little prejudice against it. For as a matter of fact, where there are sufficient proofs given of a Relators both honesty and knowledg, when I have all the assurance in the World, that such a matter is capable of, and that he could not mistake in understanding it, and that his words and thoughts do not in the least disagree, when I can object nothing but a groundless surmise, that possibly, and for ought

> I know, it may be otherwise, this will challenge my assent, and be a sufficient warrant to me to believe it, whether I have a clear *Idea* of it or no: for this unlikeliness and seeming repugnancy of it, may arise from my being ignorant of several circumstances, the knowledg of which would render it probable and easie: so is it in matter of Doctrine; whatsoever is proposed by *God*, becomes thereby immediately credible, and my assent is rational and just, though the thing be above my apprehension; and this I must ascribe to the greatness of the object, and the imperfections of my reason, which neither is nor can pretend to be an arbiter and judge in such *matters, which are too high for it*: so that before a man can safely pronounce a doctrine, that is revealed, incredible, and reject it as such, he must question the power and veracity of *God*, and maintain, that nothing is possible, but what we can comprehend; and thus under a pretence of caution, betray the greatest immodesty in the world, when he himself believes several other things, upon the bare testimony of men, which neither his wit nor curiosity, nor his reason can ever be able satisfactorily to make out and demonstrate.[1]

Kant said of the argument from design: "This proof always deserves to be mentioned with respect. It is the oldest, the clearest, and the most accordant with the common reason of mankind.... It would ... not only be uncomforting but utterly vain to attempt to diminish in any way the authority of this argument.... But," he added, "it cannot hurt the good cause, if the dogmatic language of the overweening sophist be toned down to the more moderate and humble requirements of a belief adequate to quieten our doubts, though not to command unconditional submission. I therefore maintain that [this] proof can never by itself establish the existence of a supreme being."[2] That, however, was in the next century. In the seventeenth century such arguments flourished. They can be found in every eminent writer of the period, including Boyle and Newton, Leibniz and Locke, and of course, Descartes.

By and large the arguments were less than compelling. Many were simply expansions of St. Paul's claim that "the invisible things of him from the creation of the world are clearly seen, being understood by the things that are made, even his eternal

1 Smith 1675, 16-17, 24-5.

2 Kant 1787, A623-4/B651-2.

power and Godhead."[1] William Bates, for example, offered in 1676 a "proof" based on "the visible frame of the World," which really consisted merely of the claim that design (and hence a designer) would leap out at one upon even the most casual inspection:

> [I]f we survey the Universe, and all the beings it contains, their proportion, dependence and harmony, it will fully appear that antecedently to its existence, there was a perfect mind that designed it, and disposed the various parts in that exact order, that one beautiful World is compos'd of them.... if we observe the frame of the World, the concatenation of the superior with the middle, and of the middle with the lower parts, whereby 'tis not an accidental aggregation of bodies, but an intire universe; if we consider the just disposing them conveniently to their nature and dignity, the inferiour and less noble depending on the superiour, and that so many contrary natures, with that fidelity and league of mutual love embrace and assist each other, that every one working according to its peculiar quality, yet all unite their operations for one general end, the preservation and benefit of the whole, must not we strongly conclude that 'tis the work of a designing & most wise Agent?[2]

More cautiously, Boyle remarked that "God was pleas'd to give the world a contrivance so conspicuously admirable that the proofe of his existence should be as obvious, as the objections that Atheists make against it," making it clear that he thought, as Kant was to think later, that standard design arguments could

---

1 Romans 1.20. NEB has "His invisible attributes, that is to say his everlasting power and deity, have been visible, ever since the world began, to the eye of reason, in the things he has made." Cf Pascal 1952, "nature has engraved her image and that of her author on all things" *(la nature ayant gravé son image et celle de son auteur dans toutes choses*, Fr 199 = Brunschvicg 72).

2 Bates 1676, 5-7. Bates goes on to give particular instances: the sun is just the right distance away to provide the Earth with the right temperature. It moves from East to West, causing day and night. It provides us with colours, which make the world pleasant. It gives rise to the seasons. There are oceans and they are useful. Etc, etc. Despite the generality of the initial claim, the actual examples are chosen to show that Bates thinks the universe is well designed from *our* point of view. Bates offered a number of other proofs, but by and large they achieve the difficult feat of being even less compelling than this one.

(and should) function, not as proofs in themselves, but rather as a weapon against the atheist. Although, said Kant, the considerations available to the believer provide "but leaden weapons ... they are yet as effective as those which our opponents can employ against us."[1]

However, as noted, some of these design arguments, or "moral demonstrations"[2] made use of the scientific achievements, and one of the weakest, least plausible, and most interesting is provided by the anonymous "Person of Honour," who included it in his 1685 treatise, *The Atheist Unmasked or A Confutation of such as deny the Being of a Supream Deity, that governs Heaven and Earth by Unanswerable Arguments deduc'd.* Preludes to his argument had been offered earlier by Henry More (1614-87), and by Luther (1483-1546). Here is the Person of Honour's argument:

> [I]f there be not a God, how comes it to pass, that the Sea which is agreed to be bigger and higher than the Land, should contrary to the Nature of Water (which is to diffuse it self) be restrained by a low sandy shore, from overflowing the Earth, which cannot be but by that God that has set it, its bounds, and says hitherto, shall you come, and no further, and that the Sea is higher than the Land, is demonstrable by the Springs which under *Aristotles* favour, have another cause then what he asserts.[3] The true cause of the Springs being the Waters of the Sea which passes through the small Crannies, and meatus[4] of

1 BP 2.144v; Kant 1787, A778/B806.

2 Boyle and others of the time spoke of arguments such as the argument from design as "moral demonstrations." "Demonstration" was a technical term standardly limited to the valid deduction of necessary truths from necessary premises, while "moral demonstrations" allowed a weaker standard for both the argument form and the premises. I have discussed this point at greater length in Boyle 2006, 70-81, and in MacIntosh 2005. For an interesting discussion of the use of the notion earlier in the century, particularly in the writings of Descartes, see Morrison 1989.

3 Aristotle had suggested that "just as above the earth small drops form and these join others, till finally the water descends in a body as rain, so too we must suppose that in the earth the water at first trickles together little by little, and that the sources of the rivers are formed where the earth gushes out, as it were, at a single point." He also suggests that the earth's coolness may condense any water vapour that exists in the earth. *Meteorology*, Aristotle 1984, 349b 20-35.

4 Correcting the text's "mealus" to "meatus" (a channel or tubular passage), but *meals* are banks of sand, which would allow another possible reading.

the Earth, which sweetens it by its passage, and breaks out into Springs, which we see many times rise in High Hills, the reason of which is, that the Sea being as high, or higher then those Hills, the Water is forced to rise so high, for it would else be contrary to the Nature of Water to ascend to those Hills, we see it manifest by leading Water from a Spring-head by Pipes or otherwise, that as high as the Spring-head is so high it will force the Water to rise whither it is carryed.[1]

More's claim is gentler, and unlike that of the Person of Honour, does not require divine intervention:

> [T]hose rudely-scattered *Mountains*, that seem but so many Wens and unnatural Protuberancies upon the face of the Earth, if you consider but of what consequence they are, thus reconciled you may deem them ornaments as well as useful.
>
> For these are Nature's *Stillatories*, in whose hollow Caverns the ascending vapours are congealed to that universal *Aqua vitæ*, that good *fresh-water*, the liquor of life, that sustains all the living Creatures in the world, being carried along in all parts of the Earth in the winding Channels of *Brooks* and *Rivers*.[2]

---

1 Anon 1685, 18.

2 More 1662, Bk. 2, ch. 3, 1:48. In seventeenth century England mountains had a bad press. "High Objects," wrote Dryden, "may attract the sight; but it looks up with pain on Craggy Rocks and Barren Mountains, and continues not intent on any object, which is wanting in shades and greens to entertain it [Dryden 1966, 'Dedication (to James, Duke of Monmouth,' Oct. 12, 1667)]." The young Robert Boyle found "those ... Mountains where the Rhosne takes it's source" to be "hideous," and likened the Alps to a purgatory which has to be "pass'd over" to get "to that Paradice call'd Italy [BP 37.183r]," and James Howell earlier had a similar opinion of the Alps:

> I am now got o're the *Alps*, and returned to *France*; I had crossed and clambered up the *Pyreneans* to *Spain* before, they are not so high and hideous as the *Alpes*; but for our Mountains in *Wales*, as *Eppint* and *Penwinmaur*, which are so much cried up amongst us, they are *Mole-hills* in comparison of these, they are but *Pigmeys* compared to *Giants*, but *Blisters* compared to *Impostumes*, or *Pimples* to *Warts*: Besides, our *Mountains* in *Wales* bear always something useful to Man or Beast, some Grass at least; but these uncouth huge mounstrous excrescences of Nature, bear nothing (most of them) but craggy Stones: the tops of some of them are blanched over all the year long with Snows, and the

Luther is not setting out to *derive* God's existence—that is taken as a given—but he does supply scriptural backing for the claim that the sea is higher than the land. Commenting on Genesis 1.9-10 ("And God said, Let the waters under the heaven be gathered together unto one place, and let the dry land appear: and it was so. And God called the dry land Earth; and the gathering together of the waters called the Seas: and God saw that it was good"), Luther writes:

> He calls the earth dry because the waters had been removed. So we see the ocean seething miraculously, as if it were about to swallow up the entire earth. The sea stands out higher than the land, but it cannot pass over its limits. This statement at the first creation fixes the limits of the earth and establishes a most solid embankment against the sea. Likewise Job (Job 38:10) and the Psalmist (Ps. 104:9) bear witness that although the sea is higher and is not bounded by its own bounds, nevertheless it cannot range beyond what is permitted. In view of the fact that it is the center, the earth ought to be shut in and covered by the sea; but God holds back the sea by His Word and causes that Surface to stand out to the extent necessary for habitation and for life.[1]

> People who dwell in the Valleys, drinking for want of other, *this Snow-water*, are subject to a strange Swelling in the Throat, called *Goytre*, which is common amongst them. [*To Sir* J.H. *from* Lions, Nov 6, 1621, in Howell 1705, p 62]

By the early nineteenth century there was a complete reversal, Mary Shelley (or at any rate one of her two best known characters) found the Alps "majestic," "wondrous," and "sublime." See further Thomas 1984, pp. 258 ff, and Marjorie Hope Nicholson's standard study, *Mountain Gloom and Mountain Glory* (Nicholson 1959).

1 Luther 1955, 1:34. The texts to which Luther refers are Job 38.8-10: "Who shut up the sea with doors, when it brake forth, as if it had issued out of the womb? When I made the cloud the garment thereof, and thick darkness a swaddlingband for it, And brake up for it my decreed place, and set bars and doors, And said, Hitherto shalt thou come, but no further: and here shall thy proud waves be stayed?" and Psalms 104.6-9: "The waters stood above the mountains. At thy rebuke they fled; at the voice of thy thunder they hasted away. They go up by the mountains; they go down by the valleys unto the place which thou hast founded for them. Thou hast set a bound that they may not pass over; that they turn not again to cover the earth." Thanks to Keith Hutchinson for drawing my attention to this passage in Luther.

What is interesting about the Person of Honour's version of this argument is the way in which the anonymous author attempts to meld what is taken to be the certainty of scripture with sound empirical observation, coupled with scientific theory: water will not naturally rise higher than its origin. By scripture, the sea is higher than the non-mountainous portions of the land. By natural philosophy, it should overrun the land. Therefore some mighty power must—out of benevolence, presumably—be keeping it back. Interestingly, the Person of Honour is willing to allow what amounts to constant miraculous intervention to keep the sea back (while allowing the "Nature of Water" and the sea's presumed height to raise the water in the mountains to its own level), but does not consider the equally miraculous alternative: that the sea is lower than the land, but that God allows (or compels) the water "to rise so high, ... contrary to the Nature of Water." Given a choice of two continuous miraculous interventions, neither of which is less plausible than the other, the knowledge of water's ordinary behaviour is allowed to decide the issue without, apparently, having the alternative even considered.

Appendix H: Jonathan Swift's "Broomstick" and Boyle's Occasional Reflections [see text p. 30]

As noted in Boyle's *Life* in the Introduction, *The Excellency of Theology* was probably substantially written in the year that Boyle published his *Occasional Reflections*. Famously, in the second decade after Boyle's death, Jonathan Swift composed a satire on these *Reflections*, his "Meditation upon a Broomstick." Then, in the view of many of Boyle's admirers, he worsened the situation considerably by publishing it. Thomas Birch's reaction is typical:

> [In 1665] Mr. *Boyle* gave the public his *Occasional Reflections upon several Subjects*.... This piece was drawn up when he was very young.... And this consideration, added to that of the custom of the age, in which the imagination was more indulged upon important subjects, than the severity of a true taste of writing will admit, may serve to apologise for this treatise, against the insult upon it in Dr. *Swift*'s *pious Meditation on a Broom Staff*, who has certainly not shewn in that piece a just regard to the interests of religion, any more than to the character of Mr. *Boyle*, by allowing himself to treat such subjects, and so excellent a person, with the most licentious buffoonery.[1]

Thomas Sheridan, in his *Life* of Swift, reports the occasion of Swift's writing the satire:

> During this period, Swift's pen was hardly ever employed, except in writing sermons; and he does not seem to have indulged himself even in any sallies of fancy, for some years, excepting only the Meditation on a Broom-stick, and the Tritical Essay on the Faculties of the Mind,[2] both written in the year 1703. As Swift has been much censured for writing the

---

1 Birch 1772, I:lxxii.

2 Swift coined the term "tritical" for something trite as a play on "critical." "A Tritical Essay Upon the Faculties of the Mind," was published in his *Miscellanies in Prose and Verse* (Swift, 1711), pp. 247-59.

former of these pieces, on account of the ridicule contained in it of the style and manner of so great and pious a man as Mr. Boyle, it may not be improper here to relate an anecdote[1] which I had from undoubtedly good authority, with regard to the occasion of writing that piece, and which will in a great measure exonerate Swift from the charge brought against him on that account. In the yearly visits which he made to London, during his stay there, he passed much of his time at Lord Berkeley's, officiating as Chaplain to the family, and attending Lady Berkeley in her private devotions. After which the Doctor, by her desire, used to read to her some moral or religious discourse. The Countess had at this time taken a great liking to Mr. Boyle's Meditations, and was determined to go through them in that manner; but as Swift had by no means the same relish for that kind of writing which her Ladyship had, he soon grew weary of the task; and a whim coming into his head, resolved to get rid of it in a way which might occasion some sport in the family; for which they had as high a relish as himself.

The next time he was employed in reading one of these Meditations he took an opportunity of conveying away the book, and dexterously inserted a leaf, on which he had written his own Meditation on a Broomstick; after which, he took care to have the book restored to its proper place, and in his next attendance on my Lady, when he was desired to proceed to the next Meditation, Swift opened upon the place where the leaf had been inserted, and with great composure of countenance read the title, "A Meditation on a Broom-stick." Lady Berkeley, a little surprised at the oddity of the title, stopped him, repeating the words, "A Meditation on a Broom-stick!" bless me, what a strange subject! But there is no knowing what useful lessons of instruction this wonderful man may draw, from things apparently the most trivial. Pray let us hear what he says upon it. Swift then, with an inflexible gravity of countenance, proceeded to read the Meditation, in the same solemn tone which he had used in delivering the former. Lady Berkeley, not at all suspecting a trick, in the fulness of her prepossession, was every now and then, during the reading of it, expressing her admiration of this extraordinary man, who could draw such

1 This anecdote came from Lady Betty Germaine, daughter of Lady Berkeley, and was communicated to me by the late Lady Lambert, an Intimate of Lady Betty's [Thomas Sheridan's note].

fine moral reflections from so contemptible a subject; with which, though Swift must have been inwardly not a little tickled, yet he preserved a most perfect composure of features, so that she had not the least room to suspect any deceit. Soon after, some company coming in, Swift pretended business, and withdrew, foreseeing what was to follow. Lady Berkeley, full of the subject, soon entered upon the praises of those heavenly Meditations of Mr. Boyle. But, said she, the Doctor has been just reading one to me, which has surprised me more than all the rest. One of the company asked which of the Meditations she meant. She answered directly, in the simplicity of her heart, I mean that excellent Meditation on a Broom-stick. The company looked at each other with some surprise, and could scarce refrain from laughing. But they all agreed that they had never heard of such a Meditation before. Upon my word, said my Lady, there it is, look into that book, and convince yourselves. One of them opened the book, and found it there indeed, but in Swift's hand-writing; upon which a general burst of laughter ensued; and my Lady, when the first surprise was over, enjoyed the joke as much as any of them; saying what a vile trick has that rogue played me! But it is his way, he never baulks his humour in anything. The affair ended in a great deal of harmless mirth, and Swift, you may be sure, was not asked to proceed any further in the Meditations. Thus we see that his original intention in writing this piece, was not to ridicule the great Robert Boyle, but only to furnish occasion for a great deal of innocent mirth on Lady Berkeley's enthusiasm, and simplicity of heart; and at the same time to get rid of the disagreeable task of reading to her writings which were not at all to his taste. And that it afterwards got out into the world, was owing to the eagerness of those who were acquainted with the Berkeley family, to procure copies of a piece of such exquisite humour. This was the case indeed in almost all the small things afterwards written by Swift, scarce any of which were published by himself, but stole into the world in that way.[1]

Here are two examples of the *Reflections* Swift was satirizing, followed by his "Meditation Upon a Broom-stick":

Upon his making of a Fire.[2]

---

1 Sheridan 1787, 37-9.

2 "Reflection II," *Works* 5:85.

How many fruitless Blasts have I been spending upon this sullen Fire! 'Twas not, though, the Greenness of this Wood, that made it so uneasie to be Kindled; but, 'twas alone the greatness of the Loggs, on which the Fire could take no hold, but by the intervention of such smaller Sticks as were at first wanting here: Witness, that I had no sooner laid on a little Brushwood, but the Flame, from those kindled Twiggs, invading and prevailing on the Billets, grew suddenly great enough to threaten to make the House it self part of its Fuel, and turn it to such Ashes as it makes haste to reduce the Wood into. Methinks the blaze of this Fire should light me to discern something instructive in it: These Blocks may represent our Necessary, these Sticks our less important, Religious practices, and this aspiring Flame, the subtile Inhabitor of that of Hell. 'Twil be but succeslesly, that the Devil can attempt our grand Resolves, till he have first Master'd our less considerable ones; and made his successes against these, not only Degrees, but Instruments, in the Destroying of the other: Our more neglected and seemingly trivial Affections, having once receiv'd his Fiery impressions, do easily impart them to higher Faculties, and serve to Kindle solider Materials. It is therefore the safest way, to be faithfull ev'n to our lesser Determinations, and watchfull over our less predominant Passions, and whensoever we find our selves tempted to violate the former, or neglect the latter, not so barely to cast one Eye upon the seeming inconsiderableness of what we are intic'd to, as not to fix the other upon the Consequences that may attend it; and therein, to consider the importance of what such slighted things may, as they are manag'd, prove Instrumental, either to endanger, or preserve.

Upon my Spaniel's Carefulness not to lose me in a strange place.[1]
During my stay at Home, whilst every Body this Cur chanc't to meet, made so much of their Landlord's Spaniel, that they seem'd to have added to Oracles that Proverb of *Love me, love my Dogg*, the cajoll'd Cur would never keep at home; but being welcom'd to so many places abroad, made me few Visits, that cost me not the trouble of sending for him. But now, that we are in a place, where he sees not more Men than Strangers, he stirrs not from my Heels, and waits so close, and

1 "Reflection III," *Works* 5:85-6.

carefully, that it were now more difficult to lose him, than it was formerly to keep him from wandring. Thus doth it generally fare with us; whilst we are Environed with numerous outward Objects, which, smiling on us, give our Gaddings to them, the Temptation of an inviting welcome; how inclin'd are we to forget and wander from our great Master: But when we are depriv'd of those Enveigling Courters,[1] our Maker too is freed from those seducing Rivals, and our undistracted Affections are brought to settle on their noblest Object, by the removal, and the displacing, as well as they would be by the Knowledge and the Undervaluation, of inferiour ones. Lord! when I lose a Friend, or any outward Idol of my Fondness, teach me to reduce him to leave thee his Heir, by taking that loss for a Summons, to transfer and settle my whole Love on Thee; and if Thou but vouchsafe to make me so happy, I shall think my self enough so, not to Envy him, to whom the loss of his Asses prov'd an occasion of his finding a Crown;[2] and shall not so much Regret what thy Dispensations shall have taken from me, as Gratulate[3] to my self their having reduc'd me unto Thee.

A Meditation Upon a Broom-Stick, According to the Style and Manner of the Honourable *Robert Boyl*'s Meditations.

Written *August*, 1704.

This single Stick, which you now behold Ingloriously lying in that neglected Corner, I once knew in a Flourishing State in a Forest, it was full of Sap, full of Leaves, and full of Boughs; but now, in vain does the busie Art of Man pretend to Vye with Nature, by tying that withered Bundle of Twigs to its sapless Trunk; 'tis now at best but the Reverse of what it was, a Tree turned upside down, the Branches on the Earth, and the root in the Air; 'tis now handled by every Dirty Wench, condemned to doe her Drudgery, and by a Capricious kind of Fate, destined to make other Things Clean, and be Nasty it self: At Length, worn to the Stumps in the Service of the Maids, 'tis either thrown out of Doors, or condemned to its last use of kindling a Fire. When I beheld this, I

1 Replaced by "thise Enveigling Courtiers" in the printing of 1669.

2 For this account see I Samuel 9-10.

3 I.e., congratulate.

sigh'd, and said within my self, *Surely Mortal Man is a Broom-Stick*; Nature sent him into this World Strong and Lusty, in a Thriving Condition, wearing his own Hair on his Head, the proper Branches of this Reasoning Vegetable, till the Axe of Intemperance has lopt off his Green Boughs, and left him a withered Trunk: He then flies to Art, and puts on a *Perewig*, valuing himself upon an Unnatural Bundle of Hairs, all covered with Powder, that never grew on his Head; but now should this our *Broom-Stick* pretend to enter the Scene, proud of those *Birchen* Spoils it never bore, and all covered with Dust, though the Sweepings of the Finest Lady's Chamber, we should be apt to Ridicule and Despise its Vanity; Partial Judges that we are of Our own Excellencies, and other Men's Defaults!

BUT a *Broom-Stick*, perhaps you will say, is an Emblem of a Tree standing on its Head; and pray what is Man, but a Topsy-turvey Creature, his Animal Faculties perpetually mounted on his Rational; His Head where his Heels should be, groveling on the Earth, and yet with all his Faults, he sets up to be an universal Reformer of Grievances, rakes into every Sluts Corner of Nature, bringing hidden Corruptions to the Light, and raises a mighty Dust where there was none before, sharing deeply all the while, in the very same Pollutions he pretends to sweep away: His last Days are spent in Slavery to Women, and generally the least deserving; till worn to the Stumps, like his Brother *Bezom*,[1] he is either kickt out of Doors, or made use of to kindle Flames, for others to warm themselves by.[2]

1 A besom is a type of broom.

2 Swift 1711, 231-4.

Appendix I: Coke, Boyle, and Edwards on Testimony [see text, pp. 58–62]

Coke on Testimony

In the early modern period the notion of testimony was taken to lie in the province of logic, and seventeenth-century logicians such as Zachary Coke were quite willing to discuss it in at least as much detail as Boyle or Locke. Boyle's writing on testimony should be seen against that background. Expressly following Boyle's *Excellency of Theology*, John Edwards (Edwards 1699) offers an account of the value of testimony in theology.

Here is Coke on three types of testimony. First, writing of contingent Syllogisms, he tells us:

> The Canons of humane Testimony are 13.
>
> 1. Though no humane testimony as such, be of necessary truth, yet admitteth it certain degrees, and one is more strong, or weak then another.
> 2. Proper, or ones own testimony of things, done or not done, especially on the worser part, if it be not wrong out of force, is counted for firm.
> 3. Publike testimonies of publick seals are firm.
> 4. Testimony of publick and long-lasting fame is also to be esteemed for meanly firm.
> 5. Old testimony is more worth then new.
> 6. Grammatical testimonies, to wit, which treat of the use, signification, quantity of words; syllables, &c. gathered out of the best Authors, are firm.
> 7. Testimonies Practick, that is Ethick, Politick, Legal, of honest, filthy, right, wrong, spoken of grave Authors, are firm.
> 8. Testimonies historical, of approved Historians, are firm.
> 9. Testimonies Theoretical of some great and received Author, alledged after reasons of a Theoretical conclusion, have great force.

10. Testimonies of many Wise men and Famous, is to be preferred before the testimony of one and obscure man.
11. Testimony of a skilfull Artizen, is to be preferred before the testimony of another unskilfull, however famous otherwise.
12. Testimonies of ancient Fathers, if they be subordinate to the holy Scripture, have a force in proving Theological conclusions, but no proving humane, yet greater.
13. An Argument from humane Testimony negatively, is of no force.

And thus much of a contingent Syllogism.[1]

Then, in the course of telling us about necessary syllogisms, he offers the following about God's testimony, and about the testimony of sense:

The Canons of Gods Testimony, Mediate, and Immediate, are twelve.

1. Gods Testimony is believed for God himself, and his Authotiy, not for the mans sake by whom it was uttered.
2. There is no Divine Testimony written this day; But in the Bible.
3. All Principles of Theological conclusions, pertaining to the perfection and Salvation of the Elect, are sufficiently delivered in the Scriptures.
4. Argumentation from Gods Testimony, proceedeth both Affirmatively and Negatively in things pertaining to Salvation.
5. It ceaseth to be the Testimony of God, if wrested either to a wrong sence or unmeet Allegories.
6. From places or testimonies doutfull, Doctrines of faith are not firmly stablished.
7. That which by good consequence is gathered from any Divine testimony, it hath the same force with it.
8. What is proved or explained by the Scripture, that is under-

1 Coke 1654, 163-4.

stood to be also proved and explained by the true Church, Lawful Councels, and Antient Doctors.

9. From Gods revealed will to his power, the argument alwayes is of force; But it follows not, because he will not, that therefore he cannot.

10. From Gods will Indefinite and Hypothetical unto the simple execution thereof, an argument is not of Force: As, God would all men should be saved: therefore, they shall all be saved; It follows not; For that will is Hypothetical or Conditional, if they believe.

11. Gods Affirmative Commandments are to be taken with limitation.

12. Gods Negative Commandments do bind simply.

Finally, Coke tells us that

Testimony of sense, is that which every ones sense telleth him.

And it is { Outward / Inward

Inward, is [that] which Laws of nature and Conscience tells us.

Outward, is that with the outward senses (as seeing, hearing, &c.) rightly disposed, and so the sensual observation and experience doth confirm: Mat. 11.

Go tell John what ye hear and see; come see the place where the Lord was layed.[1]

Boyle on Testimony

First I consider what Qualifications men require in a testimony, & Secondly, How much they judge it not reasonable to beleeve

1 Coke 1654, 170-1. Coke's texts are from Matthew 11.4 and Matthew 28.6.

upon Testimony. I. A Testimony is recommended. 1. When a witnes may know the Truth of what he testify's. 2. When there is just Cause to beleive he hath the will to testify the Truth. 3. When other Things concurre to ascertaine his Testimony. That these 3 Qualifications are found in the Testimony of the Apostles about the Resurrection of Christ (which is held the most incredible of Miracles & therefore fittest to be here instanc'd in). I evince. 1. Because the Apostles were ... Eyewitnesses[1] of what they relate & sufficiently indispos'd to believe it. 2. That they wanted not will to tell the truth appears 1. By their Illiteratenes & unfitnes to devise Fictions.[2] 2. By the Holynes of their Doctrine & its severe Prohibition of Lyes. 3. By its being in the highest Degree against their Interest to promulgate such a matter. 4. By the miracles attesting their mission from God. 5. By their ingenuous & impartiall Recording their owne Faults, and Errors. 6. By their syncerity in recording things wherein if they would have written Lyes, they might have done it without feare of being found out. 7. By their great & yet reconcileable Variations from one another, which cleares them from the suspition of complotting. 8. By the very Incredibility of the thing they relate, which they could not hope would find Beleefe in the World, if they knew it to be a Fiction.[3]

---

1 Luke 1.2.

2 This is a problematic claim in the context. For Boyle and his contemporaries, moral certainty normally required expertise along with moral probity (as in Coke's point 11), not "Illiteratenes & unfitnes to devise Fictions." Concerning the Royal Society's assessment of the reliability of testimony, Barbara Shapiro remarks, "Credibility was assessed on the basis of a range of considerations that included social status but also the experience, skill, fidelity, impartiality and number of observers" (Shapiro 2002, 253). And Boyle himself makes the same point in *Christian Virtuoso I*: "'Tis as Justly as Generally granted, that the better qualify'd a Witness is ... the Stronger Assent his Testimony deserves; ... For the two grand Requisites of a Witness [are] the *knowledge* he has of the things he delivers, and his *faithfulness* in truly delivering what he knows" [*Works* 11:313, V:529]. (Boyle was making this point in order to stress the fact that "Human Testimony must ... be inferior to Divine Testimony.")

3 Locke, too, suggests that miracles provide a case where implausibility entails acceptability:

> Though the common Experience, and the ordinary Course of Things have justly a mighty Influence on the Minds of Men, to make them give or refuse Credit to anything proposed to their Belief; yet there is one Case, wherein the strangeness of the Fact lessens not the Assent

3ly Auxiliary Testimony's

1. The Jews not being able to produce his Body, notwithstanding their Care to secure it.

2. The Consonancy of his Resurrection both to his owne Predictions & those of the Prophets. 3. The Gifts of Tongues & miracles pour'd out upon the Beleivers of his Resurrection. 4. The Beleife it found in the world both amongst supremly indispos'd Persons, as St Paul & others, & amongst Philosophers and such as had both opportunity to examine the Truth of it & all the Reason in the world not to embrace it, unles they were fully convinc'd of it.

II. Wise Men believe upon unsuspected Testimony otherwise altogether Improbable Relations the most unlikly & unnaturall Crimes, & indeed any thing which is not irreconcileably inconsistent with the cleare Principles of Reason. Now I deny that any Narrative or Doctrine in the Scripture is such. For by our Vindication of the Testimony & witnesses of the Resurrection of Christ (by whom the old Testament is confirm'd) God is interested in the Miracles recorded, which are therefore not to be rejected as Impossible unles they be prov'd to be impossible to Omnipotence it selfe. And here I consider the Difference betwixt a things being impossible or against right Reason & its seeming soe to Men furnish'd only with such & such Principles & Notions of Reason; <& such measures & ways of estimating> which I evince, by sundry Chymicall Instances. This premis'd I consider that ev'n Wise Men beleive upon unsuspected Testimony, things contrary to the Principles & Notions they had before, & which may as plausibly & strongly be argu'd against as the things scrupl'd at in the Scripture. This I instance in Mens venturing without scruple to sayle to the Indy's, upon the Beleife that a Needle once excited by the Loadstone will retaine its Verticity though carry'd a thousand Leagues off from the stone,

---

> to a fair Testimony given of it. For where such supernatural Events are suitable to ends aim'd at by him, who has the Power to change the course of Nature, there, under such Circumstances, they may be the fitter to procure Belief, by how much the more they are beyond, or contrary to ordinary Observation. This is the proper Case of *Miracles*, which, well attested, do not only find Credit themselves; but give it also to other Truths, which need such Confirmation. (Locke 1975, 4.16.13)

See further MacIntosh 1994.

which yet noe Man can take but upon Testimony, the first time he ventures upon it & which is inconsistent with the most received Principles of Philosophy. Then I instance Witches & their Converse with the Devil, which the Gravest Judges in all Nations beleive (and sentence accordingly) upon Testimony: though otherwise the things related are altogether incredible & as obnoxious to objections from humane Reason & Philosophy as the distrusted Relations and Doctrines of the Scripture. Whence I conclude that there are some things which Reason herselfe must judge of after the rate of her owne Principles & that it is not against Reason as to the Trinity (about which the over bold & over nice Decisions are left to their Justifying that make them) that God being the increated & transcendent Being should have a Manner of Subsistence differing from all others & that That should be incomprehensible to man & therefore to be learn'd from Revelation only.[1]

Edwards on Testimony

Assent or *Belief* naturally follows on the *Clearness of Evidence;* and the more Clear and Demonstrative the Evidence is, the Firmer and Stronger will the Belief be. For as the Testimony is, such must this needs be: and therefore if the former be not only Human but Divine, and consequently be Infallible, the latter must be proportionable. What is Divine, saith an Excellent Writer,[2] doth by its Excellency conciliate Belief, and by its Truth gain Authority. For this Reason no Art or Science can pretend to that *Certainty* which is in *Divinity.* Politicks are fallible, Philosophy goes upon contrary Hypotheses, Medicks guess rather than know the inward Causes and Springs of Diseases. The Lawyer hath his *Ieofail,*[3] Law it self is very Uncertain and Arbitrary, if you consider the infinite Disagreement of divers Nations even about the same thing. Yea, even *Mathematicks* (if we may believe those that best understand them) are mixt with Uncertainties and Falshoods: there are Fallacies and Paralogisms in *Geometry:* all is not plain downright *Demonstration,* as appears from the Quarrels and Contests among *Mathematicians*

1 BP 3:117-20 (Boyle 2006, 4.6.8, pp. 380-2). This passage is also transcribed in Stewart 1993. My transcription differs in minor details from his.

2 Maximus Tyrius, Dissertation III. [Jonathan Edward's note.]

3 I.e., jeofail: a mistake or oversight in a legal proceeding.

themselves.[1] But *Divinity* is truly a Science, and surpasseth all others, because the Ground of it is supernatural Light, and the very Testimony of God himself. Particularly the Articles of *Christianity* are founded on Divine Revelation, and therefore are unquestionable. The Doctrine of the Gospel is built on this Rock, this Stable and Impregnable Rock. *The Foundation of God standeth sure,*[2] it continues the same, and cannot be moved. *Christian Theology* is founded on a sure Bottom; *Christ Iesus* the Son of God (and who is himself God) having fixed it. Heaven and Earth shall pass away, but this Word shall not pass away.[3]

With relation to this, Mr. Boyle's Treatise of the *Excellency of Theology compared with Natural Philosophy* is well worth our perusal. That admirable Person, so well skill'd in the Study of Physiologie, shews the Preeminence of the Study of Divinity above it on this account, that Theological Truths are evidenced by Divine Testimony, and therefore we may firmly acquiesce in them, and require no further or greater Proof (as indeed there can be no greater) tho, as I have shew'd, they are not destitute of other Evidences. The *Evangelical* Truths especially are the True *Theologie* (That of *Plato* and *Aristotle* and other Philosophers, to which they were pleased to vouchsafe *This Name*, being but a sorry and ill contrived Rhapsodie) therefore the *Christian Church* gave the Title of theologian to St. *Iohn*, because he, above all the rest of the Evangelists, so expresly declared the Divinity of the Son of God, which is the Noblest and Sublimest Point of Christianity, and is matter of pure Faith, and Divine Revelation. Be convinced then of the True Grounds of your *Christian Belief*, of the solid Foundations and undeniable Evi-

---

1 "Mathematician" was a term with a wide application in the seventeenth century. Some "mathematicians" were more or less self-appointed, and some of the quarrels between "mathematicians" may be put down to this feature (see, in particular, Jesseph 1999 for Hobbes's quarrel with the Oxford mathematicians, which may well be what Edwards has in mind). Nonetheless, leaving aside disputes about priority, etc., some of the quarrels involved practicing mathematicians (in our sense of the term) and concerned genuine mathematical issues. Edwards is right to think that there were quarrels among the mathematicians. More recently Einstein, asked, with reference to the quarrel between the intuitionist Brouwer and the formalist Hilbert, "What is this frog and mouse battle among the mathematicians?"

2 2 Timothy 2.19.

3 Matthew 24.35, Mark 13.31, Luke 21.33.

dences which *Christianity* is built upon. Know this, that God could not have done more for the begetting of a strong Faith and Assurance.[1]

1 Edwards 1699, 564-6.

Appendix J: A Review of the Excellency and Grounds of the Mechanical Hypothesis, Philosophical Transactions, *103, May 1674, pp. 53-55*[1]

This discourse is annexed to another, entituled, *The Excellency of THEOLOGY, compar'd with NATURAL PHILOSOPHY*, which though it be not of a direct tendency to the design of these Tracts, yet doth it occasionally mention divers things, fit to be taken notice of by a Student of Natural Philosophy; such as are the useful Hints and Directions to guide him in the making Experiments skilfully and warily (p. 118, 119 [170-71];)[2] now that the *Mechanical Hypothesis* is sufficiently settled, and the right Methods of Inquiring are found out (p. 171, [198-99]) to instruct him how injurious *Systematical* Writers are to the true search of Nature (p. 193. [208]) and what care is to be had of establishing *Philosophical Hypotheses* (p. 208. [214]) as also how much remains yet to be discover'd of Nature (p. 174, 176, 178. [200-02]) and how Philosophy hath recoiled by the *Aristotelians* laying aside Mathematicks, and disputing of Generals (p. 204. [213]) and by whom the Experimental and Mathematical Way of Philosophizing hath been restored and brought into esteem (p. 205, 206: [213]) Among which particulars there occur also several notable Considerations about the Nature of Body and Sensation (p. 144, 145, 153; [185-86, 190]) and divers Instances of Philosophy improved (p. 209, 210, 211; [215-16]) not only in reference to the understanding of the sensible Qualities of things, and their Causes, (p. 211, 212; [216]) but also as to Practical Inventions and Instruments (p. 213, [217]) &c.

But to pass to that dissertation, which is more within our sphere, *viz*. Concerning the *Excellency* and *Grounds* of the *Mechanical Hypothesis*; the Noble author thereof maketh it his business to evince, that the other *Hypotheses*, entertain'd by the several Sects of Philosophers, are so far from overthrowing the *Mechanical*, that they will either be foiled by it, or found reconcileable to it. In the doing whereof, having first declared his meaning about the subject

1 For the background to the reception of the *Excellencies*, see Harrison 2005 and, though it deals centrally with other theological works of Boyle, Wojcik 1997.

2 Bracketed numbers are the page numbers in this edition.

discours'd of, (*viz.* the *Mechanical Philosophy,*) he succinctly and plainly delivers the particulars that recommend it.

1. Of the Principles of things *Corporeal* (for such only he here treats of;) none can be more few without being insufficient, or more *primary*, than *Matter* or *Motion*.

2. The natural and genuine effect of variously determin'd *Motions* in portions of *Matter*, is, to divide it into parts of different *Sizes*, and *Shapes*, and to put them into *different Motions*; the consequences of which are, *Posture, Order, Scituation* and peculiar *Textures*.

3. The parts of *Matter* endow'd with these *Catholick affections* are by various associations reduced to Natural Bodies of several kinds, according to the plenty of the matter, and the various Compositions and Decompositions of the Principles; which all suppose the common Matter they diversify: And these several Kinds of Bodies, by Vertue of their Motion, Rest, and other Mechanical Affections, which sit them to act and to suffer, become endowed with several Kinds of Qualities, and with those that work upon the peculiarly fram'd Organs of Sense, whose Perceptions by the animadversive Faculty of the Soul are Sensations.

4. These Principles *Matter, Motion, Rest, Bigness, shape, Posture, order, Texture,* being so *simple, clear*, and *comprehensive*, are by our Author shown to be applicable to all the real *Phænomena* of Nature, which seem not explicable by any other not consistent with these. For, *saith he*, if recourse be had to an Immaterial Principle, it may be such an one, as is not intelligible; and however it will not enable us to explain the *Phænomena*, because its *manner* and *way* of working upon things Material would probably be more difficult to be *Physically* made out, than a Mechanical account of such Effects. And as to an Immaterial *created* Agent, we cannot conceive, how it should produce changes in a Body without the help of Mechanical Principles, especially *Local motion*; and accordingly we find not, that the Reasonable Soul in Man is able to produce what changes it pleaseth in the body, but is confin'd to such as it may produce by determining or guiding the Motions of the Spirits, and other Parts of the Body, subservient to voluntary Motion.

5. And if the Active Principles resorted to, be not Immaterial, but Corporeal, they must either in Effect be the same with those lately mention'd; or, because of the great universality and simplicity of the same, the new ones propos'd must be less general then *they*, and consequently capable of being subordinated or reduced to those asserted by our Author, which by various Com-

positions may afford matter to several *Hypotheses*, and by several Conditions afford minute Concretions exceedingly numerous and durable, and consequently fit to become the Elementary Ingredients of more compounded Bodies, being in most Trials Similar, and as it were the Radical Parts, which may after sever manners be diversified, as in a Language the Themes are by *Præpositions*, *Terminations*, &c. So that the fear, that so much of a *New* physical Hypothesis, as is *true*, will overthrow or make useless the *Mechanical* Principles, is, as if one should fear, there will be a Language propos'd, that is discordant from, or not reducible to, the Letters of the Alphabet.

Appendix K: John Evelyn to Boyle, 20 June 1674, in response to having received Boyle's Excellency of Theology[1]

Sir.

I have been too long a debter to you for the many obligations you have been pleased to accumulate upon me; but for none more, then for the Booke, Lately brought me by Mr. Oldenburg; and I am sorry the Returne I make you, beares so small proportion, to the Inestimable Treasure I have received:[2] I confesse I have (as well as all the world) been ever an admirer of the Excellent Talents and of the many great endowments, with which God hath blessed you; but for nothing do I so sincearly love, and really esteem you, as for that rare piety, and those beames of Heavenly, light which I find to Illustrate all your writings and Conversations; After all you have seene, and read, and tryd, what a blessed Choyce have you made. But thus I remember you began,[3] Thus you proceede, and thus (I argue) you will conclude: I must acknowledge, and deplore how vaine, and unhappy I have hitherto beene, to have ever with any solicitude, sought for satisfaction in the studies to my vanity has at any time Imported me: very shallow, and trifeling have been all my, parsutes, compared with the many usefull, and solid things which you have so happiely produced: But still you find me blotting Paper: Forgive me this one folly, and be assur'd, that I was not altogether the Cause of this publication; so nor has the argument any sort of affinity with my Genious: It has been now some yeares my endeaver, and resolution to serve God, and to devote the rest of the time which he shall please to assigne me here, to the contemplation of those things which you have Cælebrated with so much reason, and pius argument: I have a little enter'd into that glorious vestibule, and find so much satisfaction superiour to all the pleasures that I ever tooke in other speculations, that fortifyd, as I am, by your excellent discourse, and Example, I doe not doubt, but I shall go on

1 *Correspondence* 4:383-84.

2 The Editors of the *Correspondence* point out that "Boyle's gift and Evelyn's return gift were respectively, *Excellency of Theology*, and *Navigation and Commerce*, both first published in 1674" (4:383).

3 Seraph: love [Evelyn's note, i.e., "Seraphic Love,"*Works* vol. 1].

and persevere: I am every day more and more amazed at men of Learning and reason (as they would be thought) that they should not be the most Religious persons in the world: But you have hit the white; their is a certaine pride, which that knowing spirit, doth Infuse into them, which hinders the operation of that more divine, and knowing spirit, who only dwells with the Humble, and those who sincerely submit unto his wisdome, however opposite, and contradictory it appeares to our Corrupted and arrogant Inclinations: Methinkes one Chapter of St paules[1] were enough to bring downe these high thoughts, as well as the lives and confessions of so many saintes, and eminently, knowing persons as have in all ages submitted their science, will and prodigious Parts to the scandall of the Crosse, and the foolishnes of Preaching, I meane, to the Doctrine of the Gospell: but either men do not belive those things, or will not give themselves Leasure to Consider them: Blessed be God, that you are not only none of them, but all Emulous Example of that sanctified, and true knowledge, which you so piously recommend:

Sir, the best, and most acceptable Returne, I can ever make you for this noble Present, will be to Cultivate the Choyce which you prefer and to become your Proselyte, who am

Sir
with all sincerity and affection, Most thankfull,
most obliged & humble servant.

20 June (74)
J Evelyn

---

1 1 Cor. 1 [Evelyn's note]

Works Cited

Ackrill 1981: John Ackrill, *Aristotle the Philosopher* (Oxford, Oxford UP, 1981)

Akenside 1744: Mark Akenside, *The Pleasures of Imagination* (London: Printed for R. Dodsley, 1744)

Alexander 1962: A.F.O'D. Alexander, *The Planet Saturn: A History of Observation, Theory and Discovery* (New York: Dover, 1962)

Anon 1685: *The Atheist Unmasked, or, A Confutation of such as deny the Being of a Supream Deity, that governs Heaven and Earth By Unanswerable Arguments deduc'd ... By A Person of Honour* (London: Printed for Langley Curtiss, 1685)

Anstey 1999: Peter Anstey, "Boyle on occasionalism: an unexamined source," *Journal of the History of Ideas*, 60.1, 1999, 57-81

Anstey 2000: Peter Anstey, *The Philosophy of Robert Boyle* (London: Routledge, 2000)

Anstey 2002: Peter Anstey, "Locke, Bacon and Natural History," *Early Science and Medicine*, 7, 2002, 65-92

Anstey 2005: Peter Anstey, "Experimental versus Speculative Natural Philosophy," in Peter Anstey and John A. Schuster, eds., *The Science of Nature in the Seventeenth Century: Patterns of Change in Early Modern Natural Philosophy* (Dordrecht: Springer, 2005), 215-42

Aquinas, St. Thomas: *QD de Potentia Dei* (*On the Power of God*), 2 vols. translated Lawrence Shapcote (London: Burns Oates & Washbourne, 1932; reprinted Westminster, MD: The Newman Press, 1952)

Aquinas, St. Thomas, *Summa Theologica* [cited as ST], translated by the Fathers of the English Dominican Province, 5 vols. (Westminister, MD: Christian Classics, 1981, reprinting the revised 1920 ed. [1st ed. 1911])

Aristotle 1984: *The Complete Works of Aristotle*, Jonathan Barnes, ed. (Princeton: Princeton UP, 1984)

Aristotle 2002: *Invitation to Philosophy*, edited and translated D.S. Hutchinson and Monte Ransome Johnson; available online at <http://www.chass.utoronto.ca/~phl102y/Protrepticus.pdf>

AT: Descartes, Ch. Adam and P. Tannery, *Oeuvres de Descartes* 11 vols. (Paris: J. Vrin, 1964-76)

Aubrey 1957, John Aubrey, *Brief Lives*, Oliver Lawson Dick, ed. (Ann Arbor: U of Michigan P, 1957)

Bacon, Francis: *The Works of Francis Bacon*, James Spedding, Robert Leslie Ellis, Douglas Denon Heath, eds., 14 vols. (London: Longman & Co., 1857-75; Facsimile reproduction Stuttgart-Bad Cannstatt: Friedrich Fromann Verlag Gunther Holzboog, 1963)

Bacon 1612: Francis Bacon, *The Essaies of Sr Francis Bacon Knight, the Kings Sollicitere Generall* (London, Iohn Beale, 1612)

Bacon 1733: Roger Bacon, *Opus Maius* (London: Gulielmi Bowyer, 1733)

Barnes 1982: Jonathan Barnes, *Aristotle* (Oxford: Oxford UP, 1982)

Barber 1999: Sarah Barber, "'Nothing but the First Chaos': Making Sense of Ireland," *Seventeenth Century*, 14, 1999, 24-42

Bates 1676: William Bates, *Considerations of the Existence of God, and of the Immortality of the Soul* (London: Brabazon Aylmer, 1676)

Bayle 1734: Pierre Bayle, *Dictionaire Historique et Critique*, 5th ed., 5 vols. (Amsterdam, 1734)

Bennett and Remnant 1978: Jonathan Bennett and Peter Remnant, "How Matter Might at First be Made," in C.E. Jarrett, J. King-Farlow, and F.J. Pelletier, eds., *New Essays on Rationalism and Empiricism*, *Canadian Journal of Philosophy* Supp. vol. 4 (Guelph: Canadian Association for Publishing in Philosophy, 1978), 1-11; available on-line at <http://www.earlymoderntexts.com/jfb/howmat.pdf>

Bentley 1699: Richard Bentley, *The Folly and Unreasonableness of Atheism* (London: Printed by J.H. for H. Mortlock, 1699, The fourth edition, corrected)

Berman 1988: David Berman, *A History of Atheism in Britain: From Hobbes to Russell* (London: Croom Helm, 1988)

Birch 1772: *The Works of the Honourable Robert Boyle*, Thomas Birch, ed., 6 vols. (London, 1772; reprinted Hildesheim: George Olms, 1966). Birch's *Life of the Honourable Robert Boyle* is in Volume I.

Boyle *Works*: Robert Boyle, *The Works of Robert Boyle*, Michael Hunter and Edward B. Davis, eds., 14 vols. (London: Pickering and Chatto, 1999-2000)

Boyle 2006: Robert Boyle, *Boyle on Atheism*, transcribed and edited by J.J. MacIntosh (Toronto: U of Toronto P, 2006)

BP: Robert Boyle, *Letters and Papers of Robert Boyle*, Michael Hunter, ed. (Bethesda, MD: University Publications of America, 1990). available online at <http://www.bbk.ac.uk/Boyle/boyle_papers/boylepapers_index.htm.>

Broad 1952: C.D. Broad, *Ethics and the History of Philosophy* (London: Routledge and Kegan Paul, 1952)

Brown 2006: Deborah Brown, *Descartes and the Passionate Mind* (Cambridge: Cambridge UP, 2006)

Budgell 1732: Eustace Budgell, *Memoirs of the Life and Character of the Late Earl of Orrery And of the Family of the Boyles* (London, 1732)

Burnet 1989: Thomas Burnet, *Remarks on John Locke with Locke's Replies*, George Watson, ed. (Doncaster: The Brynmill Press, 1989)

Burns 1972: Norman T. Burns, *Christian mortalism from Tyndale to Milton* (Cambridge, Mass: Harvard University Press, 1972)

Burton 1638: Robert Burton, *The Anatomy of Melancholy* (Oxford: Henry Cripps, 1638)

Canny 1982: Nicholas Canny, *The Upstart Earl: A study of the social*

and mental world of Richard Boyle, first Earl of Cork, 1566-1643 (Cambridge: Cambridge UP, 1982)
Cardano 1663: Girolamo Cardano, *Opera Omnia*, 10 vols. (Lyon: Jean Antoine Huguetan/Marc Antione Ravaud, 1663)
Cardano 2002: Girolamo Cardano, *The Book of My Life (De Vita Propria Liber)* (New York: New York Review Books Classics, 2002)
Casaubon 1999: Casaubon, Meric, *Generall Learning*, Richard Serjeantson, ed. (Cambridge: RTM publications, Renaissance Texts from Manuscript, No. 2, 1999)
Chillingworth 1638: William Chillingworth, *The Religion of Protestants* (Oxford: Printed by Leonard Lichfiel[d], 1638)
Cicero: *De natura deorum*, translated H. Rackham (London: William Heinemann, The Loeb Classical Library, 1933)
Clarke 1738: Samuel Clarke, *The Works of Samuel Clarke, D.D.*, 4 vols. (London, 1738, reprinted New York: Garland Publishing, 1978)
Clericuzio 2000: Antonio Clericuzio, *Elements, Principles and Corpuscles: A Study of Atomism and Chemistry in the Seventeenth Century* (Dordrecht: Kluwer, 2000)
Coke 1654: Zachary Coke, *The Art of Logick* (London, 1654, reprinted Menston: The Scolar Press, 1969)
Correspondence: *The Correspondence of Robert Boyle*, Michael Hunter, Antonio Clericuzio, and Lawrence M. Principe, eds., 6 vols. (London: Pickering and Chatto, 2001)
CSMK: René Descartes, *The Philosophical Writings of Descartes*, 3 vols. (Cambridge: Cambridge UP, 1984 [vol. 2], 1985 [vol. 1], 1991 [vol. 3]), vols. 1 & 2 translated J. Cottingham, R. Stoothoff, D. Murdoch, vol. 3 translated J. Cottingham, R. Stoothoff, D. Murdoch, A. Kenny)
Cudworth 1678: Ralph Cudworth, *The True Intellectual System of the Universe* (London, 1678, reprinted Stuttgart-Bad Cannstatt: Friedrich Frommann Verlag, 1964)
Cudworth 1731: Ralph Cudworth, *A Treatise Conderning Eternal and Immutable Morality* (London: printed for James and John Knapton, 1731)
Curtius Rufus, Quintus, *The History of Alexander*, translated by John Yardley, with an introduction and notes by Waldemar Heckel (Harmondsworth: Penguin, 1984)
Daston 1988: Lorraine Daston, "The Factual Sensibility," *Isis*, 79, 1988, 452-67
Daston 1991: Lorraine Daston, "Marvelous Facts and Miraculous Evidence in Early Modern Europe," *Critical Inquiry* 18, 1991, 93-124
Debus 1965: Allen G. Debus, *The English Paracelsians* (London: Oldbourne, 1965)
de la Forge 1666: Louis de la Forge, *Treatise on the Human Mind*, translated Desmond M. Clarke (Dordrecht: Kluwer, 1997)
Descartes 1954: René Descartes, *The Geometry of René Descartes*,

translated David Eugene Smith and Marcia L. Latham (New York: Dover, 1954)

Descartes 1998: René Descartes, *Principles of Philosophy*, translated G. Macdonald Ross, 1998-9, available online at <http://www.philosophy.leeds.ac.uk/GMR/hmp/texts/modern/descartes/principles/dcprinc.html>

Dewhurst 1966: Kenneth Dewhurst, *Dr. Thomas Sydenham (1624-1689): His Life and Original Writings* (Berkeley and Los Angeles: U of California P, 1966)

Digby 1644: Kenelm Digby, *Two Treatises. In the one of which The Nature of Bodies; in the other, The Nature of Mans Sovle; is looked into: in way of discovery, of the Immortality of Reasonable Sovles* (Paris, 1644, reprinted New York: Garland, 1978)

Dijksterhuis 1961: E.J. Dijksterhuis, *The Mechanization of the World Picture* (Oxford: Oxford UP, 1961)

Dryden 1966: John Dryden, *The Indian Emperour*, in *The Works of John Dryden*, vol. IX, ed. J. Loftis and V.A. Dearing (Berkeley and Los Angeles: The University of California Press, 1966)

Duchesneau 1970: François Duchesneau, "La Philosophie Medicale de Sydenham," *Dialogue* 9, 1970, 54-68

Edwards 1699: John Edwards, *A Compleat History or Survey of all the Dispensations and Methods of Religion, From the beginning of the World to the Consummation of all things* (London: Printed for Daniel Brown et al., 1699)

Epicurus 1994: *The Epicurus Reader: Selected Writings and Testimonials*, translated and edited Brad Inwood and L.P. Gerson (Indianapolis and Cambridge: Hackett, 1994)

Fell 1661: John Fell, *The Life of the Most Learned, Reverend and Pious Dr H. Hammond* (London: Jo. Martin, Ja. Allestry, and Tho. Dicas, 1661)

Foster 1924: Michael Foster, *Lectures on the History of Physiology During the Sixteenth, Seventeenth and Eighteenth Centuries* (Cambridge: Cambridge UP, 1924)

Fraser 1984: Antonia Fraser, *The Weaker Vessel* (New York: Alfred A. Knopf, 1984)

Freind 1737: John Freind, *Chymical Lectures: In which almost all the Operations of Chymistry are Reduced to their True Principles, and the Laws of Nature* (London: Printed for Aaron Ward ... and Thomas Longman, 2nd ed., 1737; a translation of Freind's 1704 Oxford lectures, originally printed as *Prælectiones Chymicæ* ... [London: John Bowyer, 1709])

Galileo 1967: Galilei Galileo, *Dialogue Concerning the Two World Systems*, translated Stillman Drake (Berkeley and Los Angeles: U of California P, 2nd revised ed., 1967)

Gaukroger 2001: Stephen Gaukroger, *Francis Bacon and the Transformation of Early-Modern Philosophy* (Cambridge: Cambridge UP, 2001)

Geach 1969: Peter Geach, *God and the Soul* (London: Routledge & Kegan Paul, 1969)

Gerhardt: Gottfried Wilhelm Leibniz, *Philosophische Schriften*, C.I. Gerhardt, ed., 7 vols. (Berlin: Weidmannsche Buchhandlung, 1875-90)

Geulincx 1965: Arnold Geulincx, *Sämtliche Schriften in fünf Bänden*, H.J. de Vleeschauwer, ed., 5 vols. (Stuttgart-Bad Cannstatt: Friedrich Frommann, 1965-8)

Goethe 1948: Johann Wolfgang Goethe, *Materialen zur Geschichte der Farbenlehre, Werke*, E. Beutler, ed., 24 vols. (Zürich: Artemis-Verlag, 1948-54)

Goodrum 2002: Matthew R. Goodrum, "Atomism, Atheism, and the Spontaneous Generation of Human Beings: The Debate over a Natural origin of the First Humans in Seventeenth-Century Britain," *Journal of the History of Ideas*, 63, 2002, 207-24

Greek 1992: Cecil Greek, "Drug Control And Asset Seizures: A Review of The History of Forfeiture In England And Colonial America," in *Drugs, Crime and Social Policy: Research, Issues, and Concerns*, Thomas Mieczkowski, ed. (Boston: Allyn and Bacon, 1992), 109-37

Harrison 2005: Peter Harrison, "Physico-theology and the Mixed Sciences: the Role of Theology in Early Modern Natural Philosophy," in *The Science of Nature in the Seventeenth Century: Patterns of Change in Early Modern Natural Philosophy*, Peter Anstey and John A. Schuster, eds. (Dordrecht: Springer, 2005), 165-83

Harwood 1991: John T. Harwood, ed., *The Early Essays and Ethics of Robert Boyle*, (Carbondale and Edwardsville: Southern Illinois UP, 1991)

Heath 1921: Thomas Heath, *A History of Greek Mathematics*, 2 vols. (New York: Dover, 1981; reprinting Oxford: Clarendon Press, 1921)

Hill 1972: Christopher Hill, *The World Turned Upside Down* (London: Temple Smith, 1972)

Hill 2004: James Hill, "Locke's account of cohesion and its Philosophical Significance," *British Journal for the History of Philosophy*, 12, 2004, 611-30

Hooke 1705: Robert Hooke, *Lectures of Light*, in *Robert Hooke, Posthumous Works*, Richard Waller, ed. (London, 1705; reprinted London: Frank Cass, 1971)

Horace, *Ars Poetica* (London: W. Bowyer, 1749)

Howell 1705: James Howell, *Epistolae Ho-Elianae Familiar Letters, Domestick and Foreign* (7th ed., London, 1705)

Howell 2002: Kenneth J. Howell, *God's Two Books: Copernican Cosmology and Biblical Interpretation in Early Modern Science* (Notre Dame: U of Notre Dame P, 2002)

Hume 1975: David Hume, *An Enquiry Concerning Human Understanding*, ed. L.A. Selby-Bigge and P. Nidditch (Oxford: Clarendon Press, 1975)

Hunter 1981: Michael Hunter, *Science and Society in Restoration England* (Cambridge: Cambridge University Press, 1981)

Hunter 1993: Michael Hunter, "Casuistry in Action: Robert Boyle's Confessional Interviews with Gilbert Burnet and Edward Stillingfleet, 1691," *The Journal of Ecclesiastical History*, 44.1, 1993, 80-98, reprinted in Hunter 2000, 72-92

Hunter 1994: Michael Hunter, ed., *Robert Boyle by Himself and His Friends* (London: William Pickering, 1994)

Hunter 1995a: Michael Hunter, "How Boyle Became a Scientist," *History of Science* 33, 1995, 59-103, reprinted in Hunter 2000, 15-57

Hunter 1995b: Michael Hunter, "How to Edit a Seventeenth-Century Manuscript: Principles and Practice," *The Seventeenth Century*, 1995, 277-310

Hunter 2000: Michael Hunter, *Robert Boyle 1627-1691: Scrupulosity and Science* (Woodbridge: The Boydell Press, 2000)

Hunter 2006: Michael, Hunter, *Editing Early Modern Texts: An Introduction to Principles and Practice* (Basingstoke: Macmillan Palgrave, 2006)

Hunter 2007: Michael Hunter, "Robert Boyle and the Early Royal Society: A Reciprocal Exchange in the Making of Baconian Science," *British Journal for the History of Science*, 40 2007, 1-23

Hunter and Davis: See under Boyle *Works*

Hurka 2006: Thomas Hurka, "Games and the Good," *Proceedings of the Aristotelian Society*, Supplementary Volume LXXX, 2006, 217-35

Hussey 1972: Edward Hussey, *The Presocratics* (London: Duckworth, 1972)

Huygens 1888: Christiaan Huygens, *Œuvres Complètes*, 30 vols. (La Haye: Martinus Nijhoff, 1888-1950)

Iamblichus 1965: Iamblichus, *Life of Pythagoras*, translated Thomas Taylor (London: John M. Watkins, 1965)

Jesseph 1999: Douglas M. Jesseph, *Squaring the Circle: The War Between Hobbes and Wallis* (Chicago: U of Chicago P, 1999)

Justin Martyr, "On the Resurrection," at <http://www.earlychristianwritings.com/text/justinmartyr-resurrection.html>

Kant 1787: Immanuel Kant, *Critique of Pure Reason*, translated N. Kemp Smith (London: Macmillan, 1933 [2nd ed. 1787])

Kant 1793: Immanuel Kant, *Religion Within the Limits of Reason Alone*, translated Theodore M. Greene and Hoyt H. Hudson (revised, John R. Silber) (New York: Harper Torchbooks, 1960 [1793])

Kant 1956: Immanuel Kant, *Groundwork of the Metaphysic of Morals*, translated H.J. Paton as *The Moral Law* (London: Hutchinson's, 3rd ed., 1956)

Kemp Smith 1952: Norman Kemp Smith, *New Studies in the Philosophy of Descartes* (London: Macmillan & Co., 1952)

Kim 2001: Jaegwon Kim, "Lonely Souls: Causality and Substance Dualism," in *Soul Body and Survival: Essays on the Metaphysics of Human Persons*, Kevin Corcoran, ed. (Ithaca: Cornell UP, 2001)

Kirk, Raven, and Schofield 1983: G.S. Kirk, J.E. Raven and M. Schofield, *The Presocratic Philosophers* (Cambridge: Cambridge UP, 2nd ed., 1983)

Laertius, Diogenes: *Lives of Eminent Philosophers*, translated R.D. Hicks, 2 vols. (London: William Heinemann, Loeb Classical Library, 1925)

Le Grand 1694: Antoine Le Grand, *An Entire Body of Philosophy According to the Principles of the Famous Renate Descartes*, translated R. Blome (London: Samuel Roycroft, 1694)

Leibniz 1672: Gottfried Wilhelm von Leibniz, *The Labyrinth of the Continuum: Writings on the Continuum Problem, 1672-1686*, translated and edited Richard Arthur (New Haven: Yale UP, 2001)

Leibniz 1981: G.W. Leibniz, *New Essays on Human Understanding*, translated and edited Peter Remnant and Jonathan Bennett (Cambridge: Cambridge UP, 1981)

Leibniz 1994: Gottfried Wilhelm Leibniz, *Writings on China*, translated Daniel J. Cook and Henry Rosemont, Jr. (Chicago : Open Court, 1994)

Lennon 1993: Thomas M. Lennon, *The Battle of the Gods and Giants* (Princeton: Princeton UP, 1993)

Locke 1669: John Locke, *De Arte Medica*, in Dewhurst 1966, 79-84

Locke 1823: John Locke, *The Works of John Locke* (10 vols., London, 1823; reprinted Aalen: Scientia Verlag, 1963)

Locke 1975: John Locke, *An Essay Concerning Human Understanding*, ed. P.H. Nidditch (Oxford: Clarendon Press, 1975)

Locke 1979: *The Correspondence of John Locke*, E.S. de Beer, ed., 8 vols. (Oxford: Clarendon Press, 1979)

Loemker 1969: *Gottfried Wilhelm Leibniz: Philosophical Papers and Letters*, edited and translated Leroy E. Loemker (Dordrecht: D. Reidel, 2nd ed., 1969)

Luther 1955: Martin Luther, *Works*, 55 vols. Various editors and publishers; Vol. 1 ed. Jaroslav Pelikan (Saint Louis: Concordia Publishing House, 1955)

MacIntosh 1978: J.J. MacIntosh, "Berkeley's Views on Time," in *New Essays on Rationalism and Empiricism*, C.E. Jarrett, J. King-Farlow, and J. Pelletier, eds. (Guelph: Canadian Association for Publishing in Philosophy, 1978), 153-63

MacIntosh 1983: J.J. MacIntosh, "Perception and Imagination in Descartes, Boyle and Hooke," *Canadian Journal of Philosophy*, 13, 1983, 327-52

MacIntosh 1991: J.J. MacIntosh, "Robert Boyle on Epicurean Atomism and Atheism," in *Atoms, Pneuma, and Tranquillity: Epicurean and Stoic Themes in European Thought*, M.J. Osler, ed. (New York: Cambridge UP, 1991), 197-219

MacIntosh 1992: J.J. MacIntosh, "Robert Boyle's Epistemology: The Interaction between Scientific and Religious Knowledge," *International Studies in the Philosophy of Science*, 6, 1992, 91-121

MacIntosh 1994: J.J. MacIntosh, "Locke and Boyle on Miracles and God's Existence," in *Robert Boyle Reconsidered*, M. Hunter, ed. (Cambridge: Cambridge UP, 1994), 193-214; reprinted in *John Locke: Critical Assessments*, P. Anstey, ed., 4 vols. [London: Routledge, 2006])

MacIntosh 1996: J.J. MacIntosh, "Animals, Morality, and Robert Boyle," *Dialogue*, 35, 1996, 435-72

MacIntosh 2001: J.J. MacIntosh, "Boyle, Bentley and Clarke on God, Necessity, Frigorifick Atoms and the Void," *International Studies in the Philosophy of Science*, 15, 2001, 33-47

MacIntosh 2005: J.J. MacIntosh, "Boyle and Locke on Observation, Testimony, Demonstration and Experience," *Croatian Journal of Philosophy*, vol. V, no. 14, 2005, 275-88

Maddison 1969: R.E.W. Maddison, *The Life of the Honourable Robert Boyle F. R. S.* (London: Taylor & Francis, 1969)

Magalotti 1980: Lorenzo Magalotti, *Relazione d'Inghilterra*, translated and edited W.E. Knowles Middleton as *Lorenzo Magalotti at the Court of Charles II* (Waterloo: Wilfrid Laurier UP, 1980)

Maimonides, Moses, *The Guide for the Perplexed*, translated M. Friedlander (New York: Dover, 1956)

Malcolm and Stedall 2005: Noel Malcolm and Jacqueline Stedall, *John Pell (1611-1685) and his Correspondence with Sir Charles Cavendish: The Mental World of an Early Modern Mathematician* (Oxford: Oxford UP, 2005)

Mancosu 1996: Paolo Mancosu, *Philosophy of Mathematics and Mathematical Practice in the Seventeenth Century* (New York: Oxford UP, 1996)

Mathew 1662: Richard Mathew, *The Unlearned Alchymist his Antidote* (London: Ioseph Leigh 1662)

McMullen 1978: E. McMullen, *Newton on Matter and Activity* (Notre Dame: U of Notre Dame P, 1978)

Mintz 1969: S. Mintz, *The Hunting of Leviathan* (Cambridge: Cambridge UP, 1969)

Moote and Moote 2004: A. Lloyd Moote and Dorothy C. Moote, *The Great Plague: The Story of London's Most Deadly Year* (Baltimore and London: Johns Hopkins UP, 2004)

More 1662: Henry More, *An Antidote Against Atheism, in A Collection of Several Philosophical Writings of Dr. Henry More*, 2 vols. (London, 1662, reprinted New York: Garland, 1978)

More 1671: Henry More, *Enchiridion Metaphysicum: sive, de Rebus Incorporeis Succincta & luculenta Dissertatio* (London: J. Flesher for William Morden, 1671)

Morrison 1989: Margaret Morrison, "Hypotheses and Certainty in Cartesian Science," in *An Intimate Relation*, ed. J.R. Brown and J. Mittelstrass (Dordrecht: Kluwer, 1989), 43-64

Newton 1972: Isaac Newton, *Philosophiae Naturalis Principia Mathematica*, Alexandre Koyré and I. Bernard Cohen, eds., 2 vols. (Cambridge, Mass: Harvard UP, 1972)

Newman 2005: Lex Newman, "Descartes' Epistemology," *The Stanford Encyclopedia of Philosophy* (Summer 2005 Edition), Edward N. Zalta. ed., available online at <http://plato.stanford.edu/archives/sum2005/entries/descartes-epistemology/>

Nicholson 1959: Marjorie Hope Nicholson, *Mountain Gloom and Mountain Glory: The Development of the Aesthetics of the Infinite* (New York: Norton, 1959)

OED: *Oxford English Dictionary*, John Simpson, ed. (Oxford: Oxford UP, 2000)

Oldenburg 1965: *The Correspondence of Henry Oldenburg*, translated and edited, Rupert A. Hall and Marie Boas Hall, 11 vols. (Madison: The U of Wisconsin P, 1965-).

Osler 1992: Margaret J. Osler, "The intellectual sources of Robert Boyle's philosophy of nature: Gassendi's voluntarism and Boyle's physico-theological project," in *Philosophy, Science, and Religion in England 1640-1700*, R. Kroll, R. Ashcraft, and P. Zagorin, eds. (Cambridge: Cambridge UP, 1992), 178-98

Osler 1994: Margaret J. Osler, *Divine Will and the Mechanical Philosophy* (New York: Cambridge UP, 1994)

Oster 1989: Malcolm Oster, "The 'Beame of Diuinity': Animal Suffering in the Early Thought of Robert Boyle," *British Journal for the History of Science*, 1989, 22, 151-80

Ovid 1693: *Metamorphoses*, translated John Dryden in *Examen poeticum* (London: Printed by R.E. for Jacob Tonson, 1693)

Parker 1993: Michael St. John Parker, *The Civil War, 1642-51* (Andover, Hampshire: Pitkin Pictorials, 1993)

Parker 1666: Samuel Parker, *A Free and Impartial Censvre of the Platonick Philosophie, being a letter written to his much honoured friend Mr. N.B.* (Oxford: printed by W. Hall, for Richard Davis, 1666)

Partington 1961: J.R. Partington, *A History of Chemistry*, 2 vols. (London: Macmillan, 1961)

Pascal 1952: Blaise Pascal, *Pensées sur la Religion et sur quelques autres sujets*, L. Lafuma, ed., 3 vols. (Paris: Éditions du Luxembourg, 1952)

Peirce 1931: C.S. Peirce, *The Collected Papers of Charles Sanders Peirce*, Charles Hartshorne and Paul Weiss (vols. 1-6), Arthur W. Burks (vols. 7-8), eds., 8 vols. (Cambridge, MA: Harvard UP, 1931-58)

Penelhum 1970: Terence Penelhum, *Survival and Disembodied Existence* (London: Routledge & Kegan Paul, 1970)

Penington 1656: Isaac Penington, *Expositions with observations sometimes, on several Scriptures* (London: J. Macock, 1656)

Pepys 1932: *The Letters and Second Diary of Samuel Pepys*, R.G. Howarth, ed. (London: J.M. Dent, 1932)

Philo Judaeus, *Life of Moses, II*, translated C.D. Yonge (London: H.G. Bohn, 1854)

Plot 1677: Robert Plot, *The Natural History of Oxford-shire* (Oxford: printed at The Theatre, 1677)

Plutarch 1961: Plutarch, *Moralia*, 15 vols. various translators (Cambridge, MA: Harvard UP, and London: William Heinemann, Loeb Library, 1961), *Moralia* Book 8 translated Edwin L. Minar, Jr.

Porter 1984: Noah Porter, "Marginalia Locke-a-na," in Thomas Burnet, John Locke, Noah Porter, *Remarks Upon an Essay Concerning Human Understanding: Five Tracts* (New York: Garland, 1984)

Principe 1994: Lawrence M.Principe, "Style and Thought of the Early Boyle: Discovery of the 1648 Manuscript of *Seraphic Love*," *Isis*, 85, 1994, 247-60

Principe 1995: Lawrence M. Principe, "Virtuous Romance and Romantic Virtuoso: The Shaping of Robert Boyle's Literary Style," *Journal of the History of Ideas*, 1995, 377-97

Principe 1998: Lawrence M. Principe, *The Aspiring Adept: Robert Boyle and his Alchemical Quest* (Princeton: Princeton UP, 1998)

Principe and Newman 1998: Lawrence M. Principe and W.R. Newman, "Alchemy vs. Chemistry: The Etymological Origins of a Historiographic Mistake," *Early Science and Medicine*, 3, 1998, 32-65

Prior 1967: A.N. Prior, *Past, Present and Future* (Oxford: Clarendon Press, 1967)

Proclus 1970: Proclus, *A Commentary on the First Book of Euclid's "Elements,"* trans. and ed. Glen R. Morrow (Princeton: Princeton University Press, 1970)

Ray 1691: John Ray, *The Wisdom of God Manifested in the Works of the Creation* (London: Christopher Wilkinson, 1691)

Ross 1645: Alexander Ross, *Medicus Medicatus:* Or the Physicians Religion Cured ... With some Animadversions upon Sir *Kenelme Digbie*'s Observations on *Religio Medici* (London: Printed by James Young, 1645)

Ross 1923: D. Ross, *Aristotle* (London: Methuen, 1923)

Ross 1965: Sutherland Ross, *The Plague and the Fire of London* (London: Faber and Faber, 1965)

Ruestow 1973: Edward G. Ruestow, *Physics at Seventeenth and Eighteenth-Century Leiden: Philosophy and the New Science in the University* (The Hague: Martinus Nijhoff, 1973)

Russell 1937: Bertrand Russell, *A Critical Exposition of the Philosophy of Leibniz* (London: George Allen & Unwin, 2nd ed., 1937 [1900])

Ryle 1954: Gilber Ryle, *Dilemmas* (Cambridge: Cambridge University Press, 1954)

Salmon 1671: William Salmon, *Synopsis Medicinæ or A compendium of Astrological, Galenical, & Chymical Physick, Philosophically deduced from the Principles of Hermes and Hippocrates* (London: Printed by W. Godbid for Richard Jones, 1671)

Salmon 1970: Wesley C. Salmon, ed., *Zeno's Paradoxes* (New York: Bobbs-Merrill, 1970)

Sarton 1950: George Sarton, "Boyle and Bayle: the sceptical chemist and the sceptical historian," *Chymia*, 3, 1950, 155-89

Scot 1584: Reginald Scot, *The discouerie of witchcraft, Wherein the lewde dealing of witches and witchmongers is notablie detected, the knauerie of coniurors, the impietie of inchantors, the follie of soothsaiers, the impudent falshood of cousenors, the infidelitie of atheists, the pestilent practises of Pythonists, the curiositie of figurecasters, the vanitie of dreamers, the geggerlie art of Alcumystrie, The abhomination of idolatrie, the horrible art of poisoning, the vertue and power of naturall magike, and all conueiances of Legerdemaine and iuggling are deciphered: and many other things opened, which have long lien hidden, howbeit verie necessarie to be knowne* (London: William Brome, 1584)

Scott 1952: J.F. Scott, *The Scientific Work of René Descartes (1596-1650)* (London: Taylor and Francis, 1952)

Sennert 1637: Daniel Sennert, *The Weapon-salves Maladie: or, A declaration of its insufficiencie to perform what is attributed to it* (London: Iohn Clark, 1637)

Shapin 1994: Steven Shapin, *A Social History of Truth* (Chicago: U of Chicago P, 1994)

Shapin and Schaffer 1985: Steven Shapin and Simon Schaffer, *Leviathan and the Air-Pump: Hobbes, Boyle, and the Experimental Life* (Princeton: Princeton UP, 1985)

Shapiro 1983: Barbara J. Shapiro, *Probability and Certainty in Seventeenth-Century England* (Princeton: Princeton UP, 1983)

Shapiro 1994: Barbara J. Shapiro, "The Concept 'Fact': Legal Origins and Cultural Diffusion," *Albion*, 26.2, 1994, 227-52

Shapiro 1999: Barbara J. Shapiro, *A culture of Fact: England, 1550-1720* (Ithaca: Cornell UP, 1999)

Shapiro 2002: Barbara J. Shapiro, "Testimony in seventeenth-century natural philosophy: legal origins and early development," *Studies in History and Philosophy of Science Part A*, 33.2, 2002, 243-63

Sharrock 1659: Robert Sharrock, *The History of the Propagation & Improvement of Vegetables by the Concurrence of Art and Nature ... Written according to Observations made from Experience and Practice* (Oxford: printed by A. Lichfield for Tho. Robinson, 1659/60)

Sheridan 1787: Thomas Sheridan, *The Life of the Rev. Dr. Jonathan Swift, Dean of St. Patrick's, Dublin* (London: Printed for J.F. and C. Rivington, et al., 2nd ed., 1787)

Smith 1907: Logan Pearsall Smith, *The Life and Letters of Sir Henry Wootan*, 2 vols. (Oxford: Clarendon Press, 1907)

Smith 1675: Thomas Smith, *The Credibility of the Mysteries of the*

Christian Religion (London: Printed by Tho. Roycroft, for Ric. Davis bookseller in Oxford, 1675)

Stanley 1687: Thomas Stanley, *History of Philosophy*, 3 vols. (2nd ed., London, 1687; reprinted New York: Garland, 1978)

Stewart 1979: M.A. Stewart, ed., *Selected Philosophical Papers of Robert Boyle*, (Manchester: Manchester UP, 1979; reprinted Indianapolis and Cambridge: Hackett, 1991)

Stewart 1993: M.A. Stewart, "Locke's 'Observations' on Boyle," *The Locke Newsletter*, 24, 1993, 21-34

Strabo: *The Geography of Strabo*, translated H.L. Jones, 8 vols. (Cambridge, MA: Harvard University Press, Loeb Library, 1917-33)

Swift 1711: Jonathan Swift, *Miscellanies in Prose and Verse* (London: Printed for John Morphew, 1711)

Thomas 1973: Keith Thomas, *Religion and the Decline of Magic* (Harmondsworth: Penguin, 1973)

Thomas 1984: Keith Thomas, *Man and the Natural World* (Harmondsworth: Penguin, 1984)

Townshend 1904: Dorothea Townshend, *The Life and Letters of the Great Earl of Cork* (London: Duckworth, 1904)

Underdown 1971: David Underdown, *Pride's Purge: Politics in the Puritan Revolution* (Oxford: Clarendon Press, 1971)

Ussher 1658: James Ussher, *The Annals of the World* (London: printed by E. Tyler, for J. Crook, and for G. Bedell, 1658)

van Helmont 1648: Johann B. van Helmont, *Ortus medicinae* (Amsterdam, 1648), translated along with *Opuscula medica inaudita* (Amsterdam, 1648), by John Chandler as *Oriatrike* (London: Lodowick Loyd, 1662)

van Maanen 1986: J.A. van Maanen, "The refutation of Longomontanus' quadrature by John Pell," *Annals of Science*, 43, 1986, 315-52

Vaucher 1951: G. Vaucher, "Le XVIIe siècle—La politique intérieure" [de Genève], in A. Jullien, ed., *Histoire de Genève des Origines à 1798* (Geneva: Société d'histoire et d'archéologie de Genève, n.d. [c. 1951])

Verney 1892: F.P. and M.M. Verney, *Memoirs of the Verney Family*, 4 vols. (London: Longmans, Green, and Co., 1892-99)

Walker 1678: Anthony Walker, *Eureka, Eureka, The Virtuous Woman found Her Loss Bewailed, and Character Exemplified in a Sermon Preached at ... the Funeral of that most Excellent Lady, the Right Honourable ... Mary, Countess Dowager of Warwick ... with ... The Life of that Noble Lady, to which are Annexed some of her Ladyships Pious and Useful Meditations* (London: Nathanael Ranew, 1678)

Webster 1975: Charles Webster, *The Great Instauration: Science, Medicine and Reform, 1626-1660* (London: Duckworth, 1975)

Whitehead 1929: A.N. Whitehead, *Process and Reality* (New York: The Macmillan Co., 1929)

Willis 1683: Thomas Willis, *Two Discourses Concerning the Soul of Brutes, Which is that of the Vital and Sensitive of Man* (London, 1683; reprinted Gainesville, Florida: Scholars' Facsimiles & Reprints, 1971), with an introduction by Solomon Diamond

Wojcik 1997: Jan Wojcik, *Robert Boyle and the Limits of Reason* (New York: Cambridge UP, 1997)

Index